AF183866

Italian Yearbook of Human Rights 2015

P.I.E. Peter Lang

Bruxelles · Bern · Berlin · Frankfurt am Main · New York · Oxford · Wien

Director
Antonio Papisca

Research and editorial committee
Andrea Cofelice, Pietro de Perini,
Paolo De Stefani, Marco Mascia,
Antonio Papisca, Claudia Pividori

Editors
University Human Rights Centre
University of Padua
via Martiri della Libertà, 2
35137 Padua

tel. 049.8271817; fax 049.8271816

centro.dirittiumani@unipd.it
www.italianhumanrightsyearbook.eu
http://unipd-centrodirittiumani.it/en/

Italian Yearbook of Human Rights 2015

Italian Yearbook of Human Rights

UNIVERSITÀ DEGLI STUDI DI PADOVA | HUMAN RIGHTS CENTRE

UNESCO Chair
Human Rights, Democracy and Peace

REGIONE DEL VENETO

ARCHIVIO PACE DIRITTI UMANI
peace human rights

Cover picture: © *The ideal city (interpolation)*, 2011, Venezia, Marsilio Editori.

First Italian edition: *Annuario italiano dei diritti umani 2015*, Venezia, Marsilio Editori, 2015.

This edition of the Yearbook has been realised in the framework of the Scientific Research Programme of Relevant National Interest (PRIN) "Italian Foreign Policy in front of the new challenges of the international system: actors, institutions and policies".

No part of this book may be reproduced in any form, by print, photocopy, microfilm or any other means, without prior written permission from the publisher. All rights reserved.

© P.I.E. PETER LANG S.A.
Éditions scientifiques internationales
Brussels, 2015
1 avenue Maurice, B-1050 Bruxelles, Belgique
info@peterlang.com ; www.peterlang.com

ISSN 2294-8848
ISBN 978-2-87574-293-3
eISBN 978-3-0352-6564-4
D/2015/5678/52

Printed in Germany

CIP available from the British Library, GB and the Library of Congress, USA.

Bibliographic information published by "Die Deutsche Nationalbibliothek"

"Die Deutsche Nationalbibliothek" lists this publication in the "Deutsche Nationalbibliografie"; detailed bibliographic data is available in the Internet at http://dnb.d-nb.de.

Table of Contents

Part IV. National and International Case-law

List of Acronyms

AGCM	Regulatory Authority for Electricity and Gas (Autorità garante della concorrenza e del mercato)
AGCOM	The Communications Regulatory Authority (Autorità per le garanzie nelle comunicazioni)
ANCI	National Association of Italian Municipalities (Associazione Nazionale dei Comuni Italiani)
C.l.	Constitutional law (Legge costituzionale)
CARA	Reception Centre for Asylum Seekers (Centro di accoglienza per richiedenti asilo)
CAT	Convention against Torture and other Cruel, Inhuman or Degrading Treatment or Punishment
CEDAW	Convention on the Elimination of all Forms of Discrimination against Women
CFREU	Charter of Fundamental Rights of the European Union
CFSP	Common Foreign and Security Policy of the European Union
CIDU	Inter-Ministerial Committee for Human Rights (Comitato interministeriale per i diritti umani)
CIE	Identification and Expulsion Centre (Centro di identificazione ed espulsione)
CM	Committee of Ministers of the Council of Europe
CoE	Council of Europe
CPED	International Convention for the Protection of All Persons from Enforced Disappearance
CPT	European Committee for the Prevention of Torture and Inhuman or Degrading Treatment or Punishment
CRC	Convention on the Rights of the Child
CRPD	Convention on the Rights of Persons with Disabilities
CSDP	Common Security and Defence Policy of the European Union

D.p.c.m.	Decree of the President of the Council of Ministers (Decreto del Presidente del Consiglio dei Ministri)
D.p.r.	Decree of the President of the Republic (Decreto del Presidente della Repubblica)
ECHR	European Convention for the Protection of Human Rights and Fundamental Freedoms
ECJ	Court of Justice of the European Union
ECOSOC	United Nations Economic and Social Council
ECRI	European Commission against Racism and Intolerance
ECtHR	European Court of Human Rights
EP	European Parliament
ESC-R	European Social Charter (revised)
EU	European Union
FAO	Food and Agriculture Organisation of the United Nations
FRA	Fundamental Rights Agency of the European Union
GA	General Assembly of the United Nations
ICC	International Criminal Court
ICCPR	International Covenant on Civil and Political Rights
ICERD	International Convention on the Elimination of all Forms of Racial Discrimination
ICESCR	International Covenant on Economic, Social and Cultural Rights
ICRMW	International Convention on the Protection of the Rights of all Migrant Workers and their Families
ILO	International Labour Organisation
IOM	International Organisation for Migration
L.	Law
L.d.	Law-decree (decreto legge)
LGBT/LGBTI	Lesbian, Gay, Bisexual, Transexual (and Intersex)
Lgs.d.	Legislative decree (decreto legislativo)
MIUR	Ministry of Education, University and Research
NATO	North Atlantic Treaty Organisation
NGO	Non-governmental Organisation

ODIHR	Office for Democratic Institutions and Human Rights (OSCE)
OHCHR	Office of the High Commissioner of the United Nations for Human Rights
OPCAT	Optional Protocol to the Convention against Torture
OSCE	Organisation for Security and Cooperation in Europe
P.l.	Provincial law
PACE	Parliamentary Assembly of the Council of Europe
R.g.d.	Regional Government deliberation
R.l.	Regional law
SPRAR	Protection System for Asylum Seekers and Refugees (Sistema di protezione per richiedenti asilo e rifugiati)
TEU	Treaty on European Union
TFEU	Treaty on the Functioning of the European Union
UN-HABITAT	United Nations Human Settlements Programme
UNACLA	United Nations Advisory Committee of Local Authorities
UNAR	Office for the Promotion of Equal Treatment and the Fight against Racial Discrimination (Ufficio per la promozione della parità di trattamento e la rimozione delle discriminazioni fondate sulla razza e sull'origine etnica)
UNDP	United Nations Development Programme
UNEP	United Nations Environmental Programme
UNESCO	United Nations Educational, Scientific and Cultural Organisation
UNHCR	United Nations High Commission for Refugees
UNICEF	United Nations Children's Fund
UPR	Universal Periodic Review
WHO	World Health Organisation

Italy and Human Rights in 2014: the Challenge of National/International Constitutional Synergism

Just as this edition of the *Italian Yearbook of Human Rights*, the fifth in the series, is going to press, a host of events are taking place to celebrate the 800th anniversary of the *Magna Charta Libertatum Ecclesiae et Regni Angliae* which, as is well known, was sealed by King John of England on June 15th 1215, on the water-meadow of Runnymede, near Windsor. The commemoration of this solemn act, conventionally considered the antecedent of modern legislations as far as human rights and fundamental freedoms are concerned, offers an opportunity to reflect on the intrinsic, substantially unilinear development force of a normative paradigm which touches on the supreme value of human dignity. Certain privileges and discriminations remain in the Magna Carta, and yet it contains the roots of *Habeas Corpus*, of the rule of law and of representative democracy; in other words, the beginning of a long road whose milestones are acts such as the Petition of Right, for example, and the Bill of Rights in the XVII Century in England, the Constitution of the United States of America and the French Declaration of the Rights of Man and of the Citizen in the XVIII Century.

From the second half of the XIX Century onwards, the first part of more and more national Constitutions is devoted to recognising human rights and fundamental freedoms. Universal ethical values are translated into norms and principles of *ius positum* within each State's legislation, each separately from the other. Similarly to a karst process, these virtuous rivulets rise to the surface and merge, thanks to the United Nations Charter and the Universal Declaration of Human Rights, in their shared riverbed of a new International Law which sets the respect of human dignity and of the rights inherent to it, as the foundation for freedom, justice and world peace.

1945–1948 were the years of the "great new time in global history" that Giuseppe Dossetti defined a "burning and universal crucible", a kind of fertile construction site for producing radically innovative norms in the mark of respect for human dignity. It was in this context of a broader, universalist approach that the Constitution of the Italian Republic took shape. The first part of it cannot be fully understood in its everlasting validity without taking into consideration how it relates, or more correctly, how it is anchored, to the new international law which took organic shape starting from the United Nations Charter and the Universal Declaration. Indeed, the content of national and international human rights law is substantially the same, and this welds them together. In the case of Italian legislation, this union is further strengthened, and constantly fuelled, by the original and innovative fact that thousands of municipal Statutes, and a number of regional ones, make specific reference, as concerns the values of human dignity and peace, to the norms and principles of international human rights law, together with those enshrined in the Italian Constitution. From this, one can deduce that the Constitution lives with dual, converging support coming both from above and from below.

It is from this perspective of reciprocal exchange and strengthening between the various levels of legislation that the complex network of monitoring actions and encouragement carried out by the supranational bodies which are part of the global and regional human rights systems, and the relative reporting requirements Italy must meet, should be considered. The dynamics of these exchanges have a substantial content of reciprocal learning and educating, to the benefit of both national and international good governance, within the "glocal" space of actionability which is proper to the fundamental rights of the person. The competent and organically continuous participation of national institutions in this practice of enacted legality affords a better understanding of what the actual implementation on the ground of norms such as, for example, articles 2, 3, 10 and 11 of the Italian Constitution involves. Faithfulness to the Constitution, besides being an obligation, is a virtue that is exercised synoptically, so to speak, holding the national Constitution in one hand and the Universal Declaration and the corpus of the many international legal instruments deriving from it in the other.

The main purpose of the *Italian Yearbook of Human Rights* is to offer a service to the Nation, to help develop within the Country an ever more organic and systematic vision of the instruments and procedures which touch on the most sensitive part of the Constitution: in short, a humble but heartfelt contribution to exercising the virtuous synopticity mentioned above.

The introductory pages of the Yearbook highlight certain "special focus" issues which the research and editorial committee consider particularly significant and urgent. One of these, which has recurred in every edition of the Yearbook, is the failure to establish a National Human Rights Commission in line with the Paris Principles recommended by the United Nations and the Council of Europe. What arcane reason is hidden behind this persistent refusal? Who is afraid of an independent body that is capable of monitoring and making proposals following the sapiential idea *de lege semper perficienda* (laws must perennially be perfected)?

Less mystery surrounds the reason why "National action plans", the logical consequence of international legislative acts regarding specific life conditions deserving of special protection are not implemented. One may reasonably suppose that, rather than being due to budget restrictions, it is above all a question of incompetence, lack of political sensitivity and bureaucratic sloth. This is the case, for example, of the Plan for implementing two fundamental international instruments concerning the right to education: the European Charter on Education for Democratic Citizenship and Human Rights Education (Council of Europe, 2010) and the United Nations Declaration on Human Rights Education and Training (2011). As well as being a soft law obligation, they are two excellent pedagogical and didactic aids for the genuine civic education which is so urgently needed; and they were designed in line with the principle of subsidiarity, the glocality of its scope and the synopticity of the reference legislative sources. It is hoped that civic education will finally be called by the name that is immanently proper to it: education for human rights, democracy and peace. It should be noted that quality education is measured, primarily, on the quality of the civic education imparted, inasmuch as it is the bearer of the universal reference values underlying any education and training plan.

National plans, together with the functioning of the relevant specialist institutions, contribute to ensuring the structural sustainability of Italy's human rights system. An evaluation of this sustainability should be carried out every year in Parliament, in the course of a special session.

As concerns Italy's contribution to the functioning of the international bodies working on human rights, from data examined relative to the timeframe considered by the Yearbook, it emerges that Italy's overall financial contributions to these organisations have decreased. Considering the fundamental importance of their role in promoting and monitoring human rights, which is instrumental to developing a robust and consistent constitutional praxis at the national level, one cannot but denounce the ingratitude and short-sightedness of those who are responsible for grasping the opportunities for civic and democratic growth that still remain at their disposal.

The 2015 edition of the Yearbook falls in a year which has plenty of celebrations providing food for reflection: besides the 800th anniversary of the Magna Charta, the most significant are the seventieth anniversary of the end of the Second World War and the birth of the United Nations. In Italy, these last two anniversaries are intertwined in their history and in their perspective. This intertwining has taken on the original shape of a widespread, capillary campaign for the international recognition of peace as a fundamental right of the person and of peoples. The previous edition of the Yearbook described the structure of this Italian campaign supporting the Human Rights Council's initiative setting up an inter-governmental working group, which is debating a draft United Nations Declaration precisely on the right to peace, amid bitter disagreements and *a priori* rejections of the document. To date, over three hundred municipal Councils have approved a petitionary motion, almost always unanimously, calling for the inclusion of the right to peace in international legislation, starting from the recognition already operative in their respective Statutes. Further, motions similar to those of the local administrations have been approved by the Regional Councils of Veneto, Marche, Emilia-Romagna, Friuli-Venezia Giulia and Apulia. A number of Mayors and Regional Governors have to our knowledge sent the text of their motions to the members of the United Nations Human Rights Council, in an exercise of "city diplomacy" to support the action of the Italian Mission to the United Nations in Geneva. This is an implicit reference to the principle of subsidiarity, which is to be implemented in a multi-level governance structure and fully respecting the dignity of the human person and his or her inherent rights.

I. New Legislation and Infrastructure

Ratification Processes: Few Steps Forward but Some Signs of Willingness to Move

The number of international legal instruments concerning human rights accepted by Italy has remained more or less unchanged compared to the previous year. Indeed, there were only two ratification processes on which Italy made partial progress in 2014. Specifically, on 3 October 2014, the Italian Parliament adopted the law ratifying and implementing the Optional Protocol to the International Covenant on Economic, Social and Cultural Rights, and the relative instrument of ratification was deposited only on 20 February 2015; and concerning disarmament, on 2 April 2014, the ratification process of the Arms Trade Treaty, which had begun in 2013 with the adoption of the relevant law of ratification and implementation (l. 118/2013), was completed. On the other hand, as concerns the legal instruments of the Council of Europe, there have been no developments.

Consequently, not even 2014 saw any progress on certain essential legal instruments for which Italy has already begun the respective acceptance processes, in some cases quite some time ago. This is the case, out of the treaties with a global reach, for the International Convention for the Protection of All Persons from Enforced Disappearance (signed in 2007) and the Third Optional Protocol to the Convention on the Rights of the Child on a Communications Procedure (signed in 2012); of the Council of Europe instruments, the ratification processes still to be completed are those of the XII Additional Protocol to the ECHR (signed in 2000) and the Convention on Human Rights and Biomedicine (Oviedo Convention). To be specific, the law ratifying and implementing the latter was adopted in 2001 (l. 145/2001), but the ratification instrument has still not been deposited.

Over the year being examined, a few timid signs of willingness to move can be recorded as concerns the ratification of the core human rights treaties to which Italy is still not party. Indeed, during the Universal Periodic Review (UPR) which Italy underwent in October 2014, the Government committed to becoming party to the first two legal instruments mentioned above, accepting in full all the recommendations on this issue received from the United Nations Human Rights Council Working Group (recommendations 7–14). On the contrary, the Italian Government rejected the 6 recommendations (1–6) concerning ratification of the 1990 International Convention on the Protection of the Rights of all Migrant Workers and Members of their Families. The Italian authorities justified their rejection by stating that the human rights of regular and irregular migrants are already protected by domestic legislation, specifically by the application of the ILO conventions Nos. 143 and 189 (on migrant workers and domestic workers respectively). And so this Convention remains the only one of the core treaties which not only has not yet been the object of any actions towards acceptance by Italy, but for which no progress is planned in future years either.

Pending Legislative Interventions: Introduction of the Crime of Torture, Law on Defamation and Protection of the Roma Minority in Italy

Three significant legislative actions regarding human rights have recently received a boost from the authorities, but they have still not been concluded. These specifically concern the introduction of the crime of torture into the Italian criminal code, the adoption of a law on defamation in line with international standards and the protection of the rights of people belonging to the Roma and Sinti minorities present in Italy. The speedy conclusion of these legislative processes becomes a priority issue in Italy's commitment to human rights, particularly in the light of the many requests and recommendations made to the authorities in recent years through several different human rights protection and monitoring mechanisms at both the global and European level, not least the aforementioned UPR.

As is well known, the issue of the introduction of the crime of torture into the Italian criminal code has been debated since at least 1989, the year the 1984 United Nations Convention against Torture came into effect for Italy. Article 4 of this Convention requires each State Party "to ensure that all acts of torture are offences under its criminal law". However, over the years, the Italian authorities have substantially rejected the repeated requests from the international human rights monitoring bodies to fulfil this obligation, considering that the framework of the Italian Constitution and legislation was sufficient to punish the criminal behaviours to which the 1984 Convention refers. This position was also reiterated during Italy's first Universal Periodic Review in February 2010. On that occasion, the Netherlands, the Czech Republic and New Zealand had recommended the introduction of the crime of torture into the criminal code (recommendation 8). Several draft bills were proposed over the years, but never completed, for a variety of reasons which can substantially be put down to a lack of political will. These issues and the relative problems were recently brought back to the attention of the Italian authorities and public opinion, both following incidents in the news and because of the broad media coverage of some of the ECtHR judgments concerning pushback of migrants (*Hirsi Jamaa* case) and overcrowding in prisons (*Torreggiani* case). In both cases, indeed, Italy was found guilty of violating the norm prohibiting torture (art. 3 ECHR).

At the end of the second cycle of UPR in 2014, Italy showed a change of attitude on this issue, and fully accepted the recommendations from Australia and France, respectively on the necessity of adopting effective domestic measures to ensure that all acts of torture are considered crimes under the Italian criminal code, and on introducing further provisions to prevent all forms of cruel, inhuman and/or degrading treatment of detainees. The 2015 ECtHR judgment on the *Cestaro v. Italy* case (complaint No. 6884/11) gave further impulse to this process. The *Cestaro* judgment found Italy guilty of violation of the prohibition of torture in connection with the anti-G8 protests in Genoa in 2001, in particular the repressive actions carried out against demonstrators lodging in the Diaz school. The ECtHR ruled that the inadequacy of the provisions of the criminal code which could be used to punish police behaviour in those circumstances, not only prevented the investigative and judicial bodies from being able to bring effective prosecutions for the acts of torture committed, but also contributed to creating a substantial situation of impunity for those who took part in the violence. Following publication of the ruling, the passage through Parliament of draft bill No. 10 of 2013 had a sudden acceleration. In 2015 a greatly improved version of the bill as compared to the first draft was approved by the Chamber of Deputies (Act C.2168) and is now being examined by the Senate. It is hoped that after a number of failed attempts, there will finally be the right conditions for this process to be concluded without further delays.

As concerns the protection of the human rights of Roma and Sinti people, the observations of the international bodies, particularly of the European Commission against Racism and Intolerance, have placed some hope in draft bill No. 770 (Norms for the protection and equal opportunities for the Roma minority). This was presented in the Senate by Francesco Palermo in June 2013, however no progress worth mentioning has been achieved to date. In early 2015 the bill was assigned to the Senate institutional affairs commission, but the process of examining it has not yet started. In this situation of stalemate, a particularly interesting initiative is that taken in autumn 2014 by a network of NGO spokespersons and Roma and Sinti associations or associations working for the rights of people from these communities; they have set up a national committee for a citizens' bill on "Norms for the protection and equal opportunities of the historical-linguistic Roma and Sinti minority". The bill repeats most of the measures contained in the 2013 draft bill, placing strong emphasis on the need to recognise the Roma as a historical-linguistic minority. This is because to date Italian legislation on minority groups (specifically law 482/1999) recognises and protects only the linguistic minorities which have a long history of occupying a limited area; consequently this excludes the Roma as they are not concentrated in specific areas but scattered over the whole of Italy. According to the promoters, legal recognition of this minority would give a substantial contribution to enhancing the respect of all the human rights of Roma, Sinti and Travellers living in Italy, and tackle the various issues (housing, education, employment, health) on which the main recommendations made by both international institutions and civil society organisations have focused. The Italian Constitution (art. 71(2)) requires the promoters to collect at least 50,000 signatures from people on the electoral roll before they can present the initiative in Parliament.

Alongside the gradual implementation of the National Strategy for Inclusion of the Roma and Sinti, approved by the Prime Minister's Office in 2012, the adoption of a law to protect the Roma minority in Italy would represent a significant step forward, and not only for the protection of the human rights of these people. This act would also contribute to turning the page as far as the approach to them is concerned: as of 2005 they had been treated purely as an emergency and a security problem, starting with the State-Region "security pacts" and continued in 2008 with the "nomad emergency" decrees (declared illegitimate by the Supreme Administrative Council in 2011). Indeed, this would allow the complex issues surrounding the situation of Roma and Sinti in Italy to be tackled in a way that is inclusive, respectful of human rights and sustainable over time. This appears to be the only viable solution, considering that the results of the previous security-based approach to the Roma issue did not show any appreciable improvements, neither as regards the effective enjoyment of human rights for Roma and Sinti in Italy, nor as concerns the social tension deriving from the uneasy relationship between the resident population and the members of these communities.

The third piece of legislation still pending is about the promised changes to the law on defamation and, in particular, the provisions of the Italian criminal code allowing for a custodial sentence of up to three years for journalists and editors found guilty of aggravated defamation. Parliament's commitment to adopting bill 925 (the so-called "defamation bill") was mentioned in the report the Italian Government submitted at the time of the second cycle of its periodic review, in answer to recommendations received in the past, during the first UPR in 2010. The bill in question, submitted to the Chamber of Deputies in 2013 and approved there within the year, was amended in the Senate in October 2014 and is now back still waiting to be examined by the justice commission of the Chamber of Deputies. Consequently, Parliament should bring the bill's passage through Parliament to a conclusion without further delay. It should be noted that the approval of this bill represents an important step, but not the definitive one, towards bringing Italian legislation fully in line with international standards on defamation. Indeed, although the bill met with the substantial approval of the international monitoring bodies (including the Council of Europe Venice Commission and the OSCE Representative on Freedom of the Media), the text currently being examined by Parliament does not appear to fully satisfy the recommendations expressed by the European and international community, since it merely provides for custodial sentences for the offence of defamation being replaced by fines, rather than the hoped-for and recommended complete decriminalisation of this type of offence.

Domestic Infrastructure: is Italy Moving towards an Imminent Appointment of the National Commission?

At the close of 2014, Italy remained one of the few Countries which still did not have an independent national human rights institution in line with the "Paris Principles". This serious gap in infrastructure is underlined by the 25 recommendations on this subject made to the Government during the recent Universal Periodic Review. This issue was the subject of the second largest number of recommendations made to Italy, outnumbered only by the 33 recommendations made on the far broader area of racial discrimination. During the first cycle of UPR (2010), Italy received 16 requests on establishing this national institution, making those requests the fifth most frequent recommendation. And so the creation of this institution is a priority for Italy, now more than ever.

On this issue, it should be pointed out that among the 25 recommendations on this subject during the 2014 UPR, all fully accepted by Italy, a time limit for completing this process emerged. Indeed, the Italian Government accepted that it would create this institution by the end of 2015, as recommended by Denmark (recommendation No. 43). After the failure to get the bills submitted in 2013 through, a new bill was submitted to the Chamber of Deputies (first signatories Marazziti and Nicoletti) on 9 July 2014, hence prior to Italy's second UPR. Bill 2529 (Establishment of the National Commission for the Promotion and Protection of Human Rights), has been assigned to the commission for constitutional affairs. However, in early 2015, there is no news of its having begun to examine the bill. The hope is that, after a number of failed attempts, and in the light of Italy's formal commitment made at the international level, Parliament will finally be able to carry through the parliamentary process for this law to be adopted and then allow the National Commission to be established without further delay. The hopes on this front are slightly dampened by the consideration that after the previous UPR in 2010, too, Italy had fully accepted a recommendation, again from Denmark, which gave a short deadline for the establishment of the Commission, and yet did not manage to give any tangible follow-up to this commitment.

Regarding Ombudspersons, no legislative measures to appoint an Ombudsperson at the national level have been taken. However, worthy of note is the fact that, following an initiative by the National Coordinating Body of Ombudspersons, a national Ombudsperson's Office has been created and, in October 2014, a first report was published on the activities that this Office had carried out. The report provides an update on the coverage of Ombudspersons all over Italy, lists the main objectives established by the Coordinating Body for the two-year period 2013–2014 and summarises the activities carried out in 2013. Moreover, on 5 November 2014, Parliament approved motion No. 9/2681/127, submitted by Deputy Bruno Tabacci, which commits the Government to adopting, alongside its actions to reform civil justice, purpose-designed initiatives to enhance the value of the Ombudsperson's role by increasing its duties, powers and areas of expertise.

On the contrary, there is nothing new to report concerning the appointment of members to the National Ombudsperson for the rights of persons deprived of their personal freedom. This office is collegial and was established in December 2013 with watchdog functions to ensure the execution of custodial sentences and of other forms of restriction of personal freedom is implemented in compliance with the regulations and principles established by the Constitution, by international human rights conventions and by the laws of the State. While waiting for the appointment of the three members of this independent authority, the regional and local Ombudspersons for detainees have undertaken to set up a "coordinating committee" made up of six members (three regional and three local), to tackle issues of a general nature such as the right to health, to work and to education relationships with people deprived of freedom, prison conditions, overcrowding and relations with the National Ombudsman, once its members have been appointed.

II. Implementation of International Obligations and Commitments: Moving between Conforming and the "Counter-limits" Theory

One fundamental element in evaluating a Country's level of implementation of its international human rights obligations is its capacity to conform to international standards and to how these are understood and applied by the case-law of the international courts, including, most importantly for Italy, the European Court of Human Rights (ECtHR) and the Court of Justice of the European Union (ECJ).

Regarding the dialogue between the Italian courts and the international ones, 2014 saw the positive trend continue whereby Italian judges, from those of the Constitutional and the Supreme Courts downwards, drew extensively and consciously on European Union and international human rights law sources including, in the case of Italy, the European Convention on Human Rights, the EU Charter of Fundamental Rights, the 1989 United Nations Convention on the Rights of the Child and the 2006 United Nations Convention on the Rights of Persons with Disabilities.

As concerns 2014, one can consider as instances of successful convergence, or exemplary openness to ECtHR case-law, ruling 135/2014, by which the Constitutional Court declared unconstitutional the provisions of the Italian code of criminal procedure by which, in cases regarding the application of security measures, hearings have to take place in closed chambers – rather than in public hearings; or the central role case-law from the Strasbourg Court played, even in cases not concerning Italy, on issues concerning adoption and heterologous embryo transfer.

Whereas there are increasing numbers of examples of "good osmosis" between legal orders, on some specific issues, opposing fronts remain between the Italian case-law and the Court of Strasburg's consolidated positions. For example, there continue to be differences in approach between ECtHR practice and a certain type of Italian case-law on subjects such as the compliance with fair trial standards of some legal instruments presented as "interpretative", but which in actual fact make retroactive changes to legal positions which citizens believed established, based on consolidated case-law orientation; the same problem exists with regard to the effectiveness of investigations into treatments in violation of article 3 ECHR suffered by individuals in the hands of State officials.

However, the development of a distinctive Italian profile in the way of interpreting international human rights standards should not necessarily always be considered in negative terms; not only could it be a sign of heightened awareness on the part of the Italian judiciary of the qualifying essential principles based on inviolable rights, but it could also pave the way for a highly innovative series of interpretations. Along these lines, mention must certainly be made of the Constitutional Court's ruling 238/2014, not least because of the inevitable international repercussions it will have: in this case, applying the so-called counter-limits theory, the Court declared customary international law on State immunity inapplicable in the Italian legal order as far as damages deriving from war crimes and crimes against humanity are concerned, as the International Court of Justice held in the case *Germany v. Italy* (see *2012 Yearbook*, p. 292).

Against an ever-stronger link forged by the judiciary, despite some points of friction, between the domestic and international level, the data regarding the execution of European Court of Human Rights rulings paint a disheartening picture of the capacity of the Italian Government as a whole to promptly and fully satisfy the commitments it has made regarding human rights. According to the annual report on the execution of ECtHR judgments compiled by the CoE Committee of Ministers on 2014 activity, there are 2,396 cases regarding Italy which are still being supervised (making up 35% of the total number of cases), of which 26 *leading cases* and 2,370 repetitive cases subject to enhanced supervision. Concerning the duration of the execution of Italian cases closed before the Committee of Ministers, the report shows that on average it takes 5.2 years (against a general average of 4.1). Added to this is the fact that as regards payment of just satisfaction established by the ECtHR, in 2014 Italy respected the payment terms in only 11 cases, whereas there are 21 cases which have been pending for over 5 years. The main cases or groups of cases which Italy has not yet executed, and which are listed here because of the structural or complex nature of the underlying issues are: *Ceteroni*, *Luordo*, *Mostacciuolo and Gaglione*, *Abenavoli*, regarding the excessive length of civil, criminal and administrative proceedings and the problems regarding the "Pinto" proceedings; the *Costa and Pavan* case on medically-assisted procreation; the *Di Sarno and Others* case on waste service issues in Campania; the *Godelli* case on the right of adopted children to access information concerning their biological mother; the *M.C. and Others* case, a "pilot judgment", on the non-payment of the annual reassessment of the supplementary component of the allowance granted under law 201/1992 to people accidentally contaminated through blood transfusions.

There is one improvement to report since the Committee of Ministers published its data on Italy's performance in executing ECtHR judgments: the response of the Government and Italian lawmakers to the issues of prison overcrowding raised by the pilot judgment in the *Torreggiani and Others* case. In compliance with the Court's ruling, as of 2013 Italy has adopted a number of measures on crime policy and prison organisation with the objective of tackling the causes of prison overcrowding and, in parallel, has amended the law on the penitentiary system, creating a new internal remedy of a preventive nature which allows detainees to lodge a complaint to a supervising magistrate about the material conditions of his or her detention, as well as a compensatory remedy offering redress for people who have already been subjected to detention in violation of ECtHR standards (l.d. 146/2013 and 92/2014).

On the issue of prison overcrowding, partial confirmation, albeit in strictly statistical terms, on the impact of the provisions adopted by Italy to reduce the numbers and improve the living conditions of detainees can be found in the data on prison population provided by the Prison Administration Department (DAP): as of 31 December 2014 there were 53,623 detainees in Italian prisons (where the official capacity is 49,635), the lowest figure recorded since 2007 and marking a decrease of 8,910 people compared to the previous year (DAP data as at December 2013). Despite the improved trend recorded, further systemic efforts in the area of non-custodial detention and penalty systems are still necessary to keep up the achievements over the long term. Indeed the results are still partial and subject to fluctuation, as proven by a further, albeit limited, increase in the prison population in the first quarter of 2015 (+ 499 people against a decrease in places officially available of 141, DAP data for March 2015).

Regarding the preventive and compensatory judicial remedies introduced by the Italian Government, their impact, or at least potential impact, is confirmed by some important rulings issued by the Strasburg Court in September 2014: the Court declared a large number of complaints pertaining to overcrowding issues inadmissible because not all domestic remedies had been exhausted. Although it has reserved the right to re-examine the cases should doubts emerge in the future on the effectiveness of these new domestic remedies, the Court's position is particularly important if one considers that there are approximately 3,500 similar cases currently pending before the ECtHR.

III. Adoption and Implementation of Policies

One of the critical issues most frequently raised by the international human rights monitoring bodies is the lack of systemic planning of human rights policies at the national level. There are two aspects which are particularly evident in this area: first of all, the lack of "action plans" which could set up proper multi-level governance of human rights policies, in which the appropriate Ministries, Regions, local authorities and civil society should play a part; secondly, the lack of systematic monitoring of the level of implementation of existing action plans, so as to enhance the impact of the measures and the protection of victims (two functions which should properly be taken on and coordinated by the National Commission).

Consequently, no significant progress can be recorded in 2014 on the adoption of new national action plans. Indeed, with reference to the hopes expressed in the *Italian Agenda of Human Rights*, no action plans have yet been adopted on: the human rights situation within detention structures; the national programme on education for democratic citizenship and education and training on human rights; the fourth national action plan for the protection of rights and the development of children and adolescents (the third plan covered the period 2010–2011); the national plan against racism, xenophobia and intolerance for the three-year period 2013–2015 (despite the draft plan having been adopted by UNAR back in 2013).

On the other hand, there are some developments to report on other measures:

– *National action plan against trafficking of human beings.* One of the novelties introduced by lgs.d. 4 March 2014, No. 24 (Implementation of directive 2011/36/EU, on the prevention and repression of trafficking of human beings and the protection of victims, replacing the framework decision 2002/629/GAI), which entered into force on 28 March 2014 was the adoption of the first "National Action Plan against Trafficking and Serious Exploitation of Human Beings". This decree states that the objective of the plan is to identify multi-year action strategies to prevent and combat these situations as well as taking social prevention and awareness-raising actions and helping hidden victims to come out and achieve social integration.

– *Extraordinary action plan against sexual and gender-based violence.* On 22 July 2013, the Government set up the "Inter-institutional Task-force against Violence Against Women", coordinated by the Department for Equal Opportunities and comprising representatives from several Ministries (Justice, Interior, Health, Education, Foreign Affairs, Defence, Economy and Finance, Labour, Economic Development), Regions, local authorities and NGOs working in this area at the national level (*UDI, Telefono Rosa, D.i.RE, Pangea Onlus, Maschile plurale* and *Centro di Ascolto Uomini Maltrattanti*). The Task Force has adopted a draft national plan built around the following lines of action: communications (use of the female image by the media); awareness-raising amid the general public; teaching mutual gender respect; training professionals who come into contact with women victims of violence; social inclusion and employment for female victims of violence; recover and return to society of male perpetrators of violence; setting up databases; evaluating risk factors; and adopting a specific protocol for action when a woman victim of violence accesses a hospital structure (a so-called "pink code"). The draft was published online for public consultation from 10 December 2014 to 10 January 2015.

– *Two-year action plan for the promotion of rights and the integration of persons with disabilities.* In April 2015, the Ministry of Labour Directorate-general for inclusion and social policy, with the agreement of the National Observatory for the rights of persons with disabilities, began collecting the information required to write a report to Parliament on the status of implementation in Italy of policies on disabilities, from 2009 to date, at both the national and regional level.

– *National strategy for the inclusion of Roma, Sinti and Traveller communities – 2012–2020.* During 2014 and the early months of 2015, the process of setting up the so-called "roundtables for the inclusion and social integration of the Roma, Sinti and Traveller communities" whose aim is to promote and coordinate the policies for social inclusion of these people, through the involvement of a very wide-ranging group of public institutions and third sector bodies. However, at over two years since its launch, there is still no systematic monitoring of the state of implementation of the Strategy. As often happens, civil society has taken on the burden of filling this gap. Indeed, in October 2014, a coalition of non-governmental organisations, coordinated by the "*Associazione 21 luglio*", published the report *La Tela di Penelope* (Penelope's Web), a civil society survey on the implementation status of the National Strategy for the Inclusion of Roma, Sinti and Travellers in Italy. This report, although it recognises the great novelty of the aims and guidelines of the Strategy, criticises a series of delays in setting the bodies responsible for its implementation in motion, and some highly critical areas as regards its impact on the ground for the lives of the Roma, particularly those who are living in extremely deprived and vulnerable conditions.

Furthermore, as happens in other policy areas too, Italian human rights education policies are subject to monitoring by international organisations, particularly those operating at the worldwide level, that is, the United

Nations and UNESCO. What are the main mechanisms for dialogue between Italy and international bodies in this area? How does Italy respond to pressing requests and recommendations from the international institutions?

First of all, there have been a number of resolutions adopted from 1995 onwards by the General Assembly and the Human Rights Commission/Council, in the context of the United Nations Decade for Human Rights Education (1995–2004) and the World Programme for Human Rights Education (launched in 2005 and now in its third phase), which invite States to develop national action plans to promote human rights education (see, specifically, General Assembly resolutions 49/184, 50/177 and 51/104, and the Human Rights Commission resolutions 1995/47 and 1996/44). The process is currently coordinated by the Office of the High Commissioner for Human Rights, which has adopted some guidelines to help States preparing their national action plans. As of 2014, however, Italy still did not have such a national strategy.

A further mechanism for dialogue is the "Education for All" programme (EFA), launched by UNESCO at the time of the 1990 World Conference on Education for All, aiming to provide high quality primary education for all (children, young people and adults) by 2015. Within the context of this initiative, Member States have on several occasions been requested to submit monitoring reports to evaluate progress in reaching the EFA objectives, precisely in 1996, 2000, 2005, 2010 and finally in 2015. To date, Italy has presented only one report, in 1999, whereas at the moment of writing this Yearbook, it has not yet prepared the final 2015 report.

There are another two UNESCO educational instruments which require constant monitoring of their implementation: the Convention against Discrimination in Education (adopted in 1960), and the recommendation concerning Education for International Understanding, Co-operation and Peace and Education relating to Human Rights and Fundamental Freedoms (1974). As concerns the 1960 Convention, Italy submitted its last report (covering the period 2000–2005) in 2007, on the occasion of the VII Consultation of Member States, whereas it did not submit a report in 2013, when the last Consultation of Member States (the eighth) was held. On the other hand, Italy is up to date with its reports on the 1974 Recommendation: the most recent was submitted in 2013 (reference period 2009–2012), at the V Consultation of Member States.

The Rights of Migrants, Refugees and Asylum-Seekers

One of the particularly sensitive issues for Italy and for Europe as a whole, and which was strongly in evidence in 2014 due to its dramatic consequences, especially in terms of lives lost, was that of the arrival by sea, across the Mediterranean, of large mixed migratory flows; these arrivals were made more dramatic by the difficult geo-political conditions in Countries such as Libya, Syria, Iraq, Somalia and Nigeria.

According to UNHCR data, 170,000 migrants arrived in Italy by sea (out of a total of 219,000 who arrived in the Southern European Countries) in 2014, whereas in the first three months of 2015 there have already been over 10,000 arrivals. Partly due to those arrivals, a total of 65,700 asylum requests were recorded in Italy in 2014 (+140% compared to 2013, making Italy the Country with the fifth highest number of asylum requests out of 44 industrialised nations).

In this situation, despite recognising and appreciating the commitment and effort Italy has put into search and rescue operations at sea (according to UNHCR estimates, thanks to Operation *Mare Nostrum* and other initiatives, since October 2013 almost 150,000 people have been rescued at sea), and into the various stages of receiving migrants, there have been many instances of international bodies, including the United Nations, the IOM and the Council of Europe pinpointing some critical areas in the overall management of migrants and migratory flows.

Particularly serious inasmuch as it concerns the prohibition of both *refoulement* and collective expulsions, was the ruling against Italy in the *Sharifi and Others* case, in which the Strasburg Court censured the practice of automatic readmission of irregular migrants arriving from Greece at ports on Italy's Adriatic coast. Also significant as far as the suitability of reception facilities for migrants and asylum seekers is concerned is another ruling by the ECtHR, in this case against Switzerland, in which the SPRAR structures were judged totally unfit to house a family of eight, including six children.

Considering the critical issues the Italian migrant reception system has – a system which nonetheless offered refuge to over 66,000 people in 2014 – there is one positive development to mention, at least because it shows signs of political will to tackle the problem. This is the decision adopted by the Chamber of Deputies on 7 November 2014 to establish a (single chamber) Parliamentary Enquiry Commission into the whole system of reception and identification and on the conditions in which migrants are held in the reception centres (CDA), the reception centres for asylum seekers (CARA) and the identification and expulsion centres (CIE). The objectives of the Commission include: ascertaining the living conditions of migrants and the efficiency of the facilities; monitoring the procedures for contracting out management of these centres; evaluation of the performance of the authorities responsible for overseeing the centres and an evaluation of the financial sustainability of the system, also considering possible new regulations on managing the migrant issue.

Finally, mention is made of the positive development marked by the State-Regions-local authorities agreement made on 10 July 2014 for a National Reception Plan 2014–2016, as it appears to adopt a systemic, multi-level approach to one of the many issues connected with managing migration.

IV. Structure of the 2015 Yearbook

The objective of the *Italian Yearbook of Human Rights 2015* is to provide a snapshot of the human rights situation in Italy, both from the legislative and "infrastructural" point of view and from that of the practical implementation of policies and initiatives to promote and protect them. The reference timeframe of the book is calendar year 2014. The level of detail and further background provided in the various sections allow for cross-cutting and targeted reading, which can also be developed by consulting the analytical indexes.

The information presented in the first three Parts of the Yearbook come from documents in the public domain, normally consultable via the official web pages of each body examined. For Part IV the databases of the courts mentioned were used (for Italian case-law the Giuffrè "De Iure" database was that used the most). The complete and updated lists of the international legal instruments adopted and Italy's behaviour in relation to them (ratifications, signatures, no action) are available online in the specific section hosted on the site of the "Pace Diritti Umani" Regional Archive (www.italianhumanrightsyearbook.eu, Attachments), managed by the University of Padua Human Rights Centre pursuant to art. 2 of Veneto regional law 55/1999.

Part I of the Yearbook illustrates the main developments in Italy's incorporation of international and regional laws into its domestic legislation. This overview starts from the global level (United Nations), moves on to the regional level, comprising legislation drawn up by the Council of Europe and the European Union, before presenting domestic legislation which has implemented international obligations through national and regional laws.

Part II illustrates the human rights infrastructure in Italy and is divided into three chapters. The first is on the structure, functions and activities of State bodies: Parliament, Government, the Judiciary and independent authorities; it also covers the activities of civil society organisations and academic institutions which operate at the State level. The second chapter considers the sub-national level of the Italian order and illustrates the variegated local and regional human rights infrastructure and the relative coordinating bodies at the national level. The third chapter is devoted to the "peace human rights infrastructure" and the local and international initiatives in this area developed by the Region of Veneto. The specific focus on this Region is explained by the pioneering commitment shown by Veneto, dating back to its 1988 regional law No. 18, in promoting a culture of human rights, peace and international solidarity.

Part III examines Italy's position with reference to the regional and international bodies and mechanisms for monitoring the implementation of human rights. The evaluations and recommendations that these bodies have addressed to Italy as a result of specific missions to the Country and periodic monitoring are included. Italy's role within these organisations and the contribution of its diplomatic representatives for the promotion of human rights at the regional and global level are highlighted. This Part is subdivided into five chapters. The first focuses on the United Nations system, with particular attention devoted to the activities of the General Assembly, the Human Rights Council (mostly concentrating on Italy's second round of UPR) and the specialised Agencies. The second chapter is on the Council of Europe, and the third on the European Union. These two chapters complement the information presented in Part I (concerning legislation) and in Part IV (concerning case-law), relative to Council of Europe and EU activities in 2014. The fourth chapter is on the Organisation for Security and Cooperation in Europe (OSCE) and its bodies for the promotion of the human dimension of security. The fifth and final chapter is on international humanitarian and criminal law and in this area, in addition to providing updates on Italy's level of conformity, there is a list of the international peace missions to which Italian troops contributed in 2014.

Finally, *Part IV* presents a selection of domestic and international case-law concerning Italy over the reference period. It comprises three chapters, into which the cases are subdivided according to the bodies pronouncing the various judgments. The chapters address domestic case-law (mainly the Constitutional Court, the Supreme Court and the Supreme Administrative Council), case-law of the European Court of Human Rights and case-law of the Court of Justice of the European Union respectively, the last two with reference to cases directly involving Italy. A targeted reading of the case-law can also be made using the index of referenced case-law at the end of the book.

Italian Agenda of Human Rights 2015

For the fourth consecutive year, the research and editorial committee of the *Italian Yearbook of Human Rights*, based at the Human Rights Centre of the University of Padua, has compiled an "Italian Agenda of Human Rights", drawing on the analysis of the recommendations made to Italy at the international level and the most critical issues identified in the successive editions of the Yearbook itself. The Agenda can be seen as an updated instrument for choosing the main initiatives to be undertaken on the legislative, infrastructural and policy-making fronts in order to strengthen the Italian system for promoting and protecting human rights (the 2012, 2013 and 2014 Agendas are available online at www.italian-humanrightsyearbook.eu).

There are only 3 items (and sub-items) on the *2014 Agenda* on which the research and editorial committee found Italy had made significant progress during the year under scrutiny.

The first item concerns the normative level. On 3 October Italy adopted the law of ratification and implementation of the Optional Protocol to the International Covenant on Economic, Social and Cultural Rights (and the ratification instrument was deposited on 20 February 2015).

The second item was on the need to allocate UNAR sufficient resources to fulfil its functions. According to the conclusions adopted by ECRI in December 2014 on the implementation of the recommendations subject to follow-up monitoring, UNAR currently has sufficient human resources (25 members of staff) and financial resources (2 million from the regular budget and European funds) to manage its workload. Consequently, this item and that relative to the ratification of the Optional Protocol to the ICESCR have been removed in the *2015 Agenda.* However, as concerns the UNAR, the research and editorial committee has decided to add a new item to the Agenda, based on the aforementioned observations made by the ECRI. It is on the need for the Italian authorities to formally recognise the broadening of UNAR's remit to act on a wider range of types of discrimination, including those based on language, religion, Country of origin, disability, sexual orientation and gender identity.

The third item on last year's *2014 Agenda* on which significant progress has been recorded concerns measures to tackle overcrowding in Italian penitentiary facilities. On this issue, the various international bodies operating in this area have welcomed alternative measures to imprisonment and other deflationary mechanisms Italy adopted in execution of the ECtHR ruling on the *Torreggiani* case. While awaiting data showing the efficacy of these measures, the Agenda sees these advances in a positive light and encourages the authorities to continue with the efforts already undertaken and follow up on the initiatives they have put in place thus far.

On the remaining points, on the other hand, some distinctions should be made. In certain areas, some improvements have been noted, but a longer time-frame is considered necessary to assess whether Italy has actually met its commitments. Consequently, these points are reformulated based on the developments observed and appear again in the *2015 Agenda*, to allow for a longitudinal assessment of their implementation. Other issues have not been the object of any specific initiatives by the Italian authorities and so the research and editorial committee considers it particularly important to keep a focus on them. These points are therefore confirmed again, in the same words as last year, in the *2015 Agenda*.

Generally speaking, the points listed in the *Italian Agenda of Human Rights 2015* cover most of the recommendations which Italy fully accepted out of those made to the Country during the second cycle of UPR in October 2014 (see Part III, The United Nation System, II, B). And so the *2015 Agenda* is also put forward as a tool to strengthen and support the commitments Italy made recently before the United Nations Human Rights Council through the coming months.

Italian Agenda of Human Rights 2015

Normative Level	1) Ratify the following legal instruments (United Nations and Council of Europe): a. International Convention on the Protection of the Rights of All Migrant Workers and Members of their Families; b. International Convention for the Protection of All Persons from Enforced Disappearances; c. Optional Protocol to the Convention on the Rights of the Child on a Communications Procedure; d. United Nations Convention on the Reduction of Statelessness; e. Protocol XII to the Convention for the Protection of Human Rights and Fundamental Freedoms; f. Protocol XV to the Convention for the Protection of Human Rights and Fundamental Freedoms; g. Protocol XVI to the Convention for the Protection of Human Rights and Fundamental Freedoms; h. European Convention on Nationality; i. Additional Protocol to the Criminal Law Convention on Corruption.

	2) Deposit the instruments of ratification for the following legal instruments for which Parliament has already adopted the relative ratification and implementation laws: a. Convention on Human Rights and Biomedicine (Oviedo Convention); b. Additional Protocol to the Convention on Human Rights and Biomedicine concerning Transplantation of Organs and Tissues of Human Origin.
	3) Support the adoption of the draft Declaration on the right to peace (A/HRC/20/31), presented to the Human Rights Council by its own Advisory Committee in February 2012, containing the explicit recognition of peace as a right of the person and of peoples.
	4) Accept article 25 of the European Social Charter (revised), on the right of workers to protection of their claims in the event of insolvency of their employer.
	5) Withdraw the declaration that excludes the application for Italy of Chapter C of the European Convention on the Participation of Foreigners in Public Life at Local Level and, accordingly, provide for the introduction of active and passive voting rights in local elections for foreigners who have been residing in Italy for a certain number of years.
	6) Include hate motivation as an aggravating circumstance in article 61 of the Italian criminal code.
	7) Include the crime of torture in domestic legislation.
	8) Expressly recognise representative non-governmental organisations within Italian jurisdiction having particular competence in issues regulated by the European Social Charter (revised) the right to present collective complaints pursuant to the 1995 Protocol.
	9) Complete the adoption process of parliamentary bill No. 925 on defamation in light of the of United Nations, Council of Europe and OSCE standards.
	10) Continue efforts to reform the system for the prevention and repression of corruption in both the public and private sector, with special reference to the most recent recommendations made by GRECO.

Infrastructural Level	11) Complete the system of independent national human rights institutions in line with the Paris principles adopted by the United Nations: a. establish the National Human Rights Commission; b. establish the National Ombudsperson; c. appoint the members and allocate the necessary resources to the National Ombudsperson for the rights of detainees and persons deprived of their personal freedom, established by law-decree 146/2013; d. establish an independent and adequately funded national preventive mechanism against torture (OPCAT), pursuant to law 195/2012.
	12) Ensure the existence of a permanent parliamentary Human Rights Commission, in one or both Chambers.
	13) Assign all Ministries an ad hoc human rights office.
Implementation of International Obligations and Commitments	14) Complete the legislative process for the implementation of the Statute of the International Criminal Court as concerns substantive law.
	15) Submit reports due to the international monitoring bodies, particularly: a. VI report to the United Nations Committee on Civil and Political Rights (overdue since October 2009); b. I report to the Council of Europe European Committee of Social Rights on the provisions of the European Social Charter (revised) which have not been accepted (overdue since 31 July 2004).
	16) Increase the timeliness and full execution of European Court of Human Rights rulings, including paying out compensation awarded, and improve Italy's capacity to conform to the standards defined by the same Court.
	17) Address as a matter of urgency the issue of the excessive duration of legal proceedings, including those initiated to seek remedy for their excessive duration.
Adoption of Policies	18) Hold an annual debate on Human Rights in Parliament.
	19) Adopt the following national action plans, providing them with suitable tools for monitoring and assessment: a. National action plan against trafficking of human beings; b. National action plan on the human rights situation within detention structures; c. National programme on education for democratic citizenship and education and training on human rights; d. Fourth National action plan for the protection of rights and of the development of children and adolescents;

	e. National plan against racism, xenophobia and intolerance for the three-year period 2013–2015, based on the outline prepared by UNAR in 2013; f. Extraordinary action plan against sexual and gender-based violence, as per art. 5 of law-decree 14 August 2013, No. 93, as amended and converted into law by law 15 October 2013, No. 119.
	20) Provide information on the impact of the following national action plans: a. National strategy for the inclusion of Roma, Sinti and travellers – 2012–2020; b. National strategy for preventing and combating discrimination on grounds of sexual orientation or gender identity; c. Two-year action plan for the promotion of rights and the integration of persons with disabilities.
	21) Formally extend the remit of UNAR to include all forms of discrimination, including those based on language, religion, nation of origin, disabilities, sexual orientation and gender identity.
	22) Allocate sufficient public social spending in the various categories (illness, disability, family support, unemployment, social housing and combating social exclusion).
	23) Continue with efforts to resolve the problem of overcrowding in prisons, making further progress on the structural measures and deflation mechanisms introduced.
Initiatives in specific areas	
Women's Rights	24) Promote actual equality between men and women in all aspects of public and private life, specifically through adoption of policies and actions directed at: a. reducing the deficit in the number of women represented in the highest decision-making roles in political bodies, including Parliament and Regional Councils, public administration including the Diplomatic Service and in the private sector; b. reducing the salary gap between men and women; c. fostering a more balanced sharing of family duties between men and women, both in running the home and in care-giving duties; d. eliminating stereotypical attitudes on the roles and responsibilities of women and men in the family, in society and in the workplace; e. encouraging plans for the integration of foreign women; f. tackling and resolving the phenomenon of resignations without a justified reason ("blank resignation letters") for pregnant women and working mothers.

	25) Adopt further institutional, political and administrative initiatives to continue to combat the phenomenon of violence against women and reinforce the support services for victims of violence, including: a. correcting the current fragmentation of legislation on violence against women and fostering the use of current legislation which is best able to ensure effective protection of victims; b. completing the framework of regional laws on violence against women; c. carrying out an audit on the performance of the activities to prevent and combat gender-based violence and stalking described in the relevant National Plan; d. encouraging growth in the numbers of anti-violence centres and in multi-agency work done on the issue, including in the prevention of violence stage; e. encouraging correct information on the real circumstances and dimensions of the phenomenon of violence against women, with a particular regard to femicides.
Children's Rights	26) Adopt a general legislative measure which enshrines the right of children to be listened to in court, in administrative bodies, in the institutions, at school and in the family in every issue which concerns them directly and establish suitable mechanisms and procedures to this end, to ensure that the participation of children really takes place.
	27) Amend the criminal code so as to explicitly forbid and criminalise the recruitment and the deployment, by either the armed forces or armed groups, of young people under the age of 18 in the course of armed conflicts.
	28) Adopt legislation prohibiting and criminalising the sale of light and small calibre arms to Countries which deploy child soldiers.
	29) Amend legislation so as to prohibit the expulsion of children, even on public order or State security grounds, when there are substantiated reasons to believe there is a real risk of irreparable damage to the child.

Rights of Migrants, Refugees and Asylum Seekers	30) Address migratory flows as a structural phenomenon, the systematic planning for which must be assigned to instruments of an ordinary nature (rather than to emergency measures linked to a purely security-oriented viewpoint) and to multi-level governance with the involvement of the relevant Ministries, Regions, local administrations and civil society.
	31) Respect the principle of *non-refoulement*, the right of asylum seekers to an individual examination of their case, as well as immediate access to asylum procedures and other forms of national and international protection, including where there are bilateral agreements for return or for cooperation in management of migratory flows.
	32) Support the activities of the "Roundtable on the Legal Status of Roma", established on 30 January 2013 as part of the National Strategy for Inclusion of the members of these communities, with the objective of finding solutions to the situation of statelessness of large numbers of Roma and Sinti originally from the former Yugoslavia, and of their children born in Italy (the so-called "de facto stateless people").
	33) Develop a more expeditious identification system, in order to reduce as far as possible the period that migrants are detained while waiting for the identification procedures to be completed.
	34) Re-examine laws on citizenship in the light of the principle of *ius humanae dignitatis*, continuing in the direction taken by the simplification of the process for acquiring citizenship status pursuant to art. 33 of l.d. 21 June 2013, No. 69.

Part I

Implementation of International Human Rights Law in Italy

International Human Rights Law

The first Part of the Yearbook is divided into two chapters. The first is devoted to the review of the major international human rights instruments that Italy has ratified, as well as to the identification of both those international instruments signed but not ratified by the Country and those adopted in 2014 that have not been subjected to any initiative of acceptance yet.

The framework of Italy's international obligations takes into consideration the universal conventions adopted within the system of the United Nations, the conventions of the Council of Europe as well as the European Union treaties and secondary law. Accordingly, the information provided are preliminary to the presentation of the national normative apparatus – the Constitution, national and regional laws – which is the subject of the following chapter.

The complete list, updated to December 2014, of the 111 international legal instruments on human rights considered into this publication (43 of the United Nations, 16 on disarmament and non-proliferation and 52 of the Council of Europe) and of Italy's acceptance status (ratification, signature, no initiative) is available online at: www.italianhumanrightsyearbook.eu, in the section "attachments".

I. Legal Instruments of the United Nations

In 2014, Parliament ratified the Optional Protocol to the International Covenant on Economic, Social and Cultural Rights (l. 3 October 2014 No. 52); however, as of 31 December 2014 the act of ratification was yet to be deposited.

The complete list, updated to December 2014, of the legal instruments of the United Nations, and of Italy's acceptance status (ratification, signature, no initiative) is available online at: www.italianhumanrightsyearbook.eu, in the section "attachments".

II. Legal Instruments on Disarmament and Non-proliferation

On 2 April 2014 Italy deposited the instrument of ratification of the Arms Trade Treaty.

The complete list, updated to December 2014, of the legal instruments on disarmament and non-proliferation, and of Italy's acceptance status (ratification, signature, no initiative) is available online at: www.italianhumanrightsyearbook.eu, in the section "attachments".

III. Legal Instruments of the Council of Europe

In 2014 Italy neither signed nor deposited instruments of ratification concerning legal instruments adopted by the CoE. The only addition in this area derives from the coming into force on 1 August 2014 of the Convention on preventing and combating domestic violence and violence against women (Istanbul Convention), ratified by Italy on 10 September 2013.

The complete list, updated to December 2014, of the legal of the Council of Europe, and of Italy's acceptance status (ratification, signature, no initiative) is available online at: www.italianhumanrightsyearbook.eu, in the section "attachments".

IV. European Union Law

A. Treaties

As envisaged by the Treaty of Lisbon, since 1 December 2009 the EU legal framework has consisted of two fundamental instruments: the Treaty on the European Union (TEU) and the Treaty on the Functioning of the European Union (TFEU). Article 6 of the TEU attributes the status of primary law to the Charter of Fundamental Rights of the EU, and also refers specifically to the rights guaranteed by the European Convention for the Protection of Human Rights and Fundamental Freedoms (ECHR) and those deriving from the constitutional traditions common to the Member States, which are part of EU law insofar as they are general principles.

Furthermore, in the Preamble of the TEU, explicit reference is made to the 1989 Community Charter of Fundamental Social Rights of Workers and the 1961 European Social Charter of the Council of Europe (revised in 1996). Both these instruments are also mentioned in the TFEU in the context of Title X on Social Policy (art. 151).

On 18 December 2014 the EU Court of Justice (ECJ) adopted opinion 2/13 on the compatibility of the revised Draft agreement on accession of the Union to the European Convention on Human Rights (ECHR), presented in Strasbourg on 10 June 2013. Highlighting the specific features of the Union's legal system, the ECJ identified six main points of incompatibility of the Draft with primary Union law regarding the following: the application of article 53 ECHR regarding rights recognised by the Charter of Fundamental Rights of the European Union (CFREU); the preservation of the principle of mutual trust between the Member States of the EU; the autonomy and effectiveness of the preliminary ruling procedure in light of Protocol XVI to the ECHR; the compatibility between art. 344 of the TFEU and art. 33 of the ECHR; the co-respondent mechanism and prior involvement of the ECJ; and exclusive attribution of the competency of the ECHR to provide an opinion on the violation of rights regarding CFSP/CSPD. In view of all the points identified, the Court concluded that the draft agreement on the accession of the European Union to the ECHR is not compatible with the provisions of Union law. Taking into account the legal effect of Opinions adopted by the ECJ pursuant to art. 218(11) of the TFEU on one hand, and the requirement created by the Lisbon Treaty for the Union to accede to the ECHR (art. 6(2) TEU) on the other, the Council and the Commission must now take action to reopen negotiations with the Council of Europe in order to adopt a new accession agreement in line with the opinion of the ECJ.

B. *EU Law in 2014*

During 2014 the European Parliament and Council of the EU adopted a number of directives, regulations and decisions with particular relevance to human rights. For its part the European Commission presented significant draft legislation and communications.

During 2014, directives were adopted on measures facilitating the exercise of rights conferred on workers in the context of freedom of movement (2014/54/EU of 16 April 2014), and on the return of cultural objects unlawfully removed from the territory of a Member State (2014/60/EU of 15 May 2014).

Among the regulations adopted in 2014 with particular relevance to the issue of human rights were: Commission implementing regulation (EU) No. 775/2014 of 16 July 2014 amending Council regulation (EC) No. 1236/2005 concerning trade in certain goods which could be used for capital punishment, torture or other cruel, inhumane or degrading treatment or punishment; Regulation (EU) No. 235/2014 of the European Parliament and of the Council of 11 March 2014 establishing a financing instrument for democracy and human rights worldwide; Commission implementing regulation (EU) No. 118/2014 of 30 January 2014 amending regulation (EC) No. 1560/2003 laying down detailed rules for the application of Council regulation (EC) No. 343/2003 establishing the criteria and mechanisms for determining the Member State responsible for examining an asylum application lodged in one of the Member States by a third-country national; Council regulation (EU) No. 390/2014 of 14 April 2014 establishing the "Europe for Citizens" programme for the period 2014–2020; Regulation (EU) No. 223/2014 of the European Parliament and of the Council of 11 March 2014 on the Fund for European Aid to the Most Deprived Persons.

Furthermore, some decisions were adopted which are particularly relevant to the theme considered here: 2014/333/EU Commission decision of 5 June

2014 on the protection of personal data in the European e-Justice Portal; 2014/322/EU Council decision of 6 May 2014 on guidelines for the employment policies of the Member States for 2014; 2014/52/EU Council decision of 28 January 2014 authorising Member States to ratify, in the interests of the European Union, the Convention concerning Safety in the Use of Chemicals at Work, 1990, of the International Labour Organization (Convention No. 170); 2014/51/EU Council decision of 28 January 2014 authorising Member States to ratify, in the interests of the European Union, the Convention concerning decent work for domestic workers, 2011, of the International Labour Organisation (Convention No. 189); Council decision 2014/385/CFSP of 23 June 2014 extending the mandate of the European Union Special Representative for Human Rights.

Finally, regarding communications adopted by the Commission, in 2014 those relating to the consequences of depriving Union citizens who exercise their right to free movement of the right to vote, and a new EU framework to strengthen the rule of law, are of particular interest.

Since the adoption of l. 24 December 2012, No. 234, two instruments have been employed to bring Italian legislation into line with European law: the European law and the law of European delegation. While the former contains norms for the direct implementation of EU law, designed to remedy situations where European norms have been implemented incorrectly, the latter contains the authorisation provisions necessary for implementing the directives and other acts of the Union.

On 7 October 2014 Parliament adopted the law of European delegation 2013 relating to the second semester. With particular reference to the protection of fundamental rights, the parliamentary proxy to the Government empowers it to transpose the following: the directive on common procedures for granting and withdrawing international protection (2013/32/EU of 26 June 2013); and the directive laying down standards for the reception of applicants for international protection (2013/33/EU of 26 June 2013). Furthermore, within the scope of this measure, Parliament charged the Government with adopting a consolidated act by 20 July 2019 containing provisions for the implementation of European Union regulations on international protection and temporary protection.

On 30 October 2013 law 161/2014 was adopted, setting out provisions for complying with obligations resulting from Italy's membership of the European Union – European law 2013-*bis*. In the context of this measure, actions concerning the protection of fundamental rights were: amendments to law 30 November 1989 No. 398, adopting regulations relating to study bursaries for continued learning abroad (EU Pilot 5015/13/EACU case); amendments to provisions for immigration and returns as set out in the preliminary ruling of the Court of Justice of the European Union of 6

December 2012 in case C-430/11 (EU Pilot 6534/14/HOME case); amendments to legislative decree of 9 April 2008 No. 81 on health and safety of workers in the workplace (infringement proceeding 2010/4227); amendments to legislative decree 17 August 1999 No. 298 on health and safety for work on board fishing vessels (infringement procedure 2011/2098); amendments to article 24 of law 23 July 1991, No. 223, on collective redundancies (infringement procedure 2007/4652; ruling of the Court of Justice of the European Union of 13 February 2014 in case C-596/12).

Data provided by the Department of European Affairs of the Prime Minister's Office show that as of 28 January 2015, 92 infringement proceedings were pending against Italy, of which 23 began in 2014. Among those which began in 2014, those of particular note in relation to human rights issues are: the letters of formal notice ex art. 258 TFEU 2014/0134 for failure to incorporate into Italian law directive 2011/93/EU of 13 December 2011 on the fight against sexual abuse and exploitation of minors and child pornography; and procedure 2014/0135 for failure to incorporate directive 2011/95/EU of 13 December 2011, on standards for the qualification of third-country nationals or stateless persons as beneficiaries of international protection, for a uniform status for refugees or for persons eligible for subsidiary protection, and for the content of the protection granted; procedure 2014/2126 for the alleged violation of the reception conditions directive (2003/9/EC) and the Dublin regulation (343/2003) in connection with push-backs to Greece; procedure 2014/2171 for the alleged violation of directives 2003/9/EC and 2005/85/EC relating to the situation of unaccompanied minors seeking asylum; procedure 2014/2235 for incorrect transposition of directive 2008/115/EC on common standards and procedures in Member States for returning illegally staying third-country nationals (return directive); and the alleged violation of directive 2003/9/EC, laying down minimum standards for the reception of asylum seekers in Member States (reception directive).

Finally, regarding the evolution of some infringement proceedings initiated in previous years, it should be noted that on 16 October 2014 the European Commission referred Italy to the EU Court of Justice under art. 258 TFEU for not adequately implementing directive 2004/80/EC on compensation for victims of crime (infringement procedure 2011/4147). However, during 2014 the following infringement procedures were closed: No. 2006/2441 for incorrect transposition of directive 2000/78/EC on equal treatment in employment and occupation; No. 2013/0398 on failure to transpose directive 2010/64/EU of 20 October 2010 on the right to interpretation and translation in criminal proceedings; No. 2013/4009 on the non-conformity of some Italian provisions with the principle of equal treatment of directive 2003/109/EC (purchase cards and family and maternity allowance).

Italian Law

I. The Constitution of the Italian Republic

"The Republic recognises and guarantees the inviolable rights of the persons, both as an individual and in the social group where the human personality is expressed. The Republic expects that the fundamental duties of political, economic and social solidarity be fulfilled" (article 2).

"All citizens have equal social dignity and are equal before the law, without distinction of sex, race, language, religion, political opinion, personal and social conditions.

It is the duty of the Republic to remove those obstacles of an economic or social nature which constrain the freedom and equality of citizens, thereby impeding the full development of the human person and the effective participation of all workers in the political, economic and social organisation of the Country" (article 3).

"The Italian legal system conforms to the generally recognised principles of international law. The legal status of foreigners is regulated by law in conformity with international provisions and treaties. A foreigner who, in his home Country, is denied the actual exercise of the democratic freedoms guaranteed by the Italian constitution shall be entitled to the right of asylum under the conditions established by law. A foreigner may not be extradited for a political offence" (article 10).

"Italy rejects war as an instrument of aggression against the freedom of other peoples and as a means for the settlement of international disputes. Italy agrees, on conditions of equality with other States, to the limitations of sovereignty that may be necessary to a world order ensuring peace and justice among the Nations. Italy promotes and encourages international organisations furthering such ends" (article 11).

The whole of Part I of the Constitution (articles 1–54) is devoted to the fundamental rights and duties of citizens, which are grouped into four areas: civil relations, ethical and social relations, economic relations and political relations.

II. National Legislation

During the year 2014, Parliament and the Government passed a number of legislative acts (laws, law-decrees, legislative decrees) relating, directly or indirectly, to the safeguarding and protection of internationally recognised human rights. The following list of legislative acts is structured on the same lines as the classification of international instruments:

a) general legislative acts (the judiciary in general)
b) legislative acts dealing with specific issues (right to a home; peacekeeping missions and international cooperation; treaty ratification; crimes, criminal procedure and issues relating to the prison system; culture and mass media; education)
c) legislative acts concerning the protection of particular social groups (migrants, refugees, asylum seekers; children and adolescents; workers; disaster victims).

a) General Legislative Acts

The Judiciary in General

L. 11 August 2014, No. 114 (Conversion into law, with amendments, of law-decree 24 June 2014, No. 90, containing urgent measures on simplification, administrative transparency and the efficiency of legal offices).

b) Legislative Acts Dealing with Specific Issues

Right to a Home

L. 23 May 2014, No. 80 (Conversion into law, with amendments, of law-decree 28 March 2014, No. 47, containing urgent measures on the housing emergency, the building market and for Expo 2015).

Peacekeeping Missions, International Cooperation, Treaty Ratification

L. 14 March 2014, No. 28 (Conversion into law, with amendments, of law-decree 16 January 2014, No. 2, containing provisions for the extension of the international missions of the armed forces and police, cooperation and initiatives to develop support processes of reconstruction, and participation in the initiatives of international organisations for the consolidation of peace and stabilisation processes).

L. 11 August 2014, No. 125 (General regulations on international co-operation for development).

L. 3 October 2014, No. 152 (Ratification and execution of the Optional Protocol to the International Covenant on Economic, Social and Cultural Rights, done in New York, on 10 December 2008).

Crimes, Criminal Procedure and Issues Relating to the Prison System

L. 21 February 2014, No. 10 (Conversion into law, with amendments, of law-decree 23 December 2013, No. 146, containing urgent measures relating to the protection of fundamental rights of prisoners and controlled reduction of the prison population).

L. 28 April 2014, No. 67 (Parliamentary proxies to the Government relating to house arrest and reforming of the punishment system; provisions on the suspension of proceedings with probation and for absconded persons).

L. 30 May 2014, No. 81 (Conversion into law, with amendments, of law-decree 31 March 2014, No. 52, containing urgent measures relating to the definitive closure of criminal psychiatric hospitals).

L. 11 August 2014, No. 117 (Conversion into law, with amendments, of law-decree 26 June 2014, No. 92, containing urgent measures relating to compensation in favour of prisoners and detainees who have been treated in violation of article 3 of the European Convention on Human Rights, as well as changes to the criminal proceedings code and implementing regulations, the rules for the penitentiary police and the prison system, including the juvenile prison system).

Culture and Mass Media

L. 22 July 2014 No. 110 (Amending the Cultural Heritage and Landscape Code as per law-decree 22 January 2004, No. 42, in relation to heritage professionals and the creation of national lists of those professionals).

L. 29 July 2014 No. 106 (Conversion into law, with amendments, of law-decree 31 May 2014, No. 83, containing urgent measures for the protection of cultural heritage, cultural development and the revival of tourism).

Education

L. 5 June 2014, No. 87 (Conversion into law, with amendments, of law-decree 7 April 2014, No. 58, containing urgent measures to ensure the regular provision of education services).

c) Legislative Acts Devoted to the Protection of Social Groups

Migrants, Refugees and Asylum Seekers

L. 17 October 2014, No. 146 (Conversion into law, with amendments, of law-decree 22 August 2014, No. 119, containing urgent measures countering illegal and violent activities at sporting events, recognising international protection, and ensuring the functioning of the Ministry of Interior).

Workers

L. 16 May 2014, No. 78 (Conversion into law, with amendments, law-decree 20 March 2014, No. 34, containing urgent measures to help boost employment and simplifying the administrative burden imposed on businesses).

Disaster Victims

L. 26 June 2014, No. 93 (Conversion into law, with amendments, law-decree 12 May 2014, No. 74, containing urgent measures in favour of the people of Emilia-Romagna affected by the earthquake and subsequent flooding which took place between 17 and 19 January 2014, as well as measures to ensure that the National Emergency Fund is operational).

III. Municipal, Provincial and Regional Statutes

Since 1991, after the adoption of law 8 June 1990, No. 142 (Local authorities system), the so called "peace human rights norm", originally contained in article 1 of Veneto regional law 30 March 1988, No. 18 (then updated by regional law 55/1999) on "Regional measures for the promotion of a culture of peace", has been included in the Statutes of several Italian Municipalities, Provinces and Regions. The original wording of this norm reads:

> The Municipality [...] (the Province [...], the Region [...]), consistent with the Constitutional principles sanctioning the repudiation of war as a means of resolving international controversies, and the promotion of human rights, the democratic freedoms and international cooperation, recognises peace as a fundamental human and peoples' right.
>
> To this end the Municipality [...] (the Province [...], the Region [...]) promotes the culture of peace and human rights through cultural, research, education, cooperation and information initiatives aimed at making the Municipality a land of peace.
>
> In order to achieve these goals, the Municipality [...] (the Province [...], the Region [...]) will take direct initiatives and foster the initiatives by local authorities, associations, cultural institutions, volunteers and international cooperation groups.

With r.l. 18 April 2014, No. 10, the Molise Regional Council adopted a new Statute which includes the "Peace Human Rights" norm in art. 2, setting out its fundamental principles (the previous Statute dated back to 1971). Below are some extracts from the article in question.

1. The Region is founded on the values of Republican Democracy, human rights and sustainable development. It is based on the principles of freedom, equality, solidarity and subsidiarity and works to entrench awareness of the universal value of peace. It recognises the values of its Christian and civil traditions.
2. The Region adopts the principles of the Constitution and of the European Union. [...]

There are also many other local and regional bodies whose Statutes include a specific reference to international norms and principles relating to human rights and territorial autonomy, particularly to the United Nations Charter, the Universal Declaration of Human Rights, the International Covenant on Civil and Political Rights, the International Covenant on Economic, Social and Cultural Rights, the International Convention on the Rights of the Child, the Charter of Fundamental Rights of the EU, and the European Charter of Local Self-Government (see *2011 Yearbook*, pp. 65–69).

IV. Regional Laws

This section lists the laws on human rights, equal opportunities, development cooperation, fair trade, minorities, migration, Ombudspersons and the protection of children's rights, workers' rights, the rights of persons with disabilities, solidarity, social advancement, family assistance, and citizenship and legality education adopted by the Councils of the Italian Regions and Autonomous Provinces in 2014. The laws are divided according to topics and listed, for each authority, in chronological order.

Peace, Human Rights, Development Aid, Fair Trade

R.l. Abruzzo 4 January 2014, No. 5 (Regional interventions to promote development aid activities and international partnership).

R.l. Abruzzo 28 April 2014, No. 28 (Amending r.l. 4 January 2014, No. 5 (Regional interventions to promote development aid activities and international partnership)).

R.l. Apulia 1 August 2014, No. 32 (Provisions to support and promote fair trade).

R.l. Campania 21 July 2014, No. 14 (Promotion of the regional ethical label).

R.l. Emilia-Romagna 12 May 2014, No. 4 (Amending r.l. 13 November 2001, No. 34 (Participation of the Emilia-Romagna Region in establishing the Fondazione Scuola di Pace di Monte Sole (Peace School)).

R.l. Tuscany 1 October 2013, No. 56 – cited below: Solidarity, social advancement and support to families.

Equal Opportunities, Gender

R.l. Apulia 4 July 2014, No. 29 (Regulations for the prevention and combating of gender-based violence, victim support, promotion of women's freedom and self-determination).

R.l. Apulia 8 October 2014, No. 40 (Provisions for the protection of women affected by endometriosis).

R.l. Emilia-Romagna 27 June 2014, No. 6 (Framework law for equality and against gender discrimination).

R.l. Lazio 19 March 2014, No. 4 (Reorganisation of provisions to combat gender-based violence against women and promotion of a culture of respect for fundamental human rights and the differences between men and women).

R.l. Tuscany 23 December 2014, No. 81 (Amending r.l. 15 December 2009, No. 76 (Regional equal opportunities commission)).

Ombudspersons and Children's Ombudspersons

R.l. Umbria 26 February 2014, No. 1 (Further integration of r.l. 18 October 2006, No. 13 (Creation of an Ombudsperson for persons subject to restricted or limited personal freedom).

Persons with Disabilities

R.l. Abruzzo 17 April 2014, No. 17 (Provisions promoting social inclusion of deaf people and recognition of Italian sign language and integration of r.l. 13 January 2014, No. 7).

R.l. Basilicata 27 October 2014, No. 31 (Establishment of the special dentistry service at the emergency dental service for persons with disabilities and at-risk patients).

R.l. Basilicata 12 November 2014, No. 34 (Amendments and integrations to r.l. 18 August 2014, No. 26, article 17 on "Reordering of regulations relating to the prevention of blindness. Amendments and integrations to art. 16 of r.l. 16 April 2013, No. 7").

R.l. Basilicata 12 December 2014, No. 38 (Establishment of the Regional Observatory on the condition of persons with disabilities).

R.l. Lazio 29 December 2014, No. 13 (Contributions towards the adaptation of vehicles used to transport persons with permanent disabilities and severe limitations in walking ability).

R.l. Marche 9 October 2014, No. 25 (Provisions for those with autism spectrum disorders).

Workers' Rights

R.l. Apulia 10 March 2014, No. 8 (Regulations for safety, quality and wellbeing at work).

R.l. Calabria 13 January 2014, No. 1 (Guidelines encouraging the elimination of insecure employment as per l.d. 31 August 2013, No. 101, converted into l. 30 October 2013, No. 125).

R.l. Campania 21 July 2014, No. 14 – cited above: Peace, human rights, development aid and fair trade.

R.l. Marche 22 April 2014, No. 7 (Regulations on preventative measures and protection from the risk of falls from a height to be implemented in buildings to ensure that maintenance work on roofs is carried out safely).

R.l. Tuscany 1 October 2014, No. 56 (Amendments to r.l. 2 August 2013 No. 45 (Funding support measures on behalf of families and workers in financial difficulty, to promote social cohesion and combat social alienation) regarding microcredit for workers in difficulty).

R.l. Tuscany 16 December 2014, No. 78 (Amendments to r.l. 2 August 2013 (Funding support measures on behalf of families and workers in financial difficulty, to promote social cohesion and combat social alienation) regarding family support provisions).

R.l. Umbria 2 April 2014, No. 3 (Provisions to encourage new farming businesses and job creation, to promote sustainable agriculture. Provisions concerning the processing of small quantities of agricultural produce.

Amendments and integrations to r.l. 29 May 1980, No. 59 and r.l. 18 April 1997, No. 14).

Solidarity, Social Promotion and Assistance to Families

R.l. Abruzzo 4 January 2014, No. 2 (Urgent measures to reduce housing problems. Establishment of Territorial Commissions to revise eviction dates).

R.l. Basilicata 27 October 2014, No. 30 (Measures to combat the spread of pathological gambling).

R.l. Emilia-Romagna 28 March 2014, No. 2 (Regulations for recognition and support of family caregivers).

R.l. Emilia-Romagna 30 June 2014, No. 8 (law simplifying regional regulations governing voluntary work, social advancement associations and civil service. Creation of the Citizen Solidarity Day).

R.l. Emilia-Romagna 23 July 2014, No. 19 (Regulations for promotion and support of the solidarity economy).

R.l. Liguria 13 October 2014, No. 25 (Creation of the donated breast milk bank in Liguria).

R.l. Liguria 2 December 2014, No. 39 (Measures to simplify and facilitate access to financial support for Ligurian businesses affected by exceptional meteorological events).

R.l. Lombardy 24 June 2014, No. 18 (Provisions for the protection of separated or divorced spouses in difficult conditions, particularly those with dependent children).

R.l. Lombardy 16 December 2014, No. 33 (Creation of the Voluntary Regional Civic Service).

R.l. Marche 30 May 2014, No. 11 (Amendments to r.l. 3 April 2002, No. 5 (Integration of r.l. 26 December 1983, No. 41 on benefits to the population of Ancona affected by the landslide of 13 December 1982)).

R.l. Marche 3 October 2014, No. 24 (Amendments to r.l. 2 September 1996, No. 38 (Restructuring of the rules relating to the right to university study)).

R.l. Marche 1 December 2014, No. 32 (Regional integrated system of social services for the protection of the person and of the family).

R.l. Molise 2 December 2014, No. 21 (Creation of the regional body for social housing).

R.l. Piedmont 18 April 2014, No. 5 (Urgent normative-legal measures. Amendments to r.l. 3 September 1991, No. 43 (New regulation on the Institute of Economic and Social Research of Piedmont I.R.E.S. Repeal of r.l. 18 February 1985, No. 12) and amendments to r.l. 18 March 1992, No. 16 (Right to university study)).

R.l. Piedmont 29 September 2014, No. 10 (Further normative-legal amendments to r.l. 18 March 1992, No. 16 (Right to university study)).

R.l. Piedmont 29 September 2014, No. 11 (Restructuring of the Territorial Housing Agencies. Amendments to r.l. 17 February 2010, No. 3 (regulations relating to social housing)).

R.l. Piedmont 11 November 2014, No. 17 (Further amendments to r.l. 28 December 2007, No. 28 (Regulations on education, the right to study and free choice of education)).

R.l. Tuscany 14 February 2014, No. 8 (Extraordinary contributions to the population of Municipalities affected by the floods of the period 4 January – 11 February 2014).

R.l. Tuscany 15 April 2014, No. 21 (Rules governing the Permanent Conference of Local Social Organisations. Repeal of r.l. 20/2007).

R.l. Tuscany 30 July 2014, No. 45 (Amendments to r.l. 24 February 2005, No. 41 (Integrated system of programmes and services to protect social citizenship rights)).

R.l. Tuscany 26 September 2014, No. 53 (Amendments to r.l. 25 July 2006, No. 35 (Formation of the regional civic service), relating to regional civic service financed with European funds).

R.l. Tuscany 29 September 2014, No. 54 (Extraordinary contributions for the inhabitants and local authorities affected by the exceptional meteorological events of the days of 21 – 22 July and 19 – 20 September 2014).

R.l. Tuscany 1 October 2014, No. 56 – cited above: Workers' Rights.

R.l. Tuscany 1 October 2014, No. 57 (Recognition of the social and cultural role of mutual benefit societies and actions to protect their heritage).

R.l. Tuscany 24 November 2014, No. 70 (Extraordinary contributions to the inhabitants of towns affected by the exceptional meteorological events of 10 – 14 October and 5–7 November 2014).

R.l. Tuscany 16 December 2014, No. 78 – cited above: Workers' Rights

R.l. Tuscany 23 December 2014, No. 85 (Amendments to r.l. 18 October 2013, No. 57 (Provisions for responsible gambling and for the prevention of problem gambling). New provisions for combating the problem of gambling).

R.l. Umbria 21 November 2014, No. 21 (Regulations to prevent, combat and reduce the risk of pathological gambling).

R.l. Umbria 28 November 2014, No. 25 (Restructuring and transformation of Public assistance and charitable institutions (IPAB) and regulations on Public providers of services to the person (ASP). Further amendments to r.l. 28 December 2009, No. 26 (Regulations on the creation of an integrated system of interventions and social services. Further amendments to r.l. 16 September 2011, No. 8 (Administrative and regulatory simplification of the regional and the local authorities' systems)).

R.l. Veneto 28 November 2014, No. 39 (Amendments to r.l. 7 April 1998, No. 8 (Regulations for the implementation of the right to university study) and subsequent amendments).

Education for Citizenship and Legality

R.l. Marche 7 July 2014, No. 16 (Provisions for the implementation of regional policy for the promotion of the culture of legality).

R.l. Marche 9 July 2014, No. 17 (Amendments to the legislative deliberation approved at the meeting of 1 July 2014, No. 162, concerning: "Provisions for the implementation of regional policy for the promotion of the culture of legality").

Part II

The Human Rights Infrastructure in Italy

National Bodies with Jurisdiction over Human Rights

International human rights law requires States to set up structures that are adequately specialised in promoting and protecting fundamental rights. In this regard, a distinction shall be made between, on one hand, strictly governmental bodies, and on the other, independent structures directly emanating from civil society. The latter in particular, through channels different from those classically used by governmental powers, aim to participate in policy-making and to promote and develop a human rights culture, as well as to prevent violations.

In this Part the composition, mandate and activities of the following institutions will be illustrated:

- *Parliamentary bodies*: the Special Commission for the Promotion and Protection of Human Rights of the Italian Senate; the Permanent Committee on Human Rights instituted within the Foreign Affairs Commission (III) of the Italian Chamber of Deputies; the Parliamentary Commission for Children and Adolescents; the Parliament-Government Observatory Monitoring the Promotion and Protection of Fundamental Rights (data are lacking on the actual functioning of this Observatory in 2014).
- *Governmental bodies*: Bodies established within the Prime Minister's Office: Committee of Ministers for Orientation and Strategic Guidance for the Protection of Human Rights (data are lacking on the actual functioning of this Observatory in 2014); Department for Equal Opportunities; Commission for International Adoptions; National Committee on Bioethics. Bodies established within the Ministry of Foreign Affairs: Inter-Ministerial Committee for Human Rights; National Commission for UNESCO. Bodies established within the Ministry of Labour and Social Policy: National Observatory for Children and Adolescents; National Observatory Monitoring the Condition of Persons with Disabilities; and other departments and bureaus of the Ministry of Justice which work specifically on human rights matters.
- There is no data available on the actual functioning of the Committee of Ministers on Orientation and Strategic Guidance for the Protection of Human Rights in 2014.
- The *Constitutional Court*.
- *Judicial authorities:* the Court of Cassation, acting as the supreme judge of legitimacy.

- *Independent authorities*: the Communications Regulatory Authority; the Data Protection Authority; the Committee Guaranteeing the Implementation of the Law on Strikes Affecting Essential Public Services; the National Ombudsperson for Children and Adolescents.
- Italy's national human rights infrastructure is completed by academic institutions promoting not only research, but also education and training in human rights issues, and by several non-governmental organisations, some of which function through networking.

I. Parliamentary Bodies

A. *Senate of the Republic: Special Commission for the Protection and Promotion of Human Rights*

The Senate's Special Commission for the Protection and Promotion of Human Rights was first set up during the 14th legislature (motion 20, 1 August 2001) and is the fruit of long experience by the Committee against Capital Punishment (1996–2001). Since the Commission is not permanent, it must be instituted formally at the beginning of each legislature, and the Senate did so during the 15th legislature (motion 20, 12 July 2006), the 16th legislature (motion 13, 26 June 2008) and the 17th legislature (motion 7, 26 March 2013). In the latter motion, the Senate decided to commence the proceedings for the establishment of a permanent human rights commission.

The Commission has the task of studying, observing and taking initiatives on issues concerning the protection and promotion of internationally recognised human rights. To this end, it can establish relations with institutions of other Countries and with international bodies; carry out missions in or outside Italy, in particular with foreign Parliaments, even – if necessary – in order to establish agreements fostering human rights or to facilitate other forms of collaboration; it can carry out informational procedures and formulate proposals and assembly reports; and provide its advisory opinions on proposed legislation as well as on matters deferred to other commissions.

The Commission is made up of 25 members, present in proportion to the size of the parliamentary groups to which they belong. Among these members, the Commission elects the bureau, made up of the Chair, two Vice Chairs and two Secretaries.

In 2014 the Commission was composed as follows: Chair: Luigi Manconi; Vice Chairs: Ciro Falanga, Daniela Donno; Secretaries: Giovanni Bilardi, Paola De Pin; Members: Bruno Alicata, Silvana Amati, Federica Chiavaroli, Franco Conte, Peppe De Cristofaro, Aldo Di Biagio, Enzo Fasano, Emma Fattorini, Elena Ferrara, Miguel Gotor, Sergio Lo Giudice, Riccardo Mazzoni, Emanuela Munerato, Venera Padua, Francesco Palermo, Lucio Romano, Francesco Russo (until 6 March 2014), Manuela Serra, Ivana Simeoni, Daniela Valentine (from 6 March 2014), Guido Viceconte.

In the ambit of the survey of the various levels and systems of human rights protection currently in place in Italy and abroad, in 2014 the Commission held 33 hearings of representatives from associations, organisations and institutional bodies, and of individual experts, as reported below.

- 15 January: Messaud Romdhani, Director of the *Forum Tunisien pour les Droits Economiques et Sociaux* (FTDES).
- 23 January: Antonio Apruzzese, director of the Postal and Communications Police.
- 29 January: Alberto Berbieri, general coordinator of Physicians for Human Rights, Giulia Anita Bari, researcher at the same organisation, and Salvatore Fachile, member of the Governing Council of the Association for Legal Studies on Immigration.
- 5 February: Antonio Mumolo, President of the Association *Avvocato di Strada*.
- 12 February: Hilary Sedu, President of the association *Nova Italia*.
- 26 February: Antonella Napoli, President of the association *Italians for Darfur*, and Abu Gasim Mohamed, spokesperson for the Darfur community in Italy.
- 5 March: Maurizio Del Bufalo of the Human Rights Cinema Festival, Francesca Saudino from the association *Osservazione*, and Nuria Seferovic, resident of the Masseria del Pozzo camp.
- 12 March: Francesca Zuccari and Daniela Pompei of the *Comunità di Sant'Egidio*.
- 18 March: Professor Carlo Fiorio, on the detention regime under article 41-*bis* of the Italian Penitentiary Act.
- 1 April: Deborah Lucchetti, coordinator of the *Abiti Puliti* campaign, and Shila Begum, survivor of the Rana Plaza collapse.
- 2 April: Sebastiano Ardita, Assistant Prosecutor at the Public Prosecutor's Office of Messina.
- 16 April: Riccardo Compagnucci, deputy head of the Department for Civil Liberties and Immigration of the Ministry of Interior.
- 8 May: Daniele Ozzimo, Housing Policy Councillor at the Municipality of Rome.
- 8 May: Gian Ludovico De Martino, President of the Inter-Ministerial Committee for Human Rights (CIDU), on the United Nations Universal Periodic Review (UPR) procedure.
- 22 May: Dr. Soulangduoji, President of the Economic, Population, Resources and Environment Commission of the Tibet Autonomous Region's Political Consultative Conference.

- 3 June: Renato De Nicola and Gianfranco Crua of the International Help NPO.
- 4 June: Nicola Gratteri, Assistant Prosecutor of the Republic at the Court of Reggio Calabria, on the detention regime relating to article 41-*bis* of the Penitentiary Act.
- 10 June: Gabriele Eminente, Director General, and Loris de Filippo, President, of Médecins Sans Frontières Italy.
- 25 June: Mauro Palma, President of the Council for Penological Cooperation of the Council of Europe.
- 26 June: Franco Roberto, National Anti-Mafia Prosecutor.
- 9 July: Angelino Alfano, Minister of the Interior.
- 17 July: Franca Biondelli, Undersecretary of State for Labour and Social Policy, on the reception of unaccompanied foreign minors.
- 30 July: Andrea Pugiotto, Tenured Professor of Constitutional Law at the University of Ferrara.
- 16 September: Gian Ludovico De Martino, President of the Inter-Ministerial Committee for Human Rights (CIDU).
- 24 September: Admiral Giuseppe De Giorgi, Chief of Staff of the Italian Navy, on operation *Mare Nostrum*.
- 25 September: Maria Teresa Agai, Chair of the Centre for Study and Research on Technical Aids for Disabled Persons of Confindustria, on updating the Prostheses Tariff Nomenclature.
- 4 November: Razen Kader, High Representative of the Regional Government of Kurdistan to Italy and the Holy See.
- 18 November: Giuseppe Scifo, representative of the Federation of Agro-Industrial Workers CGIL in Ragusa, and Antonello Mangano, journalist.
- 2 December: Gian Ludovico De Martino, President of the Inter-Ministerial Committee for Human Rights (CIDU).
- 3 December: François Crépeau, United Nations Special Rapporteur on the human rights of migrants.
- 9 December: Admiral Giuseppe De Giorgi, Chief of Staff of the Italian Navy, on operations *Mare Nostrum* and *Triton*.
- 10 December: Franca Biondelli, Undersecretary of State for Labour and Social Policy, on implementing the "National Strategy for the inclusion of Roma, Sinti and Travellers".
- 16 December: Giovanni Maria Bellu, President of the *Carta di Roma* association, presenting the results of the 2013 report "*Notizie alla deriva*" on media and immigration.

Furthermore, in 2014 the Commission adopted the report on identification and expulsion centres in Italy (24 September 2014), and made four resolutions on:

- the conclusion of their study on the implementation of the National Strategy of inclusion for Roma, Sinti and Travellers in Italy (14 January 2014).
- the conclusions of the group's study on measures to adopt with reference to the identification and expulsion centres (5 March 2014).
- the conclusion of the group's study on the respect of fundamental rights in Tibet (5 March 2014).
- the conclusion of the group's study of the respect of the fundamental rights of people belonging to Falun Gong, with particular reference to organ harvesting from prisoners in China (4 March 2014).

B. Chamber of Deputies: Permanent Committee on Human Rights

The international protection of human rights is one of the focal points of the activities performed by the Commission for Foreign and European Union Affairs (3rd Commission) of the Chamber of Deputies. As from the 10th legislature (1987–1992), the Commission set up within it the Permanent Committee on Human Rights, which, especially through hearings, ensures that Parliament is kept continually informed and up-to-date with regard to the status of international human rights. The Committee also has the task of following the course of individual human rights measures, performing preliminary tasks pertinent to the activities of the Commission. The Committee for the current legislature (17th) was set up on 16 July 2013.

In 2014, the Committee convened 18 times:

- 29 January: hearing of representatives of the Ukrainian community in Italy.
- 6 February: hearing of the activist from the International Campaign for the Abolition of the Death Penalty, Lidia Guerrero de Saldano.
- 20 March: hearing of the advocacy officer of the Palestinian NGO *Addameer* (Arabic for 'conscience') Prisoner Support and Human Rights Association, Randa Wahbe.
- 2 April: hearing of Mariela Castro, campaigner for rights for homosexuals and transsexuals in Cuba.
- 8 April: hearing of campaigners for human rights in Colombia, representing the associations *Cavida* and *Justicia y Paz*. Hearing of the chair of the Inter-Ministerial Committee for Human Rights, Minister Plenipotentiary Gian Ludovico de Martino.
- 29 April: hearing of representatives of Action Aid and Children's Development Association on the violation of human rights in cane sugar production in Cambodia.

- 6 May: hearing of Ahmed Bashar, President of the Parliament of the Iraqi province of Nineveh.
- 8 May: hearing of Maherzia Labidi, Vice President of the Constituent Assembly of the Republic of Tunisia.
- 15 May: informal meeting with a delegation from the Commission for Human Rights of the National Assembly of the Republic of Turkey.
- 12 June: hearing of Matteo Meccacci, President of the International Campaign for Tibet.
- 15 July: hearing of activists for human rights in Ukraine.
- 22 July: hearing of the President of the Inter-ministerial Committee for Human Rights, Minister Plenipotentiary Gian Ludovico de Martino, on Italy's Universal Periodic Review (UPR) at the United Nations Human Rights Council.
- 29 July: hearing of representatives of the Palestinian community in Rome and Lazio.
- 22 September: hearing of Mukesh Kapila, former UN Resident Representative in Sudan.
- 24 September: hearing of Sheila B. Keetharuth, United Nations Special Rapporteur on the situation of human rights in Eritrea.
- 19 November: informal meeting with representatives of the Central Committee of the Chinese Communist Party regarding the situation in the Tibet Autonomous Region.
- 26 November: hearing of the President of the Inter-Ministerial Committee for Human Rights, Minister Plenipotentiary Gian Ludovico de Martino, on the outcomes of the first stage of Italy's Universal Periodic Review at the Human Rights Council of the United Nations.
- 3 December: hearing of François Crépeau, United Nations Special Rapporteur on the human rights of migrants.

In addition, in 2014 the Committee carried out four missions: to Budapest (26–28 February 2014), to address constitutional reforms and protection of fundamental rights in Hungary; to Geneva (12–14 March 2014), on the occasion of the 25th Session of the United Nations Human Rights Council; to Berlin (11–13 November 2014), visiting the *Bundestag* Committee on Petitions; and to Geneva (27 October 2014), for the 20th Session of the Working Group of the United Nations Human Rights Council.

C. Bicameral Bodies: Parliamentary Commission for Children and Adolescents

The Parliamentary Commission for Children and Adolescents was set up by law 23 December 1997, No. 451, although its name and responsibilities were modified by law 3 August 2009, No. 112.

Essentially, the Commission is entrusted with a supervisory and policymaking role related to the enforcement of international obligations and domestic law on children's rights. It may also present to the two Houses of Parliament observations and proposals concerning the effects and limitations of current legislation, and the possible need to amend it to ensure compliance with international law concerning the rights of the child.

The Commission is composed of 20 Senators and 20 Representatives appointed, respectively, by the Chair of the Italian Senate and the Chair of the Italian Chamber of Deputies, proportionately to the total number of members in the various parliamentary groups. The Commission then elects its Chair, two Vice Chairs and two Secretaries. In 2013 the Commission was composed as follows: *Chair*: Michela Vittoria Brambilla; *Vice Chairs*: Rosetta Enza Blundo, Sandra Zampa; *Secretaries*: Antimo Cesaro, Maria Antezza; *Members from the Chamber of Deputies*: Luigi Bobba (until 2 July 2014), Renata Bueno, Annagrazia Calabria, Chiara di Benedetto (from 30 October 2014), Vittoria D'Incecco, Gabriella Giammanco, Silvia Giordano (until 2 October 2014), Maria Tindara Gullo, Vanna Iori, Roberta Lombardi (from 1 October 2014), Loredana Lupo, Michela Marzano (from 2 July 2014), Gaetano Nastri, Marisa Nicchi, Giovanna Petrenga, Chiara Scuvera, Giorgio Girgis Sorial (until 29 October 2014), Irene Tinagli, Giorgio Zanin; *Members from the Senate*: Ornella Bertorotta, Valeria Cardinali, Nunzia Catalfo, Mario Ferrara (until 10 February 2014), Rosanna Filippin, Antonio Gentile, Stefania Giannini, Manuela Granaiola (until 22 December 2014), Pietro Langella (from 10 February 2014), Donella Mattesini, Alessandra Mussolini (until 30 June 2014), Venera Padua, Franco Panizza (until 22 September 2014), Francesca Puglisi, Antonio Razzi, Maria Rizzotti, Mariarosaria Rossi, Annalisa Silvestro, Maria Spilabotte, Erika Stefani, Mara Valdinosi (from 22 December 2014).

In 2014 the Commission carried out three fact-finding surveys:

– *Survey on poverty and troubled childhoods*. The aims of the survey are: to investigate the impact and consequences of the protracted economic crisis in Italy on minors; and to identify legislative and administrative instruments that could be adopted by Government institutions to combat the phenomenon and to deliver concrete responses to the difficulties faced by children and adolescents. In the ambit of the survey, the following were heard:

- 23 January: Arianna Saulini, coordinator of Gruppo CRC, Diego Cirpani, Gruppo CRC/Caritas Italy, and Matteo Rebesani, Gruppo CRC/Save the Children Italy.
- 13 February: Giacomo Guerrera, President of UNICEF Italy, and Federica Aguiari from the UNICEF Italy Advocacy Office.
- 18 February: Concetta Vaccaro, head of the welfare and health sector at CENSIS.

- 18 March: Vincenzo Spadafora, National Ombudsman for Children and Adolescents.
- 20 March: Antonio Di Pinto, national coordinator of the communities working on the reception of unaccompanied foreign minors; Barbara Ferrari, regional delegate of CICAM Apulia; Salvatore Angellotti, CICAM national Vice President; and Savlatore Barcellona, CICAM national Vice President.
- 3 April: Marilisa Martelli, member of the Board of Directors of the Italian Children's Mental Health Association (AISMI) with responsibility for relations with public bodies and the media.
- 15 April: Sivana Mordeglia, President of the National Council of Social Workers.
- 6 May: Representatives from the organisation Agevolando: Federico Zullo, President; Merita Gasi, Vice President; and Denise Pergher, National Councillor.
- 8 May: Vincenzo Spadafora, National Ombudsman for Children and Adolescents.
- 29 May: Samantha Tedesco, planning and development manager at the not-for-profit *SOS Villaggio dei Bambini*; and Laura Bononcini, institutional relations official at Facebook Italy.
- 5 June: Vincenzo Curatola, President of the Forum for Distance Support in Rome; and Simona Chiapparo and Pasquale De Sole, National Councillors of the Forum.
- 12 June: Christian Morabito, Scientific Head of the Save the Children Project on Educational Poverty.
- 19 June: Lucia Piacentini, Director of the *DarVoce* association; Anna Canapini, coordinator of the "*Non più soli*" ("No Longer Alone") project; and Erica Brindisi, legal consultant of the *DarVoce* association.
- 24 June: Franca Biondelli, Undersecretary of the Ministry of Labour and Social Policy.
- 22 July: Grazia Sestini, Ombudsperson for Children and Adolescents of the Tuscany Region; and Sabrina Breschi, head of the Tuscan regional documentation centre for children and adolescents.
- 29 July: Tiziano Vecchiato, director at the *Fondazione Zancan*; and Marzia Sica, representative of the *Compagnia di San Paolo*.
- 11 September: Luigi Fadiga, Ombudsperson for Children and adolescents of the Emilia-Romagna Region.
- 18 September: Francesco Alvaro, Ombudsperson for Children and adolescents of the Lazio Region.
- 25 September: Marilina Intrieri, Ombudsperson for Children and adolescents of the Calabria Region.

- On 16 December 2014, the Commission unanimously approved the "Concluding Document of the Survey on Poverty and troubled childhoods" (Document XVII-*bis* No. 2).

– *Child prostitution survey*. The main aim of the survey is to update the overall picture built up by the survey conducted in the previous legislature (16th), in order to gauge whether and to what extent forms of systematic monitoring have been introduced by the institutionally competent bodies. Such monitoring is a prerequisite for developing effective instruments to combat and eliminate this form of exploitation of minors. In addition, the survey seeks more information about the social context of the problem, and analyses the underlying causes (economic, educational and social) with a view to identifying possible preventative initiatives. In the ambit of the survey, the following were heard:

- 4 March 2014: Melita Cavallo, President of the Juvenile Court of Rome.
- 10 July: Antonio Apruzzese, Director of the Postal and Communications Police.
- 6 November: Cosimo Maria Ferri, Undersecretary of State at the Ministry of Justice.
- 27 November: Gianna Maria Nanna, Assistant Public Prosecutor at the Juvenile Court of Bari.

– *Survey on the right of children to enjoy their national artistic and cultural heritage* In the ambit of the survey, launched in January 2014, Cristina Marchini, school and education sector official at the Italian Environmental Fund (FAI), was heard (13 May 2014).

D. Parliamentary Initiatives Concerning Human Rights

Presented below is a brief overview of the main human rights legislation produced by the Italian Parliament in 2014, subdivided into bills and guidelines and watchdog initiatives (motions, interpellations, questions for an oral or written answer, resolutions, agenda proposals). The proposer or first signer, the code (the letter 'C' indicating that the initiative was presented in the Chamber of Deputies and the letter 'S' that it was presented in the Senate), the title, the date of presentation and the most recent update are listed for each initiative.

In 2014, Parliament adopted 168 human rights initiatives overall, including 35 bills, 14 motions, 12 interpellations, 13 questions for an oral answer, 42 questions for a written answer, 11 questions submitted to Commissions, four Commission resolutions, one final resolution, 22 Assembly agenda proposals and seven Commission agenda proposals.

Bills

The 35 bills presented concerned the following issues: the right to vote (12); the right to a private and family life (7); the ratification of international instruments (4); prison conditions and the rights of prisoners (3); the rights of migrants (including citizenship rights), refugees and asylum seekers (2); national human rights institutions (2); freedom of opinion and expression (2); economic, social and cultural rights (1); the rights of children (1); the protection of victims of crime (1).

Date	Initiative	Latest update
07/01/2014	Pierpaolo VARGIU (SCpI) – C.1926 Amendments to the Consolidated text as per Decree of the President of the Republic 30 March 1957, No. 361, concerning the exercising of the right to vote in a place other than the place of residence, and to l. 27 December 2001, No. 459, regarding the exercising of the right to vote on the part of Italian citizens temporarily living abroad.	31/03/2014 assigned (examination not yet begun)
10/01/2014	Giuseppe LUMIA (PD) – S. 1231 Civil union between persons of the same sex.	24/02/2015 under examination by the Commission
10/01/2014	Luigi ZANDA (PD) – S. 1235 Amendments to l. 27 December 2001, No. 459, regarding the exercising of the right to vote of Italian citizens resident abroad.	27/02/2014 assigned (examination not yet begun)
15/01/2014	Roberto SPERANZA (PD) – C.1955 Amendments to l. 27 December 2001, No. 459, regarding the exercising of the right to vote of Italian citizens resident abroad.	10/03/2014 assigned (examination not yet begun)
19/01/2014	Roberto OCCHIUTO (FI-PdL) – C.2825 Addition of art. 17-*bis* of l. 25 May 1970, No. 352, on exercising the right to vote by post in referenda provided for in the Constitution.	05/02/2015 assigned (examination not yet begun)
21/01/2014	Marco MELONI (PD) – C.1977 Amendments to the consolidated text regulating the election to the Chamber of Deputies, as per the Decree of the President of the Republic 30 March 1957, No. 361, regarding exercising the right to vote for non-resident students within the national territory.	11/03/2014 atypical conclusion by withdrawal
27/01/2014	Antonella INCERTI (PD) – C.2001 Regulation of the integrated public system for children to ensure the right to education and learning from birth to age six.	12/05/2014 assigned (examination not yet begun)

30/01/2014	Riccardo NENCINI (Aut(SVP-UV-PATT-UPT)-PSI) – S. 1277 Amendments to art. 48 of the Constitution and the consolidated text as per Decree of the President of the Republic 20 March 1967 No. 223, on granting the right to vote in all sub-national elections to citizens who have reached the age of sixteen.	05/03/2014 assigned (examination not yet begun)
03/02/2014	Alessandro DI BATTISTA (M5S) – C.2038 Amendments to l. 27 December 2001, No. 459, regarding the exercising of the right to vote on the part of Italian citizens resident abroad.	11/03/2014 atypical conclusion by withdrawal
12/02/2014	Emma BONINO – C.2085 Ratification and implementation of the Optional Protocol to the International Covenant on Economic, Social and Cultural Rights, done at New York on 10 December 2008.	04/06/2014 approved
14/02/2014	Maurizio SACCONI (AP (NCD-UDC)) and others – S. 1316 Provisions regarding civil unions.	24/02/2015 under examination by the Commission
05/03/2014	Emma FATTORINI (PD) – S. 1360 Regulation of civil unions between persons of the same sex.	24/02/2015 under examination by the Commission
05/03/2014	Khalid CHAOUKI (PD) – C.2159 Amendments to art. 2 of law-decree 24 June 1994, No. 408, converted, with amendments, into l. 3 August 1994, No. 483, regarding the right to vote in elections to the European Parliament on the part of citizens of another Member State of the European Union resident in Italy.	12/05/2014 assigned (examination not yet begun)
11/04/2014	Daniele FARINA (SEL) – C.2300 Amendments to art. 111 of the Constitution, regarding the guarantee of rights to victims of crime.	11/04/2014 to be assigned
14/04/2014	Nicola LATORRE (PD) – S. 1452 Provisions regarding the right to asylum and the rights of migrants	24/06/2014 assigned (examination not yet begun)
30/04/2014	Pia LOCATELLI (Mixed) – C.2342 Regulation of civil unions.	09/07/2014 assigned (examination not yet begun)
28/05/2014	Alessio TACCONI (Mixed) and others – C.2413 Amendments to l. 27 December 2001, No. 459, regarding the exercising of the right to vote on the part of Italian citizens resident abroad.	19/09/2014 assigned (examination not yet begun)

Date	Initiative	Latest update
29/05/2014	Emanuele SCAGLIUSI (M5S) – C.2424 Establishment of the independent National Commission for the promotion and protection of human rights and fundamental freedoms.	23/10/2014 assigned (examination not yet begun)
06/06/2014	Emma BONINO – S. 1510 Ratification and implementation of the Optional Protocol to the International Covenant on Economic, Social and Cultural Rights, done at New York on 10 December 2008.	03/09/2014 passed as law
17/06/2014	Andrea GIORGIS (PD) – C.2460 Amendments to the consolidated text as per legislative decree 18 August 2000, No. 267, on the right to vote and stand as a candidate on the part of foreigners legally resident in Italy in municipal and district elections.	17/06/2014 to be assigned
27/06/2014	Andrea ORLANDO and others – C.2496 [Prisoner Compensation Decree] Conversion into law, with amendments, law-decree 26 June 2014, No. 92, containing urgent provisions on compensatory remedies for prisoners and internees who have undergone treatment in violation of art. 3 of the European Convention for the Protection of Human Rights and Fundamental Freedoms; also, amendments to the Code of Criminal Procedure and implementing provisions, to the regulation of the Italian prison guard system and to the prison system, including the juvenile prison system.	24/07/2014 approved
09/07/2014	Mario MARAZZITI (PI-CD) and others – C.2529 Establishment of the National Commission for the promotion and protection of human rights.	10/10/2014 assigned (examination not yet begun)
10/07/2014	Alessandro PAGANO (AP (NCD-UDC)) and others – C.2535 Ban on the production and sale of goods produced by the labour of workers in conditions of slavery or serious intimidation.	10/07/2014 to be assigned
14/07/2014	Laura GARAVINI (PD) – C.2540 Amendments to law-decree 24 June 1994, No. 408, converted, with amendments, into l. 3 August 1994, No. 483, and to l. 24 January 1979, No. 18, regarding the right to vote in elections to the European Parliament of Italian citizens resident in other Member States of the European Union.	14/07/2014 to be assigned

22/07/2014	Edmondo CIRIELLI (FdI) and others – C.2559 Establishment of a Parliamentary Commission of Enquiry on the responsibilities for failure to adapt prisons and on prison overcrowding.	19/09/2014 assigned (examination not yet begun)
23/07/2014	Luca D'ALESSANDRO (FI-PdL) – C.2560 Introduction of Title VI-*bis* of Book One of the Civil Code, concerning the rules of the civil solidarity pact.	17/09/2014 assigned (examination not yet begun)
24/07/2014	Andrea ORLANDO and others – S. 1579 [Prisoner Compensation Decree] Conversion into law, with amendments, law-decree 26 June 2014, No. 92, containing urgent provisions on compensatory remedies for prisoners and internees who have undergone treatment in violation of art. 3 of the European Convention for the Protection of Human Rights and Fundamental Freedoms; also, amendments to the Code of Criminal Procedure and implementing provisions, to the regulation of the Italian prison guard system and to the prison system including the juvenile prison system.	02/08/2014 passed as law
28/07/2014	Alessandro ZAN (PD) and others – C.2570 Establishment of and framework for civil unions between persons of the same sex.	28/07/2014 to be assigned
04/09/2014	Elena FATTORI (M5S) – S. 1603 Organic framework of regulations on the right to asylum, international protection and other humanitarian protection measures.	04/03/2015 assigned (examination not yet begun)
19/09/2014	Lodovico SONEGO (PD) – S. 1623 Regulations against covering one's face.	19/09/2014 to be assigned
24/09/2014	Luis Alberto ORELLANA (Mixed) and others – S. 1633 Ratification and implementation of Protocol No. 12 of the Convention for the Protection of Human Rights and Fundamental Freedoms.	12/11/2014 assigned (examination not yet begun)
15/10/2014	Gian Luigi GIGLI (PI-CD) and others – C.2666 Provisions and parliamentary proxy to the Government on the establishment of a register of stable cohabitation.	30/11/2014 assigned (examination not yet begun)
30/10/2014	Enrico COSTA (AP (NCD-UDC)) and others – C.925-B [Defamation act] Amendments to l. 8 February 1948, No. 47, to the criminal code, to the code of criminal procedure and the code of civil procedure with regard to defamation, libel in print or other media, insult and conviction of the plaintiff, as well as professional secrecy. Further provisions for the protection of the defamed party.	27/01/2015 under examination in Commission

Date	Initiative	Latest update
14/11/2014	Maurizio SACCONI (AP (NCD-UDC)) and others – S. 1675 Recognition of the right to multiple weighted votes to parents of minors.	03/02/2015 assigned (examination not yet begun)
30/12/2014	Paolo GENTILONI SILVERI and others – C.2801 Ratification and implementation of the following Protocols: a) Protocol No. 15 containing amendments to the Convention for the Protection of Human Rights and Fundamental Freedoms, done at Strasbourg 24 June 2013; b) Protocol No. 16 containing amendments to the Convention for the Protection of Human Rights and Fundamental Freedoms, done at Strasbourg 2 October 2013.	05/02/2015 assigned (examination not yet begun)

Sources: *openparlamento* (search criteria: "human rights", "rights of the person").

Motions

Date	Initiative	Latest update
28/01/2014	Emma FATTORINI (PD) – S. 1/00208 "Whereas: Ukraine is a member of the United Nations and is obliged to observe its principles, to respect the Universal Declaration of Human Rights and all documents approved at…"	28/01/2014 accepted
27/02/2014	Aldo DI BIAGIO (AP (NCD-UDC)) and others – S. 1/00224 "Whereas: In Venezuela since the beginning of February 2014 there have been many protests against the president Nicolás Maduro, which determined…"	27/02/2014 presented
06/03/2014	Lia QUARTAPELLE PROCOPIO (PD) – C.1/00358 "Whereas: The Italian Parliament, in the Senate of the Republic and the Chamber of Deputies, has for years been closely following the situation in Myanmar, a strategic Country…"	11/06/2014 concluded
13/03/2014	Elena FERRARA (PD) – S. 1/00233 "Whereas: The term 'cyber bullying' is a neologism describing the phenomenon of aggression from an individual (the 'cyber bully') who, online and mainly through…"	13/03/2014 presented
02/04/2014	Andrea CIOFFI (M5S) – S. 1/00242 "Whereas: It has now been around 40 years since Spain gave up its former West Sahara colony. After so much time there is still no definition of the State…"	03/04/2014 not accepted

03/04/2014	Paola BINETTI (AP (NCD-UDC)) and others – C.1/00423 "Whereas: Freedom of religion is one of the fundamental rights of the person which every State should protect and respect; the Universal Declaration of Human Rights…"	02/07/2014 accepted
05/08/2014	Manuela SERRA (M5S) – S. 1/00297 Italy's role in the Israeli-Palestinian conflict.	05/08/2014 presented
30/09/2014	Ivana SIMEONI (Misto) e altri – S. 1/00315 "Whereas: Italy has been facing a dramatic situation for several months: boats full of migrants from Africa and the Middle East continue to arrive on our shores…"	Further signatures being added
03/10/2014	Michele NICOLETTI (PD) – C.1/00603 "Whereas: The phenomenon of refugees and asylum seekers in Europe who, due to dramatic and violent conflict, are investing in the Mediterranean and, further…"	18/12/2014 accepted
13/10/2014	Roberto SPERANZA (PD) – C.1/00615 "Whereas: Consolidating and affirming a culture of equality, equal opportunities and women's rights has by rights become, in recent years, one of the…"	11/11/2014 accepted
25/11/2014	Giorgio TONINI (PD) – S. 1/00354 Combating the phenomenon of violence against women.	26/11/2014 concluded
25/11/2014	Paolo ROMANI (FI-PdL) – S. 1/00355 "Whereas: The 'disease' that causes the most damage to a child and which parents pass on to children is poverty, as it carries an extremely high risk of social exclusion…"	26/11/2014 accepted
25/11/2014	Ornella BERTOROTTA (M5S) – S. 1/00348 "Whereas: On 25 November 1960 Patria Mercedes, María Argentina Minerva and Antonia María Teresa Mirabal were killed for their opposition to the dictatorial regime of Rafael…"	25/11/2014 presented
19/12/2014	Manuela SERRA (M5S) – S. 1/00369 "Whereas: On 4 November 2014 the "21 Luglio" association, which promotes the rights of Roma, Sinti and Travellers on a national level in Italy, publicised how…"	19/12/2014 presented

Sources: *openparlamento* (search criteria: "human rights", "rights of the person").

Interpellations

Date	Initiative	Latest update
08/01/2014	Nicola FRATOIANNI (SEL) – C.2/00355 The images presented on 16 December 2013 by TG2, concerning the Contrada Imbriacola Rescue and Initial Reception Centre at Lampedusa show an inhumane situation in which…	10/01/2014 concluded
17/01/2014	Maria Edera SPADONI (M5S) – C.2/00372 Mario Pescante, IOC member, on the occasion of the National Council of the Italian National Olympic Committee (Coni) in Milan, said of the upcoming Winter Olympic Games in Sochi: "It is absurd that a…	17/01/2014 presented
22/01/2014	Adele GAMBARO (Mixed) and others – S. 2/00114 To the Minister of the Interior – "Whereas: Thousands of children, women, elderly people and men are fleeing from Syria due to the war unleashed by…"	22/01/2014 presented
11/02/2014	Alessia MORANI (PD) – C.2/00407 The website of the *Corriere della Sera* on 6 February 2014 published a video investigation on the dramatic phenomenon of deaths in prison, of which there have been 2230 in little over a decade…	21/03/2014 concluded
04/03/2014	Luigi MANCONI (PD) – S. 2/00129 To the Ministers of Foreign Affairs and of Defence – "Whereas: There are ever more victims of the conflict in the south of Sudan and human rights continue to be violated…"	04/03/2014 presented
06/03/2014	Alessandro PAGANO (AP (NCD-UDC)) and others – C.2/00443 With the Decree of the Prime Minister 11 December 2003 the UNAR (National Anti-Racial Discrimination Office) was established at the Prime Minister's office…	28/03/2014 concluded
20/03/2014	Sergio LO GIUDICE (PD) – S. 2/00139 The phenomenon of surrogacy.	31/03/2014 amended by responsible Minister
10/07/2014	Carlo GIOVANARDI (AP (NCD-UDC)) and others – S. 2/00179 To the Prime Minister and the Minister of Foreign Affairs – "Whereas: On 25 June 2014 the United Nations Human Rights Council approved a resolution on the protection of the family and its members…"	10/07/2014 presented
05/09/2014	Erasmo PALAZZOTTO (SEL) – C.2/00665 Eritrea is living completely closed off from the rest of the world due to the dictator Isaias Afewerki being in power since independence was established…	05/09/2014 presented

17/09/2014	Gian Luigi GIGLI (PI-CD) and others – C.2/00682 On 14 July 2013 in Naples at Palazzo San Giacomo city hall, in the presence of Mayor Luigi de Magistris, the registry office recorded a marriage…	25/09/2014 concluded
07/10/2014	Erasmo PALAZZOTTO (SEL) – C.2/00709 After a siege lasting more than 20 days on Kobane Canton in western Kurdistan, the ISIS militia entered the city of Kobane, Syria's third-largest city on the border…"	10/10/2014 concluded
21/10/2014	Arturo SCOTTO (SEL) – C.2/00722 The prisons issue.	24/10/2014 concluded

Sources: *openparlamento* (search criteria: "human rights", "rights of the person").

Questions for an Oral Answer

Date	Initiative	Latest update
22/01/2014	Sergio LO GIUDICE (PD) – S. 3/00665 In January 2013 Russia passed a law against homosexual propaganda, which is extremely harmful to fundamental human rights…	06/02/2014 concluded
23/01/2014	Adriano ZACCAGNINI (SEL) and others – C.3/00585 On 21 November information was released about the arrest, by the Italian police in Milan, of Bahar Kimyongür, Belgian anti-imperialist militant of Turkish origin, who reached Italy…	23/01/2014 presented
19/02/2014	Enrico CAPPELLETTI (M5S) – S. 3/00738 Following the regrettable situation characterising our prison system…	assigned to a commission
26/02/2014	Michela MONTEVECCHI (M5S) – S. 3/00759 To the Minister of Education, Universities and Research – Whereas: Many Italian schools have decided to give up…	09/09/2014 concluded
18/06/2014	Luigi MANCONI (PD) – S. 3/01049 On some shipwrecks which occurred between 2012 and 2013 in the sea between Tunisia and Italy and involved a number of people who are missing…	30/10/2014 concluded
23/07/2014	Vincenzo SANTANGELO (M5S) – S. 3/01129 To the Minister of Defence – Whereas: In the Middle East armed conflict is ongoing…	23/09/2014 amended by responsible Minister
04/08/2014	Josefa IDEM (PD) and others – S. 3/01159 Over the next decade the Qatari Government will be obliged to take on over a million workers to complete the infrastructure for the 2022 Football World Cup on time: the toll of workplace deaths is bound to increase…	04/08/2014 presented

Date	Initiative	Latest update
01/10/2014	Stefano VACCARI (PD) – S. 3/01252 On the conflict in the Western Sahara.	assigned to a commission
11/11/2014	Franco CARDIELLO (FI-PdL) – S. 3/01394 To the Minister of Justice – Whereas: The problem of overpopulation of our penal institutions has not been solved. The imbalance…	assigned to a commission
19/11/2014	Peppe DE CRISTOFARO (Mixed) – S. 3/01444 On 26 September 2014 during a student protest in Iguala, in the State of Guerrero (Mexico), police killed three students, injured a further 25 and carried out an unspecified number of arrests…	assigned to a commission
02/12/2014	Mario MARAZZITI (PI-CD) and others – C.3/01200 Since October 2014 the flag of Islamic State has been flying in the city of Derna in Lybia, now being called by its former name Barqa, and now the first caliphate ISIS has managed to…	03/12/2014 concluded
18/12/2014	Venera PADUA (PD) – S. 3/01525 Whereas autism, as defined in national and international guidelines, is a behavioural syndrome…	assigned to a commission
19/12/2014	Peppe DE CRISTOFARO (Mixed) – S. 3/01528 To the Minister for the Interior – Whereas it is the questioner's understanding that those living in the Roma camp in via Cupa Perillo, Scampia (Naples), since Tuesday 16 December…	19/12/2014 presented

Sources: *openparlamento* (search criteria: "human rights", "rights of the person").

Questions for a Written Answer

Of the 42 questions for a written answer, 10 concerned the protection of human rights on an international level (with particular reference to Russia, Venezuela, Equatorial Guinea, Georgia, Israel/Palestine, and Kazakhstan); 9 the issues of prison conditions and prisoners' rights; 6 the right to a private and family life; 5 the rights of migrants (including citizenship rights), refugees and asylum seekers; 3 the fight against homophobia and transphobia; three torture; 1 the right to health; 1 the rights of children; 1 the right to the environment; 1 civil and political rights; 1 the rights of persons with disabilities; and 1 the international arms trade.

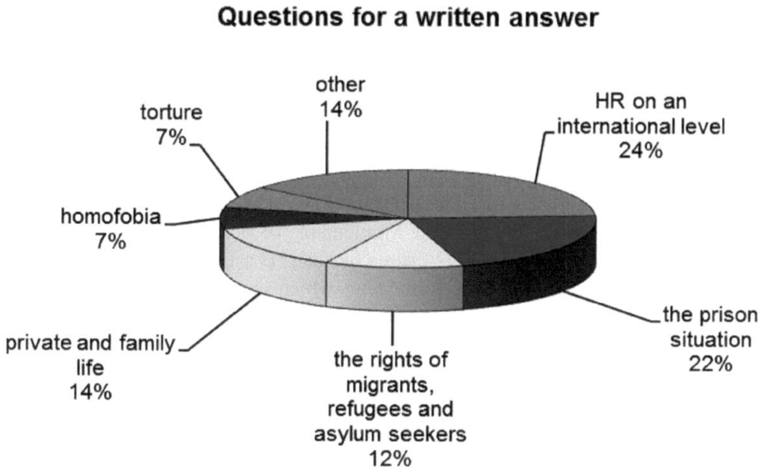

Sources: *openparlamento* (search criteria: "human rights", "rights of the person").

Questions Submitted to Commissions

Date	Initiative	Latest update
15/01/2014	Eleonora CIMBRO (PD) – C.5/01871 In the last five years the European Union has allocated over 500 million euro to improve our national control and assistance system for refugees; and of the 122 million…	15/01/2014 amended by commission being questioned
27/01/2014	Vincenzo AMENDOLA (PD) – C.5/01990 Since the end of November 2013 Ukraine has witnessed demonstrations against President Viktor Yanukovich's decision not to sign the association agreement with the European Union and to sign…	30/01/2014 concluded
04/03/2014	Khalid CHAOUKI (PD) – C.5/02248 We have learned from the Repubblica newspaper, dated 21 February 2014, that the UK Supreme Court recognises the grounds for accusations of the violation of human rights which four refugees, three…	04/03/2014 amended by commission being questioned
02/04/2014	Riccardo FRACCARO (M5S) – C.5/02528 Recent violence and disorder in Ukraine have caused many victims; this been one of the most tragic moments in recent decades; President Viktor Janukovich and his entourage…	02/04/2014 amended by commission being questioned
08/04/2014	Arturo SCOTTO (SEL) – C.5/02594 In the collective imagination of almost the entire Country, the terrorist attack on the Italian military base at Nassiriya in Iraq is one of the most dramatic events of…	08/04/2014 amended by commission being questioned

Date	Initiative	Latest update
07/07/2014	Arturo SCOTTO (SEL) – C.5/03171 In October 2013 an Italian citizen, Romeo Pulitelli, was arrested in the Dominican Republic; according to information from the Dirección Nacional de Control de Drogas, Pulitelli…	18/11/2014 concluded
25/07/2014	Lia QUARTAPELLE PROCOPIO (PD) – C.5/03338 On 4, 5 and 6 July 2014 the Municipality of Bologna held an event called the "Eritrea Festival" (Festival d'Eritrea) in the Parco Nord Arena, which saw substantial direct heavy involvement of the Eritrean Government and of the…	25/07/2014 amended by commission being questioned
28/07/2014	Lia QUARTAPELLE PROCOPIO (PD) – C.5/03346 The recent Italy-Africa initiative has brought to the fore the very real possibility of reciprocal collaboration between our Country and the African continent in the fields of politics, economics…	28/07/2014 amended by commission being questioned
10/10/2014	Maria IACONO (PD) – C.5/03776 From the press and, in particular, from an inquiry by Antonello Mangano published in Espresso magazine, we have learned of the very serious and disturbing situation concerning women, in…	28/10/2014 Further signatures being added
16/10/2014	Enza BRUNO BOSSIO (PD) – C.5/03810 Recent reports from the Praesidium organisations (Save the Children and UNHCR) tell us of the recent arrival of 124 Syrian migrants on 20 October 2014 on the territory of Crotone, among…	16/10/2014 amended by commission being questioned
04/11/2014	Demetrio BATTAGLIA (PD) – C.5/03935 Law No. 89 of 2001, better known as the "Pinto law", established the right of reimbursement for moral and material damages to a citizen who has a case pending…	04/11/2014 amended by commission being questioned

Sources: *openparlamento* (search criteria: "human rights", "rights of the person").

Assembly Resolutions

Date	Initiative	Latest update
21/01/2014	Loredana DE PETRIS (Mixed) – S. 6/00039 Administering justice and fighting crime.	21/01/2014 concluded
21/01/2014	Daniele FARINA (SEL) – C.6/00046 Administering justice and fighting crime.	21/01/2014 accepted
04/03/2014	Edmondo CIRIELLI (FdI) and others – C.6/00052 The prisons issue.	04/03/2014 not accepted
04/03/2014	Andrea COLLETTI (M5S) – C.6/00054 The prisons issue.	04/03/2014 not accepted

Sources: *openparlamento* (search criteria: "human rights", "rights of the person").

Commission Resolutions

Date	Initiative	Latest update
28/01/2014	Alessandro DI BATTISTA (M5S) – C.7/00234 Whereas: ALBA, the Bolivarian Alliance for the Americas (Alianza bolivariana para América Latina y el Caribe) is a system of political, social and economic co-operation between the…	11/06/2014 accepted
05/02/2014	Gabriele ALBERTINI (AP (NCD-UDC)) and others – S. 7/00072 Procedural rights of suspected or accused persons in criminal proceedings.	05/02/2014 approved
14/02/2014	Marietta TIDEI (PD) – C.7/00264 Whereas: The Chinese Government has decided to proceed with an almost complete elimination of nomadism in China between now and 2015. According to the report from Human Rights Watch…	14/02/2014 presented
27/02/2014	Arturo SCOTTO (SEL) – C.7/00277 Whereas: On 24 February 2014 the President of Uganda, Yoweri Museveni, signed a law approved by the Ugandan Parliament on 20 December 2013 dramatically criminalising homosexuality…	25/03/2014 accepted
25/03/2014	Alessandro DI BATTISTA (M5S) – C.7/00315 Whereas: On 11 January 2002 the Government of the United States, under the Bush administration, opened a prison camp in the US military base in Guantanamo, Cuba, for the purpose…	25/03/2014 presented
28/10/2014	Emanuele SCAGLIUSI (M5S) – C.7/00501 The human rights situation in Sudan.	28/10/2014 presented
25/11/2014	Lia QUARTAPELLE PROCOPIO (PD) – C.7/00536 Whereas: Women's rights constitute an integral, inalienable part of the heritage of universal rights which are recognised by democratic societies; the…	25/11/2014 presented

Sources: *openparlamento* (search criteria: "human rights", "rights of the person").

Final Resolutions

Date	Initiative	Latest update
25/03/2014	Arturo SCOTTO (SEL) – C.8/00041 On the violations of human rights and discrimination based on sexual orientation in Uganda.	25/03/2014 approved

Sources: *openparlamento* (search criteria: "human rights", "rights of the person").

Assembly Agenda Proposals

Date	Initiative	Latest update
04/02/2014	Walter RIZZETTO (Mixed) and others – C.9/01921-AR/0 The question of prison overcrowding.	04/02/2014 accepted
27/02/2014	Cristina DE PIETRO (Mixed) and others – S. 9/01248/005 Whereas: Only a few days ago, very peaceful democratic protests from citizens protesting with the Ukrainian Government were strongly repressed by the…	27/02/2014 concluded
27/02/2014	Luis Alberto ORELLANA (Mixed) and others – S. 9/01248/011 Whereas: Instability in the Mediterranean area is progressively increasing and is characterised by numerous violent episodes, such as the coup d'état in Egypt with the aim of…	27/02/2014 concluded
13/03/2014	Lia QUARTAPELLE PROCOPIO (PD) – C.9/02149/002 Whereas: The "missions decree" allows for refinancing and renewal of military personnel's participation in the European Union mission known as EUTM Somalia…	13/03/2014 accepted
13/03/2014	Chiara DI BENEDETTO (M5S) – C.9/02149/009 Whereas: Subparagraph 2 of article 2 of the decree under examination, authorises spending between 1 January 2014 and 30 June 2014 to extend military personnel in…	13/03/2014 not accepted
13/03/2014	Sergio BATTELLI (M5S) – C.9/02149/016 Whereas: Subparagraph 2 of article 2 of the decree under examination, authorises spending between 1 January 2014 and 30 June 2014 to extend military personnel in…	13/03/2014 not accepted
13/03/2014	Davide CRIPPA (M5S) – C.9/02149/029 Whereas: Instability in the Mediterranean area is progressively increasing and is characterised by numerous violent episodes, such as the coup d'état in Egypt with the aim of…	13/03/2014 not accepted
02/08/2014	Giacomo CALIENDO (FI-PdL) – S. 9/01579/002 Prison conditions.	02/08/2014 declared precluded
17/09/2014	Filiberto ZARATTI (SEL) – C.9/02598-AR/0 Whereas: In accordance with the provisions of the law-decree under examination, further allocations are envisaged for the Active Endeavour mission, on which Italy has already…	17/09/2014 not accepted

17/09/2014	Carlo SIBILIA (M5S) – C.9/02598-AR/0 Whereas: PKK and YPG are among the main organisations which immediately, in the silence of the international community, opposed ISIS in Iraq and Syria to defend…	17/09/2014 not accepted
17/09/2014	Emanuele SCAGLIUSI (M5S) – C.9/02598-AR/0 Mandate of the MINURSO mission.	17/09/2014 accepted
17/09/2014	Daniele DEL GROSSO (M5S) – C.9/02598-AR/0 Whereas: Subparagraph 2 of article 2 of the decree under examination, authorises spending between 1 July 2014 and 31 December 2014 to extend military personnel in…	17/09/2014 not accepted
25/09/2014	Peppe DE CRISTOFARO (Mixed) – S. 9/01613/012 Whereas: In accordance with the provisions as per the law-decree under examination, further allocations are envisaged for the Active Endeavour mission, on which Italy has already…	25/09/2014 not accepted
25/09/2014	Peppe DE CRISTOFARO (Mixed) – S. 9/01613/027 Commit the Government to adopt every useful initiative on an international level favouring reopening direct negotiations, under the auspices of the United Nations, between the Kingdom of Morocco and the Polisario Front…	25/09/2014 accepted
25/09/2014	Luis Alberto ORELLANA (Mixed) and others – S. 9/01613/029 During discussions on the bill: Conversion into law, with amendments, law-decree 10 August 2014, No. 109, concerning extending international missions of the Armed Forces and…	25/09/2014 accepted
23/10/2014	Enrico BUEMI (Aut(SVP-UV-PATT-UPT)-PSI) – S. 9/01612/003 During examination of law-decree No. 132 of 12 September 2014, concerning urgent de-juridicalisation measures and other interventions to define the backlog of procedure…	23/10/2014 declared precluded
28/10/2014	Gian Luigi GIGLI (PI-CD) and others – C.9/02629-AR/0 Whereas: Recognised private schools within the integrated public education system, despite making up 24 per cent of Italian schools, host around 10 per cent of the…	29/10/2014 accepted as recommendation
26/11/2014	Peppe DE CRISTOFARO (Mixed) – S. 9/01329/001 During discussions of the bill ratifying and implementing the Treaty on Criminal Judicial Cooperation between the Government of the Italian Republic and the Government of the United Mexican States…	26/11/2014 accepted

Date	Initiative	Latest update
27/11/2014	Aldo DI BIAGIO (AP (NCD-UDC)) and others – S. 9/1–00328/001 Whereas: The latest figures released by the Ministry of Labour and Social Policy, updated to 30 November 2013, show a total of 8,655 unaccompanied minors reported…	26/11/2014 accepted
30/11/2014	Vittoria D'INCECCO (PD) – C.9/02679-*bis* Whereas: The full participation of persons with disabilities in society and the economy for intelligent, sustainable and inclusive growth is one of the key points in the…	30/11/2014 accepted
18/12/2014	Michele ANZALDI (PD) – C.9/02279/001 Whereas: In Mexico, between January 2000 and September 2014, a total of 102 male and female journalists have been assassinated and 17 have disappeared, with proof of connection…	18/12/2014 declared inadmissible
22/12/2014	Pia LOCATELLI (Mixed) – C.9/02679-*bis* Whereas: Italy's six-month presidency of the European Council has confirmed Italy's central geopolitical role for stability, dialogue and peace in the Mediterranean…	22/12/2014 accepted

Sources: *openparlamento* (search criteria: "human rights", "rights of the person").

Commission Agenda Proposals

Date	Initiative	Latest update
06/02/2014	Cristina DE PIETRO (Mixed) and others – S. 0/01248/008/ Whereas: Only a few days ago, very peaceful democratic protests from citizens protesting with the Ukrainian Government were strongly repressed by the…	12/02/2014 accepted
06/02/2014	Luis Alberto ORELLANA (Mixed) and others – S. 0/01248/016/ Whereas: Instability in the Mediterranean area is progressively increasing and is characterised by numerous violent episodes, such as the coup d'état in Egypt with the aim of…	06/02/2014 accepted
15/07/2014	Rita GHEDINI (PD) – S. 0/01519/001/ Whereas: Article 10 of the Constitution recognises the right of asylum for foreigners who do not enjoy democratic freedoms in their own Country, proving of the high value that such…	30/07/2014 partially accepted

30/07/2014	Nadia GINETTI (PD) – S. 0/01579/001/ Whereas: Article 1, subparagraph 1, of law-decree 26 June 2014, No. 92, establishes the amount and the terms of compensatory remedies for prisoners and detainees who have...	30/07/2014 accepted
30/07/2014	Sergio LO GIUDICE (PD) – S. 0/01579/002/ Whereas: law-decree 26 June 2014, No. 92, concerning urgent measures relating to compensatory measures for detainees and prisoners who have undergone treatment...	30/07/2014 accepted
30/07/2014	Luigi D'AMBROSIO LETTIERI (FI-PdL) – S. 0/01579/003/ In discussions on Senate Act 1579 concerning "urgent measures relating to compensation for detainees and prisoners who have undergone treatment in violation..."	30/07/2014 accepted
30/07/2014	Luigi D'AMBROSIO LETTIERI (FI-PdL) – S. 0/01579/004/ In discussions on Senate Act 1579 concerning "urgent measures relating to compensation for detainees and prisoners who have undergone treatment in violation..."	30/07/2014 accepted

Sources: *openparlamento* (search criteria: "human rights", "rights of the person").

II. Prime Minister's Office (Presidency)

The organisation of the Prime Minister's Office is regulated by the decree of the Prime Minister of 1 October 2012. The Prime Minister's Office has a number of departments and offices (the so-called general structures), which the Prime Minister draws on for guideline and coordination functions regarding specific political and institutional fields. Of particular importance for human rights is the Department for Equal Opportunities.

A number of committees and commissions with specific tasks of economic and social relevance operate within the ambit of the Prime Minister's Office. These include the Commission for International Adoptions and the National Committee on Bioethics.

In addition, in 2007 the Committee of Ministers for Orientation and Strategic Guidance for the Protection of Human Rights was established, in order to ensure effective policy and coordination between Ministries with regard to the protection of human rights; however, no data are available about the actual functioning of this Committee in 2014.

A. Department for Equal Opportunities: UNAR and Observatory for the Fight against Paedophilia and Child Pornography

The Department for Equal Opportunities, established under the auspices of the Prime Minister's Office, plans and coordinates legislative, administrative and research initiatives in all areas pertaining to equal opportunities policies. Since September 2014, the management of the Department has been entrusted to Giovanna Martelli, who has been appointed Advisor to the Prime Minister's Office for Equal Opportunities.

The Department was instituted by the d.p.c.m. of 28 October 1997, No. 405, subsequently amended by various decrees (the most recent being ministerial decree 4 December 2012). It comprises three offices: the Office of General Affairs, International Affairs and Social Measures; the Office for Measures to Promote Equality and Equal Opportunities; and the National Anti-Racial Discrimination Office (UNAR).

UNAR was established by lgs.d. 9 July 2003, No. 215, in compliance with the European Community directive 2000/43/CE. Its mission is to guarantee observance of the principle of equal treatment of individuals, to monitor the efficacy of current instruments against discrimination, and to help to stamp out forms of discrimination based on race or ethnic origin, while analysing their diversified impact on gender, and their connection with other forms of racism of a cultural and religious nature.

In October 2014, the new edition of the Statistical Dossier on Immigration "From discrimination to rights", edited by the IDOS/ Immigration Study and Research Centre in collaboration with UNAR, was presented. The Dossier estimates that the number of foreign citizens resident in Italy at the end of 2013 was 4,922,085, in a population of 60,782,668; this figure equates to 8.1% of the total population. Women made up 52.7% of these, and of over a million minors, 802,785 were enrolled in schools in the school year 2013/2014, making up 9% of the overall school population. 11,470 of these were Roma. Over half of all foreign citizens (51.1%) were from just five Countries: Romania, Albania, Morocco, China and Ukraine. A quarter of the foreign population lived in four Provinces: Rome, Milan, Turin and Brescia.

According to Dossier data, there is an increase in the number of refugees arriving from Africa and Middle Eastern Asia. As of 31 August 2014, a total of 112,689 people had landed in Italy; operation *Mare Nostrum*, launched on 18 October 2013, saved over 130,000 people over 12 months. In 2013 there were 26,620 requests for asylum. However, the numbers of people not authorised to enter, intercepted at the Italian borders (7,713), repatriated (8,769) and those ordered to leave but not complying (13,529), making a total of 30,011 people, have decreased. Their numbers have constantly decreased since 2006, when there were 124,381. According to estimates in the Dossier, the foreign population residing without authorisation is lower than half a million. The existence of identification and expulsion centres is a harsh reality: of 420 such centres in the whole of the EU (for a total of 37,000 places), ten are in Italy, where in 2013, 5,431 men and 585 women were held (including 395 Romanians and many who had come from prisons), with an expulsion rate of 45.7%. These centres have critically poor living conditions as concerns the respect of human rights, as recognised by the Senate Extraordinary Commission for Human Rights.

Finally, the Dossier includes 1,142 cases of discrimination reported to UNAR in 2013, 68.7% of which were based on grounds of race and ethnicity. Mass media make up the largest single source (34.2% of reports compared with 19.6% the previous year), particularly after the appointment of Cécile Kyenge as a Minister. There are also significant cases of discrimination in public life (20.4% of the total). Reports of discrimination in access to work and public services each represented slightly over 7%, while 5.1% concerned access to housing. Reported discrimination relating to schools and the police forces made up around 4%.

In addition to the three offices mentioned above, the following collegial bodies also have their secretariat within the Department for Equal Opportunities: the Inter-Ministerial Commission for Support to Victims of Trafficking, Violence and Severe Exploitation (as per presidential decree 14 May 2007, No. 102); the Committee for Prevention and Combating Female Genital Mutilation; the Committee to Evaluate the Legitimacy to Act on Behalf of People with Disabilities; the Committee for Equal Opportunities for Men and Women; the Observatory for the Fight against Paedophilia and Child Pornography.

The Observatory for the Fight against Paedophilia and Child Pornography was established in accordance with l. 3 August 1998, No. 269, as amended by l. 6 February 2006, No. 38, with the task of acquiring and monitoring data and information relating to activities carried out by all Government bodies to prevent and stamp out the sexual abuse and exploitation of minors. A further significant task of the Observatory is to prepare the National Plan for preventing and combating sexual abuse and exploitation of minors.

B. Commission for International Adoptions

Article 6 of the Hague Convention on the Protection of Minors and Cooperation in Respect of Inter-country Adoption, which was adopted on 29 May 1993 and came into force on 1 May 1995, requires State Parties to establish a central authority to ensure that adoptions of foreign children adhere to the principles established by the Convention itself. To comply with this requirement, via law 31 December 1998, No. 476, Italy instituted the Commission for International Adoptions, which operates through the Prime Minister's Office. The Commission is Italy's central authority for the implementation of the Hague Convention.

The Commission comprises a Chair, nominated by the Prime Minister (in 2014, Silvia Della Monica, Counsellor to the Court of Cassation), and the following members: three representatives from the Prime Minister's office; one from the Ministry of Foreign Affairs; one from the Ministry of Education; one from the Ministry for Labour and Social Policy; one from the Ministry of the Interior; two from the Ministry of Justice; one from the Ministry of Health; one from the Ministry of the Economy; four from the Unified Conference between State and Region; three from family associations; and experts.

Within the framework of international reports, in 2014 the Commission invited and hosted many delegations to important working sessions, notably from Burundi, Cambodia, Belarus, China and Mongolia. Important bilateral agreements were signed or renewed with some of these Countries, particularly with Burundi, Cambodia, the Russian Federation and Belarus. The agreement put in place with Belarus is particularly important: it was brokered personally by the President of the Commission and the Belarusian Ambassador in October 2014, and will allow adoptions in Belarus to resume, with the preparation of a new list of children whom Italian families are applying to adopt. The creation of a mixed Italian-Belarusian working group is a key element of the agreement reached in October 2014.

C. National Committee on Bioethics

The National Committee on Bioethics performs an advisory role vis-à-vis the Government, Parliament and other institutions, with a view to providing guidelines on legislative and administrative instruments designed to define the criteria to use in medical and biological practice in order to protect human rights. It also has a role in informing the public and in raising awareness with regard to ethical problems arising in connection with progress in scientific research and in technological applications in the life sciences and in healthcare.

The Committee was established by the d.p.c.m. of 28 March 1990. It is made up of the following bodies: Chair (Francesco Paolo Casavola, President Emeritus of the Constitutional Court); Vice Chairs (Riccardo Di Segni, Chief Rabbi of Rome; Lorenzo d'Avack, Professor in the Philosophy of Law; Laura Palazzani, Professor in the Philosophy of Law); Office of the President (made up of the Chair and the Vice Chairs); Assembly.

One of the tasks of the Committee is to produce studies and make recommendations that can also be used for legislative purposes. The Committee's documents offer in-depth focus and reflection on ethical and legal issues that arise as knowledge in the field of the life sciences advances. According to their nature and purpose, the documents are classified as: opinions (approved in the Committee's assembly on the basis of inquiries conducted by working groups); motions (urgent documents approved with a two-thirds majority of those present in the assembly); responses (documents in which the Committee makes recommendations on issues about which its opinion has been sought by other bodies or by physical persons).

In 2014 the following opinions were approved:

– Regarding some bioethical problems raised by law 6 August 2013, No. 96 (Criteria for delegating to the Government for transposing Directive 2010/63/EU of the European Parliament and of the Council of 22 September 2010) (24 January 2014)

– Lifestyles and protecting health (20 March 2014)

– Paediatric biobanks (11 April 2014)

– Ethical considerations concerning dementia and Alzheimer's disease (20 June 2014)

– Bioethical considerations on accidental swapping of embryos (11 July 2014).

III. Ministry of Foreign Affairs

The Ministry of Foreign Affairs has a number of directorate-generals and offices that deal specifically with human rights, disarmament and cooperation. In 2014, the delegated responsibility for issues arising in the United Nations was held by the Deputy Minister Lapo Pistelli.

Particularly worthy of note is Office II – Human rights advocacy and international humanitarian law, Council of Europe, which falls within the Directorate-general for Political Affairs and Security. Other offices in the same directorate are: Office I – The United Nations system and the institutional reform process, peacekeeping operations and preventive diplomacy; Office V – Disarmament, arms control and nuclear, biological and chemical non proliferation, Office of the national authority for the banning of chemical weapons; Office VI – Organisation for Security and Cooperation in Europe. The theme of human rights also relates across the board to the Directorate-general for Global Affairs (Office IV – Energy, environmental protection and sustainable global development policies), the Directorate-general for the European Union (Office III – European space of freedom, security and justice, the free movement of people and migratory flows towards the European Union) and the Directorate-general for Development Cooperation (Office I – Development of cooperation policies within the European Union; Office II – Multilateral development cooperation; Office VI – Emergency and humanitarian aid; Office VIII – Planning and monitoring of the cooperation budget; gender issues, the rights of children and people with disabilities).

A. Inter-Ministerial Committee for Human Rights (CIDU)

The Inter-Ministerial Committee for Human Rights (CIDU) was established by decree of the Minister of Foreign Affairs on 15 February 1978, No. 519; its composition was updated by d.p.c.m. on 11 May 2007. Over 2012–2013 the CIDU was involved in a restructuring process: initially phased out as a result of the spending review, it was re-established on 5 September 2013. It maintained its functional competences because it was regarded as indispensable, both for its advice and its strategic guidance regarding the promotion and protection of human rights, and in ensuring correct compliance with the obligations that Italy assumed following the signature and ratification of conventions and international agreements in this field.

CIDU is chaired by a functionary of the diplomatic service appointed by the Minister of Foreign Affairs: in 2014, Gian Ludovico De Martino. Committee members include representatives of the Prime Minister's Office, of various Ministries and of many different institutions (such as the Association of Italian Municipalities (ANCI); the Conference of Presidents of the Regions and Autonomous Provinces; the Union of Italian Provinces (UPI); the National Commission for UNESCO; the Italian Committee for UNICEF; the Italian Society for International Organisation (SIOI); as well as three eminent personalities in the field of human rights.

CIDU has the following tasks: to promote measures necessary for ensuring full compliance with international obligations assumed by Italy; to facilitate the implementation of international conventions in Italy; to draft the reports Italy is required to submit to the pertinent international organisations; to maintain and develop appropriate relations with civil society organisations engaged in promoting and protecting human rights.

On 29 December 2014 Foreign Minister Paolo Gentiloni sent a report on the activities of the CIDU and on the protection and respect of human rights in Italy in 2013 (doc. CXXI, No. 2) to the Presidency of the Chamber of Deputies. The report provides Parliament with the results of collaboration with United Nations and Council of Europe bodies on presenting the periodic reports stipulated in international human rights instruments to which Italy is party, and reports on arranged visits of those bodies to obtain specific information or seeing for themselves the situations in areas considered particularly sensitive for human rights. It is in this context that CIDU carried out the following activities in 2013.

United Nations

– Contributed to drafting the Report on implementing the UN Convention on the Rights of the Child (CRC);

– Prepared the national response to the Concluding Observations of the UN Committee for the Elimination of All Forms of Racial Discrimination, formulated following Italy's examination in March 2012;

– Prepared the national response to the Concluding Observations of the UN Committee for the Elimination of All Forms of Discrimination against Women, formulated following Italy's examination in August 2011;
– Began drafting the second National Action Plan on "Women, Peace and Security" in accordance with Security Council resolution No. 1325 of 2000;

– Contributed to drafting the Foundations of the National Action Plan on "Business and Human Rights" in accordance with the "UN Guiding Principles on Business and Human Rights" and participated in the "Business and Human Rights" forum (December 2013);

– Preparatory activities for the National Report in view of the second cycle of UPR by the United Nations Human Rights Council;

– Arranged the visit to Italy by the United Nations Special Rapporteur on trafficking in persons, especially women and children, Joy Ngozi Ezeilo (12–20 September 2013);

– Arranged the visit to Italy by United Nations Special Rapporteur on Promotion and Protection of the Right to Freedom of Opinion and Expression, Frank La Rue (11–18 November 2013);

– Follow-up actions after the visit to Italy by the Working Group on Arbitrary Detention, which took place in November 2008;

– Follow-up actions after the visit to Italy by the United Nations Special Rapporteur on Violence against Women, which took place in January 2012.

Council of Europe

– Visit to Italy by the Venice Commission of the Council of Europe in relation to criminal convictions relating to defamation in the press (21–22 October 2013);

– Visit to Italy by the expert group on the fight against people trafficking of the Council of Europe (GRETA, 2–6 December 2013);

– Drafted Italy's response to the report of the Council of Europe Committee for the Prevention of Torture (CPT), prepared following the periodic visit of 13–25 May 2012 (June 2013);

– Arranged the procedural follow-up of the 4th monitoring cycle of Italy by the Council of Europe's European Commission against Racism and Intolerance (ECRI);

Further, in 2013 the CIDU promoted the following meetings and conferences related to study and analysis;

– Presentation of the *Italian Yearbook of Human Rights*, edited by the University Centre for Human Rights of the University of Padua (Extraordinary Commission of the Senate for the Protection and Promotion of Human Rights, 13 September 2013);

– Fifth congress of *Nessuno Tocchi Caino* ("Hands Off Cain" – campaigners for the worldwide abolition of the death penalty) (December 2013).

B. Italian National Commission for UNESCO

The Commission was established by inter-ministerial decree on 11 February 1959, at the Ministry of Foreign Affairs, two years after Italy entered the Organisation, and pursuant to article 7 of the UNESCO Charter.

> Its composition has been regulated and updated by a series of successive decrees, the most recent one dating back to 24 May 2007. Members of the Commission include representatives from Parliament, the Prime Minister's Office, various Ministries, public and private agencies, local authorities and civil society.
>
> The Commission's mission is to promote the implementation of UNESCO programmes in Italy; to spread the ideals of the Organisation, especially among the younger generations; to disseminate information on its principles, goals and activities, thus stimulating action by institutions, civil society and the world of culture, education and science. The Commission also advises the Government regarding its dealings with UNESCO.

In 2014 the President, nominated by the Ministry of Foreign Affairs, was Giovanni Puglisi, while the post of Secretary General was held by Lucio Alberto Savoia.

The National Commission receives funding for institutional activities and its functioning through chapter 2471/10 of the budget forecast of the Ministry of Foreign Affairs. Funding has continued to drop over the years, with allocated funds in 2014 falling to around 15,000 euro (in 2013 it was 17,000 euro and in 2012 it was 25,000), which covers no more than the basic functioning of the Commission, making it extremely difficult to perform its public activities.

Despite these shortages, in 2014 the Commission carried out many activities (seminars, conferences, meetings in schools, competitions, exhibitions, workshops, shows) in various Italian cities, particularly on the various UN International Days, including International Mother Language Day (21 February), World Poetry Day (21 March), World Book and Copyright Day (23 April) and International Jazz Day (30 April). Moreover, the Commission ran specific projects in schools, and further reinforced the network of UNESCO associated schools. Finally, between 24 and 30 November the Commission celebrated the end of the UNESCO Decade of Education for Sustainable Development 2005–2014 with the ninth and final Week of Education for Sustainable Development. This initiative focused in particular on taking stock of the activities carried out, on one hand consolidating the good practices and educational methods introduced over the course of the Decade, on the other identifying the results which will outlive the mere Decade and will continue to promote education on sustainability all over Italy.

IV. Ministry of Labour and Social Policies

A number of the departments and offices belonging to the Ministry of Labour and Social Policies deal specifically with human rights.

The following are particularly worthy of note:

- *Directorate-general for employment service policies*. Functions: guidance, promotion and coordination of employment services in order to sustain employment policies; initiatives to combat irregular labour; guidance, coordination and initiatives to facilitate entry and reentry to the labour market of persons with disabilities; promotion of female employment; promotion of equal opportunities for entry into the labour market; support for the activities of parity advisors.
- *Directorate-general for inclusion and social policies*. Functions: promoting policies to combat poverty, social exclusion and severe marginalisation; promoting and monitoring policies for children and adolescents, and the protection of minors; coordination policies for the social inclusion, protection and promotion of the rights and opportunities of persons with disabilities; managing the National Fund for Social Policies, the National Fund for the Non-self-sufficient, the National Fund for Childhood and Adolescence and other funds for financing social policies and monitoring transferred resources; study, research and investigations concerning social policies; participation in all the pertinent internationally significant activities, and managing relations with the European Union, the Council of Europe, the International Labour Organisation, the United Nations and the Organisation for Economic Cooperation and Development.
- *Directorate-general for the third sector and social groups*. Functions: promoting and supporting the activities carried out by third sector subjects, especially initiatives relating to social promotion and voluntary

associations, in order to facilitate the growth of an active society welfare to support policies of social inclusion and integration.

- *Directorate-general for immigration and integration policies*. Functions: programming migratory flows, and managing and monitoring entry quotas of foreign workers as well as bilateral cooperation agreements with Countries of origin; coordinating policies for social and job integration of foreign immigrants and initiatives designed to prevent and combat discrimination, xenophobia and racism; developing international cooperation for activities to prevent and study social and employment emergencies, and for initiatives regarding work-related migratory flows.

In 2012 the Directorate-general for immigration and integration policies took over the functions of the Committee for Foreign Minors, which was abolished in accordance with the decree on the so-called spending review (article 12, para. 20 of l.d. 95/2012, converted into law, with amendments, in l. 135/2012). The Directorate-general is consequently now responsible for monitoring the presence, and modes thereof, of foreign minors temporarily present on Italian territory, whether they be unaccompanied minors present on Italian soil or admitted minors.

As regards unaccompanied minors, the Directorate-general may adopt two kinds of measures: the first is "no repatriation", which amounts to activating the procedures for integrating the person into Italy; the second is "assisted repatriation", designed to reunite the child with his or her family in their Country of origin. As regards the first option, responsibility for managing and monitoring the measures is placed in the hands of local authorities. The most frequent choice made for unaccompanied minors in Italy is to place them in residential care facilities for children.

As regards admitted minors, the Directorate-general makes decisions, following due appraisal and according to predetermined criteria, at the request of organisations, associations or Italian families, regarding the temporary admission of children into the framework of humanitarian programmes. The Committee then makes decisions on temporary fostering and repatriation. It keeps a register of minors already admitted into the framework of humanitarian programmes and predefines criteria for assessing requests for the admission of temporarily admitted minors.

During 2014, 14,243 unaccompanied foreign minors were referred to the Directorate-general (compared to 8,461 in 2013 and 7,066 in 2012), of which 13,400 were boys (94%) and 843 girls (6%). The chief Countries of origin were Egypt (23%), Eritrea (12%), Gambia (10%), and Somalia (10%). Approximately 60% of these reports originated in three Regions: Sicily (44%), Apulia (10%), and Calabria (8%).

A. National Observatory for Children and Adolescents

The Observatory performs a role of coordination among central administrations, local and regional bodies, associations, professional groups and non-governmental organisations dedicated to children's issues.

It was instituted by law 23 December 1997, No. 451, and is currently regulated by decree of the President of the Republic (d.p.r.), No. 103, 14 May 2007, which assigns it joint chairmanship by the Ministry of Labour and Social Policies and the Undersecretary of State to the Prime Minister's Office mandated with family policies. It is made up of representatives from national and local public administrations, associations and professional orders, voluntary and third sector organisations as well as experts in the field of children's rights.

Presidential decree 103/2007 assigns to the Observatory the task of preparing three documents about the condition of childhood and adolescence in Italy:

– The *National plan of action and of measures to safeguard the rights and development of children and adolescents*. Drawn up every two years, the plan contains the fundamental strategic guidelines and concrete commitments that the Government intends to pursue in order to develop a satisfactory policy for children and adolescents in Italy. The third action plan (2010–2011) was adopted by presidential decree on 21 January 2011 (see *2012 Yearbook*, p. 113).

– The *Report on the condition of children and adolescents in Italy*, which aims to provide an updated picture of the aspects and phenomena characterising the condition of children and adolescents in Italy, and of the system of social services and measures for promoting and protecting the rights of children and adolescents. The latest report published by the Observatory refers to the two-year period 2008–2009.

– The *Periodic report of the Government to the UN Committee on the Rights of the Child regarding the application of the 1989 International Convention on the Rights of the Child*, pursuant to article 44 of the Convention. The latest report (combining the 3rd and 4th reports) was sent by Italy in January 2009, and discussed in October 2011 (see *2012 Yearbook*, p. 114).

In carrying out its functions, the National Observatory makes use of the National Centre of Documentation and Analysis for Children and Adolescents, which performs documentation, analysis, research, monitoring and training tasks. In 2013, the chair of the Centre was Simonetta Matone, while the Coordinator of scientific activities was Maria Burani Procaccini.

More specifically, the National Centre of Documentation deals with:

- collecting and disseminating regional, national, European and international norms and regulations, as well as statistical data and scientific studies;
- creating an annually updated map, based on information provided by regional authorities, of public, private and non-governmental services, including social and health care services, and of financial resources dedicated to children at the national, regional and local level;
- analysing the situation of childhood and adolescence in Italy, including the conditions of foreign minors;
- preparing an outline, based on National Observatory directives, of the biennial report on the condition of children in Italy, and of the Government report to the United Nations Committee on the Rights of the Child on the domestic implementation of the Convention on the Rights of the Child;
- formulating proposals, also at the request of local authorities, for the creation of pilot projects designed to improve children's living conditions as well as to assist mothers during the prenatal period.

B. National Observatory Monitoring the Condition of Persons with Disabilities

The Observatory is an advisory body offering technical and scientific support in defining national policies regarding disabilities.

It was instituted by law 3 March 2009, No. 18, at the Ministry of Labour, Health and Social Policies. It is chaired by the Ministry of Labour and includes a maximum number of 40 members, who are appointed by ministerial decree and represent central administrations involved in defining and implementing disability-related policies; regional and local authorities; social security institutions; the National Statistics Institute; trade unions; and most representative associations and organisations of persons with disabilities, joined by a maximum number of five experts of proven experience in the field of disabilities.

The Observatory's tasks include the following: to promote the implementation of the United Nations Convention on the Rights of Persons with Disabilities and to prepare, together with CIDU, the national report for the monitoring procedure established by that Convention; to prepare a biennial Plan of action on disability implementing national and international laws; to promote and develop statistic-based studies and research that may contribute to defining priorities and needs.

During 2014, the Observatory began to implement the *Two-year action plan for promoting the rights and for the integration of persons with disabilities*, adopted by Presidential Decree 4 October 2013 (see *2014 Yearbook*, p. 109).

V. Ministry of Justice

Within the Ministry of Justice there are various departments and bureaus specifically involved with human rights. The most relevant are:

– *Office for studies, research, legislation and international relations* (Office of the Head of Department – Department of penitentiary administration): it deals in particular with coordinating activities with international organisations devoted to the protection and promotion of human rights of adult prisoners; it also handles pleas lodged by inmates with the European Court of Human Rights;

– *Office II*: (Directorate-general for litigation and human rights – Department of legal affairs): it is actively involved in examining cases pending before the European Court of Human Rights and in procedures relating to compliance with international obligations, and to the amendment of domestic law in accordance with the provisions of international instruments;

– *Office III*: Protection and support for the rights of minors. Promotion of measures in favour of subjects who risk the greatest degree of social exclusion (Directorate-general for the enforcement of judgments – Department of juvenile justice): the office deals with promoting and protecting the rights of unaccompanied foreign minors and of persons at risk of social exclusion.

VI. Judicial Authorities

The judiciary, that is to say the various organs of justice – ordinary, administrative and auditing – constituting judicial power, is the fundamental guarantee of rights and legality in a State that respects the principles of democracy, the division of powers and the rule of law. The Italian courts – the Constitutional Court, which delivers judgments regarding the constitutionality of laws, the Supreme Court, which is the court of last resort, the penal and civil tribunals and trial courts, and those concerned with administrative, audit and military matters – deal in a contentious manner with cases which often affect human rights in the most various ways and according to the most disparate perspectives. Access to a judge to obtain a ruling on a right that a plaintiff claims has been breached is a fundamental human right, linked to which are the many other procedural rights that distinguish the fair trial.

Besides ruling on individual cases, the justice system contributes to building and to the evolution of applicable law, through its own case-law. In recent years, and in relation to the theme of fundamental rights in particular, Italian rulings have been strongly influenced by that of international courts, especially the European Court of Human Rights and the

Court of Justice of the European Union. The interaction between national judicial organs and international courts with jurisdiction over human rights stresses the universal nature of the latter. The dialogue with international courts and with those of other Countries called upon to apply the same standards regarding individual human rights does not just concern the supreme courts of a State, but all judges, who can draw on rulings made in foreign or international courts to improve existing guarantees regarding fundamental rights, fully respecting the Constitution and the law.

Part IV of this Yearbook is specifically devoted to a summary presentation of cases in the Italian courts on which rulings were delivered in 2014 (with particular reference to those made by the Constitutional and the Supreme Court), and of case law elaborated by the European Court of Human Rights or the Court of Justice of the European Union which directly concerns Italy, either because the Italian State was the "defendant" or because the intervention of the European judge regarded pleas presented by Italian citizens or related to Italian legal norms.

VII. Independent Authorities

There are nine independent authorities in Italy: the Communications Regulatory Authority (AGCOM); the Data Protection Authority; the Committee Guaranteeing the Implementation of the Law on Strikes Affecting Essential Public Services; the Authority Protecting Free Competition and the Market (Antitrust Authority); the Italian Companies and Stock Exchange Commission (CONSOB); the Institute for Vigilance on Private Insurance and Insurances of Collective Interest (ISVAP); the Regulatory Authority for Electricity and Gas; the Authority for Vigilance on Contracts for Public Works, Services and Supplies; the National Ombudsperson for Children and Adolescents.

Furthermore, in December 2013 the Council of Ministers adopted l.d. 146/2013 (Urgent measures regarding the protection of the fundamental rights of prisoners and the controlled reduction of the prison population). Article 7 of the l.d. made provision for the establishment, in the Ministry of Justice, of the National Ombudsperson for the Rights of Persons in Prison or Deprived of Liberty. The National Ombudsperson is collegial, and consists of the Chair and two members, and will have the function of acting as a watchdog to ensure that the execution of custodial sentences and of other forms of restriction on liberty is implemented in compliance with the regulations and principles established by the Constitution, by international human rights conventions and by the laws of the State. It will also have the faculty to visit, without prior authorisation, prison institutions and any other structure used to house persons subject to measures depriving them of their liberty.

The four authorities that relate more pertinently to human rights are described below.

A. Communications Regulatory Authority (AGCOM)

AGCOM was set up by law 31 July 1997, No. 249. It has a dual mandate: to ensure correct competition among market actors and to guarantee the fundamental freedoms of citizens in the area of communications, particularly as regards the protection of minors.

The composition of the Authority is disciplined by decree 6 December 2011, No. 201 (the so-called Save Italy decree), and its conversion into law (22 December 2011, No. 214). In 2013 the Authority was made up as follows: Chair: Angelo Marcello Cardani; members of the Services and Products Commission: Antonio Martusciello and Francesco Posteraro; members of the Commission for Infrastructure and Networks: Maurizio Dècina (until November 2013, replaced by Antonio Nicita) and Antonio Preto. The Council consists of the Chair and all the Commissioners.

As detailed in the 2014 annual report of its activities and work programmes (referring to the period May 2013-April 2014), the Authority devoted particular attention to its role as a watchdog on behalf of minors and users, especially in relation to local and national broadcasters, in order to ascertain whether violations had been committed, and, if so, to punish broadcasters accordingly.

In January 2014 the Authority adopted the White Paper on Media and Minors, created in collaboration with CENSIS. The Paper considered which safeguard measures are best suited to the new context of digital communication, in which various forms of media other than television are consumed. In particular, the Paper contains an accurate review of national and international scientific literature and focuses on media consumption by minors, and on the opinions of adults and parents.

In the period considered, the Authority also adopted two regulations regarding the protection of minors. These measures are, firstly, the regulation on classification criteria of television broadcasts which may seriously damage the physical, mental or moral development of minors (as referred to in art. 34, paragraphs 1, 5 and 11 of lgs.d. 31 July 2005, No. 177, as modified and amended in particular by lgs.d. 15 March 2010, No. 44 and by lgs.d. 28 June 2012, No. 120), and secondly the regulation on technical measures to prevent minors from viewing or listening to broadcasts made available by on-demand audiovisual media service providers, that may seriously damage the physical, mental or moral development of minors (so-called parental control tools) in compliance with article 34 of lgs.d.

31 July 2005, No. 177, as amended and integrated in particular by lgs.d. 15 March 2010, No. 44, and lgs.d. 28 June 2012, No. 120.

In relation to reports received on audiovisual safeguards, it should be noted that in the period considered there were various issues raised concerning protecting users and, in particular, safeguarding minors, human dignity and minorities. Furthermore, many of the questions raised did not relate to audiovisual services, but to content distributed online. Indeed, on analysing reports received, it emerges that 55% concerned the latter, whereas only 17% referred to content broadcast on television and 1% related to the press. The reasons for reporting were as follows: defamation (36%); issues relating to privacy (16%); human dignity (13%); and the protection of minors (also 13%); followed by unfair trade practices, intellectual property and advertising.

B. Data Protection Authority

The Data Protection Authority was instituted by l. 31 December 1996, No. 675, later substituted by lgs.d. 30 June 2003, No. 196 (Personal data protection code), with the aim to ensure protection of the fundamental rights and freedoms and respect for the dignity of persons, in the processing of personal data.

The Data Protection Authority is a collegial body made up of four members elected by Parliament, who remain in office for a seven-year non-renewable mandate. The current body is made up of Antonello Soro (Chair), Augusta Iannini (Vice Chair), Giovanna Bianchi Clerici and Licia Califano.

During 2014 the Authority issued 554 *provisions* to protect the fundamental rights of individuals with regard to the processing and diffusion of personal data, with particular reference, to the following issues among others: the right to be forgotten; freedom of the press; the right to education, work, health and scientific research; the rights of minors; the handling of sensitive data; and internet and social media.

C. Commission Guaranteeing the Implementation of the Law on Strikes Affecting Essential Public Services

The Commission was instituted by law 12 June 1990, No. 146, modified by law 11 April 2000, No. 83. It comprises nine members designated by the Chairs of the Chamber of Deputies and the Senate among experts in matters of constitutional law, labour law and industrial relations, and appointed by decree of the President of the Republic. In 2014, the members of the Commission were: Roberto Alesse (Chair), Pietro Boria, Alessandro Forlani, Elena Montecchi, Iolanda Piccinini, Nunzio Pinelli, Salvatore Vecchione.

Some of the Commission's main tasks are:

- assessing the capacity of essential services to guarantee protection of both the right to strike and the enjoyment of constitutionally guaranteed human rights;
- requesting that those calling the strike delay the date of abstention from work if the Commission intends to attempt conciliation, or if it finds that the abstention violates legal and/or contractual obligations for strikes in essential public services;
- pointing out to those calling the strike any violations of norms concerning advance notice or any other requirements relative to the phase preceding collective abstention;
- notifying the appropriate authority which can order strikers back to work of situations where the strike or collective abstention could give rise to an imminent, probable risk of infringing constitutionally protected human rights;
- taking note of behaviour by administrations or enterprises which provide essential public services in clear violation of the law;
- assessing behaviour of both parties and if any non-compliance or violation of legal or contractual obligations relative to essential services emerges, inflicting penalties pursuant to art. 4 of law 146/1990 as amended by art. 3 of law 83/2000, ordering the employer to apply the disciplinary actions.

On 1 July 2014 the Commission presented its annual report on activities carried out in 2013. The data in the report show how the 2013 conflict in the essential services sector reflected the protracted duration of the economic crisis, bringing recession to both the public and private sectors – a situation which contributed to social tension remaining relatively high. Indeed, the number of national general strikes was identical to the previous year (7 strikes); the Commission intervened with advance warnings in three of these as per art. 13, para. 1, point d), of law 146/1990 and subsequent amendments. In most cases the warnings were of the failure to comply with rules concerning the minimum period of time between strikes. All the trade unions calling for strike action accepted the interventions and responded by adjusting their calls to strike taking into consideration the Commission's points.

As regards the development of conflict in various essential public service sectors, in 2013 there were 2,339 strike calls, a figure broadly in line with that of the previous year. In particular, the level of conflict remains high in the transport sector (293 strikes), the environmental health, cleaning and multi-service sectors (186 and 105 strikes respectively), and health and justice.

D. National Ombudsperson for Children and Adolescents

The National Ombudsperson for Children and Adolescents was established with law No. 112 of 12 July 2011. A monocratic organ, the holder of the post is appointed by the Presidents of the Chamber of Deputies and of the Senate, who choose a figure of unquestioned morality, independence and professional competence in the field of children's rights. The term of office is four years. In 2013 the post of Ombudsperson was held by Vincenzo Spadafora.

The Ombudsperson has, amongst others, the following responsibilities:

- to promote the implementation of the UN Convention on the Rights of the Child, and of other pertinent international and European instruments, and to ensure appropriate forms of collaboration with all the national and international bodies and organisations engaged in promoting and protecting children and adolescents;
- to express opinions on legislative initiatives concerning the protection of the rights of children and adolescents, and the report that the Government presents periodically to the UN Committee on the Rights of the Child;
- to inform the Government, Regions and other local or territorial bodies involved, in relation to their respective responsibilities, of all appropriate measures to ensure full promotion and protection of the rights of children and adolescents;
- to inform judicial authorities and bodies concerned of problem cases or risks of minors' rights being infringed, as well as serious cases of neglect of minors, so that they can be taken into care by the appropriate authorities;
- to enhance knowledge of the rights of children and adolescents, organising, to this end, awareness-raising activities, studies and research.

Article 6 of law 112 also allows anyone to address the Ombudsperson to report violation of rights or the risk thereof. Finally, article 3 states that the Ombudsperson is to establish appropriate forms of cooperation with the regional Ombudspersons or similar figures. The National Conference for the Rights of Children and Adolescents was set up for this purpose; coordinated by the National Ombudsperson, it brings together all the other Ombudspersons, where these have been established (see in this Part, Sub-national Human Rights Structures, IV).

In April 2014, the Ombudsperson presented his third report to Parliament on the actions undertaken over the course of 2013 to benefit the approximately 11 million children and adolescents living in Italy (comprising about 17% of the population). The following are of particular note:

– *Participation and listening to children and adolescents*. The Ombudsperson fostered this action through a series of integrated measures, with the dual aim of placing minors at the centre of interest, both in public opinion and on the political agenda, and of promoting listening to them and encouraging their participation on policy and laws, as well as in everyday life. These aims were met through visits on the ground (specifically to Bari, Palermo, Naples, other parts of Campania in the area known as *Terra dei Fuochi* (Bonfire land), and Lampedusa), as well as through collaboration with associations and groups working in this field, particularly with the umbrella organisation Children's and Adolescents' Rights (PIDIDA).

– *Creation of institutional networks*. In 2013 the Ombudsperson established a partnership with the main organisations with competence, or with a potentially significant role, in promoting a culture of rights within the national system of protection of children and adolescents. Primarily, on several occasions the Ombudsperson used moral suasion to urge Parliament and the Government to reconvene the Parliamentary Commission for Children and adolescents and the National Observatory for Children and adolescents.

In the context of collaboration with police forces, the attention of the Technical Group, established in accordance with the Memorandum of Understanding signed with the Police Chief Director General of Public Security in December 2012 (see *2014 Yearbook*, p. 117), has been particularly focused on the issue of unaccompanied foreign minors and related issues regarding the methodology used to establish age, the need to provide migrants with comprehensive information about their rights, and the protection procedure.

With the Ministry of Justice, and more specifically with the Department for Juvenile Justice, important issues such as the lack of a juvenile penitentiary system and the need to reform the justice system for minors were addressed.

Cooperation was established with the Ministry of Labour and Social Policies, with the aim of promoting activities to combat child poverty, for children in alternative care and for unaccompanied foreign minors.

With the Ministry of Education, Universities and Research the Ombudsperson collaborated mainly on the issues of safety, including online safety, and health in school environments. In particular, a National training programme for school staff on health and safety in schools has been developed, with the aim of training those working in schools (teachers and ATA – administrative, technical and ancillary – staff) on what to do and, more importantly, what not to do in case of accidents involving children.

Valuable dialogues were also established with RAI, to create awareness-raising campaigns on the rights of children and adolescents, and with ISTAT, to promote a detailed study on adolescents and on wellbeing measures for them and for children.

Also, in 2013, an agreement was signed between the National Ombudsperson for Children and Adolescents and the University of Molise. A suggested first joint venture is to begin monitoring institutions dealing with children and adolescents: mapping "places" which, in various ways, have responsibilities in this area, to understand how they work and potentially to make proposals to increase their effectiveness, in a system-oriented approach.

– *Reports*. In 2013, the Ombudsperson's Office received 193 reports from individuals, associations and structures working with children and adolescents, but none of these came directly from minors. The reports received were mainly relative to the following areas: contested custody; international abductions; difficulties at school; school buildings; the media and minors; and minors with disabilities.

VIII. Non-governmental Organisations

In Italy, numerous non-governmental organisations are active in promoting and protecting human rights. Some of them, organised in networks at national and international levels, have gained consultative status with international organisations and actively participate in their programmes.

As of 31 December 2014, 103 Italian non-governmental organisations held consultative status with the United Nations Economic and Social Council (+8 compared to 2013), nine of which have general status (equal to 2013); 77 have special status (+8 compared to 2013) and 17 have roster status (equal to the 2013 figure). There are 150 non-governmental organisations with headquarters or representative offices in Italy enjoying participatory status with the Council of Europe dealing specifically with human rights.

In addition, some of the most important international non-governmental organisations have local branches in Italy. These include Amnesty International, the International Federation on Human Rights, Save the Children, Médecins sans Frontières and Action Aid. The Italian associations Nessuno tocchi Caino (Hands off Cain) and Non c'è pace senza giustizia (No Peace without Justice) also have high profiles internationally.

In addition to these, the *Comitato per la Promozione e Protezione dei Diritti Umani* is particularly worthy of note. This is a network of 90 non-governmental organisations working to promote human rights. It was created in January 2002 on the initiative of the Fondazione Basso (Basso

Foundation) with the support of a group of human rights experts. Barbara Terenzi acted as coordinator in 2014.

> This Committee's main goal is to stimulate and support the Italian legislative process in order to create an independent national institution for human rights, in full compliance with the standards promoted by the United Nations General Assembly (resolution 48/134 of 20 December 1993) and with the "Paris Principles". Alongside activities linked to the creation of the National Institution for Human Rights, since 2005 the Committee has designed and implemented a systematic process to monitor the respect of human, civil, political, economic, social and cultural rights in Italy, using the legal framework of the two relevant international covenants in an integrated fashion.

In 2014 the Committee took part in Italy's Universal Periodic Review in Geneva (20th UPR session, 27 October 2014: see Part III, The United Nation System, II, B). On that occasion the Committee presented a formal declaration of support for the creation of an independent National Institution for Human Rights in Italy, together with its consolidated four-yearly monitoring report on the UPR recommendations made to Italy during the first UPR cycle (2010–2014).

Finally, it is of note that in 2014 the Working Group for the Convention on the Rights of the Child (CRC Group), a network of 87 non-governmental organisations, published its seventh Update Report monitoring the Convention on the Rights of the Child in Italy (2013–2014). The Report focused mainly on the following areas: civil rights and liberty; family environment, and alternative measures; health and assistance; education, play and cultural activities; special measures for the protection of minors.

IX. Human Rights Teaching and Research in Italian Universities

The Italian academic world has shown growing interest in research and education in the area of human rights. This issue is now included in teaching programmes across a number of disciplines and in the curricula of various degree courses at undergraduate and post-graduate levels, as well as in interdisciplinary research programmes. The following pages offer an overview of the universities and research centres which are specifically involved with human rights issues, including the teaching of three- and five-year degree, Masters and PhD courses which were available in 2014 or which opened for registration during that year, on the subject. In the interests of precision, the list comprises only the courses and structures which include the phrase "human rights" or equivalent expressions (rights of man, rights of the person, fundamental rights) in their full title. The picture thus obtained offers reasonably reliable evidence as to how widespread and penetrating issues regarding the multifaceted aspects of the rights of the person have become in Italian academia.

University Institutions and Research Centres

University	Name	Founding year
University of Padua	University Human Rights Centre	1982
University of Salento	Inter-University Centre on Bioethics and Human Rights	1992
41 European universities in partnership	European Inter-University Centre for Human Rights and Democratisation (EIUC)	2002
University of Naples	Centre for Studies on Human Rights in the era of globalisation and conflicts	2003
University of Ca' Foscari, Venice	Interdepartmental Human Rights Research Centre (CIRDU)	2003
University of Salerno	Department of Individual Rights and Comparison	2011

Source: elaboration by the research and editorial committee of the 2015 Yearbook.

Bachelor's Degree Courses

University	Name	Scientific Area
University of Padua	Political Science, International Relations, Human Rights	L-36: Political science and International Relations

Source: elaboration by the research and editorial committee of the 2015 Yearbook.

Master's Degree Courses

University	Name	Scientific Area
University of Bergamo	Human Rights and the Ethics of International Cooperation	LM-81: Cooperation development sciences
University of Bologna	International Cooperation, Protection of Human Rights and Ethno-cultural Heritage in the Mediterranean and Eurasia	LM-81: Cooperation development sciences
	International cooperation, development and human rights	LM-81: Cooperation development sciences
University of Padua	Human rights and multi-level governance	LM-52: International Relations

Source: elaboration by the research and editorial committee of the 2015 Yearbook.

Teachings

In 2014, a total of 98 human rights teachings were run in 37 universities: over half of these were delivered via degree courses in the political and social science area (52 programmes, or 53%), while slightly over one third related to the area of law (34 programmes, or 35%), nine to history, philosophy, pedagogy and psychology (9%), and three to the area of economics and statistics (3%).

As in 2010, 2011 and 2012, the university with the greatest number of human rights courses was Padua (14 teaching courses), followed by Turin (8), Bologna (6), Milan (6), Bari (5), and Palermo (5). 11 out of 98 human rights teachings are taught in English: 8 in Padua, two in Milan (Università degli Studi), and 1 in Cagliari.

University	Area	Degree Course	Teaching	Lecturer/Professor
Aldo Moro University of Bari	Law	BA in Science of Law Service	International protection of human rights – human rights protection in the European Convention on Human Rights	Vito Sandro Leccese
		5-Year Degree in Law	Human rights	Maurizio Sozio
			International protection of human rights	Andrea Cannone
	Political and social science	MA in International Relations	Theory of human rights	Gabriella Sforza
			International protection of human rights	Egeria Nalin
University of Bergamo	History, philosophy, pedagogy and psychology	BA in Philosophy	Pedagogy of Human rights and international cooperation	Stefania Gandolfi
		5-year degree in Pedagogy	Pedagogy of marginalisation and human rights	Ivo Lizzola

University	Area	Degree Course	Teaching	Lecturer/Professor
University of Bologna	Political and social science	MA in Local and Global Development	Human rights, constitutions and institutions	Raffaella Gherardi
		MA in International Relations and Diplomatic Affairs	International protection of human rights (seminar)	Marco Balboni
		MA in International Cooperation, Protection of Human Rights and Ethno-cultural Heritage in the Mediterranean and Eurasia	International human rights law and European law on cooperation	Lorenzo Gradoni
			Public law and protection of fundamental rights	Caterina Drigo
			Human rights and history of international law	Gustavo Gozzi
	Law	5-Year Degree in Law	Fundamental rights	Luca Mezzetti
University of Cagliari	Law	5-Year Degree in Law	European governance and human rights	Marco Betzu
University of Camerino	Economics and statistics	BA in Social Sciences for Nonprofit Organisations and International Cooperation	International protection of human rights	Agostina Latino
University of Ferrara	Law	5-Year Degree in Law	Human rights and humanitarian law in armed conflicts	Francesco Salerno
University of Florence	History, philosophy, pedagogy and psychology	BA in Social Education	Human rights	Antonio Bultrini
	Law	BA in Science of Law Service	Legal systems and protection of rights	Beatrice Gambineri
			Welfare state and rights	Emilio Santoro, Giovanni Tarli Barbieri, Sara Landini

University	Area	Degree Course	Teaching	Lecturer/Professor
University of Genova	Law	5-Year Degree in Law	Civil and social rights	Lara Trucco
University of L'Aquila	Economics and statistics	BA in Economics	Theory of interpretation and human rights	Francesca Caroccia
University of Macerata	Political and social science	MA in Theories, Cultures and Techniques for Social Work	Social and citizenship-related rights	Angela Cossiri
	History, philosophy, pedagogy and psychology	MA in Philosophy	Philosophy of rights and cultures	Carla Canullo, Sergio Labate, Donatella Pagliacci
			Philosophy of rights and cultures II	Carla Danani
University of Messina	Political and social science	MA in International Relations and Development Aid	International organisations and human rights	Carmela Panella
Sacro Cuore Catholic University	Political and social science	BA in Political Science and International Relations	International protection of Human rights	Marinella Fumagalli Meraviglia
	Law	5-Year Degree in Law	Human rights	Pasquale De Sena
University of Milan	Political and social science	BA in International Studies and European Institutions	International protection of human rights	Ilaria Viarengo
		MA in Political Science and Government	Theories of fundamental rights	Alessandra Facchi
	Law	5-Year Degree in Law	Rights of religions and human rights	Cristiana Cianitto
			International investment law and human rights	Angelica Bonfanti, Albert Henke
			International refugee and human rights law	José Henrique Fischel De Andrade

University	Area	Degree Course	Teaching	Lecturer/Professor
Bicocca University of Milan	Political and social science	MA in Sociology	Rights and European citizenship	Marina Calloni
		MA in Planning and Managing Social Policy and Social Services	Cooperation and human rights protection	Gabriella Citroni
	Law	5-Year Degree in Law	European constitutional law (fundamental rights)	Stefania Ninatti
			International protection of human rights	Gabriella Citroni
University of Modena and Reggio Emilia	Law	5-Year Degree in Law	Theory and practice of human rights	Thomas Casadei
University of Molise	Political and social science	BA in Communication	Human rights and globalisation	Lorenzo Scillitani
Federico II University of Naples	Political and social science	MA in Social Services and Social Policy	International protection of human rights	Oreste Pallotta
	Economics and statistics	MA in Economics and Business Law	International protection of human rights	Rossella De Rosa
Second University of Naples	Political and social science	BA in Political Science	Protection of rights in multi-cultural states	Domenico Amirante
		MA in International Relations and Organisations	Human rights	Pasquale Femia
	Law	5-Year Degree in Law	International protection of human rights	Andrea Saccucci
Suor Orsola Benincasa University (Naples)	History, philosophy, pedagogy and psychology	BA in Education	Human Rights	Paola Giordano

University	Area	Degree Course	Teaching	Lecturer/Professor
Università degli Studi di Padova	Political and social science	BA in Political Sciences, International Relations, Human Rights	Human rights	Elena Pariotti
			Public policy and human rights	Paola Degani
			General sociology and human rights sociology	Giuseppe Giordan
			Economic development and human rights	Mario Pomini
			International protection of human rights	Paolo De Stefani
		MA in European Studies	Fundamental rights and European citizenship	Costanza Margiotta Broglio Massucci
		Master's Degree in Human Rights and Multi-Level Governance	Human Rights and international justice	Costanza Margiotta Broglio Massucci
			International law of human rights	Paolo De Stefani
			International Organisation for Human Rights and Peace	Leonce Bekemans
			Women's human rights	Paola Degani
			Culture, society and human Rights	Andrea Maria Maccarini
			Human rights monitoring and electoral observation	Sara Pennicino
			Economic globalization and human rights	Roberto Antonietti
			Religions and human rights	Giuseppe Giordan
	Law	5-Year Degree in Law	Human rights and public ethics	Umberto Vincenti
	History, philosophy, pedagogy and psychology	BA in Primary Education	Pedagogy of childhood, adolescence and rights of the child	Emanuela Toffano

University	Area	Degree Course	Teaching	Lecturer/Professor
University of Palermo	Political and social science	BA in Political Sciences and International Relations	Human rights and international criminal law	Maurizio Gemelli
		BA in Cooperation and Development	Theory and policy of human rights	Serena Marcenò
	Law	5-Year Degree in Law (Trapani)	Human rights	Clelia Bartoli
		5-Year Degree in Law (Agrigento)	Human rights	Aldo Schiavello
		5-Year Degree in Law	Human rights	Bruno Celano
University of Pavia	Law	5-Year Degree in Law	Constitutional law and fundamental rights	Francesco Rigano
University of Perugia	Political and social science	MA in International Relations	Human rights and international crime	Amina Maneggia
Amedeo Avogadro University of Eastern Piemonte	Law	5-Year Degree in Law	Protection of fundamental rights	Joerg Luther
Università degli Studi di Pisa	Political and social science	BA in Sciences for Peace: international cooperation and conflict transformation	Legal and political theories of human rights	Vittorio Benedetti
			Technology, development aid and peace	Fabio Fineschi
	Law	5-Year Degree in Law	Multilevel protection of human rights	Elena Malfatti
Libera Università Internazionale degli Studi Sociali "Guido Carli" – LUISS – Rome	Law	5-Year Degree in Law	International protection of human rights	Pietro Pustorino

University	Area	Degree Course	Teaching	Lecturer/Professor
Roma Tre University	Political and social science	BA in Political Science for Cooperation and Development	International organisations and protection of human rights	Raffaele Cadin
		MA in International Relations	Protection of fundamental rights in comparative law	Salvatore Bonfiglio
La Sapienza University of Rome	Political and social science	MA in Development and International Cooperation Sciences	Human rights and bioethics	Luca Marini
		MA in International Relations	International human rights law	Luigino Manca
		MA in Integrated Communication for Public and Non-for-profit Organisation	Communication of rights and active citizenship	Marco Binotto, Gaia Peruzzi
University of Salento	Political and social science	BA in International Relations	Human rights	Attilio Pisanò
University of Salerno	Law	5-Year Degree in Law	Human rights	Stefano Pietropaoli
			Human rights and biolaw	Anna Malomo
			International protection of human rights	Stefania Negri
University of Siena	Political and social science	BA in Communication	History of human rights	Marcello Flores D'Arcais
		MA in International Studies	International protection of human rights	Alessandra Viviani
University of Teramo	Law	5-Year Degree in Law	Human rights	Gianluca Sadun Bordoni

University	Area	Degree Course	Teaching	Lecturer/Professor
University of Torino	Political and social science	MA in Sociology	Theories of human rights	Valentina Pazé
		MA in International Studies	Human rights and immigration	Alessandra Algostino
			History of human rights	Franco Motta
		MA in Social Policy and Social Services	Citizenship, social rights, justice	Franco Prina
			Vulnerable groups and human rights protection	Maurizio Riverditi
	Law	5-Year Degree in Law	International humanitarian law and human rights protection	Edoardo Greppi
			Fundamental rights guarantees	Matteo Losana
			Social order, juridical hermeneutics and protection of fundamental rights	Sergio Dellavalle
University of Udine	Law	5-Year Degree in Law	Theory of human rights	Giovanni Turco
Carlo Bo University of Udine	Law	5-Year Degree in Law	Human Rights	Enrico Moroni
Ca' Foscari University of Venice	History, philosophy, pedagogy and psychology	MA in Cultural Anthropology, Ethnology, Anthropological Linguistics	Citizenship-related rights	Lauso Zagato
			Human rights	Lauso Zagato
University of Verona	Political and social science	MA in Social Services and Social Policies	Social and citizenship-related rights.	Donata Maria Assunta Gottardi
			Protection of fundamental rights	Elisabetta Crivelli, Giampietro Ferri

Source: elaboration by the research and editorial committee on data available on universities' websites.

Doctoral programmes (academic years 2013–2014 and 2014–2015)

University	Name	Area of scientific discipline
University of Camerino, School of Advanced Studies	Doctorate in Law, Politics and Social Science – Curriculum on Fundamental rights in the global society	M-STO/02; M-STO/04; M-DEA/01; M-FIL/03; M-FIL/06; IUS/04; IUS/08; IUS/09; IUS/13 – IUS/21 SECS-P/01; SECS P/02; SECS-P/04; SPS/01; SPS/02; SPS/04; SPS/06; SPS/07; SPS/11; SPS/12
University of Florence	Theory and history of law – Theory and history of human rights	IUS/18, IUS/19, IUS/20
University of Palermo	International Doctorate in Human rights: evolution, protection and limits	IUS/01, IUS/09, IUS/12, IUS/20, SPS/02, IUS/13, IUS/19, IUS/10, SPS/09, SECS-P/01, IUS/08
Amedeo Avogadro University of Eastern Piedmont	Local autonomies, public services and citizenship rights	IUS/05, IUS/08, IUS/09, IUS/10, IUS/21
Sant'Anna School of Advanced Studies of Pisa	Politics, human rights and sustainability	SPS/01, SPS/06, IUS/13, IUS/03, IUS/14, SPS/04, SECS-P/02, SECS-P/06, SECS-P/08
La Sapienza University of Rome	International order and human rights	IUS/13, IUS/14, IUS/08, IUS/07, IUS/01
Libera Maria Santissima Assunta University – LUMSA	Fundamental rights and freedoms in contemporary legal systems	IUS/01, IUS/11, IUS/13, IUS/17, IUS/20, IUS/18, IUS/07
	International adoptions: issues on the protection of fundamental human rights	IUS/01, IUS/11, IUS/13
University of Salerno	Comparative human rights	IUS/01, IUS/02, IUS/07, IUS/13, IUS/14, IUS/16, IUS/17
University of Teramo	Protection of fundamental rights – Italian and European public law	IUS/08, IUS/09, IUS/10, IUS/21
Carlo Bo University of Urbino	Human rights and fundamental social rights	IUS/01, IUS/02, IUS/07, IUS/10, IUS/11, IUS/13, IUS/15, IUS/16, IUS/17, IUS/18, IUS/19, IUS/21, SECS-P/03

Source: elaboration by the 2015 Yearbook research and editorial committee.

Master's degree programmes – postgraduate

University	Name	Level
University of Bologna	Human rights, migration and development	I
European Inter-University Centre for Human Rights and Democratisation (EIUC, 41 European university partners)	European master's degree in human rights and democratisation	I
Sant'Anna School of Advanced Studies of Pisa	Human rights and conflict management	I
University of Siena	European Joint Master of Human Rights and Genocide Studies	I
La Sapienza University of Rome	"Maria Rita Saulle" International protection of human rights	II
Roma Tre University	Peace studies: international cooperation, human rights and policies of the European Union	II
Italian Society for International Organisation (SIOI)	International relations and international protection of human rights	-

Source: elaboration by the research and editorial committee of the 2015 Yearbook.

Finally, in 2014 the University of Padua and its University Human Rights *Centre*, in collaboration with the *Iversity* platform, launched the first *Massive Open Online Course* (MOOC) in English on the topic of *Human Rights: Global and Local Protection.*

Sub-national Human Rights Structures

I. Peace Human Rights Offices in Municipalities, Provinces and Regions

At the sub-national level, especially by virtue of the inclusion of the "peace human rights norm" in thousands of Municipal, Provincial and Regional Statutes, and of the adoption of dedicated regional laws on this topic (see Part I, Italian Law, III), Italy has a number of consultancies, offices, departments, bureaux and centres for human rights, peace, equal opportunity, development cooperation, fair trade and international solidarity. Statistical data on the spread of these structures were given in the *2011 Yearbook* p. 133–134.

During 2014, the Italian Municipalities, together with some Provincial and Regional Councils, were at the centre of an important initiative of "city diplomacy" aimed at promoting recognition of the human right to peace. Since June 2012, an Inter-governmental Working Group has been active at the UN Human Rights Council; it is charged with developing the text of a Declaration on the Right to Peace. However, positive advancement of this initiative has been hindered from the outset by some States which declared a position of a priori opposition to the draft document under discussion. On a proposal from the Human Rights Centre and the UNESCO Chair at the University of Padua, and in collaboration with them, the National Coordination of Local Communities for Peace and Human Rights (see this Part, Sub-national Human Rights Structures, VI) invited municipal and provincial Councils to adopt a petitionary motion showing their support for the Human Rights Council initiative.

By the end of 2014 several hundred local and regional authorities in Italy were supporting this initiative. The Municipalities include: Assisi; Aviano; Bari; Crotone; Genoa; Naples; Novara; Palermo; Pistoia; Potenza; Reggio Emilia; Rovereto; Senigallia; Sondrio; Venice and Viterbo; and the five Provinces of Chieti, Parma, Perugia, Prato and Rimini. Finally, five Regional Councils, Marche, Veneto, Emilia-Romagna, Friuli-Venezia Giulia and Apulia adopted the petitionary motion.

On 23 June 2014 at the *Palais des Nations* in Geneva, a delegation of local administrators met with Ambassador Christian Guillermet Fernandez, President of the Human Rights Council Inter-governmental Working Group charged with drafting the Declaration, diplomatic representatives of Italy and the Holy See and United Nations officials. One highly significant moment for this civil society initiative, carried out in the spirit of the subsidiarity principle, was the official handover of the first 100 petitionary motions in favour of international recognition of the right to peace approved by Italian local authorities, with mayors donning the tricolour sash for the occasion. On 3 July in Rome, representatives from local authorities presented the President of the Senate and President of the Extraordinary Commission for Human Rights, Luigi Manconi, with the motions adopted and renewing their appeal to the national institutions.

II. Ombudspersons in the Italian Regions and Provinces

In 2014 there were 15 incumbent Ombudspersons, of a total of 19 Regions and Autonomous Provinces (17 + 2) whose respective Statutes or specific regional laws included provisions for such an institution: Abruzzo; Basilicata; Campania; Emilia-Romagna; Lazio; Liguria; Lombardy; Marche; Piedmont; Sardinia; Tuscany; Valle d'Aosta and Veneto; and the Autonomous Provinces of Bolzano and Trent. The post is currently vacant in Umbria, while no Ombudsperson has ever been appointed in Calabria and Apulia. No legislative provision is made for the role by the Regions of Sicily and Trentino-Alto Adige (where, however, the Region has delegated full responsibility in their respective territories to the Ombudspersons of the Autonomous Provinces), while in Friuli-Venezia, Giulia and Molise, the laws establishing this institution were abrogated in 2008 (r.l. 14 August 2008, No. 9) and 2013 (r.l. 20 December 2013, No. 25) respectively.

At European and international levels, Burgi Volgger, who served as Ombudsperson of the Autonomous Province of Bolzano until July 2014 (succeeded by Gabriele Morandell), is President of the European Ombudsman Institute (EOI) Executive Committee, of which the President of the National Coordinating Body of Ombudspersons and Ombudsperson of the Region of Tuscany, Lucia Franchini, is also a member. Many regional and provincial Ombudspersons are also members of the EOI (Abruzzo, Basilicata, Emilia-Romagna, Marche, Lombardy, Piedmont, Valle d'Aosta, Veneto, Bolzano, Trent, Rome, Milan, and Massa Carrara).

The Ombudspersons of the Autonomous Province of Bolzano and the Regions of Basilicata, Lombardy, Tuscany and Valle d'Aosta are members of the International Ombudsman Institute (IOI).

III. National Coordinating Body of Ombudspersons

The National Coordinating Body of Regional and Autonomous Provinces' Ombudspersons is an associative body working to harmonise and enhance the institutional role of the Ombudsperson in Italy, and to guarantee every citizen, regardless of where he or she resides, protection in dealing with the public administration at all levels, whether State, regional or local.

> The Coordinating Body is made up of the incumbent Ombudspersons in the Regions and the Autonomous Provinces. It operates through the office of the Ombudsperson collectively elected from time to time and its Headquarters are in Rome, at the Network of the Presidents of the Legislative Assemblies of the Regions and the Autonomous Provinces, where it usually meets.

Since March 2013, the National Coordinator has been Lucia Franchini, Ombudsperson of the Region of Tuscany. The previous incumbent (2011–2013) was Antonio Caputo, Ombudsperson of the Region of Piedmont. The Coordinator also takes action if requested by the European Ombudsman towards the central State offices or those of the Italian Regions and local authorities which do not have their own regional or local Ombudsperson. Moreover, the incumbent interfaces as the Italian National Ombudsperson with the European Ombudsman and interacts with the other European Ombudsmen also through a liaison officer, who in 2014 was Vittorio Gasparrini.

During 2014, the Coordinating Body held four meetings to discuss a range of issues central to the consolidation of the institution of Ombudspersons in Italy. These included: revising the regulations on obligations on advertising, transparency and the circulation of information by the public administration; maximising existing opportunities to create greater cohesion and visibility for Ombudspersons in Italy; electing the new European Ombudsman; the circulation and management of new common software for archiving complaints; and the development of the Italian Ombudsman Institute based in part on a proposal from the Human Rights Centre of the University of Padua.

On 23 January the Coordinating Body signed a Memorandum of Understanding with the National Ombudsperson of Albania, Igli Totozani, aimed at guaranteeing assistance to citizens of both Countries in immigration and emigration procedures, and in their interactions with the public administrations in both Countries.

On 2 October the Coordinating Body presented to the Chamber of Deputies its first annual report on Ombudspersons in Italy, in the presence of European Ombudsman Emily O'Reilly. The report gave an update on the reach of the Ombudsperson function in Italy, presented the main aims the Coordinating Body established for the period 2013–2014, and gave a summary of the activities carried out in 2013. According to the report, in 2013 the National Ombudsperson Bureau opened 59 cases in all, concerning the following thematic areas: emigration and immigration; social issues; employment and welfare; health; public services; taxes and administrative sanctions.

On 5 November, motion No. 9/2681/127, presented by Deputy Bruno Tabacci, was approved, committing the Government to supplementing civil justice reform initiatives with specific measures to enhance the institution of Ombudsperson as a means of decreasing judicial disputes between citizens and the public administrations by strengthening the Ombudsperson's functions, powers and remit, particularly regarding his or her role in guaranteeing and protecting essential delivery levels of civil and social rights.

Finally, the Coordinating Body, together with the Human Rights Centre of the University of Padua and the Office of the Ombudsperson of the Region of Veneto, promoted a seminar on 21 February 2014 on "The contribution of Regional Ombudspersons in implementing human rights: a European commitment". This was the last in a series of meetings relating to "Ombudspersons and the rights of citizens", launched in December 2012.

IV. Network of Ombudspersons for Children and Adolescents

As of today, 18 Italian Regions and the Autonomous Provinces of Trent and Bolzano have approved legislation introducing a local Ombudsperson for Children and Adolescents at a regional level. Ombudspersons have actually been nominated in 15 regions (Apulia, Basilicata, Calabria, Campania, Emilia-Romagna, Friuli-Venezia Giulia, Lazio, Liguria, Marche, Molise, Tuscany, Umbria, Veneto and the Autonomous Provinces of Trent and Bolzano).

Some of these are exclusively charged with ensuring rights for children and adolescents (Apulia, Basilicata, Calabria, Campania, Emilia-Romagna, Lazio, Molise, Tuscany, Umbria and the Autonomous Province of Bolzano), whereas others have additional competence in areas such as those dealt with by Ombudspersons and/or ensuring rights for persons of restricted personal liberty (Liguria, Marche, Friuli-Venezia Giulia, Veneto and the Autonomous Province of Trent).

The approval of l. 12 July 2011, No. 112 established the figure of Ombudsperson for Children and Adolescents at the national level and formally defined and established the National Network for the Protection of the Rights of Children and Adolescents, made up of the Regional Ombudspersons for Children (or equivalent). The Network is charged with creating common lines of action to protect the rights of children and adolescents for regional and national Ombudspersons, to promote and support at the international level. It is also charged with identifying consistent means for a constant exchange of data and information on the condition of minors living in Italy. The Network has drawn up a set of internal regulations governing its functioning.

The Network met three times in 2014, to exchange information concerning actions undertaken at the territorial level on emerging issues and on any transversal initiatives, to further examine and promote the rights of children and adolescents, to be carried out jointly.

The Network focused in particular on the issue of reforming juvenile justice; the Ombudspersons, after raising this issue on several occasions, compiled a joint document which was sent to the Minister for Justice as a contribution to the ongoing reform of juvenile justice. The document, summarised in fifteen principles, contains some essential, fundamental recommendations for the creation of a new juvenile justice system.

V. National Coordinating Network of Ombudspersons for the Rights of Detainees

In 2014, the position of Ombudsperson for the rights of detainees existed in 13 Regions (Apulia, Campania, Emilia-Romagna, Friuli-Venezia Giulia, Lazio, Lombardy, Marche, Piedmont, Sicily, Tuscany, Umbria, Valle d'Aosta and Veneto) and in the Autonomous Province of Trent. In some areas, such as Lombardy, Marche, Umbria, Valle d'Aosta and Veneto, the Ombudsperson for the rights of detainees is also Ombudsperson in another field (general Ombudsperson or for the rights of children). The position of Ombudsperson for detainees has also been introduced in a further nine Provinces and 24 Municipalities.

While awaiting the appointment of a national body for the rights of detainees (National Ombudsperson), established pursuant to l.d. 146/2013 (converted into l. 10/2014), the Ombudspersons are active within two associative organisations at the national level: the National Coordinating Network of Local Ombudspersons for the Rights of Detainees and the National Network of Regional Ombudspersons. The Coordinating Network is open to Municipal, Provincial and Regional Ombudspersons, and has the broad aims of undertaking joint actions relating to the rights of detainees, finding consensual solutions to the main problems encountered by individual Ombudspersons in Italy, and putting their experience at the disposal of the whole community. The National Network, established in 2008, is tasked with planning national initiatives to better deal with issues linked to protecting the fundamental rights of detainees, enforcing sentences, and reintegrating detainees into society. During 2014 the Network was coordinated by Adriana Tocco, Ombudsperson of Campania.

To answer the need for a single coordinating body for the regional and territorial Ombudspersons for the rights of detainees, the Network met on 11 March in Rome and established a new national coordinating body to address general issues such as: the rights to health, work and study; relationships with persons deprived of their liberty; detainees' conditions; overcrowding; and their future relationship with the National Ombudsperson, Operationally, the new network will be called a committee and will be made up of six members, three representing regional Ombudspersons and three representing local ones.

During meetings of the Network in 2014, the Ombudspersons focused their attention on the issues of health and the difficulties in accessing necessary treatment in prisons, on changes introduced by l.d. 146/2013 on complaints and on establishing a National Ombudsperson, and on transfers in compliance with the principle of "territorialisation of the sentence". The Network also agreed on the need to highlight to the Minister for Justice the reservations held by Ombudspersons on the procedure for nominating the National Ombudsperson, and on the need to discuss the duties and institutional framework of the new body, in the light of the Network's general opinion that it has been granted a very limited autonomy.

VI. National Coordinating Body of Local Authorities for Peace and Human Rights

The National Coordinating Body is an association founded in 1986 which brings together over 600 Italian Municipalities, Provinces and Regions committed to promoting peace, human rights, solidarity and international cooperation. The Chair of this association is Andrea Ferrari, Councillor for Peace in the Municipality of Lodi and it is managed by Flavio Lotti.

2014 was the year of the Perugia-Assisi Peace March, and hundreds of thousands of individuals, groups, associations, local authorities and institutions from across Italy played an active part. On Sunday 19 October 2014, 904 bodies participated, including schools (111), local authorities (303), and national and local associations (80 and 410 respectively); 575 towns from 97 Provinces were involved. For the first time, the March, jointly organised with the *Tavola della pace* (Peace Roundtable), saw thousands of young students centre stage, as they and their teachers opened, helped organise and closed the event with outstanding energy and creativity. A century after the outbreak of the First World War, the Perugia-Assisi event of 19 October was a march for peace and brotherhood, against the ongoing third world war and for recognition of the human right to peace, for disarmament, and for a Europe of fraternity.

The Perugia-Assisi event was the climax of a number of educational, learning and awareness-raising programmes and actions for peace. These included 39 peace marches in as many towns under the banner "peace starts in our towns!" Many of the citizens involved had never taken part in a peace demonstration before.

In 2014 the Coordinating Body promoted the "international campaign for the international recognition of the right to peace", along with the Human Rights Centre and the UNESCO Chair of "human rights, democracy and peace" from the University of Padua, and the Perugia-Assisi network (see this Part, Sub-national Human Rights Structures, I).

On 4 April 2014 the Coordinating Body celebrated its 10th National Assembly, entitled "Facciamo come Giorgio La Pira" (Let's do as Giorgio La Pira did). The Assembly offered the chance for in-depth reflection on the responsibilities towns have for peace, human rights, solidarity and cooperation, and to jointly redesign the future of Local Authorities' and Regions' commitment to them, following in the footsteps left sixty years earlier by the Mayor of Florence, Giorgio La Pira.

On 14 and 15 April, in Assisi, the Coordinating Body organised the National Meeting of peace schools, "*Pace, fraternità e dialogo. Sui passi di Francesco*" (Peace, fraternity and dialogue: in St Francis' footsteps) in which three thousand students, teachers, local administrators, journalists, academics, and religious and secular representatives from various associations participated, along with experts from fifteen Italian regions. This meeting gave rise to the creation of a National Network of Peace Schools, the approval of the Assisi Charter and the start of new programmes of activities aimed at encouraging young people to get involved in working for peace. These include the National Programme for Democratic Citizenship Education, "*Dalla Grande Guerra alla Grande Pace*" (From the Great War to the Great Peace) 2014–1018. A training and research course specifically for teachers, school directors, local administrators and social workers took place in Monfalcone (Gorizia) on 14–16 November 2014.

During 2014 the Coordinating Body continued its efforts for peace in the Middle East with the national programme "*100 Città per la Pace in Medio Oriente*" (100 Towns for Peace in the Middle East), aiming to strengthen and enhance collaboration between Italian local authorities and Israel and Palestine for peace in the Middle East. In the context of this project, local authorities were invited to: vote to join the "100 Towns for Peace in the Middle East" project and the European Network of Local Authorities for Peace in the Middle East; approve the agenda "Stop the war in Gaza, build peace in the Middle East"; and contribute to the national solidarity fund for victims in Gaza, promoted in conjunction with Caritas Jerusalem.

VII. Archives and Other Regional Projects for the Promotion of a Culture of Peace and Human Rights

Besides the "Pace Diritti Umani – Peace Human Rights" Archive of the Region of Veneto, established by r.l. 18/1988 and managed by the Human Rights Centre of the University of Padua (see this Part, Region of Veneto, IV), there are other more recent archives and similar projects set up by Italian Regions and Autonomous Provinces to foster the promotion and dissemination of a culture of human rights and peace.

The "Peace and Human Rights" project in the Region of Emilia-Romagna was set up by the Regional Council in collaboration with the Department for Social Policies, Immigration, Youth Projects and International Cooperation and the Regional Government's Management Control and Statistics Systems Department. This project, managed by the *Europe Direct* centre of the Legislative Assembly of Emilia-Romagna, follows the principles laid out in r.l. 24 June 2002, No. 12 (Regional interventions for cooperation with developing countries and countries in transition, international solidarity and the promotion of a culture of peace), aims to support activities described in the law. Their website is at http://www.paceediritti.it/.

During 2014, the Regional Service for European Policy and International Relations – International Cooperation, which has been associated with the project since 2013, continued to expand the website with news and information on projects in the Region's provinces, as well as on peace and international cooperation negotiation tables; and publications of interest on the issues on which the project focuses.

The forum "*Trentino per la pace e i diritti umani*" (Trentino for peace and human rights), a standing body, was established in 1991 at the behest of the Provincial Council of Trent with p.l. 10 June 1991 No. 11 (Promotion and dissemination of the culture of peace). Its website is at http://www.forumpace.it/.

For the period 2014–2015 the Forum decided to centre its activities around the issue of *rights denied*, taking as its starting point the idea that one cannot build peace and then assert rights, but that it is by asserting rights that one can create a society of widespread and lasting peace. In this context, the Forum helped organise and run a number of events, conferences, exhibitions and public meetings in the Autonomous Province of Trent.

Region of Veneto

The Region of Veneto has been operating organically for the promotion of human rights, the culture of peace and international cooperation, ever since 1988, the year when the first specific law on such issues was adopted (regional law 30 March 1988, No. 18). During the same year, the Regional Council established the Ombudsperson (r.l. 28/1988) and the Ombudsperson for Children and Adolescents (r.l. 42/1988). In 1999, regional law 18/1988 was replaced by the current r.l. 16 December 1999, No. 55, on "Regional measures for the promotion of human rights, a culture of peace, development cooperation and solidarity". With r.l. 24 December 2013, No. 37, the Region has established the post of *Regional Ombudsperson for the Rights of the Person* who will integrate the functions of the Ombudsperson, of the Ombudsperson for Children and Adolescents as well as those of promotion and protection of the rights of persons deprived of their liberty. In the context of the Regional Government, issues concerning human rights pertain to the Councillor on Economy, Development, Research and Innovation, Marialuisa Coppola. Measures and activities concerning international relations and development cooperation respond directly to the Regional Governor, Luca Zaia, assisted by the Minister Plenipotentiary Stefano Beltrame.

In virtue of r.l. 55/1999, the Committee on Human Rights and the Culture of Peace (articles 12–13) and the Committee on Development Cooperation (articles 14–15) operate to fulfil their mandate of formulating three-year programmes and annual plans of implementation according to their respective areas of competence and intervention. In addition, the law promotes and supports the Regional Archive "Pace Diritti Umani – Peace Human Rights" (article 2), the Venice for Peace Research Foundation (article 17) (both established with r.l. 18/1988), the activities of the European Commission for Democracy through Law (Venice Commission) of the Council of Europe (article 19) and initiatives of decentralised cooperation promoted by the Ministry of Foreign Affairs and by the European Union (article 7). The regional infrastructure for peace and human rights is completed by the Commission for the Realisation of Equal Opportunities between Men and Women, the Regional Observatory on Social Policies and the Regional Observatory for Immigration. Moreover, by way of r.l. 28 December 1998, No. 33, the Region promotes and supports financially the European Master's degree Programme in Human Rights and Democratisation (E.MA), located in Venice. With the adoption of r.l. 22 January 2010, No. 6, the Region has recognised the social and cultural value of fair trade, proclaiming its support for the organisations which operate in this sector. Finally, regional law 23 April 2013, No. 5 established a Regional Coordination Table for Preventing and Combating the Violence against Women within the Regional Government. Regional deliberation 594/2014 has decided the composition of this body, including representatives of regional bodies and institutions as well as experts in matters concerning violence against women.

I. Regional Section for International Relations

The International Relations Section is part of the Department for International Policy and Co-operation and is responsible for the implementation of r.l. 55/1999. The Section was managed in 2014 by Diego Vecchiato, Director of the Department.

The Regional Section oversees a series of international activities undertaken by the Region, including: the management of international relations; the signature of memoranda of understanding with national and foreign institutions; the participation in international bodies and initiatives; international solidarity; and all activities in the sectors of human rights, the culture of peace, the promotion of equal opportunities and the protection of linguistic minorities. The Section also hosts the Veneto Regional Committee for UNICEF.

In the specific area of promotion of human rights, the Section provides technical support to the Committee for human rights and the culture of peace; it oversees the organisation of events, takes part in the activities of the Council of Europe Venice Commission and fulfils the obligations deriving from the Region's promotion and financial support of the European Master's Programme in Human Rights and Democratisation (E.MA).

On 20 October 2014, the Director of the International Policy and Cooperation Department adopted a measure which assigned vouchers for educational projects on human rights to primary schools and junior secondary schools in Veneto, allocating euro 25,000 to the non-profit bodies which ran these projects. The vouchers are an experimental new method of funding for the Region, aiming to create opportunities for schools and associations to meet to compare ideas on human rights issues. In 2014, 50 vouchers were funded in total, for 28 projects organised by 22 authorities and delivered in 30 primary and secondary schools in the region.

II. Committee for Human Rights and the Culture of Peace

Established pursuant to art. 12 of r.l. 55/1999, the Committee contributes to drawing up three-year programmes and annual plans regarding initiatives promoted by the Region of Veneto on human rights and a culture of peace (art. 13). The Committee comprises representatives from local authorities, civil society, academia, the business world and social partners.

With regional deliberation 1123 of 1 July 2014, the Council adopted their *2014 Annual Plan* to implement regional interventions promoting human rights and a culture of peace in the context of the three-year programme 2013–2015 (adopted with deliberation of the Regional Council on 16 July 2013).

The general objectives of the three-year programme are as follows: to strengthen coordination networks on issues of interest which are already active on the territory; to encourage information and exchange of best practices of local actors in the area of human rights; to incentivise and support the nomination of projects expressed by the Veneto territory for funding of programmes promoting human rights and a culture of peace called by the Italian Government and international organisations; to promote activities assessing, measuring and evaluating the level of implementation and effectiveness at the regional level of human rights enshrined in international Conventions; to promote, through the new social media, the spread of a culture of respect for human rights and dignity of the person, within and outside of the school environment; to make human rights issues, expanded to include the new generation of human rights easier to access and enjoy; to enhance diversity as a foundation for promoting peaceful coexistence and social cohesion; to encourage an inclusive society, with particular reference to more vulnerable groups and individuals such as minors, the elderly, the disabled and the unemployed; and to solicit and support positive and innovative experimental action in Veneto which implement a model of development combined with respect for human rights in a context of social, economic and environmental sustainability.

To promote these aims, the Annual Plan was allocated a total of 250,000 euro from the regional budget for 2014. As well as guaranteeing financial support, provided for in r.l. 55/1999 for the "Peace Human Rights" Archive and for the Venice for Peace Research Foundation, the Regional Council helped to fund contributory initiatives for a total of 155,000 euro, of which 25,000 euro to cover education vouchers (see this Part, Region of Veneto, I). On the other hand, it proved impossible to undertake direct actions on human rights issues during the past year.

The 14 contributory initiatives financed within the framework of the 2014 Annual Plan were: Percorsi di pace, polis e partecipazione, by Alternativa Nord/Sud per il XXI secolo (Vicenza); *Spazi comuni* by Adelante onlus soc. coop. sociale. (Bassano del Grappa, VI), *Intrecci di relazioni: per una cittadinanza consapevole*, by Gruppo Missioni Africa (Montagnana, PD); *Nutrire i giovani, energia per la vita*, by Ispettoria Salesiana San Marco (Mogliano Veneto, TV); *Acquisto potere: il valore della scelta*, by Associazione di cooperazione e solidarietà-ACS (Padua); *Giovani, attori di cittadinanza, cooperazione e partecipazione (II year)*, by NATs per... onlus (Treviso); *Essere in rete: make peace visible*, by Associazione bNET (Treviso); *Incontri di pace*, by Associazione di Volontari per Iniziative di Pace – AVIP onlus

(Sant'Angelo di Piove di Sacco, PD); *I luoghi dei diritti umani e della pace a Vicenza e provincia*, by Il Mosaico Società Cooperativa Sociale (Vicenza); *Carcere, cittadinanza attiva e inclusione sociale*, by Associazione Fratelli dell'Uomo Onlus (Milano); *Diritti in scena*, by Jonathan Cooperativa Sociale (Piazzola sul Brenta, PD); *Run 4 Unity – In corsa verso la fraternità*, by Associazione culturale "i ponti" Onlus (Padua); *Camminare insieme per un nuovo umanesimo*, by the Comitato d'intesa tra le associazioni volontaristiche (networking committee for volunteering associations) della Provincia di Belluno (Belluno); *L'integrazione a scuola e nel mondo*, by SOS Bambino International Adoption Onlus (Vicenza).

III. Committee for Development Cooperation

The Committee for Development Cooperation was established pursuant to art. 14 of r.l. 55/1999. The Committee is charged with contributing to the drafting of the three-year programmes and annual plans for decentralised development cooperation and international solidarity activities. The Committee comprises representatives from local administrations, civil society, academia, the business world and social partners.

In 2014 the Regional Government adopted deliberation 15 July 2014, No. 1192, concerning the 2014 Annual Plan on decentralised cooperation operations for development and international solidarity and the promotion of fair trade, which allocated funds for the Region's direct initiatives in partnership with public bodies from Veneto and for those in which the Region is a partner, in collaboration with national and supranational authorities and bodies, as well as for contributory initiatives. The strategic priorities for the new Plan are those detailed in the *2013–2015 Three-Year Programme* (adopted in 2012): promoting human and sustainable development; protecting, safeguarding and enhancing the territories, their natural resources and environmental heritage; strengthening the role of women; protecting children; strengthening democratic institutions and local administrations; supporting the active role of migrants in co-development initiatives.

To promote these aims, the Annual Plan allocated 830,000 euro from the 2014 Regional budget for decentralised development cooperation, and 150,000 euro for initiatives promoting fair trade.

IV. Regional Archive «Pace Diritti Umani – Peace Human Rights»

The Regional Archive was created pursuant to r.l. 18/1988 and reconfirmed by the subsequent r.l. 55/1999. The Archive is managed by the Human Rights Centre of the University of Padua, as laid down in art. 2

of the aforementioned law, which reads: "*1. The Region promotes and supports: [ ] c) the Archive established by regional law 30 March 1988, No. 18, in cooperation with the Centre of Studies and Training on the Rights of Man and of Peoples of the University of Padua, according to a special agreement* [...]". It is one of the main instruments through which the Region of Veneto promotes the culture of human rights, peace, development cooperation and solidarity in Italy and abroad.

> The Archive works to collect, elaborate and publish documents, thematic databases and informational resources on topics regarding regional law, particularly through the regular updating of the portal "Archivio Pace Diritti Umani" (http://unipd-centrodirittiumani.it/en/), available in Italian and in English, and the distribution of knowledge on human rights through multi-media tools and social networks. In addition, it oversees publication of books, teaching aids, in-depth studies and multi-media, and offers technical and scientific support to the actors most closely involved in the promotion and practice of the culture of peace, especially as concerns initiatives promoted by teachers, education staff and schools. In 2014 the Archive published and distributed 18 editions of the "peace human rights" newsletter in Italian and in English to a long but qualified mailing list. The newsletter aims to support development activities relating to education on human rights and the culture of peace in schools.

During 2014 the Archive updated the databases available on its website, notably the Italian translation of the database of international legal instruments on human, humanitarian, criminal and refugee law; the University of Padua Human Rights Centre publications from 1982 to the present; and the associations and NGOs active in the field of human rights and development cooperation in Veneto. In addition to its usual activities of updating, providing in-depth studies and informing, the Archive published a special edition of the review *Pace Diritti Umani Peace Human Rights* on the right to peace, as well as several in-depth articles by university professors on current issues involving human rights in the publication *Human Rights Academic Voice*. The Archive also contributed to the publication of the 2014 edition of the *Italian Yearbook of Human Rights*.

In 2014 the Archive played an active role in the "International Campaign for Recognition of the Right to Peace" (see *2014 Yearbook* pp. 20–22), for which it created a mapping of the Municipalities, Provinces and Regions which had adopted the petitionary motion on recognising the right to peace proposed by the Coordinating Body of Local Authorities for Peace and Human Rights, the Human Rights Centre and the UNESCO Chair of the University of Padua (see this Part, Sub-national Human Rights Structures, I). The same issue was the focus of an initiative of a group of students and volunteers from the national civil service, who took an active part in the "Perugia-Assisi" Peace March on 19 October with the technical and scientific support of the Archive. The Archive also helped to organise a series of events at the University of Padua, including a meeting with Mayors on the International Day of Peace (20 September) and the International Human Rights Day 2014, which in Padua was devoted to the right to peace (10 December).

In 2014, the Archive helped organise a series of events at the University of Padua, particularly as concerns the documentation and multimedia side, in collaboration with national and international organisations and experts. Particularly noteworthy are the following:

– the University Association of European Studies (AUSE) international conference on the topic of "Representative democracy and political participation. Towards a transnational European party system", held during the run-up to the European elections (5 and 6 May).

– the national conference "From the 'White Helmets Beyond Vengeance' project to the Civilian Peace Corps" (8 July).

– the cycle of seminars Towards EXPO2015, on the issue "The right to food, food and rights" (23 October).

– The start-up conference of the European project TEMVI on human trafficking and illegal economies (29 – 30 October).

V. Venice for Peace Research Foundation

As was the Regional Archive, the Foundation was established by r.l. 18/1988, and reconfirmed by r.l. 55/1999. The Foundation's main goal is to carry out research, partly in collaboration with national and international institutions, on matters of security, development and peace.

Institutional and financial reasons have impacted the Foundation's ability to plan and carry out activities of late, and so there are no specific initiatives to report on for 2014.

VI. Ombudsperson for Children and Adolescents

The Office of the Ombudsperson for Children and Adolescents was established by r.l. 9 August 1988, No. 42. The Ombudsperson is elected by the Regional Council, to which he or she presents a detailed annual report on the year's activities. Aurea Dissegna has been the Ombudsperson for Children and Adolescents in Veneto since December 2010.

The Ombudsperson works towards the non-conflictual, non-jurisdictional protection of the rights of children and adolescents, freely and independently with respect to other public institutions. The office is a monocratic authority which avails itself of a staff of experts and collaborators from various professions and disciplines; no charges are made for the Ombudsperson's services.

Over the years, the Office of the Ombudsperson for Children and Adolescents has trained and provided support to over a thousand voluntary legal guardians throughout the Region of Veneto, 75% of whom have indicated their willingness to continue to act as legal guardians. In 2014 the Office continued its support, consultancy and training activities for both voluntary legal guardians and for the local spokespersons who represent the link between the Office and the local area; it also acts as a reference-point for the groups of guardians operating in each local healthcare catchment area.

In 2014 the Office received 224 requests for voluntary legal guardians from the judicial authorities (ordinary and juvenile courts), affecting approximately 250 children and adolescents in Veneto.

The Office of the Ombudsperson has, over the years, coordinated the publication of guidelines for the social and healthcare services in Veneto on the treatment and reporting of problems concerning minors; this is an important tool which requires regular updating and reviewing, pursuant to regional Government deliberation (r.g.d.) 8 August 2008, No. 2416 (Regional guidelines to develop the services for protecting and safeguarding children and adolescents).

In connection with this, and following the success of the workshop designed and held in the previous year, the "Workshop for communications between the services and the judicial authorities", the outcome of which was recorded in the r.g.d. 779/2013 and serves as a guideline for social workers and healthcare workers, in 2014 the Office proposed and coordinated the second stage of the Workshop, which also brought in representatives of the police, the magistrates' courts, the Appeal Court (juvenile section), as well as social and healthcare professionals working on the ground. The objectives were: to strengthen and improve the means of communication and cooperation between the services and the police force, both as regards reporting to the juvenile and ordinary courts and in implementing measures ordered by the judiciary (particularly the removal of minors from their families), and between services and judiciary at juvenile, ordinary and appeal level, as well as to clarify the role, duties and responsibilities of court-appointed experts and the services in procedures involving minors.

Alongside the workshop activities, mention should also be made of some inter-institutional thematic round tables set up and coordinated by the Ombudsperson's Office on specific issues concerning minors: identifying actions to guarantee the right to education of children with health problems; defining co-operation processes between services in actions relating to minors with addiction issues; and the implementation of support pathways for the psycho-relational development of children between the ages of 0 – 6 in prison with their mothers.

In 2014, 415 files were opened concerning institutional listening, mediating and counselling, following requests from various different institutions (Municipalities, local health authorities, schools, the judiciary, etc.) and from private individuals (citizens, parents and relatives). Requests from social and healthcare services remain constantly high, comprising over half of the total.

During 2014, in agreement with the Regional Department of Health and Social Services, the Office organised a training course comprising a series of in-depth looks at judicial-legal issues entitled "Minors and Child-friendly Law", aimed at a select group of social and healthcare service workers indicated by the Mayors' Network and by local healthcare authorities in Veneto. The broad aims of this training were: to help healthcare and social workers gain and consolidate their judicial-legal knowledge and expertise, to enable them to work with greater confidence, while respecting regulations and human rights in even the most complex of cases; to enable them to manage the workings of administrative and legal proceedings with ease and awareness of their own responsibilities.

Finally, in 2014 the Office provided for various activities to advertise the outcomes of research and action on the legal institution of placing children in care promoted by the Ombudsperson for Minors in Veneto and coordinated by the Human Rights Centre of the University of Padua, with the involvement of the Regional Ombudspersons from Lazio and Emilia-Romagna.

To this end there were two opportunities for discussion and comparison of the results of this research with the main stakeholders (professional bodies, lawyers, national association of family and juvenile magistrates, social services representatives): a restricted seminar held in Bologna in January 2014, and the national conference "Entrusting minors to social services care" held in May 2014 in Rome, which led to some useful ideas for the drafting of "Guidance and recommendations on access to, interpretation and application of placing children and adolescents in social care", which was written by the Ombudspersons themselves and addressed to Parliament (in view of possible reforms to the juvenile justice system), the Regions, the judiciary and local authorities, for them to share, adopt and disseminate.

VII. Ombudsperson for Detainees

R.l. 24 December 2013 No. 37 established the role of Regional Ombudsperson for Human Rights, a new figure who will take on the functions of Ombudsperson, Ombudsperson for Children and Adolescents and Ombudsperson for Deatainees from the beginning of the next legislature.

A transitional regulation in r.l. 37/2013 allows for the functions of the Ombudsperson for Detainees to be carried out by the Ombudsperson for Children and Adolescents until a new Ombudsperson is appointed.

During 2014 the Ombudsperson for Detainees, despite no specific budget being allocated to the office, visited several penal institutions in the region and organised a meeting with the Superintendent of Prison Administration in Triveneto, the President of the Supervisory Court of Venice, the Director of the Centre for Juvenile Justice in Venice, the Director of the Mental Health Sector and Ombudspersons for Detainees appointed at a local level (Venice, Verona and Rovigo, the Municipality of Vicenza being in the process of appointing one), to discuss issues relating to persons deprived of personal freedom and living in prisons in Veneto.

In the dual role of Ombudsperson for Detainees and Ombudsperson for Children and Adolescents, on 16 June 2014 the Ombudsperson organised the regional conference "Being a parent in Prison: from the rights of adults to the rights of minors", focusing on the quality and maintenance of emotional ties between parents in prison and their children. The aim was to encourage those who are directly or indirectly involved in these situations to think about them carefully and highlighting the many examples of good practice in place in the region.

Furthermore, the Ombudsperson took part in the meetings of the Standing Inter-Institutional Observatory for Mental Health in Prisons and in various public initiatives on the issue.

VIII. Ombudsperson

The Ombudsperson of the Region of Veneto was established by r.l. 6 June 1988, No. 28.

> The Ombudsperson is a monocratic authority with freedom to act completely independently and freely to defend the rights and the interests of citizens in cases of maladministration or abuse of power by public authorities. The Ombudsperson has the support of an Office comprising a staff of legal experts who are qualified in the specific areas covered by the Ombudsperson's activities. His services are given free of charge. The Ombudsperson is elected by the Regional Council from among the citizens possessing the necessary qualifications and experience in legal and administrative matters and remains in office for five years; every year the Ombudsperson presents the Regional Assembly with a detailed report on the activity of the previous year.

The post is currently occupied by Roberto Pellegrini, who was appointed by the President of the Regional Council on 7 December 2010 and took office on 20 January 2011.

In 2014, the Veneto Regional Ombudsperson's Office received a total of 598 claims, 456 of which were resolved within the year, whereas 142 are still open and awaiting decisions. In addition, 32 cases which had been carried over from previous years were resolved.

The five main areas to which the claims referred were: territorial issues (158 new cases in 2014, of which 118 were closed and 13 cases from previous years resolved in 2014); taxes, levies, subscriptions and fines (75 new cases in 2014 of which 69 were closed, and six cases from previous years were closed in 2014); participatory instances and administrative procedures (134 new cases in 2014, of which 116 were closed, and one back case was closed in 2014); general and institutional affairs and organisation (48 new cases in 2014, of which 19 were closed, and three back cases were closed in 2014); social security (55 new cases in 2014 of which 49 were closed and four back cases resolved in 2014).

In 2014, in addition to acting on reports received from citizens, the Veneto Ombudsperson started several investigations on his own initiative, including following press reports. A specific instance involved the regional administration: the dispute concerned access to public sector employment, recalling the principle of impartiality under art. 97 of the Constitution.

As was highlighted in the previous section, from the next council legislature onwards the roles of Ombudsperson, Ombudsperson for Children and Adolescents and Ombudsperson for Detainees will be combined in the role of Ombudsperson for Human Rights.

IX. Regional Commission for Equal Opportunities between Men and Women

The Commission was established by r.l. 30 December 1987, No. 62 and it is the regional consultative body on gender policies for the actual implementation of the principles of equality and equal opportunities enshrined in the Constitution and by the Regional Statute. Chair of the Commission is Simonetta Tregnago.

> The main function of the Commission is to carry out investigations and research into the condition of women in Veneto, with particular reference to issues involving employment, labour and professional training, and to disseminate information on these areas. At the same time, the Commission respects its commitment to being present on the ground and to developing new synergies with all the actors and forces involved to promote and

support the realisation of equal opportunities in the social, political and economic life of the population of Veneto. It may offer opinions on the current state of implementation of laws and on bills, as well as drawing up proposals of its own. The Veneto Equal Opportunities Commission carries out its mission in contact with other Commissions at the local, regional and national level and maintains a constant exchange with all women's organisations in the Region.

The Commission undertook a number of activities in the Region in 2014, including research and joint study work undertaken with other bodies and organisations. Special mention is made of the following:

– the cycle of seven meeting and workshops held between 3 March and 16 April 2014 on the topic of political communication for those people, women in particular, wishing to become politically active and to present themselves convincingly and effectively during elections.

– the conference "*Pari o dispari opportunità i conti non tornano!*" (Equal or unequal opportunities – it doesn't add up!) organised by the Equal Opportunities Committee of the Association of Chartered Accountants of Venice and held in Venice on 15 May, where the results of the project "*Libere Professioniste: verifica delle pari opportunità di accesso e di attività*" (Freelance female professionals: assessing equal opportunities of access and activity") were presented.

– The conference "*In difesa della donna: il Veneto propone*" ("In defence of women: Veneto proposes"), held on 24 November at the Regional Council headquarters in Venice, with two aims: to take stock of progress in applying r.l. 5/2013 on the prevention and fight against violence against women; and to find out about the experience of reception and shelters, by listening to officials and workers from anti-violence centres as well as to the testimonies of victims of violence. At the end of the conference the President of the Commission and Sandra Miotto, Regional Councillor for Equal Opportunities, presented the regional council with the "Venice Decalogue", a document listing ten requests for action and commitment to the making gender equality a reality, a necessary condition for preventing all types of violence. The wishes expressed by the Commission and the Councillor are that the document can become a roadmap for the work of regional institutions and also a prompt for the regional council election campaign in 2015.

Furthermore, during 2014 the Commission called strongly on the Regional Council to change the electoral law to allow the introduction of the "double gender preference", by amending article 20 of r.l. 16 January 2012, No. 5 (Regulations for the Election of the President of the Regional Government and the Regional Council).

X. Regional Observatory on Social Policies

As of January 2011 the Observatory was established to replace its predecessor, the *Integrated Network of Regional Observatories on Social Policies*.

> The function of the Observatory on Social Policies is to activate an information-gathering, monitoring and evaluation system on the interventions and actions relating to regional social services and healthcare policies, in order to support decision-making and planning processes and to develop a regional social information system capable of ensuring a close connection with local information systems. This function is performed mainly through the organisation of events, training activities and consultancy on local social services and healthcare issues, but also through the development and management of databases and support activities for the regional social services headquarters. The Observatory's activities are organised according to the themes which were the object of attention by the observatories under the previous Integrated Network: minors, young people, families, senior citizens and people with disabilities, addictions and social exclusion, with a specific focus on the aspects concerning volunteering and European projects.

Among the many different activities involving the Observatory in 2014, the following, focusing particularly on action for the elderly, are highlighted:

– Conference "*I Centro Sollievo si raccontano*" (The Relief Centres Talk about Themselves), organised by the Observatory along with Health Unit ULSS No. 8 in Asolo as part of the "Progetto Sollievo". Approved by d.r.g. No. 1873/2013, the project's aim is to establish ad hoc centres throughout the region through ULSS health units, where qualified and trained volunteers welcome elderly people affected by dementia for a few hours or a few days a week, and offer activities tailored to their individual requirements.

– Conference "*Strategie europee e nuovi strumenti per le politiche abitative*" (European strategies and new instruments for housing policies), held on 24 June 2014 and promoted by the Veneto Region Health and Social Care Department. The conference was held as part of the three-year strategic plan HELPS (2011–2014) aiming to find innovative solutions to meet the challenges concerning housing and care of the elderly that many Countries face as a consequence of socio-demographic change in areas such as ageing, disability and the risk of social exclusion, by encouraging synergies between sectors with different areas of responsibility.

XI. Regional Observatory on Immigration

The Observatory is overseen by the Project Unit on Migratory Flows (the Councillor's office on migratory flows policies) and is managed by

Veneto Lavoro. Its establishment was included in the three-year programme 2007–2009 comprising measures and initiatives in the field of immigration and confirmed by the adoption of the subsequent 2010–2012 plan, pursuant to art. 3 of r.l. 9/1990 (Measures in the immigration sector).

> The Observatory is defined as a technical-scientific instrument aiming to monitor, analyse and disseminate data and information on migratory flows and integration at the regional and national level. To this end, it: collaborates with the other regional observatories which are for one reason or another involved in the migration phenomenon; assures the proper functioning and constant input for databases, the monitoring of immigration dynamics, further study on various thematic aspects, housing conditions, the social and educational integration of minors and their development; it ensures an updated collection of specialised laws, proposing training sessions to increase knowledge of these laws and their correct implementation.

In October 2014 the Observatory published its eleventh "Annual report on foreign immigration to Veneto". The report presents a systematic analysis of data and trends in migratory flows in relation to certain aspects crucial for Veneto and for Italy as a whole, such as demographic changes; employment and unemployment figures; education; services to the person; policies to encourage repatriation; recent trends and changes to entry policies; and the economic impact of immigration.

In general terms, the statistical data presented in the report show that the number of foreign nationals resident in Veneto at the end of 2013 was 514,592, constituting 10.5% of the total number of foreigners in Italy (4,922,085). Compared to the Country as a whole, Veneto has the fourth largest population of foreign residents (after Lombardy, Lazio and Emilia-Romagna). The total percentage of foreigners within the regional population is 10.5%, the fourth highest percentage after Emilia-Romagna, Umbria and Lombardy. The Provinces with the largest foreign population are Verona (11.9%), Treviso (11.4%) and Vicenza (11%). There has been a significant increase over the previous year in the number of foreign nationals in the municipal registers who have gained Italian citizenship (8,346), making a total of 14,592, equivalent to 14% of the total number of citizenships granted in the Country (around 100,000). As of 1 January 2014, the largest numbers of residence permits in Veneto were held by foreigners from Morocco (around 67,000), Albania (44,000), China (42,500) and Moldova (41,000).

Part III

Italy in Dialogue with International Human Rights Institutions

The United Nations System

I. General Assembly

The General Assembly, which is the main deliberative body of the United Nations, comprises six Committees, each of which is made up of all 193 United Nations Member States. Human rights issues are handled mainly within the Third Committee (the Social, Humanitarian and Cultural Committee). The responsibilities of this Committee include issues such as torture and other cruel, inhuman and degrading treatment or punishment; the advancement of women; the rights of refugees and displaced persons; the promotion and protection of the rights of children; the rights of indigenous peoples; the elimination of racism, racial discrimination, xenophobia and related intolerance; the right of peoples to self-determination; and social development.

In December 2014 the 69th General Assembly adopted 61 human rights resolutions which had been debated and approved by the Third Committee during October and November. In particular, with the resolution on the human rights situation in the Democratic People's Republic of Korea (A/RES/68/181), adopted with 116 votes in favour, 20 against and 53 abstentions, the Assembly decided for the first time to bring the report of the Special Rapporteur on the human rights situation in that country to the attention of the Security Council. The Assembly also asked the Council to assess the possibility of referring the situation in the Democratic People's Republic of Korea to the International Criminal Court, and to adopt effective targeted sanctions against the main actors responsible for the actions which the United Nations Commission of Inquiry defined as potential crimes against humanity.

In 2014 Italy's Permanent Representative to the United Nations in New York was Ambassador Sebastiano Cardo; Councillor of the Embassy Emilia Gatto was responsible for following the activities of the Third Committee. In June 2014, Ambassador Cardi was elected President of the Second Committee (economic and financial affairs) of the General Assembly.

The chart below shows the most significant interventions by the Italian delegation and Government representatives in General Assembly meetings in 2014.

Date	Event	Statement
20/01/2014	Interactive panel on "The threat of growing inequalities: building more just and equitable societies to support growth and sustainable development"	H.E. Cardi: opening and closing statements
3/02/2014	Interactive exchange of ideas on "Oceans and seas, forests, biodiversity", 8th session of GA Working Group on Sustainable Development Goals	Andrea Orlando, Minister for the Environment and the Protection of Land and Sea H.E. Cardi
4/02/2014	High level event on "Healthy oceans and seas: a way forward", 8th session of GA Working Group on Sustainable Development Goals	Andrea Orlando, Minister for the Environment and the Protection of Land and Sea
25/02/2014	Informal GA meeting on the humanitarian situation in Syria	H.E. Cardi
26/03/2014	GA Plenary meeting on the Peacebuilding Commission's report: Secretary General's report on the Peacebuilding Fund	H.E. Lambertini, Deputy Permanent Representative
9/06/2014	High level event of the GA President on "Contributions of human rights and the rule of law in the post 2015 development agenda"	H.E. Cardi
8/09/2014	Informal interactive GA debate on the Secretary General's report on the "Responsibility to Protect"	H.E. Lambertini, Deputy Permanent Representative

Date	Event	Statement
25/09/2014	Opening of the General Debate of the 69th General Assembly	Matteo Renzi, Prime Minister
7/10/2014	Second Committee, 69th General Assembly	H.E. Cardi: opening statement
7/10/2014	Third Committee, 69th General Assembly	H.E. Lambertini, Deputy Permanent Representative, on social development
9/10/2014	Third Committee, 69th General Assembly	H.E. Cardi, on "Crime Prevention and Criminal Justice
13/10/2014	First Committee, 69th General Assembly	H.E. Mati, Permanent Representative to the Conference on Disarmament
13/10/2014	Third Committee, 69th General Assembly	H.E. Lambertini, Deputy Permanent Representative, advancement of women
14/10/2014	Special Joint Meeting of the GA Second Committee and ECOSOC on "Lessons learned from debt crises and the ongoing work on sovereign debt restructuring and debt resolution mechanism"	H.E. Cardi: opening statement
21/10/2014	Third Committee, 69th General Assembly	H.E. Lambertini, Deputy Permanent Representative, on promoting and protecting human rights
23/10/2014	69th General Assembly	H.E. Cardi, presenting draft resolution "Strengthening the United Nations crime prevention and criminal justice programme, in particular its technical cooperation capacity"
28/10/2014	69th General Assembly	H.E. Lambertini, Deputy Permanent Representative: justifying the European Union's vote on the resolution "Necessity of ending the economic, commercial and financial embargo imposed by the United States of America on Cuba"
4/11/2014	Side-event of the GA Second Committee on "New social funding instruments"	H.E. Cardi
6/11/2014	Third Committee, 69th General Assembly	H.E. Cardi: speech on behalf of the European Union during presentation of draft resolution on the "Human rights situation in the Democratic People's Republic of Korea"

Date	Event	Statement
11/11/2014	69th General Assembly	H.E. Cardi: speech on behalf of the European Union during presentation of draft resolution "Freedom of religion or belief"
12/11/2014	69th General Assembly – annual debate on "Equitable representation and increase in membership of the Security Council"	H.E. Cardi: speech on behalf of the group Uniting for Consensus
18/11/2014	Third Committee, 69th General Assembly	H.E. Cardi: speech on behalf of the European Union during presentation of draft resolution on the "Human rights situation in the Democratic People's Republic of Korea"
21/11/2014	Third Committee, 69th General Assembly	H.E. Cardi: speech on behalf of the European Union on the adoption of the resolution on the "Moratorium on the use of the death penalty"
26/11/2014	69th General Assembly	H.E. Lambertini, on the approval of draft resolution "Strengthening the United Nations crime prevention and criminal justice programme, in particular its technical cooperation capacity"
10/12/2014	69th General Assembly – Special event for the launch of the International Decade for People of African Descent	Paolo Gentiloni, Minister for Foreign Affairs and International Cooperation, on "People of African descent: recognition, justice and development"
11/12/2014	69th General Assembly	H.E. Lambertini: speech on behalf of the European Union during the presentation of the resolution on the "Safety and security of Humanitarian Personnel and protection of United Nations personnel"

A. Resolutions on Human Rights: Italy's Voting Behaviour

As in the past, again in 2014 Italy's action in support of human rights prioritised the following thematic areas: promotion of the rule of law and strengthening of democracy; the fight against torture, xenophobia, racism and all forms of discrimination, with special attention to religious discrimination and intolerance; the rights and protection of children; the abolition of the death penalty; combating violence against women and female genital mutilation.

More specifically, Italy presented four resolutions:

– Freedom of religion or belief (A/RES/69/175), adopted by consensus; – The human rights situation in the Democratic People's Republic of Korea (A/RES/69/188) adopted with 116 votes in favour, 20 against and 53 abstentions;

– The human rights situation in Myanmar (A/RES/69/248), adopted by consensus;

– Strengthening the United Nations crime prevention and criminal justice programme, in particular its technical cooperation capacity (A/RES/69/197), adopted by consensus.

In addition, Italy sponsored 27 resolutions and was asked to pass an open vote on 15 resolutions (7 votes in favour, 5 against and 3 abstentions), the outcome of which is shown below.

Subject	**Resolution**	**Main sponsor of the resolution**	**Information regarding Italy**	**Outcome of the plenary vote**
Social development	A/RES/69/141 Literacy for life: shaping future agendas	Mongolia	Co-sponsor of the resolution	Adopted without a vote
	A/RES/69/142 Realizing the Millennium Development Goals and other internationally agreed development goals for persons with disabilities towards 2015 and beyond	Tanzania and the Philippines	Co-sponsor of the resolution	Adopted without a vote
	A/RES/69/143 Implementation of the outcome of the World Summit for Social Development and of the twenty-fourth special session of the General Assembly	Bolivia	Co-sponsor of the resolution	Adopted without a vote

Subject	Resolution	Main sponsor of the resolution	Information regarding Italy	Outcome of the plenary vote
Advancement of women	A/RES/69/147 Intensification of efforts to eliminate all forms of violence against women and girls	France and the Netherlands	Co-sponsor of the resolution	Adopted without a vote
	A/RES/69/148 Intensification of efforts to end obstetric fistula	Senegal	Co-sponsor of the resolution	Adopted without a vote
	A/RES/69/149 Trafficking in women and girls	The Philippines	Co-sponsor of the resolution	Adopted without a vote
	A/RES/69/150 Intensifying global efforts for the elimination of female genital mutilation	Burkina Faso	Co-sponsor of the resolution	Adopted without a vote
Refugees, displaced persons and humanitarian issues	A/RES/69/152 Office of the United Nations High Commissioner for Refugees	Sweden	Co-sponsor of the resolution	Adopted without a vote
	A/RES/69/154 Assistance to refugees, returnees and displaced persons in Africa	Liberia	Co-sponsor of the resolution	Adopted without a vote
Report of the Human Rights Council	A/RES/69/155 Report of the Human Rights Council	Djibouti	Abstention	125 votes in favour, 2 against, 56 abstentions
Promotion and protection of the rights of children	A/RES/69/156 Child, early and forced marriage	Canada	Co-sponsor of the resolution	Adopted without a vote
	A/RES/69/157 Rights of the child	Uruguay	Co-sponsor of the resolution	Adopted without a vote
	A/RES/69/158 Protecting children from bullying	Mexico	Co-sponsor of the resolution	Adopted without a vote

Subject	**Resolution**	**Main sponsor of the resolution**	**Information regarding Italy**	**Outcome of the plenary vote**
Rights of indigenous peoples	A/RES/69/159 Rights of indigenous peoples	Bolivia	Co-sponsor of the resolution	Adopted without a vote
Elimination of racism, racial discrimination, xenophobia and related intolerance	A/RES/69/160 Combating glorification of Nazism, neo-Nazism and other practices that contribute to fuelling contemporary forms of racism, racial discrimination, xenophobia and related intolerance	Russian Federation	Abstention	133 in favour, 4 against, 51 abstentions
	A/RES/69/161 International Convention on the Elimination of All Forms of Racial Discrimination	Belgium	Co-sponsor of the resolution	Adopted without a vote
	A/RES/69/162 A global call for concrete action for the total elimination of racism, racial discrimination, xenophobia and related intolerance and the comprehensive implementation of and follow-up to the Durban Declaration and Programme of Action	Bolivia	Abstention	134 in favour, 10 against, 42 abstentions

Subject	Resolution	Main sponsor of the resolution	Information regarding Italy	Outcome of the plenary vote
The right of peoples to self-determination	A/RES/69/163 Use of mercenaries as a means of violating human rights and impeding the exercise of the right of peoples to self-determination	Cuba	Voted against	130 in favour, 52 against, 7 abstentions
	A/RES/69/165 The right of the Palestinian people to self-determination	Egypt	Co-sponsor of the resolution, voted in favour	180 in favour, 7 against, 4 abstentions
Human rights questions, including alternative approaches to improve the effective enjoyment of human rights and fundamental freedoms	A/RES/69/166 The right to privacy in the digital age	Brazil	Co-sponsor of the resolution	Adopted without a vote
	A/RES/69/168 The role of the Ombudsman, mediator and other national human rights institutions in the promotion and protection of human rights	Morocco	Co-sponsor of the resolution	Adopted without a vote
	A/RES/69/169 International Convention for the Protection of All Persons from Enforced Disappearance	Morocco	Co-sponsor of the resolution	Adopted without a vote
	A/RES/69/171 United Nations Human Rights Training and Documentation Centre for South-West Asia and the Arab Region	Qatar	Voted in favour	182 in favour, 1 against, 3 abstentions

Subject	**Resolution**	**Main sponsor of the resolution**	**Information regarding Italy**	**Outcome of the plenary vote**
	A/RES/69/173 Globalization and its impact on the full enjoyment of all human rights	Egypt	Voted against	135 in favour, 53 against, 1 abstention
	A/RES/69/176 Promotion of peace as a vital requirement for the full enjoyment of all human rights by all	Cuba	Voted against	134 in favour, 53 against, 2 abstentions
	A/RES/69/177 The right to food	Cuba	Co-sponsor of the resolution	Adopted without a vote
	A/RES/69/178 Promotion of a democratic and equitable international order	Cuba	Voted against	129 in favour, 53 against, 6 abstentions
	A/RES/69/180 Human rights and unilateral coercive measures	Cuba	Voted against	134 in favour, 53 against, 1 abstention
	A/RES/69/181 The right to development	Cuba	Voted in favour	156 in favour, 5 against, 26 abstentions
	A/RES/69/182 Extrajudicial, summary or arbitrary executions	Finland	Co-sponsor of the resolution, voted in favour	122 in favour, none against, 66 abstentions
	A/RES/69/183 Human rights and extreme poverty	Peru	Co-sponsor of the resolution	Adopted without a vote
	A/RES/69/184 Missing persons	Azerbaijan	Co-sponsor of the resolution	Adopted without a vote

Subject	Resolution	Main sponsor of the resolution	Information regarding Italy	Outcome of the plenary vote
	A/RES/69/185 The safety of journalists and the issue of impunity	Greece	Co-sponsor of the resolution	Adopted without a vote
	A/RES/69/186 Moratorium on the use of the death penalty	Chile	Co-sponsor of the resolution, voted in favour	117 in favour, 37 against, 34 abstentions
	A/RES/69/187 Migrant children and adolescents	El Salvador	Co-sponsor of the resolution	Adopted without a vote
Human rights situations and reports by Special Rapporteurs and Representatives	A/RES/69/189 Situation of human rights in the Syrian Arab Republic	Qatar	Co-sponsor of the resolution, voted in favour	127 in favour, 13 against, 48 abstentions
	A/RES/69/190 Situation of human rights in the Islamic Republic of Iran	Canada	Co-sponsor of the resolution, voted in favour	83 in favour, 35 against, 68 abstentions

Source: United Nations, General Assembly.

II. Human Rights Council

The Human Rights Council is the subsidiary body of the General Assembly responsible for promoting worldwide respect of all human rights and fundamental freedoms for all, without distinction of any kind.

Established in 2006 under resolution 60/251, the Council is an inter-governmental body made up of 47 United Nations Member States elected by the General Assembly for an initial period of three years, extendable for not more than two consecutive terms. It meets in Geneva, usually in three ordinary sessions per year, for an overall period of at least ten working weeks. Furthermore, although it is a body of Government representatives, the Council is open to the contributions of non-governmental organisations which enjoy advisory status with the ECOSOC, which may participate in the meetings and submit written documents.

The Council has established several different "mechanisms" for monitoring human rights (resolution A/HRC/RES/5/1 of June 2007), including: the Universal Periodic Review (UPR), the Special Procedures (which include mandates by Country and thematic mandates), the Advisory Committee and a Complaints Procedure.

During 2014 the Council held:

– three ordinary sessions: the 25th (3–28 March); 26th (10–27 June); and 27th (8–26 September)

– three special sessions: on the human rights situation in the Central African Republic (the 20th session, 20 January); on the human rights situation in the occupied Palestinian territories, including East Jerusalem (21st session, 23 July); on the human rights situation in Iraq, in light of abuse committed by the Islamic State of Iraq and the Levant and groups associated with it (22nd session, 1 September)

– three UPR sessions: the 18th (27 January – 7 February); 19th (28 April – 9 May); and 20th (27 October – 7 November).

Special note is made that from 30 June to 4 July 2014 the second session of the Inter-governmental Working Group tasked with negotiating the draft *United Nations Declaration on the Right to Peace* was held. Based on recommendations from the Working Group, the 27th ordinary session of the Human Rights council adopted the resolution *Promotion of the Right to Peace* (A/HRC/27/17), with which the Council authorised a third session of the Inter-governmental Working Group in 2015, aiming to finalise the draft Declaration of the Right to Peace. The resolution was approved with 33 votes in favour, 9 against and 5 abstentions; the African and Latin American and Caribbean Groups voted unanimously in favour, as did most Countries in the Asia-Pacific Group. Austria, the Czech Republic, Estonia, Germany, Japan, the Republic of Korea, the United Kingdom and the United States of America voted against; Italy abstained along with Ireland, Montenegro, Romania and the Former Yugoslav Republic of Macedonia.

In 2011 Italy was elected to the Human Rights Council for the second time for the three-year period June 2011 – June 2014. In 2014 Italy was represented in the Council by H.E. Maurizio Enrico Serra, Permanent Representative of Italy to the International Organisations in Geneva, Deputy Permanent Representative Amadeo Trambajolo, the Councillor Paolo Cuculi, and the First Secretaries Marco Lapadura and Simona Battiloro. Listed below are the main interventions by the Italian mission in 2014.

Date	Event	Intervention
20/01/2014	20th special session on the human rights situation in the Central African Republic	H.E. Maurizio Enrico Serra
27/01–7/02/2014	18th session of UPR	Statements relative to the analysis of the human rights situation in the following States: New Zealand, Afghanistan, Chile, Cambodia, Uruguay, Yemen, Former Yugoslav Republic of Macedonia, Eritrea, Cyprus, Dominican Republic, Vietnam
3/03/2014	25th session of the Human Rights Council	Benedetto Della Vedova, Undersecretary of State – Ministry of Foreign Affairs at the High Level Segment
4/03/2014	25th session of the Human Rights Council	Benedetto Della Vedova, Undersecretary of State – Ministry of Foreign Affairs at the High Level Segment on the occasion of discussions on mainstreaming human rights
5/03/2014	25th session of the Human Rights Council	H.E. Maurizio Enrico Serra, in the discussion of the issue of the death penalty
6/03/2014	25th session of the Human Rights Council	H.E. Maurizio Enrico Serra, at the general segment
11/03/2014	25th session of the Human Rights Council	First Secretary Marco Lapadura, at the discussion on the promotion and protection of civil society space
12/03/2014	25th session of the Human Rights Council	First Secretary Simona Battiloro, in interactive dialogue with special rapporteurs on freedom of religion or belief and on the promotion and protection of human rights and fundamental freedoms in the fight against terrorism
12/03/2014	25th session of the Human Rights Council	First Secretary Simona Battiloro, at the interactive dialogue with special representatives of the Secretary General on violence against children and on children and armed conflict
13/03/2014	25th session of the Human Rights Council	First Secretary Simona Battiloro, at the discussion on justice for children
14/03/2014	25th session of the Human Rights Council	Councillor Paolo Cuculi, at the debate on the presentation of the reports of the Secretary General and the High Commissioner for Human Rights

Date	Event	Intervention
17/03/2014	25th session of the Human Rights Council	First Secretary Marco Lapadura, at the interactive dialogue with the Special Rapporteur on the human rights situation in Iran
17/03/2014	25th session of the Human Rights Council	First Secretary Marco Lapadura, at the interactive dialogue with the Special Rapporteur on the human rights situation in Myanmar
18/03/2014	25th session of the Human Rights Council	H.E. Maurizio Enrico Serra, at the interactive dialogue with the Commission of Inquiry on Syria
19/03/2014	25th session of the Human Rights Council	Councillor Paolo Cuculi, at the presentation of the report of the Forum on Minority Issues
25/03/2014	25th session of the Human Rights Council	First Secretary Simona Battiloro, at the interactive dialogue with the Independent Expert on the human rights situation in Cote D'Ivoire
27/03/2014	25th session of the Human Rights Council	Councillor Paolo Cuculi at the debate on the issue of technical assistance and capacity building
28/04–9/05/2014	19th session of UPR	Statements relative to the analysis of the human rights situation in the following States: Norway, Albania, Democratic Republic of Congo, Cote D'Ivoire, Portugal, Bhutan, Dominica, Democratic People's Republic of Korea, Brunei, Darussalam, Costa Rica, Equatorial Guinea, Ethiopia, Qatar, Nicaragua
10/06/2014	26th session of the Human Rights Council	H.E. Maurizio Enrico Serra, at the presentation of the Annual Report of the High Commissioner for Human Rights
10/06/2014	26th session of the Human Rights Council	Councillor Paolo Cuculi, in interactive dialogue with the special rapporteurs on the promotion and protection of freedom of opinion and expression, on the right to freedom of peaceful assembly and association
11/06/2014	26th session of the Human Rights Council	First Secretary Marco Lapadura, at the debate on safety of journalists
11/06/2014	26th session of the Human Rights Council	First Secretary Simona Battiloro, at the interactive dialogue with the Special Rapporteur on the rights of everyone to enjoy the highest possible standards of physical and mental health, and with the Working Group on the issue of human rights and trans-national corporations

Date	Event	Intervention
12/06/2014	26th session of the Human Rights Council	First Secretary Simona Battiloro, at the interactive dialogue with the Special Rapporteur on the rights of everyone to the enjoyment the highest possible standards of physical and mental health, and with the Working Group on the issue of human rights and trans-national corporations
12/06/2014	26th session of the Human Rights Council	First Secretary Simona Battiloro, at the interactive dialogue with the Special Rapporteur on violence against women, and on extreme poverty and human rights
13/06/2014	26th session of the Human Rights Council	First Secretary Marco Lapadura, at the interactive dialogue with the Independent Expert on human rights and international solidarity, and with the Special Rapporteur on human trafficking, particularly of women and children
16/06/2014	26th session of the Human Rights Council	First Secretary Simona Battiloro, at the debate on female genital mutilation
16/06/2014	26th session of the Human Rights Council	First Secretary Simona Battiloro, at the interactive dialogue with the Working Group on discrimination against women in law and in practice, and with the Special Rapporteur on the right to education
17/06/2014	26th session of the Human Rights Council	First Secretary Simona Battiloro at the debate on gender stereotyping
17/06/2014	26th session of the Human Rights Council	H.E. Maurizio Enrico Serra, at the interactive dialogue with the Commission of Inquiry on Syria
17/06/2014	26th session of the Human Rights Council	First Secretary Simona Battiloro, at the debate on the rights of women in sustainable development
18/06/2014	26th session of the Human Rights Council	First Secretary Marco Lapadura, at the interactive dialogue with the Special Rapporteur on the human rights situation in Eritrea
18/06/2014	26th session of the Human Rights Council	First Secretary Marco Lapadura, at the interactive dialogue with the Special Rapporteur on the human rights situation in Belarus
23/06/2014	26th session of the Human Rights Council	First Secretary Simona Battiloro, at the debate on forced marriages

Date	Event	Intervention
25/06/2014	26th session of the Human Rights Council	First Secretary Marco Lapadura, at the debate on disability.
23/06/2014	21st special session on the human rights situation in occupied Palestinian territories, including East Jerusalem	H.E. Maurizio Enrico Serra
1/09/2014	22nd special session on the human rights situation in Iraq in light of abuse committed by Islamic State of Iraq and the Levant and groups associated with it	H.E. Maurizio Enrico Serra
8/09/2014	27th session of the Human Rights Council	H.E. Maurizio Enrico Serra, at the debate on the presentation of the reports by the Secretary General and the High Commissioner for human rights
10/09/2014	27th session of the Human Rights Council	Councillor Paolo Cuculi, at the debate on the protection of human rights of persons deprived of liberty
12/09/2014	27th session of the Human Rights Council	H.E. Maurizio Enrico Serra, at the debate on the presentation of the thematic reports of the Secretary General and the High Commissioner for human rights
15/09/2014	27th session of the Human Rights Council	First Secretary Simona Battiloro, at the debate on gender perspective
16/09/2014	27th session of the Human Rights Council	H.E. Maurizio Enrico Serra, at the interactive dialogue with the Commission of Inquiry on Syria
21/09/2014	27th session of the Human Rights Council	H.E. Maurizio Enrico Serra, at the presentation of the report of the Inter-governmental Working Group on the right to peace
23/09/2014	27th session of the Human Rights Council	First Secretary Marco Lapadura, at the debate on the follow-up and implementation of the Vienna Declaration and Programme of Action

Date	Event	Intervention
23/09/2014	27th session of the Human Rights Council	First Secretary Marco Lapadura, at the debate on racism, racial discrimination, xenophobia and forms of intolerance: follow-up and implementation of the Durban Declaration and Programme of Action
24/09/2014	27th session of the Human Rights Council	First Secretary Marco Lapadura, at the debate on the presentation of the report of the High Commissioner for human rights on cooperating with and assisting Ukraine in the area of human rights
24/09/2014	27th session of the Human Rights Council	First Secretary Marco Lapadura, at the interactive dialogue with the Independent Expert on the human rights situation in Sudan
24/09/2014	27th session of the Human Rights Council	First Secretary Marco Lapadura, at the debate on the human rights situation in South Sudan
25/09/2014	27th session of the Human Rights Council	First Secretary Marco Lapadura, at the interactive dialogue with the Independent Expert on the human rights situation in Somalia
27/10/2014	20th session of UPR	Lapo Pistelli, Deputy Minister for Foreign Affairs: presentation of Italy's report and interactive debate
27/10 – 7/11/2014	20th session of UPR	Statements relative to the analysis of the human rights situation in the following States: El Salvador, Gambia, Bolivia, Fiji, San Marino, Kazakhstan, Angola, Iran, Madagascar, Iraq, Slovenia, Egypt, Bosnia and Herzegovina
31/10/2014	20th session of UPR	Deputy Permanent Representative Amedeo Trambajolo, at the adoption of the UPR report on Italy

Sources: Permanent Representative of Italy at the United Nations in Geneva and UN Web TV.

A. *Italy's Voting Behaviour at the Human Rights Council in 2014*

In 2014, Italy participated in the three ordinary sessions of the Human Rights Council as a Member State (hence, with the right to vote).

Over the course of 2014, the Human Rights Council adopted 102 resolutions (+7 compared to 2013), distributed as follows: 38 resolutions during the 25th session (3–28 March); 32 during the 26th session (10–27 June); 32 during the 27th session (8–26 September). Of these resolutions, 70 were adopted with the consensus of all Member States (68%), whereas for 32 of them (32%) it was necessary to use majority voting, thus showing a slightly higher level of disagreement than in the previous year, when majority voting was used for 29% of the resolutions adopted.

The paragraphs below aim to analyse Italy's behaviours in the Human Rights Council in 2014, with special attention to two specific aspects: Italy's diplomatic efforts in the negotiation and presentation of the resolutions, and its voting behaviour.

On the first count, it can be seen that over half of the resolutions adopted by the Council were negotiated with the direct participation (sponsoring) or diplomatic support (co-sponsoring) of Italy. Indeed, of the 102 resolutions adopted, Italy sponsored 6 (as compared to 4 in 2013) and co-sponsored 47 (48 in 2013). Three of the six resolutions sponsored by Italy were of a thematic nature and referred, respectively, to the contributions of national parliaments to the Universal Periodic Review, to the third phase of the World Programme for Human Rights Education and national policies on human rights. The other three resolutions were on the human rights situation in Syria.

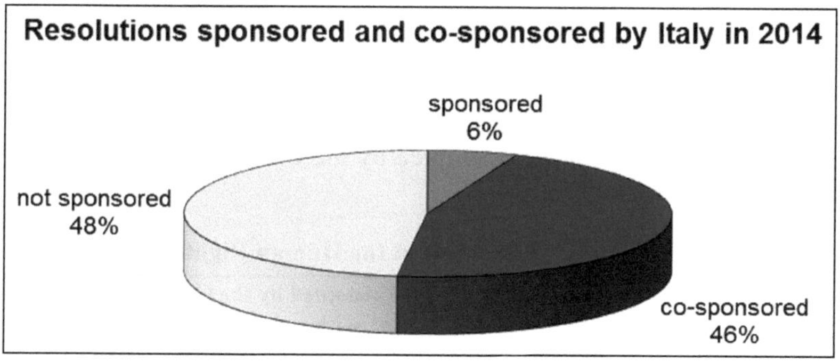

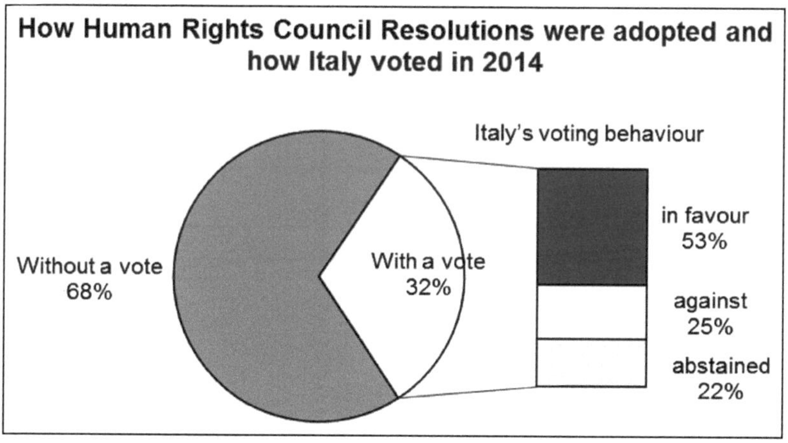

As concerns Italy's voting behaviour, it proved "winning" in 17 of the 32 votes called; whereas 8 resolutions which Italy had voted against were adopted by a majority vote; Italy abstained 7 times.

Specifically, Italy supported resolutions sponsored by Countries belonging in practice to all the regional groups represented in the Council: of its 17 votes in favour, 5 were on resolutions presented by Countries from the Asian Group (Pakistan and Iran), 1 by the Western Group (Greece), 1 by the Eastern European Group (Ukraine), 2 by the Latin American Group (joint resolutions presented by Brazil, Chile, Colombia and Uruguay and by Ecuador and Peru), and 8 'yes' votes were given in favour of transversal resolutions sponsored by Countries belonging to two or more regional groups. Resolutions voted against by Italy were sponsored by Cuba (5 out of 8), Iran (1) and jointly by Countries belonging to the Asian and the African Groups (2). Finally, the abstentions were distributed over the regional groups as follows: African Group (1: Ethiopia and Tunisia), Asian Group (2: Pakistan), Latin American Group (1: Cuba), Eastern European Group (1: the Russian Federation); 2 abstentions affected resolutions presented by Countries belonging to two or more regional groups.

The chart below summarises the data relative to both aspects examined above and also shows that, out of the resolutions sponsored or co-sponsored by Italy, 81% were adopted by the Council by consensus, and 19% by a majority vote.

Chart summarising Italy's behaviour at the Human Rights Council in 2014

	Adopted by the Council by consensus	**Adopted by the Council with a majority vote**			**Tot.**
		Italy: voted in favour	***Italy: voted against***	***Italy: abstained***	
Resolutions sponsored by Italy	3	3	-	-	4
Resolutions co-sponsored by Italy	40	7	-	-	47
Resolutions not sponsored by Italy	27	7	8	7	49
Tot.	70	17	8	7	102

Human Rights Council: resolutions sponsored by Italy in 2014

Resolution	Other sponsors of the resolution	Outcome of the voting process
A/HRC/RES/25/23 The continuing grave deterioration of the human rights and humanitarian situation in the Syrian Arab Republic	USA, France, Germany, Jordan, Kuwait, Morocco, Qatar, Saudi Arabia, Turkey and the United Kingdom	32 in favour, 4 against and 11 abstentions
A/HRC/RES/26/23 The continuing grave deterioration of the human rights and humanitarian situation in the Syrian Arab Republic	USA, France, Germany, Jordan, Kuwait, Qatar, Saudi Arabia, Turkey and the United Kingdom	32 in favour, 5 against and 9 abstentions
A/HRC/RES/26/29 The contribution of parliaments to the work of the Human Rights Council and its universal periodic review	Ecuador, Maldives, Morocco, Romania and Spain	Adopted without a vote
A/HRC/RES/27/12 World Programme for Human Rights Education: adoption of the plan of action for the third phase	Costa Rica, Morocco, The Philippines, Senegal, Slovenia and Switzerland	Adopted without a vote
A/HRC/RES/27/16 The continuing grave deterioration of the human rights and humanitarian situation in the Syrian Arab Republic	USA, France, Germany, Jordan, Kuwait, Morocco, Qatar, Saudi Arabia, Turkey and the United Kingdom	32 in favour, 5 against and 10 abstentions
A/HRC/RES/27/26 National policies and human rights	Algeria, Ecuador, Peru, Romania and Thailand	Adopted without a vote

Human Rights Council: resolutions co-sponsored by Italy in 2014

Resolution	State(s) presenting the Resolution	Outcome of the voting process
25th session (3–28 March)		
A/HRC/RES/25/1 Promoting reconciliation, accountability and human rights in Sri Lanka	USA, Macedonia and Mauritius	23 in favour, 12 against, 12 abstentions
A/HRC/RES/25/2 Freedom of opinion and expression: mandate of the Special Rapporteur on the promotion and protection of the right to freedom of opinion and expression	USA	Adopted without a vote
A/HRC/RES/25/5 Mandate of the Independent Expert on minority issues	Austria	Adopted without a vote
A/HRC/RES/25/8 The role of good governance in the promotion and protection of human rights	Poland, Australia, Chile, the Republic of Korea and South Africa	Adopted without a vote

Resolution	**State(s) presenting the Resolution**	**Outcome of the voting process**
A/HRC/RES/25/11 Question of the realization in all Countries of economic, social and cultural rights	Portugal	Adopted without a vote
A/HRC/RES/25/13 Torture and other cruel, inhuman or degrading treatment or punishment: mandate of the Special Rapporteur	Denmark	Adopted without a vote
A/HRC/RES/25/17 Adequate housing as a component of the right to an adequate standard of living	Finland and Germany	Adopted without a vote
A/HRC/RES/25/18 Mandate of the Special Rapporteur on the situation of human rights defenders	Norway	Adopted without a vote
A/HRC/RES/25/20 The right to education of persons with disabilities	Mexico and New Zealand	Adopted without a vote
A/HRC/RES/25/21 Human rights and the environment	Costa Rica, Maldives, Morocco, Peru, Slovenia, Switzerland and Uruguay	Adopted without a vote
A/HRC/RES/25/24 Situation of human rights in the Islamic Republic of Iran	Sweden, Panama, Moldova, Macedonia, USA	21 in favour, 9 against, 16 abstentions
A/HRC/RES/25/35 Renforcement de la coopération technique et des services consultatifs en Guinée [Strengthening of technical cooperation and consultative services in Guinea]	Ethiopia	Adopted without a vote
A/HRC/RES/25/36 Assistance à la République du Mali dans le domaine des droits de l'homme [Assistance to the Republic of Mali in the field of human rights]	Ethiopia	Adopted without a vote
A/HRC/RES/25/37 Technical assistance for Libya in the field of human rights	Libya and Morocco	Adopted without a vote
A/HRC/RES/25/38 The promotion and protection of human rights in the context of peaceful protests	Switzerland, Costa Rica and Turkey	31 in favour, 9 against, 7 abstentions
26th session (10–27 June)		
A/HRC/RES/26/2 The question of the death penalty	France, Switzerland, Belgium, Benin, Costa Rica, Mexico, Mongolia, Moldova	29 in favour, 10 against, 8 abstentions

Resolution	State(s) presenting the Resolution	Outcome of the voting process
A/HRC/RES/26/3 Extreme poverty and human rights	France, Albania, Belgium, Chile, Morocco, Peru, the Philippines, Romania and Senegal	Adopted without a vote
A/HRC/RES/26/5 Elimination of discrimination against women	Colombia and Mexico	Adopted without a vote
A/HRC/RES/26/7 Mandate of the Special Rapporteur on the independence of judges and lawyers	Hungary, Australia, Botswana, the Maldives, Mexico and Thailand	Adopted without a vote
A/HRC/RES/26/8 Mandate of the Special Rapporteur on trafficking in persons, especially women and children	Germany and the Philippines	Adopted without a vote
A/HRC/RES/26/12 Mandate of the Special Rapporteur on extrajudicial, summary or arbitrary executions	Sweden	Adopted without a vote
A/HRC/RES/26/13 The promotion, protection and enjoyment of human rights on the Internet	Sweden, Brazil, Nigeria, Tunisia, Turkey and the USA	Adopted without a vote
A/HRC/RES/26/15 Accelerating efforts to eliminate all forms of violence against women: violence against women as a barrier to women's political and economic empowerment	Canada	Adopted without a vote
A/HRC/RES/26/17 The right to education: follow-up to Human Rights Council resolution 8/4	Portugal	Adopted without a vote
A/HRC/RES/26/18 The right of everyone to the enjoyment of the highest attainable standard of physical and mental health: sport and healthy lifestyles as contributing factors	Brazil	Adopted without a vote
A/HRC/RES/26/20 Special Rapporteur on the rights of persons with disabilities	New Zealand and Mexico	Adopted without a vote
A/HRC/RES/26/25 Situation of human rights in Belarus	Greece	24 in favour, 7 against, 16 abstentions
A/HRC/RES/26/30 Cooperation and assistance to Ukraine in the field of human rights	Ukraine	23 in favour, 4 against, 19 abstentions

Resolution	**State(s) presenting the Resolution**	**Outcome of the voting process**
A/HRC/RES/26/32 Renforcement de capacités et coopération technique avec la Côte d'Ivoire dans le domaine des droits de l'homme [Capacity-building and technical cooperation with Ivory Coast in the field of human rights]	Ethiopia	Adopted without a vote
27th session (8–26 September)		
A/HRC/RES/27/1 Enforced or involuntary disappearances	France, Argentina, Japan and Morocco	Adopted without a vote
A/HRC/RES/27/3 Special Rapporteur on the promotion of truth, justice, reparation and guarantees of non-recurrence	Switzerland, Argentina, Austria, Colombia, Ivory Coast, France, the Maldives, Morocco, Peru and Uruguay	Adopted without a vote
A/HRC/RES/27/4 Local government and human rights	Republic of Korea, Chile, Egypt and Romania	Adopted without a vote
A/HRC/RES/27/5 The safety of journalists	Austria, Brazil, France, Greece, Morocco, Qatar and Tunisia	Adopted without a vote
A/HRC/RES/27/6 Panel discussion on realizing the equal enjoyment of the right to education by every girl	United Arab Emirates	Adopted without a vote
A/HRC/RES/27/7 The human right to safe drinking water and sanitation	Germany and Spain	Adopted without a vote
A/HRC/RES/27/8 Promoting human rights through sport and the Olympic ideal	The Russian Federation, Brazil, Congo, Cyprus, Greece, Japan, Lebanon, Morocco, Republic of Korea	Adopted without a vote
A/HRC/RES/27/13 Human rights and indigenous peoples	Mexico and Guatemala	Adopted without a vote
A/HRC/RES/27/14 Preventable mortality and morbidity of children under 5 years of age as a human rights concern	Ireland, Botswana, Austria, Mongolia and Uruguay	Adopted without a vote
A/HRC/RES/27/15 The right of the child to engage in play and recreational activities	Romania, Brazil and Norway	Adopted without a vote

Resolution	State(s) presenting the Resolution	Outcome of the voting process
A/HRC/RES/27/18 National institutions for the promotion and protection of human rights	Australia	Adopted without a vote
A/HRC/RES/27/19 Technical assistance and capacity-building for Yemen in the field of human rights	The Netherlands and Yemen	Adopted without a vote
A/HRC/RES/27/20 Enhancement of technical cooperation and capacity-building in the field of human rights	Thailand, Brazil, Honduras, Indonesia, Mauritius, Morocco, Norway, Qatar, Singapore and Turkey	Adopted without a vote
A/HRC/RES/27/22 Intensifying global efforts and sharing good practices to effectively eliminate female genital mutilation	Burkina Faso and Ethiopia	Adopted without a vote
A/HRC/RES/27/24 Equal participation in political and public affairs	The Czech Republic, Botswana, Indonesia, Netherlands and Peru	Adopted without a vote
A/HRC/RES/27/28 Technical assistance and capacity-building in the field of human rights in the Central African Republic	Ethiopia	Adopted without a vote
A/HRC/RES/27/31 Civil society space	Ireland, Tunisia, Chile, Japan and Sierra Leone	Adopted without a vote
A/HRC/RES/27/32 Human rights, sexual orientation and gender identity	Brazil, Chile, Colombia and Uruguay	25 in favour, 14 against, 7 abstentions

Source: United Nations, Human Rights Council.

Human Rights Council: resolutions not sponsored by Italy in 2014

Resolution	State(s) presenting the Resolution	Outcome of the voting process	Information regarding Italy
25th session (3–28 March)			
A/HRC/RES/25/3 Enhancement of international cooperation in the field of human rights	Iran	Adopted without a vote	-
A/HRC/RES/25/4 Integrity of the judicial system	The Russian Federation	27 in favour, 1 against, 19 abstentions	Abstention

Resolution	State(s) presenting the Resolution	Outcome of the voting process	Information regarding Italy
A/HRC/RES/25/6 Rights of the child: access to justice for children	Greece and Uruguay	Adopted without a vote	-
A/HRC/RES/25/7 Protection of human rights and fundamental freedoms while countering terrorism	Mexico	Adopted without a vote	-
A/HRC/RES/25/9 The negative impact of the non-repatriation of funds of illicit origin to the Countries of origin on the enjoyment of human rights, and the importance of improving international cooperation	Ethiopia and Tunisia	33 in favour, 2 against, 12 abstentions	Abstention
A/HRC/RES/25/10 Ending violence against children: a global call to make the invisible visible	Algeria	Adopted without a vote	-
A/HRC/RES/25/12 Freedom of religion or belief	Greece	Adopted without a vote	-
A/HRC/RES/25/14 The right to food	Cuba	Adopted without a vote	-
A/HRC/RES/25/15 Promotion of a democratic and equitable international order	Cuba	30 in favour, 14 against, 3 abstentions	Voted against
A/HRC/RES/25/16 Mandate of the Independent Expert on the effects of foreign debt and other related international financial obligations on States on the full enjoyment of all human rights, particularly economic, social and cultural rights	Cuba	30 in favour, 14 against, 3 abstentions	Voted against
A/HRC/RES/25/19 Promotion of the enjoyment of the cultural rights of everyone and respect for cultural diversity	Cuba	Adopted without a vote	-
A/HRC/RES/25/22 Ensuring use of remotely piloted aircraft or armed drones in counter-terrorism and military operations in accordance with international law, including international human rights and humanitarian law	Pakistan	27 in favour, 6 against, 14 abstentions	Abstention

Resolution	State(s) presenting the Resolution	Outcome of the voting process	Information regarding Italy
A/HRC/RES/25/25 Situation of human rights in the Democratic People's Republic of Korea	Greece and Japan	30 in favour, 6 against, 11 abstentions	Voted in favour
A/HRC/RES/25/26 Situation of human rights in Myanmar	Greece	Adopted without a vote	-
A/HRC/RES/25/27 Right of the Palestinian people to self-determination	Pakistan	46 in favour, 1 against, no abstentions	Voted in favour
A/HRC/RES/25/28 Israeli settlements in the Occupied Palestinian Territory, including East Jerusalem, and in the occupied Syrian Golan	Pakistan	46 in favour, 1 against, no abstentions	Voted in favour
A/HRC/RES/25/29 Human rights situation in Occupied Palestinian Territory, including East Jerusalem	Pakistan	46 in favour, 1 against, no abstentions	Voted in favour
A/HRC/RES/25/30 Follow-up to the report of the United Nations Independent International Fact-Finding Mission on the Gaza Conflict	Pakistan	46 in favour, 1 against, no abstentions	Voted in favour
A/HRC/RES/25/31 Human rights in the occupied Syrian Golan	Pakistan	33 in favour, 1 against, 13 abstentions	Abstention
A/HRC/RES/25/32 Mandate of the Special Rapporteur on contemporary forms of racism, racial discrimination, xenophobia and related intolerance	Ethiopia	Adopted without a vote	-
A/HRC/RES/25/33 International Decade for People of African Descent	Ethiopia	Adopted without a vote	-
A/HRC/RES/25/34 Combating intolerance, negative stereotyping and stigmatization of, and discrimination, incitement to violence and violence against persons based on religion or belief	Pakistan	Adopted without a vote	-

Resolution	State(s) presenting the Resolution	Outcome of the voting process	Information regarding Italy
26th session (10–27 June)			
A/HRC/RES/26/1 Implementation of the International Decade for People of African Descent: draft programme of activities	Ethiopia	Adopted without a vote	-
A/HRC/RES/26/4 Protection of Roma	The Russian Federation	Adopted without a vote	-
A/HRC/RES/26/6 Mandate of the Independent Expert on human rights and international solidarity	Cuba	33 in favour, 14 against, no abstentions	Voted against
A/HRC/RES/26/9 Elaboration of an international legally binding instrument on transnational corporations and other business enterprises with respect to human rights	Ecuador and South Africa	20 in favour, 14 against, 13 abstentions	Voted against
A/HRC/RES/26/10 International Albinism Awareness Day	Somalia and Ethiopia	Adopted without a vote	-
A/HRC/RES/26/11 Protection of the family	Bangladesh, China, Ivory Coast, Egypt, El Salvador, Mauritania, Namibia, Qatar, the Russian Federation, Sierra Leone and Tunisia	26 in favour, 14 against, 6 abstentions	Voted against
A/HRC/RES/26/14 Human rights and arbitrary deprivation of nationality	The Russian Federation	Adopted without a vote	-
A/HRC/RES/26/16 Human rights and the regulation of civilian acquisition, possession and use of firearms	Ecuador and Peru	44 in favour, 0 against, 3 abstentions	Voted in favour
A/HRC/RES/26/19 Human rights of migrants: mandate of the Special Rapporteur on the human rights of migrants	Mexico	Adopted without a vote	-

Resolution	State(s) presenting the Resolution	Outcome of the voting process	Information regarding Italy
A/HRC/RES/26/21 Promotion of the right of migrants to the enjoyment of the highest attainable standard of physical and mental health	Mexico	Adopted without a vote	-
A/HRC/RES/26/22 Human rights and transnational corporations and other business enterprises	Norway, Argentina, Ghana and The Russian Federation	Adopted without a vote	-
A/HRC/RES/26/24 Situation of human rights in Eritrea	Somalia	Adopted without a vote	-
A/HRC/RES/26/26 Promotion and protection of the human rights of peasants and other people working in rural areas	Bolivia, Cuba, Ecuador and South Africa	29 in favour, 5 against, 13 abstentions	Abstention
A/HRC/RES/26/27 Human rights and climate change	The Philippines and Bangladesh	Adopted without a vote	-
A/HRC/RES/26/28 The Social Forum	Cuba	Adopted without a vote	-
A/HRC/RES/26/31 Technical and capacity-building assistance for South Sudan in the field of human rights	Ethiopia	Adopted without a vote	-
27th session (8–26 September)			
A/HRC/RES/27/2 The right to development	Iran	42 in favour, 1 against, 4 abstentions	Voted in favour
A/HRC/RES/27/9 Mandate of the Independent Expert on the promotion of a democratic and equitable international order	Cuba	29 in favour, 14 against, 4 abstentions	Voted against
A/HRC/RES/27/10 The use of mercenaries as a means of violating human rights and impeding the exercise of the right of peoples to self-determination	Cuba	32 in favour, 14 against, 1 abstention	Voted against
A/HRC/RES/27/11 Preventable maternal mortality and morbidity and human rights	Burkina Faso, Colombia and New Zealand	Adopted without a vote	-

Resolution	State(s) presenting the Resolution	Outcome of the voting process	Information regarding Italy
A/HRC/RES/27/17 Promotion of the right to peace	Cuba	33 in favour, 9 against, 5 abstentions	Abstention
A/HRC/RES/27/21 Human rights and unilateral coercive measures	Iran	31 in favour, 14 against, 2 abstentions	Voted against
A/HRC/RES/27/23 Mandate of the Special Rapporteur on the implications for human rights of the environmentally sound management and disposal of hazardous substances and wastes	Ivory Coast and Ethiopia	Adopted without a vote	-
A/HRC/RES/27/25 Mandate of the Working Group of Experts on People of African Descent	South Africa and Ethiopia	Adopted without a vote	-
A/HRC/RES/27/27 Assistance technique et renforcement des capacités en matière de droits de l'homme en République démocratique du Congo [Technical assistance and capacity-building for human rights in the Democratic Republic of the Congo	Democratic Republic of Congo and Ethiopia	Adopted without a vote	-
A/HRC/RES/27/29 Technical assistance and capacity-building to improve human rights in the Sudan	Ethiopia	Adopted without a vote	-
A/HRC/RES/27/30 Effects of foreign debt and other related international financial obligations of States on the full enjoyment of all human rights, particularly economic, social and cultural rights: the activities of vulture funds	Argentina, Algeria Bolivia, Brazil, Cuba, Pakistan, the Russian Federation, Uruguay and Venezuela	33 in favour, 5 against, 9 abstentions	Abstention

Source: United Nations, Human Rights Council.

In 2014, Italy also took part in the following special sessions of the Human Rights Council:

– 20th special session on the situation of human rights in the Central African Republic (20 January 2014): Italy was one of the Countries which requested the convening of the special session, and was also one of the sponsors of the final resolution (A/HRC/RES/S-20/1), adopted without a vote;

– 21st special session on the human rights situation in the Occupied Palestinian Territory, including East Jerusalem (23 July 2014): Italy abstained in the vote on the final resolution (A/HRC/RES/S-21/1), adopted with 29 votes in favour, 1 against and 17 abstentions;

– 22nd special session on the human rights situation in Iraq in light of abuses committed by the Islamic State in Iraq and the Levant and associated groups (1 September 2014): Italy was one of the Countries which requested the convening of the special session, and was also one of the sponsors of the final resolution (A/HRC/RES/S-22/1), adopted by consensus.

B. *Universal Periodic Review*

Italy underwent its first Universal Periodic Review in 2010 (7th session): on that occasion, 92 recommendations were made to Italy, of which it fully accepted 78, partially rejected 2 and fully rejected 12. Detailed information on the outcome of the first Universal Periodic Review for Italy is contained in the 2011 edition of the *Italian Yearbook of Human Rights* (pp. 169–173).

On 27 October 2014, Italy underwent its second cycle of the UPR (20th session, 27 October – 7 November 2014), together with 13 other Countries: Angola, Egypt, Madagascar, Gambia, Fiji, Iran, Iraq, Kazakhstan, Bolivia, El Salvador, San Marino, Slovenia, Bosnia and Herzegovina. During the review, which was facilitated by a troika made up of Ireland, Ethiopia and the former Yugoslav Republic of Macedonia, Italy was represented by a high-level delegation of 20 members comprising officials from Ministries, Parliament and the diplomatic service, headed by Lapo Pistelli, Deputy Minister for Foreign Affairs.

Documentation relative to Italy's second cycle of UPR

Italy's National report	A/HRC/WG.6/20/ITA/1
Compilation prepared by the Office of the UNHCHR	A/HRC/WG.6/20/ITA/2
Report containing information from other sources (NGOs and Council of Europe)	A/HRC/WG.6/20/ITA/3
Final Report containing the recommendations made to Italy	A/HRC/28/4
Italy's responses to the recommendations made	A/HRC/28/4/Add.1
Date of the Universal Periodic Review before the Human Rights Council Working Group	27 October 2014, during the 20th session of the Universal Periodic Review (27 October – 7 November 2014)

In his presentation of the national report, Deputy Minister Pistelli highlighted the action that Italy has taken within the United Nations system and in other international and regional organisations for the promotion of human rights, including a moratorium on the death penalty, safeguarding and protecting migrants, asylum seekers and refugees and promoting dialogue between cultures and religions. Further, the Deputy Minister advised that Italy has implemented 74 of the 78 recommendations it had accepted in the first UPR cycle, and had also implemented several recommendations that had been not accepted.

In particular, the Deputy Minister mentioned the bill introducing the crime of torture, which had recently been approved by the Senate, and the judgment by the Constitutional Court which removed the status of being an illegal immigrant from the list of aggravating circumstances.

During the interactive dialogue that followed, the Italian delegation was called upon to answer questions, concerns and recommendations raised by the representatives of 92 United Nations Member States.

The information required for the interactive dialogue was supplied not only by the Italian Government's report, but also by two summary documents prepared by the Office of the U.N. High Commissioner for Human Rights: the summary compilation of all recommendations from Treaty Bodies and U.N. Special Rapporteurs; and the summary of additional information supplied by other stakeholders, in this case non-governmental organisations, the Council of Europe, the European Union Agency for Fundamental Rights and the OSCE Office for Democratic Institutions and Human Rights. Included among the many NGOs which supplied information for Italy's UPR are: Amnesty International, Associazione "Comunità Papa Giovanni XXIII", Associazione studi giuridici sull'immigrazione, Associazione 21 luglio, Defence for Children International – Italy, European Roma Rights Centre, Global Initiative to End All Corporal Punishment of Children, Human Rights Watch, International Centre for Advocates Against Discrimination, International Service for Human Rights, The Institute for Social Justice, Nonviolent Radical Party, Transnational Transparty, Unione forense per la tutela dei diritti umani, LGBTI Resource Centre, Gruppo CRC, Franciscans International, Antigone, VIDES International, Comitato per la promozione e protezione dei diritti umani (concerning the latter, see Part II, National Bodies with Jurisdiction over Human Rights, IX).

Italy also had to take into account the advance questions submitted to the Italian Government in writing by Norway, the United Kingdom, Germany, the Netherlands, the United States, Slovenia, Mexico and Spain.

At the end of this first stage, 187 recommendations were made to Italy on the possible measures (legal, political and institutional) they should adopt in order to strengthen the national system for the promotion and protection of human rights (doc. A/HRC/28/4). Approximately 70% of the recommendations made fall into six thematic areas, in descending order: racial discrimination (17.6%), national human rights institutions (13.4%), ratification of international instruments (12.8%), the rights of migrants, refugees and asylum seekers (10.7%), women's rights, gender equality, violence against women (9.6%), the rights of minorities (8.6%).

Number of recommendations per thematic area received by Italy in cycles I and II of the UPR

	Thematic areas	II Cycle (October 2014)	I Cycle (February 2010)	Diff. II-I Cycle	% II Cycle	% I Cycle
1	Racial discrimination	33	25	8	17.6	15.9
2	National human rights institutions	25	16	9	13.4	10.2
3	International instruments	24	18	6	12.8	11.5
4	Migrants and asylum seekers	20	24	-4	10.7	15.3
5	Women's rights, gender equality, violence against women	18	2	16	9.6	1.3
6	Minorities	16	19	-3	8.6	12.1
7	The rights of children	9	10	-1	4.8	6.4
8	Trafficking	8	9	-1	4.3	5.7
9	Torture and detention conditions	6	5	1	3.2	3.2
10	Sexual orientation and gender identity	5	4	1	2.7	2.5
11	Economic and social rights	5	2	3	2.7	1.3
12	Development cooperation	4	2	2	2.1	1.3
13	Freedom of expression and freedom of the press	3	7	-4	1.6	4.5
14	Justice and civil rights	3	4	-1	1.6	2.5

	Thematic areas	II Cycle (October 2014)	I Cycle (February 2010)	Diff. II-I Cycle	% II Cycle	% I Cycle
15	Persons with disabilities	3	0	3	1.6	0.0
16	Cooperation with the UN (UPR, Treaty Bodies…)	2	2	0	1.1	1.3
17	Other	2	1	1	1.1	0.6
18	Right to Education	1	4	-3	0.5	2.5
19	Freedom of religion	0	3	-3	0.0	1.9
	TOT	187	157	30	100.0	100.0

Italy fully accepted 177 of the 187 recommendations made (approximately 95%), considering them either already implemented or currently being implemented (doc. A/HRC/28/4/Add.1). In particular, Italy committed to:

– ratifying the Convention for the Protection of All Persons from Enforced Disappearance (recommendations 8–13);

– setting up a national institution for human rights, in line with the Paris principles, by the end of 2015 (recommendation No. 43, submitted by Denmark).

– Recommendation No. 182 ("include all migrants irrespective of their status within the national plans and programmes to integrate and ensure their human rights, Bangladesh) was accepted in part. Indeed, Italy reconfirmed that integration programmes are extended to all regular migrants entitled to stay in Italy. With particular regard to migrants arriving in Italy by sea, they are received and hosted with full respect for their human rights. As to their inclusion in national integration plans and programmes, these are only available to refugees, asylum seekers and those entitled to humanitarian protection.

Finally, Italy rejected 9 recommendations (as compared to 12 in the first UPR cycle).

– Recommendations 1–6: ratify the Convention on the protection of the Rights of All Migrant Workers and Members of Their Families (recommendations already rejected during cycle I of the UPR). Indeed, according to the Government, the Italian legal framework already guarantees the rights of regular and irregular migrants. Following ratification of ILO Conventions Nos. 143 (Migrant Workers – supplementary provisions) and 189 (Domestic Workers), Italy has accepted periodical monitoring of the implementation of both Conventions at the domestic level.

[...] Further, Italy is working to promote a debate on this issue at the European level, aimed at countering trafficking in human beings, in line with requests from both the United Nations and the Council of Europe.

– Recommendations 126–127: explicitly prohibit all corporal punishment of children and enact domestic legislation to enshrine the 1996 Supreme Court ruling against all forms of violence in child-rearing (recommendations already rejected in the course of Cycle I of the UPR). The Government states that the protection of children from all forms of violence within the family is already enshrined in articles 2, 3, 29, 30 and 31 of the Italian Constitution. In addition, article 572 of the Criminal Code punishes any ill-treatment of children within the family with a custodial sentence.

– Recommendation No. 170: suspend summary returns to Greece. The Government maintains that Italy does not effect summary returns to Greece. Operational procedures at borders are carried out according to a case-by-case approach: every migrant is properly identified and the competent authorities handle all personal details in order to review the individual case and relative support measures applicable.

C. Special Procedures

In 2014, the Human Rights Council activated two new thematic Special Procedures (Special Rapporteur on the rights of persons with disabilities and Special Rapporteur on the negative impact of unilateral coercive measures on the enjoyment of human rights) and one new Country mandate (Ivory Coast). Consequently, all told, there were 39 thematic Special Procedure and 14 Country mandates in operation at the Council.

In 2014 Italy was mentioned in two reports, by the Special Rapporteur on trafficking in persons and the Special Rapporteur on freedom of expression respectively. There were also two visits to Italy, by the Working Group on arbitrary detention and the Special Rapporteur on the human rights of migrants.

1) *Report by the Special Rapporteur on trafficking in persons, especially women and children, Joy Ngozi Ezeilo* (A/HRC/26/37/Add.4). In her report, the Special Rapporteur notes that trafficking is continually on the rise in Italy, in part following the increase in migratory flows caused by the so-called "Arab Spring". More in detail, trafficking for sexual exploitation, which involves mainly women from Nigeria and Eastern Europe, is the most widespread and best documented form of exploitation, although not the only one requiring attention from the authorities. Although she recognised that Italy does on the whole have sufficient anti-trafficking legislation, the Special Rapporteur feels that Italy has no comprehensive plan to combat trafficking and that little attention is paid to the

aspects concerning the protection of victims and the exploitation of their work. Consequently, the Special Rapporteur urges the Italian Government to strengthen and coordinate its measures against human trafficking, especially by developing mechanisms for permanent monitoring and evaluation of the situation, so as to enhance the impact of these measures and the protection of victims.

2) *Report of the Special Rapporteur on the promotion and protection of the right to freedom of opinion and expression, Frank La Rue* (A/HRC/26/30/Add.3). In his report, the Special Rapporteur focuses above all on media-related legislation, especially those concerning oversight and ownership, as well as issues relating to privacy and hate speech. In general, the Special Rapporteur asks the Italian Government to make the national media system more democratic, to distribute concessions of broadcasting frequencies fairly and ensuring that the elections of board members of the regulatory and control bodies are transparent. Of the many recommendations made, those relating to the following areas are highlighted:

– *National Human Rights Institution.* The Special Rapporteur requests Italy to establish a national human rights commission in line with the Paris Principles without further delay.

– *Access to information law.* The Special Rapporteur considers current legislation on access to information (Transparency decree of 14 March 2013) should extend further to increase the transparency and credibility of all State institutions. Moreover, access to information laws should also be accompanied with the establishment of an independent State authority to guarantee the exercise of this right and the effectiveness of this law.

– *Decriminalisation of defamation.* The Special Rapporteur recommends total decriminalisation of the offence of defamation and that it be reclassified as a civil offence, taking into consideration that a criminal action, even if it does not contemplate a custodial sentence, can still have an intimidating effect on journalists.

– *Hate speech.* The Special Rapporteur expressed particular concern over hate speech towards migrants and other minorities during election campaigns: a phenomenon which is becoming ever more frequent in many European Countries, partly as a consequence of the financial crisis. The Special Rapporteur expresses his full support for the efforts made by the Italian Government to combat this situation, including awareness-raising and education campaigns on diversity, which can contribute to eradicating prejudice and ignorance, often the root causes of these unacceptable attitudes and behaviours. The Special Rapporteur also welcomes the proposed bill on homophobia and trans phobia, however he believes that further amendments should be made in order to eliminate all exceptions for institutions or particular groups. Moreover he encourages Parliament to consider introducing a law on other forms of hate speech, such as incitements to violence against women or persons with disabilities.

– *Transparency in media ownership and control*. The Special Rapporteur renews his request to implement a legislative reform which would explicitly introduce incompatibility between holding elected or Government offices and ownership of media. This reform should also establish an obligation to disclose the full identity of the ownership of the media and the mechanisms on decision-making and control therein. This information should be made accessible to the public by the Communications Regulatory Body (AGCOM), as should information on the sources of revenue of the media. The Anti-Trust body should also be the subject of legislative reform, so that Italy can bring an end to the excessive concentration of media and the possible establishment of monopolies, which limit diversity and plurality of freedom of expression and are a threat to democracy.

– *Public broadcasting service*. While reiterating his support for the existence of a public service alongside private broadcasting, the Special Rapporteur nonetheless emphasises the necessity of ensuring the independence of the public service. For this reason, the Special Rapporteur recommends that the RAI should be controlled by a body which is independent of the State, administered as a public asset and that the appointment of members of the board be conducted in a transparent manner.

– *Protection of journalists* The Special Rapporteur requested the Italian authorities to take all measures necessary to prosecute anyone responsible for intimidating, threatening, harassing or using violence against journalists and social communicators.

3) *Visit by the Working Group on Arbitrary Detention* (7–9 July 2014). The aim of the visit by the Working Group on Arbitrary Detention was to review the implementation of the recommendations ensuing from their previous report on Italy in 2008 (A/HRC/10/21/Add.5). At the end of their visit, the Working Group requested that the Government implement important new measures to put an end to the excessive recourse to custodial sentences and which ensure the protection of migrants' rights. Despite their praise of the reforms introduced relating to the reduction of sentences, prison overcrowding and recourse to pre-trial detention, Mads Andenas, Chair and Rapporteur of the Working Group, expressed concern over the large numbers of people remanded in custody and the disproportionate use of pre-trial detention for foreigners and Roma, including juveniles.

The Working Group welcomed the abolition of the norm considering irregular immigrant status an aggravating factor in criminal proceedings, and also Parliament's efforts to decriminalise "illegal entry and stay", as it was noted that this is still an administrative offence. Further criticism came over the duration of holding times for migrants – currently up to 18 months, but it is hoped this will be reduced to 12 or 6 months – and over detention conditions inside the Identification and Expulsion Centres (CIE). The concern expressed over cases of summary return, which also included unaccompanied minors and asylum seekers, stems mainly from the inadequate procedures, or total lack of one, for the identification necessary to determine the age of individuals, and the failure to inform them of their rights.

Mention was also made of the harsh prison regime per article 41-*bis*, the definitive closure of criminal psychiatric hospitals, the continuing failure to appoint an Ombudsperson for the rights of detainees – despite having ratified the Optional Protocol to the Convention Against Torture – and the failure to introduce the crime of torture as a specific crime in the Italian criminal code.

4) *Visit by the Special Rapporteur on the human rights of migrants, François Crépeau* (2–5 December 2014). The purpose of the visit was to analyse and assess developments in the situation of migrants since his first visit in 2012, as well as actions taken by the Italian Government following his recommendations. During his visit, the Special Rapporteur met with members of the Government, officers of international organisations, representatives of civil society, journalists and migrants, with whom he discussed the complex issue of managing border control in Italy. Crépeau observes that the growing number of migrants and asylum seekers over recent months has led to a global humanitarian crisis which requires global humanitarian intervention, in other words a new strategic approach which is agreed between EU Member States and the international community.

At the end of his visit, and in advance of the conclusions of the more extensive report that will be presented to the United Nations Human Rights Council in June 2015, the Special Rapporteur expressed his thanks for the extraordinary efforts Italy made with its *Mare Nostrum* operation and invited the European Union and the international community to adopt suitable measures to support Italy's search and rescue efforts and to set up a common long-term programme for resettlement of refugees.

The Special Rapporteur did, however, point out some critical aspects in Italy's policy towards migrants which have until now prevented full protection of migrants and the safeguarding of their rights. Specifically, Crépeau emphasised the need to apply the principle of *non-refoulement* and ensure adequate individual assessments are made in the reception centres, taking into account the vulnerabilities and the specific needs of each individual migrant. Moreover, the Rapporteur stressed the importance of adopting alternative measures to unnecessary detention in the identification and expulsion centres with the aim of closing them altogether. Finally, the Special Rapporteur urged the Italian Government to ensure greater protection for vulnerable groups such as unaccompanied minors, through targeted support, and to make access to justice easier, affording timely and high quality legal support to all migrants as soon as they arrive in Italy and promptly supplying them with information on the rights and procedures which apply to them.

The table below shows the visits made by Special Rapporteurs in recent years, those agreed (but not yet carried out) and those merely requested by Special Rapporteurs.

Visits carried out and reports	**Agreed visits**	**Requested visits**
Special Rapporteur on the independence of judges and lawyers (11–14 March 2002). *Preliminary Report: E/CN.4/2002/72/Add.3*	Independent expert on extreme poverty and human rights (dates to be confirmed)	Special Rapporteur on the independence of judges and lawyers (visit requested in July 2013)
Special Rapporteur on the human rights of migrants (7–18 June 2004). *Report: E/CN.4/2005/85/Add.3*	Working group of experts on people of African descent (1–5 June 2015)	
Special Rapporteur on the right to freedom of opinion and expression (20–29 October 2004). *Report: E/CN.4/2005/64/Add.1*		
Special Rapporteur on contemporary forms of racism (9–13 October 2006). *Report: A/HRC/4/19/Add.4*		
Working group on arbitrary detention (3–14 November 2008). *Report: A/HRC/10/21/Add.5*		
Special Rapporteur on violence against women (15–26 January 2012) *Report: A/HRC/20/16/Add.2*		
Special Rapporteur on the rights of Migrants (30 September-8 October 2012). *Report: A/HRC/23/46/Add.3*		
Special Rapporteur on trafficking in persons (12–20 September 2013) *Report: A/HRC/26/37/Add.4*		

Visits carried out and reports	Agreed visits	Requested visits
Special Rapporteur on freedom of opinion and expression (11–18 November 2013) *Report: A/HRC/26/30/Add.3*		
Working group on arbitrary detention (7–9 July 2014) *Report to be presented in 2015*		
Special Rapporteur on the human rights of migrants (2–5 December 2014) *Report to be presented in June 2015*		

Source: United Nations, Human Rights Council.

III. High Commissioner for Human Rights (OHCHR)

The Office was established by the General Assembly in December 1993 with resolution 48/141.

> The High Commissioner has a very broad mandate which includes the prevention of violations of human rights, ensuring the respect of all human rights, coordinating all United Nations activities involving human rights and strengthening national systems for protecting human rights and the rule of law. In this context, one of the crucial strategic activities for the High Commissioner's Office is supporting the introduction and development of independent human rights commissions at the national level.
>
> In order to fulfil its mandate, the Office of the High Commissioner has consolidated its presence "on the ground", establishing 10 regional offices and the same number of national offices, sending its own experts on integrated United Nations peace missions or planning independent fact-finding operations, as well as mainstreaming the human rights component in United Nations teams' activities at Country or Programme level, and in those of specialised agencies of the United Nations (such as UNDP

On 1 September 2014, Zeid Ra'ad Al Hussein (Jordan) assumed his functions as High Commissioner for Human Rights, replacing Navanethem Pillay (South Africa), who had held the post since 2008. The Italian Flavia Pansieri has been Deputy High Commissioner for Human Rights since 2013.

The High Commissioner's Office is funded one-third by the ordinary budget of the United Nations, approved by the General Assembly every two years; the remaining two thirds of the budget comes from voluntary contributions, mostly from States, but also from international organisations, foundations, commercial enterprises and private citizens.

In 2014, Italy contributed to the budget of the High Commissioner's Office with funds for about 61,000 dollars (ranking 45th among donors), about 7,000 dollars less than in the previous year, when it ranked 42nd among donors (see graph below).

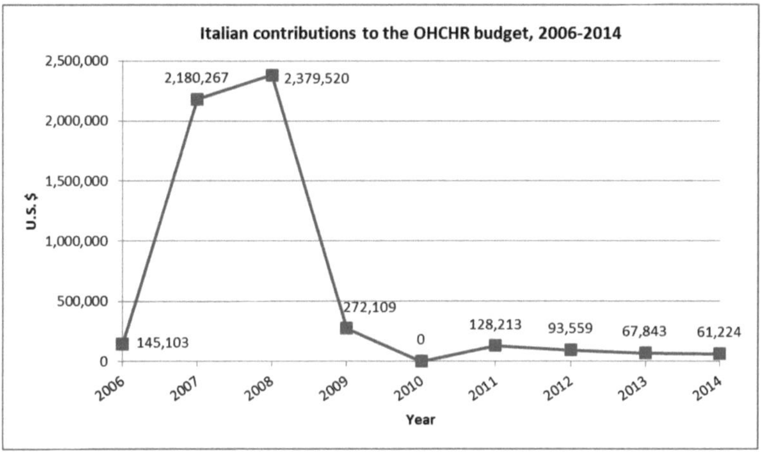

IV. High Commissioner for Refugees (UNHCR)

This Office was established by the United Nations General Assembly on 14 December 1950, with resolution A/RES/428(V).

> The mandate of the Agency is to coordinate international action for the protection of refugees and the resolution of their problems all over the world. Its primary mission is the protection of the rights and wellbeing of refugees and to ensure that all of them can exercise their right to request asylum and seek safe refuge in another State, with the option to return voluntarily to their home Country, integrate locally or to resettle into a third Country. The remit of the UNHCR also includes assistance to stateless persons.
>
> In 2014 the High Commissioner for Refugees was António Guterres (Portugal), elected by the General Assembly for the first time in 2005 and re-elected in 2010 for a second five-year mandate.

The UNHCR has had its own office in Rome since 1953. The Italian office participates in the procedures to determine refugee status in Italy and performs other duties regarding international protection, training, dissemination of information on refugees and asylum-seekers in Italy and in the various crisis areas all over the world, raising public awareness and fund-raising with Governments, companies and from individual donators. Since 2006, the Italian UNHCR Office has become a Regional Office, with responsibilities for Albania, Cyprus, Greece, Malta, Portugal, San Marino and the Holy See in addition to Italy. In January 2014, Carlotta Sami was appointed UNHCR Spokesperson in Italy.

According to data provided by UNHCR, in July 2014 there were 98,813 people coming under the agency's responsibility resident in Italy (+27,549 compared to January 2013), of whom 76,263 refugees (+11,484 compared to 2013), 22,200 asylum seekers (+16,185) and 350 stateless persons (-120).

In the first 10 months of 2014, particularly following the numerous sea rescues and landings in the Mediterranean, 51,262 asylum claims were lodged in Italy (+84% compared to 2013), a figure which places Italy sixth in the ranking of the 44 industrialised nations with the highest number of asylum seekers (with about 7% of all claims).

In 2014, Italy contributed to the UNHCR budget with an allocation of approximately 11.3 million dollars, with an increase of about 2 million dollars compared to the previous year.

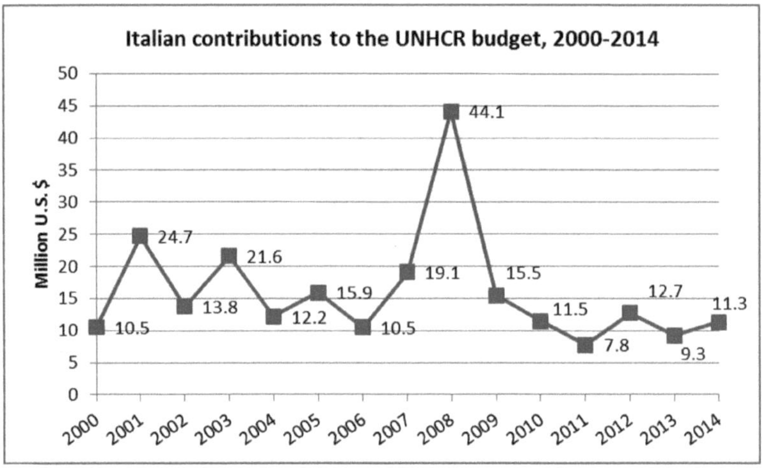

V. Human Rights Treaty Bodies

Over the years, the United Nations have created an organic International Bill of Human Rights, whose core is made up of the nine conventions listed below: the Convention for the Elimination of All Forms of Racial Discrimination (ICERD, 1965); the Covenant on Civil and Political Rights (ICCPR, 1966); the Covenant on Economic, Social and Cultural Rights (ICESCR, 1966); the Convention on the Elimination of All Forms of Discrimination against Women (CEDAW, 1969); the Convention against

Torture and other Cruel, Inhuman or Degrading Treatment or Punishment (CAT, 1984); the Convention on the Rights of the Child (CRC, 1989); the Convention on the Protection of the Rights of all Migrant Workers and Members of Their Families (ICRMW, 1990); the Convention on the Rights of Persons with Disabilities (CRPD, 2006); the Convention for the Protection of All Persons from Enforced Disappearance (CPED, 2006).

Italy has ratified seven conventions and their related optional protocols (as shown in the chart below). It has signed but not yet ratified the CPED (in 2007), the Optional Protocol to ICESCR (in 2009) and the Optional Protocol to the CRC on the communications procedure (in 2012); it has not yet signed the ICRMW. On 3 April 2013 Italy deposited the instrument of ratification of the Optional Protocol to the CAT (signed in 2003) with the Secretariat-General of the United Nations.

Convention	**Ratification law**	**Declarations/ Reservations**	**Recognition of competence of specific Committees**
ICERD	l. 13 October 1975, No. 654	Yes (art. 4)	Individual communications (art. 14): Yes
ICESCR	l. 25 October 1977, No. 881	No	-
ICCPR	l. 25 October 1977, No. 881	Yes (art. 15.1 and 19.3)	Inter-State communications (art. 41): Yes
OP – 1	l. 25 October 1977, No. 881	Yes (art. 5.2)	-
OP – 2	l. 9 December 1994, No. 734	No	-
CEDAW	l. 14 March 1985, No. 132	Yes (general)	-
OP	Deposit date of ratification instrument: 22/09/2000	No	Inquiry procedure (art. 8 and 9): Yes
CAT	l. 3 November 1988, No. 498	No	Individual communications (art. 22): Yes Inter-State communications (art. 21): Yes Inquiry procedure (art. 20): Yes
CRC	l. 27 May 1991, No. 176	No	-

Convention	Ratification law	Declarations/ Reservations	Recognition of competence of specific Committees
OP – AC	l. 11 March 2002, No. 46	Binding declaration in accordance with art. 3: 17 years old	-
OP – SC	l. 11 March 2002, No. 46	No	-
CRPD	l. 3 March 2009, No. 18	No	-
OP	l. 3 March 2009, No. 18	No	Inquiry procedure (art. 6 and 7): No

Legend:
OP = Optional Protocol
OP – AC = Optional Protocol to the Convention on the Rights of the Child on the Involvement of Children in Armed Conflict
OP – SC = Optional Protocol to the Convention on the Rights of the Child on the Sale of Children, Child Prostitution and Child Pornography.

Besides enunciating fundamental rights therein, the United Nations have set up control mechanisms for each treaty, the so-called Committees or Treaty Bodies, each comprising from 10 to 23 independent experts, selected on the basis of their high moral character and recognised expertise in the field of human rights.

In 2014, Alessio Bruni was a member of the Committee against Torture; Bianca Maria Pomeranzi was on the Committee on the Elimination of Discrimination against Women; and Maria Rita Parsi member of the Committee on the Rights of the Child.

> The principal duty of the Committees is to examine the periodic reports on the implementation in States Parties of the terms of the internationally binding rules, which the States Parties are under obligation to submit regularly (normally every 4 or 5 years). In addition to this procedure, some Committees can monitor implementation through three further mechanisms: by conducting Country enquiries (in the field); by examining inter-State communications and by examining individual complaints. Finally, the Committees publish their interpretation of the contents of provisions on human rights, the so-called General comments (for further detail on these functions, see *2011 Yearbook*, p. 180).

Italy is subject to monitoring by seven Committees, as shown in the table below. In 2014, Italy did not submit any reports to the Committees, nor were any concluding observations made.

Italy's cooperation with United Nations Treaty Bodies

Committee	Total number of reports presented	Latest report presented	Latest concluding observations	Reporting status
CERD	18	July 2011	March 2012	XIX and XX joint report to be submitted in February 2015
CESCR	5	August 2012	-	V report: submitted and awaiting discussion
CCPR	5	March 2004	April 2006	VI report: overdue since October 2009
CEDAW	6	December 2009	August 2011	VII report: to be submitted in July 2015
CAT	4	May 2004	July 2007	VI report: to be submitted in July 2015 (originally due July 2011)
CRC	4	January 2009	October 2011	V and VI joint report to be submitted in April 2017
OP – AC	2	January 2009	October 2011	Information on the implementation of the Protocol to be included in the V and VI joint report
OP – SC	2	January 2009	October 2011	Information on the implementation of the Protocol to be included in the V and VI joint report
CRPD	1	November 2012	-	I report: submitted and awaiting discussion

A. Committee on Economic, Social and Cultural Rights

In 2014 the Committee held two sessions: the 52nd (28 April-23 May) and 53rd (10–28 November). During the 52nd session, reports from Armenia, China, China (Hong Kong), China (Macau), the Czech Republic, El Salvador, Indonesia, Lithuania, Monaco, Serbia, Ukraine and Uzbekistan were considered; during the 53rd, those of Finland, Guatemala, Montenegro, Nepal, Portugal, Romania, Slovenia and Vietnam. No General Comments were adopted during the year.

Italy submitted (but has not yet discussed) its latest report in August 2012 (see *2013 Yearbook*, pp. 191–197).

B. Human Rights Committee (civil and political rights)

In 2014 the Committee held three sessions: the 110th (10–28 March), 111th (7–25 July) and 112th (7–31 October). The 110th session examined the reports from Chad, Kyrgyzstan, Latvia, Nepal, Sierra Leone and the United States of America; the 111th the reports from Chile, Georgia, Ireland, Japan, Malawi and Sudan; and the 112th the reports from Burundi, Haiti, Israel, Malta, Montenegro and Sri Lanka. During the year, General Comment No. 35 was issued, concerning art. 9 of the Convention (liberty and security of the person).

The last periodic report on Italy was discussed by the Committee in October 2005, during its 85th session (see *2011 Yearbook*, pp. 184–186). Italy should have submitted its sixth report in October 2009, but as of 31 December 2014, it had not yet discharged its duty in this respect.

C. Committee against torture

In 2014 the Committee held two sessions: the 52nd (28 April–23 May) and the 53rd (3–28 November). During the 52nd session the reports from Cyprus, Guinea, the Holy See, Lithuania, Montenegro, Sierra Leone, Thailand and Uruguay were examined; in the 53rd, those from Australia, Burundi, Croatia, Kazakhstan, Sweden, Ukraine, the United States of America and Venezuela. No General Comments were adopted during the year.

Italy's last periodic report was discussed by the Committee in May 2007, during its 38th session (see *2011 Yearbook*, pp. 187–188). Italy is to present its sixth report in July 2015 (it was originally due in July 2011). This report will have to supply detailed answers to the list of issues that the Committee prepared during its 43rd session (November 2009) and forwarded to the Italian Government in January 2010 (see doc. CAT/C/ITA/Q/6).

D. Committee on the Elimination of Racial Discrimination

In 2014 the Committee held two sessions: the 84th (3–21 February) and the 85th (11–29 August). During the 84th session, reports from Belgium, Honduras, Kazakhstan, Luxembourg, Montenegro, Poland, Switzerland and Uzbekistan were examined; during the 85th those of Cameroon, El Salvador, Estonia, Iraq, Japan, Peru and the United States of America. No General Recommendations were adopted during the year.

Italy's latest periodic report was considered by the Committee in March 2012 in the course of the 80th session (see the *2013 Yearbook*, pp. 198–201). Italy is to present its joint XIX and XX report in February 2015.

E. Committee on the Elimination of Discrimination against Women

In 2014 the Committee held three sessions: the 57th (10–28 February), 58th (30 June – 18 July) and 59th (20 October – 7 November). During the 57th session the reports from Bahrain, Cameroon, Finland, Iraq, Kazakhstan, Qatar and Sierra Leone were examined; in the 58th those of the Central African Republic, Georgia, India, Lithuania, Mauritania, Peru, Swaziland and Syria; and in the 59th those from Belgium, Brunei Darussalam, China, China (Hong Kong), China (Macau), Ghana, Guinea, Poland, the Solomon Islands and Venezuela. Two General Recommendations were also adopted: No. 31 on harmful practices (a joint general recommendation with the Committee on the Rights of the Child), and No. 32 on the gender-related dimensions of refugee status, asylum, nationality and statelessness of women.

Italy's latest report was discussed by the Committee in July 2011, during its 49th session (see the *2012 Yearbook*, pp. 191–194). Italy is due to submit its seventh report in July 2015.

F. Committee on the Rights of the Child

In 2014 the Committee held three sessions: the 65th (13–31 January), 66th (26 May – 13 June) and 67th (1–19 September). During the 65th session the reports from Congo, Germany, the Holy See, Portugal, The Russian Federation and Yemen were examined; during the 66th those of India, Indonesia, Jordan, Kyrgyzstan and Santa Lucia; and in the 67th those from Croatia, Fiji, Hungary, Morocco and Venezuela. General comment No. 18 on harmful practices was also adopted (a joint general recommendation with the Committee on the Elimination of Discrimination against Women).

Italy's latest periodic report was discussed by the Committee in September 2011, during the 58th session (see *2012 Yearbook*, pp. 195–199). Italy is due to present its joint fifth and sixth report in 2017.

G. Committee on the Rights of Persons with Disabilities

In 2014 the Committee held two sessions, the 11th (31 March – 11 April) and the 12th (15 September – 3 October). During the 11th session the reports from Azerbaijan, Costa Rica and Sweden were examined; and in the 12th those from Belgium, Denmark, Ecuador, Mexico, New Zealand and the Republic of Korea. Two General comments were adopted in 2004, regarding art. 12 (equal recognition before the law) and art. 9 (accessibility).

Italy submitted its first periodic report in November 2012 (see *2013 Yearbook*, pp. 202–212), but it has not yet been discussed.

H. Committee on Migrant Workers

In 2014 the Committee held two sessions, the 20th (31 March – 11 April) and the 21st (1–5 September), during which the concluding remarks relating to El Salvador, Mali, The Philippines, Uruguay were adopted (20th session) as were those of Ghana and Belize (21st session). No General comments were adopted during the year.

Italy has not ratified the Convention on the Protection of the Rights of all Migrant Workers and Members of their Families and, consequently, is not subject to monitoring by the Committee.

I. Committee on Enforced Disappearances

In 2014 the Committee held two sessions, the 6th (17–28 March) and the 7th (15–26 September), during which the concluding remarks regarding Germany and the Netherlands were adopted (6th session), and those on Belgium and Paraguay (in the 7th session).

Italy has not ratified the Convention for the Protection of All Persons from Enforced Disappearance and, consequently, is not subject to monitoring by the Committee.

VI. Specialised United Nations Agencies, Programmes and Funds

A. International Labour Organisation (ILO)

Established by the Treaty of Versailles in 1919, the ILO became the first specialised agency of the United Nations in 1946.

> The ILO is devoted to promoting decent and productive work for men and women in conditions of freedom, equality, safety and dignity. Its chief objectives are: to promote rights at work, to encourage decent employment opportunities, to enhance social protection and to strengthen dialogue on work-related issues. The ILO is the only United Nations agency which has a tripartite structure: representatives of Governments, employers and workers jointly elaborate the policies and programmes of the Organisation. 185 States are members of the ILO.
>
> Since its foundation, the ILO has adopted 189 conventions. Of these, the ILO has identified 8 which it defines as "fundamental" or "core" (No. 29 on Forced Labour, 1930; No. 87 on Freedom of Association and Protection of the Right to Organise, 1948; No. 98 on the Right to Organise and Collective Bargaining, 1949; No. 100 on Equal Remuneration for Men and Women Workers for Work of Equal Value, 1951; No. 105 on the Abolition of Forced Labour, 1957; No. 111 on the Elimination of All Forms of Discrimination in Employment, Occupation, Vocational Training and Terms and Conditions

of Employment, 1958; No. 138 on the Minimum Age for Admission to Employment or Work, 1973; and No. 182 on the Elimination of the Worst Forms of Child Labour, 1999) and 4 defined as "priority" (or "governance": No. 81 on Labour Inspection, 1947; No. 122 on Employment Policy, 1964; No. 129 on Labour Inspection [Agriculture], 1969; and No. 144 on Tripartite Consultation [International Labour Standards], 1976).

Italy has been a member of the ILO since 1919 (it is one of the founding members); it withdrew from the Organisation in 1937 but joined again permanently in 1945. The ILO is present in Italy with its offices in Rome, which have been operating since 1920, and the International Training Centre, established in Turin in 1965.

Italy has ratified 113 conventions adopted by the ILO (of which 82 in force and 31 denounced), including the 8 fundamental ones, the 4 priority ones and 101 of the 177 technical conventions.

The complete list, updated to December 2014, of ILO conventions and of Italy's acceptance status (ratification, signature, no initiative is available online at: www.italianhumanrightsyearbook.eu, in the section "attachments".

In order to monitor the application of conventions ratified by States, in 1926 the ILO established the *Committee of Experts on the Application of Conventions and Recommendations*, a body made up of twenty eminent jurists and social professionals, who are independent of Governments and appointed on individual merits. The monitoring mechanism requires each Member State to submit periodic reports on the steps they have taken, in law and in practice, to apply each of the conventions it has ratified. At the same time, Governments are required to submit copies of their reports to employers' and workers' organisations, which are entitled to make comments and supply further information. Government reports are initially examined by the Committee of Experts, which can make two different kinds of comments: *observations* and *direct requests*. The observations contain comments on fundamental questions raised by the application of a particular convention by a State, and are published in the Committee's annual report. On the other hand, direct requests relate to more technical requests or requests for further information; they are not published in the report but are communicated directly to the Governments concerned.

Upon conclusion of its considerations, the Committee presents an annual report to the *International Labour Conference*, the most representative body of the ILO, comprising representatives from all the ILO Member States and including all its observations and recommendations, which are carefully examined by the *Conference Committee on the Application of Standards*, a tripartite standing committee made up of Government, employer and worker delegates. This Committee selects a number of observations from the report for more in-depth discussion. The Governments referred to in these comments are invited to respond before the Conference Committee to provide information on the situation in question. In many cases, the Conference Committee adopts conclusions recommending that Governments take specific steps to remedy a problem or to invite the ILO to come on a mission to their Country or to request technical assistance.

In 2014, Italy received 2 direct requests and 4 observations from the Committee of Experts on the Application of Conventions and Recommendations.

The Committee's direct requests were made in order to obtain further information on Italy's legislative, administrative and political instruments connected with the implementation of the following conventions: No. 117 – Social Policy (basic aims and standards) and No. 160 – Labour Statistics.

The observations received were on Conventions Nos. 122 – Employment Policy; 159 – Vocational Rehabilitation and Employment (disabled persons); 181 – Private Employment Agencies and 183 – Maternity Protection.

Convention No. 122 on employment policy: articles 1, 2 and 3, measures to alleviate the impact of the crisis.

– *Employment trends.* The Committee took note of the answers provided by the Italian Government in October 2013, following the observations published by the Committee that same year. In its response, the Government stressed that the strategy implemented to tackle the impact of the global crisis on the labour market focuses on four priority points: (i) creating new jobs with permanent contracts; (ii) promoting self-employment; (iii) promoting entry into the labour market of young people who are currently not in employment, education or training ("NEETs") through apprenticeships; (iv) combating extreme poverty. However, the ISTAT annual report for 2014 shows that the only type of work which has increased as compared to 2008 is part-time employment. ISTAT data also show that in May 2014, the unemployment rate reached 12.6%, half a percentage point higher than at the same time in 2013. The number of people unemployed is 3,222,000, with an increase of 127,000 over the course of the year. Moreover, significant differences remain between the north and south of Italy in terms of unemployment rates. The nationwide unemployment rate in Italy was 12.2% in 2013 (+5.4% as compared to 2008 and +1.5% compared to 2012), but in southern Italy unemployment rates reached 19.7%. Finally, ISTAT figures confirm the continuing differences in employment levels between men and women: in July 2013, the employment rate for men was 65%, whereas it was a mere 46.8% for women.

Consequently, the Committee asked the Italian Government to illustrate how article 2 of the Convention is applied, particularly to specify how the measures and policies adopted in order to reach the objectives enshrined in art. 1 of the Convention are monitored. In addition, the Committee asked the Government to provide information on the outcome of the measures adopted to close the gap in employment levels between men and women and between different areas of the Country.

– *Youth employment.* According to ISTAT figures, youth unemployment in the 15–24 age group stood at 43% in May 2014, an increase of 4.2% over the previous year. The Committee acknowledged the measures to increase youth employment taken as of 2013, and asked the Government to supply information which would allow assessment of the outcomes of these measures.

– *Education and training policies.* The Committee asked the Government to provide information on the impact of education and training policies, including the reform of apprenticeships, on young people's and other categories of vulnerable workers' chances of obtaining employment.

Convention No. 159 on vocational rehabilitation and employment (disabled persons)

The Committee acknowledged the answers provided by the Government in November 2013, in response to the observations published by the Committee in 2011. The Government stated that the economic and employment crisis over the 2-year period 2010–2011 had an impact on the mandatory placement systems for persons with disabilities. Following implementation of law 68/99 on the right to work of persons with disabilities, 22,360 people were placed in 2010 and 22,023 in 2011. From the statistics provided, the Committee noticed significant disparities between the various regions of Italy as concerns registrations and placements: the recovery seems to have positively affected most regions, except in the south. It also noted that over half of the job placements were established under fixed-term contracts. Moreover, the Committee noted with interest that the Government adopted legislative decree No. 76 of 28 June 2013, converted into Act No. 99 of 9 August 2013, which provides that employers in the public and private sectors are required to take appropriate steps to ensure that reasonable accommodation is provided in the workplace, as defined in the United Nations Convention on the Rights of Persons with Disabilities, to ensure equality between persons with disabilities and other workers.

The Committee encouraged the Government to strengthen its efforts to promote employment opportunities for persons with disabilities in an open labour market. The Government was asked to provide an assessment, supported by statistics, of the impact of the national policy on vocational rehabilitation and employment of persons with disabilities (articles 3 and 7 of the Convention).

Convention No. 181 on private employment agencies: protection for workers employed by private employment agencies.

The Committee acknowledged the Italian Government's report of November 2013, containing general remarks on the operation of the public employment service and private employment agencies. The Government indicated that, from 2010 onwards, a large number of private employment agencies, especially smaller ones, have ceased their activities due to, inter alia, an increase in the number of computer databases available to search for jobs, and the consequent loss of importance of labour mediation services. The Committee referred back to the concerns raised by the Italian General Confederation of Labour (CGIL) on the lack of protection for agency workers with regard to their working and employment conditions.

Consequently, the Committee asked the Government to provide a report indicating how the measures adopted to date have ensured adequate protection of the rights of workers in temporary work agencies (articles 11 and 12 of the Convention).

Convention No. 183 on Maternity Protection

– *Compulsory period of postnatal leave (art. 4).* The Italian Government stated that legislative decree No. 119 of 18 July 2011 amended section 16 of the consolidated text concerning the protection of maternity and paternity, giving a female worker the option to return to work in the case of specific events and under specific conditions, thus forgoing, wholly or partially, the postnatal portion of her maternity leave. The Committee asked the Government to indicate how it intends to harmonize this provision with article 4(4) of the Convention, which provides that "maternity leave shall include a period of six weeks' compulsory leave after childbirth, unless otherwise agreed at the national level by the Government and the representative organizations of employers and workers".

– *Protection against dismissal: domestic workers* (art. 8.1). The Committee noted the Governments reference to the Supreme Court Decision No. 6199 of 1998, which limits the period of protection against dismissal for domestic workers solely to maternity leave (two months before and three months after childbirth), considering that the provisions of section 54 of the consolidated text (protection against dismissal until the child is one year old) were too burdensome for employers. The Committee observed that this decision dates from 1998, namely before Italy's ratification of the present Convention in 2001. Hence the Committee considered that, under the Italian legal system, it is the provisions of article 8(1) of this Convention that must apply.

The Committee therefore requests the Government to bring all the relevant provisions – in particular section 62 of Decree No. 151 of March 2001 into conformity with art. 8(1) of the Convention.

During 2014, none of these observations was selected by the Conference Committee on the Application of Standards for more in-depth discussions.

The overall budget of the ILO is structured through three main funding sources: the regular budget, voluntary contributions in addition to the regular budget (the Regular Budget Supplementary Account) and the extra-budgetary resources for technical cooperation. In line with previous years, in 2014 Italy contributed 4.5% of the regular budget of the ILO, an amount equivalent to approximately 17 million Swiss Francs. In the two-year period 2014–2015, Italy made a further voluntary contribution to the regular budget equivalent to approximately 154,000 dollars, making Italy one of the eight donor Countries, together with Belgium, Denmark, Germany, Luxemburg, Netherlands, Norway and Sweden. Finally, in 2014 Italy contributed to the ILO's resources for technical cooperation, allocating approximately 2.9 million dollars (see graph below).

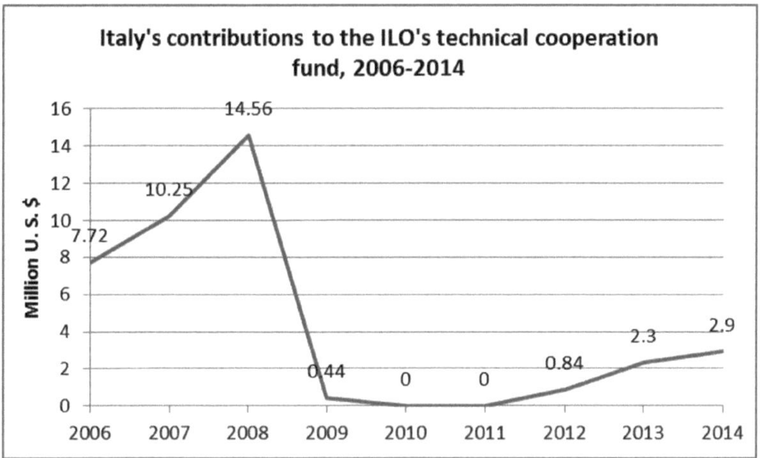

Source: ILO Development Cooperation Dashboard.

B. United Nations Educational, Scientific and Cultural Organisation (UNESCO)

The human rights which fall under the responsibility of UNESCO are the right to education, the right to benefit from scientific progress, the right to participate freely in cultural life and the right to information, including freedom of opinion and expression. In connection with these, the right to freedom of thought, conscience and religion, the right to seek, receive and impart information and ideas through any instrument and across borders, the right to protection of the moral and material interests resulting from any scientific, literary or artistic production are pertinent, as are the right to freedom of assembly and association.

Italy has been a Member State of UNESCO since 1948. In 2014, H.E. Vincenza Lomonaco was Italy's Permanent Representative to UNESCO. Since its inception, UNESCO has adopted 28 Conventions, of which Italy has ratified 20.

In the field of education, in 1991 the 26th General Conference of UNESCO established the International Programme for University Cooperation (IUC). The Programme is working to foster the creation of a network of centres of excellence (UNESCO Chairs) which will implement advanced teaching and research programmes in fields related to UNESCO policies, with special reference to the areas of peace, human rights, democracy and intercultural dialogue. There are over 650 UNESCO chairs worldwide: in 2014 Italy had 20 chairs (no change from 2013), of which 3 are specifically devoted to human rights and include these words in their name: the Chair in "Human Rights, Democracy and Peace", established in 1999 at the University of Padua (Chair: Antonio Papisca); Chair in "Human Rights and Ethics of International Cooperation" established in 2003 at the University of Bergamo (Chair: Stefania Gandolfi); and the Chair in "Bioethics and Human Rights", established in 2009 at the "Regina Apostolorum" Pontificial Athenaeum, European University of Rome (Chair: Alberto García).

The complete list, updated to December 2014, of UNESCO conventions and of Italy's acceptance status (ratification, signature, no initiative is available online at: www.italianhumanrightsyearbook.eu, in the section "attachments".

In the field of education, in 1991 the 26th General Conference of UNESCO established the International Programme for University Cooperation (IUC). The Programme is working to foster the creation of a network of centres of excellence (UNESCO Chairs) which will implement advanced teaching and research programmes in fields related to UNESCO policies, with special reference to the areas of peace, human rights, democracy and intercultural dialogue. There are over 650 UNESCO chairs worldwide: in 2014 Italy had 20 chairs (no change from 2013), of which 3 are specifically devoted to human rights and include these words in their name: the Chair in "Human Rights, Democracy and Peace", established in 1999 at the University of Padua (Chair: Antonio Papisca); Chair in "Human Rights and Ethics of International Cooperation" established in 2003 at the University of Bergamo (Chair: Stefania Gandolfi); and the Chair in "Bioethics and Human Rights", established in 2009 at the "Regina Apostolorum" Pontificial Athenaeum, European University of Rome (Chair: Alberto García).

There are two committees on bioethics operating in UNESCO: the International Bioethics Committee (IBC) and the Inter-governmental Bioethics Committee (IGBC).

The IBC was established in 1993, particularly thanks to the efforts of Director-General of UNESCO at that time, and it is a body made up of 36 independent experts coming from different geographical and disciplinary backgrounds. Its mission is to follow progress in life science and its applications in order to ensure respect for human dignity and human rights and to promote reflection on the ethical and legal issues raised by research in the life sciences and their applications. To this end, over the years it has published a number of recommendations and other documents, the most significant of which is the Universal Declaration on Bioethics and Human Rights, adopted by the UNESCO General Conference in 2005. The Committee convenes once a year upon invitation from the UNESCO Director-General. The 2013 session (twentieth) was held in Seoul from June 19–21 and debated the issue of non-discrimination and non-stigmatisation, as set forth in art. 11 of the Declaration. In 2013 the Chairperson of the Committee was Stefano Semplici, full professor of Moral Philosophy at Rome «Tor Vergata» University and member of the Committee since 2008.

The IGBC was created in 1998 pursuant to art. 11 of the IBC Statute. It is comprised of 36 Member States who are elected by the UNESCO General Conference, and meets at least once every two years to examine the proposals and recommendations of the IBC and to forward these proposals, accompanied by its own opinions, to the other UNESCO Member States. Italy was not a member of the IGBC in 2014.

From 8 – 12 September 2014, the IBC and the IGBC held a joint session in Paris to discuss two main issues: elaborating on the principle of the sharing of benefits (art. 15 of the Universal Declaration on Bioethics and Human Rights) and the human genome and human rights.

As in previous years, Italy contributed to about 4.5% of UNESCO's regular budget (which covers ongoing expenses for personnel and the main activities of the Organisation), a sum equivalent to approximately 14.4 million dollars, placing it seventh among the main contributors to the Organisation. Moreover, Italy ranked fifth in 2014 (after Japan, the European Union, Sweden and the Republic of Korea) in terms of voluntary contributions (which fund multiannual cooperation programmes managed by UNESCO), with a contribution of 5.7 million dollars (almost unchanged compared to 2013; -2.4 million dollars compared to 2012 and -5.4 million compared to 2011).

UNESCO Machinery

Italy was not involved with any of the organisation's monitoring mechanisms in 2014.

C. The Food and Agriculture Organisation of the United Nations (FAO)

The FAO was established in 1945 in Ville de Quebec, Canada, and has its headquarters in Rome. José Graziano da Silva (Brazil) has been the Director-General of the Organisation since 1 January 2012. Italy is currently appointed to the Council, with a three-year term that started on 1 July 2014.

In addition, Italy works with the FAO on the Cooperation Programme FAO/Italy, the main components of which, funded by Italian voluntary contributions, are: the Traditional Programme; the Italian Trust Fund for Food Security and the Decentralised Cooperation Programme.

D. The World Health Organisation (WHO)

The primary objective of the Organisation, established in 1948, is the attainment by all peoples of the highest possible level of health, understood not as the absence of disease but as a state of complete physical, mental and social well-being.

In Italy there are two offices of the WHO (Rome and Venice) and currently 27 accredited collaborating centres. The latter, specialised institutions which receive no funding from the WHO, are identified by the Director General of the WHO and are part of a worldwide network to support the Organisation in various medical and scientific fields. In Italy their activity is coordinated by the Ministry of Health.

E. The United Nations Development Programme (UNDP)

The United Nations Development Programme (UNDP) was established by the General Assembly in 1965 and has the role of central agency for the coordination and funding of development cooperation of the United Nations system.

UNDP action pursues the general objective of "human development", understood as not only economic growth but also as social development, based on gender equality and respect for human rights. UNDP conducts research and analysis, preparing studies and reports. Of the most significant, worth noting are the Annual Report on Human Development and the report on the state of achievement of the Millennium Development Goals. The former, in addition to in-depth studies of different themes relating to human development, surveys living conditions in 187 Countries. In the latter, also an annual report prepared by UNDP, devoted to the state of achievement of the Millennium Development Goals, analyses the success stories of each year and the challenges still to be tackled as the deadline set for their achievement, the end of 2015, draws near.

F. The United Nations Environment Programme (UNEP)

The UNEP's mission is to coordinate and facilitate the realisation of a global partnership for development projects and environmental protection activities so that nations and peoples may improve their quality of life without jeopardising that of future generations.

The current Director General is Achim Steiner. The Permanent Representative to the UNEP and also head of the Italian Embassy mission in Nairobi is H.E. Mauro Massoni.

G. The United Nations Human Settlements Programme (UN-HABITAT)

The mission of UN-HABITAT, the United Nations Human Settlements Programme, is to promote sustainable urbanisation in social and environmental terms, for the ultimate purpose of guaranteeing everyone the right to decent housing. The current Director General is Joan Clos (Spain). The Permanent Representative to UN-HABITAT and also the head of the Italian Embassy mission in Nairobi is H.E. Mauro Massoni.

UN-HABITAT works closely with local authorities, including Municipalities, Provinces and Regions, mainly due to the special relationship formed with UNACLA, the United Nations Advisory Committee on the Local Authorities. The latter consists of mayors and representatives of umbrella organisations of local authorities chosen by the Director General of UN-HABITAT on the basis of their expertise and commitment in implementing the UN agenda on human settlements.

H. The United Nations Children's Fund (UNICEF)

UNICEF in the permanent United Nations Fund mandated to protect and promote the rights of boys, girls and adolescents with the aim of improving their living conditions. Anthony Lake (USA) has been the Executive Director since 1 May 2010.

Italy hosts the UNICEF Research Centre at the Istituto degli Innocenti in Florence. Moreover, the Italian Committee for UNICEF, a non-governmental organisation whose activity is regulated by a cooperation agreement signed with UNICEF International, has been operating in Italy since 1974. Chairperson of the Committee is Giacomo Guerrera, who has held the post since November 2011.

As concerns Italy's contribution to the Fund in 2013, UNICEF'S ranking of donor Countries places Italy in 15th place, the same position as in 2012.

VII. International Organisations with Permanent Observer Status at the General Assembly

Of the 20 inter-governmental organisations of a universal or regional nature that have permanent observer status at the UN General Assembly and maintain permanent representation offices at the United Nations headquarters in New York, one of the most active in issues related to human rights is the International Organisation for Migration.

A. The International Organisation for Migration (IOM)

Established in 1951, the IOM is the major inter-governmental organisation which deals with migrant issues. Its mission is to promote orderly migration based on respect for human dignity; to this end, it collaborates with Governments and civil society.

The IOM Coordination Centre for the Mediterranean Countries is based in Rome and the main activities of the IOM offices in Italy concern: providing information services on immigration; guidance on migration for work purposes and social integration; combating trafficking in human beings and providing assistance to victims; reuniting families; projects designed to help prevent the spread of HIV and promote consideration of the health implications of migration; migration and development projects and appreciation of the African diaspora in Italy; supporting voluntary return and reintegration in their area of origin for vulnerable migrants, citizens from other Countries resident in Italy and foreigners in an irregular position.

The IOM is present in Sicily, Apulia and Calabria in the places where migrants land and in the migrant centres, where it provides information on the procedures and potential risks of staying in Italy without regular permits. It also carries out monitoring activities inside the structures. Together with the UNHCR, Save the Children and the Italian Red Cross, the IOM is part of the *Praesidium* project, funded by the Italian Ministry of the Interior. Finally, the Organisation was also active in many other initiatives in Italy in 2014, such as "Pruma", a project promoting family reunification for unaccompanied minors seeking asylum, under the Dublin Regulation, or "Partir", a programme offering the safe and dignified return home of vulnerable immigrants present in Italy who voluntarily request it, and contributing to individual resettling plans for their reintegration in their home Countries.

On 17 January 2014, the IOM made 10 proposals aiming to contribute to the resolution of some of the most critical issues defining the question of irregular immigration to Italy. Among these proposals, formulated on the basis of the organisation's findings during their 2013 visits conducted under the *Praesidium* project, the most significant ones are about: decriminalisation of the offence of entering Italy and staying illegally; the need to avoid holding migrants who have been in prison, and could be identified there, in CIEs; reducing the holding time in CIEs from the current 18 months to the time strictly necessary to identify and release the migrant, should it be clear that this identification cannot take place through no fault of the migrant; promoting voluntary assisted return to support those who wish to return to their home Country; the use of alternatives to detention, already in place in other Countries, such as introducing an Ombudsperson, providing for specific financial guarantees, etc.; implementing a code regulating the lives of immigrants inside CIEs and ensuring uniformity of treatment of migrants in all structures throughout Italy; tighter control over the management of these centres and an improvement in the quality of the services provided; promoting criteria of transparency and ease of access to these centres by allowing migrant protection organisations entry, as they can provide legal, psychological and social support; setting up an independent monitoring body/agent to oversee respect of migrants' rights, flag up critical situations and take care of particularly vulnerable subjects.

On 9 July 2014, during the Italian Presidency of the Council of the European Union, the IOM forwarded several recommendations to the Italian Government on the issue of migrant flows. While highlighting the need for these problems to be tackled through the collective action of all Member States, together with the Countries migrants pass through and, where possible, with their Countries of origin, the IOM identified the following areas as the key points of its recommendations: irregular immigration, labour migration and return programmes. On the first issue, the IOM affirms the need to assist the Countries of origin and of transit to develop proper policies for migration and border management, with special attention to migrant children. In addition to enhancing cooperation between all Countries impacted by migratory flows so as to be able to offer migrants alternatives to irregular immigration, the IOM claims that it is necessary to develop a humanitarian border management model so that all Countries subject to high migratory pressure can manage migratory flows appropriately. As concerns labour migration, the IOM highlights the importance of developing tools which can help match demand and supply of labour, while at the same time fostering a balanced and responsible discourse at the European level which can counter the myths and misinformation associated with migrants. Finally, on return programmes, the IOM stresses that more work is needed to increase cooperation between Member States in order to strengthen existing partnerships and together with the Countries of origin and transit, create effective return policies, fostering a common European approach to returns which is inclusive and respects human rights in cooperating with the Countries on the southern shores of the Mediterranean.

Council of Europe

Founded on 5 May 1949, the Council of Europe (CoE, 47 Member States) is the first and most advanced system of promotion and protection of human rights at the regional level.

The Permanent Representative of Italy to the Council of Europe is H.E. Manuel Jacoangeli. The Italian experts holding institutional posts with the organisation include Gabriella Battaini-Dragoni who is Deputy Secretary General of the CoE and Claudia Luciani heads the Democratic Governance Directorate.

In 2014, Italy contributed an overall total of 36,094,389 euro to the activities of the Council of Europe for, of which 27,369,609 euro for the ordinary budget (in 2013 the total contribution was 36,457,297 euro, of which 27,346,590 for the ordinary budget). In 2014, voluntary contributions paid by Italy amounted to 583,980 euro (501,947.79 in 2013).

The following pages will illustrate, with reference to Italy, the activities of the Parliamentary Assembly and the Committee of Ministers; those of five bodies established by a treaty: the European Court of Human Rights, the Committee for the Prevention of Torture, the European Committee of Social Rights, the Advisory Committee on the Framework Convention for the Protection of National Minorities and the Group of Experts on Action against Trafficking in Human Beings; and of four bodies established by the Committee of Ministers: Commissioner for Human Rights, the European Commission against Racism and Intolerance, the European Commission for Democracy through Law and the Group of States against Corruption.

I. Parliamentary Assembly

In the Parliamentary Assembly of the Council of Europe (PACE), made up of delegations from the national Parliaments of the Member States of the CoE, 18 members of the Senate and the Chamber of Deputies sit for Italy; there are an equal number of alternate members.

The following are the members and the alternate members (a) of PACE in 2014: Ferdinando Aiello (a), Francesco Maria Amoruso (a), Anna Ascani (a), Deborah Bergamini, Anna Maria Bernini, Maria Teresa Bertuzzi, Alessandro Bratti, Nunzia Catalfo, Elena Centemero, Massimo Cervellini (a), Khalid Chaouki (a), Vannino Chiti, Eleonora Cimbro (a), Paolo Corsini, Celeste Costantino, Jonny Crosio, Luca D'Alessandro (a), Cristina De Pietro (a), Manlio Di Stefano, Claudio Fazzone (a), Giuseppe Galati (a), Adriana

Galgano (a), Adele Gambaro, Francesco Maria Giro, Sandro Gozi, Carlo Lucherini (a), Emanuela Munerato (a), Michele Nicoletti, Luis Alberto Orellana (a), Laura Puppato (a), Lia Quartapelle Procopio (a), Andrea Rigoni, Vincenzo Santangelo, Milena Santerini (a), Maria Edera Spadoni (a), Francesco Verducci (a).

The President of the Italian delegation is Michele Nicoletti, who is also one of the 20 Vice-Presidents of the Assembly. As to the role of Italian members of Parliament in the various parliamentary commissions, in 2014, Adele Gambaro was Chairperson of the Committee on Culture, Science, Education and Media; and Andrea Rigoni was Vice-Chairperson of the Sub-Committee on co-operation with non-European Countries of origin and transit (Committee on Migration, Refugees and Displaced Persons).

The Assembly is a forum for discussion on the main issues underlying the mandate of the Council of Europe and has an advisory role in relation to all international conventions developed in this context. It elects the judges of the European Court of Human Rights, the Commissioner for Human Rights, the Secretary-General of the Council and his Deputy.

In 2014, the PACE adopted two resolutions and two recommendations on the subject of managing migratory flows, in which there are frequent references to Italy.

Resolution 1999, entitled *The "left-to-die" boat: actions and reactions* was adopted on 24 June 2014 on the basis of the report presented to the Committee on Migration, Refugees and Displaced Persons (*Rapporteur*: Strik). It follows the earlier resolution 1872 from 2012, entitled *Lives lost in the Mediterranean Sea: Who is Responsible?* Referring to the recommendations contained in resolution 1872 (see *2013 Yearbook*, pp. 235–236) spurred on by the series of dramatic incidents which between 2012 and 2014 led to the deaths of migrants coming from the southern shores of the Mediterranean resolution 1999 reinforces its previous recommendations and urges the adoption of further measures designed to avoid any gaps in communications and responsibilities when it comes to saving people whose lives are in danger.

Specifically, on the question of rescue at sea and the loss of human life, the PACE recommends that member States adopt clear, binding and enforceable common standards, which are consistent with international maritime law and international human rights and refugee law, and that they extend the rules on surveillance of the maritime borders of the European Union to national operations performed outside the framework of Frontex. Furthermore, it asks states to commit to improving the recording and identification of deceased or missing migrants, ensuring their relatives have immediate access to this data and that family links are maintained or restored following rescue operations. With regard to criminalisation of irregular migration, the PACE recommends eliminating any factors which dissuade private vessels from taking aboard people they have rescued, including ending the threat to rescuers of prosecution on charges of aiding and abetting irregular immigration. In this field, the Assembly asks shipmasters and fishermen to comply with their international obligations to assist any migrant boats in distress and to report them to the relevant authorities. The Assembly also asks Member States to: end all push-back practices and ensure that practices of rescue are compliant with the right to seek international protection; ensure the credibility of any judicial proceeding concerning push-back incidents, publicly condemn all forms of collective expulsion and ensure that any accelerated asylum procedures to assess personal circumstances in the context of search and rescue operations respect a person's right to be protected from *refoulement*, ensure access to individual procedures to seek international protection and have access to an effective remedy against any decision regarding return. The PACE also urges that any bilateral readmission agreement should be drafted and implemented consistently with international human rights and refugee law standards and include effective safeguards of human rights.

The Assembly also focuses on the 2011 incident of the "left-to-die" boat on which *Rapporteur* Strik's work was based and which gave rise to resolutions 1872 and 1999. In this respect, the PACE asks member States to cooperate in providing answers to the outstanding questions and to grant the right to residence for the survivors whose applications for asylum or residence on humanitarian grounds are still pending. Moreover, with a view to encouraging the creation of safe legal migration channels and preventing irregular migrants, asylum seekers and refugees from undertaking hazardous journeys to Europe, and to sharing the responsibility for asylum seekers inside the European Union, the Assembly recommends that the European Union, encourage its Member States to increase resettlement quotas for persons in need of international protection and adopt a common approach to humanitarian visas and take further steps to harmonise asylum standards and procedures throughout the EU. The Assembly considers that Frontex should make the protection of human rights a priority issue and should also apply its own rules to migrant boats within the territorial waters of third Countries, and should establish an effective mechanism for individual complaints of violations of human rights. The Assembly recommends that NATO take into account possible movements of people in need of international protection in all military operations and that they ensure all vessels deployed on NATO missions are equipped appropriately. Finally, the Assembly makes some recommendations to the

International Maritime Organization (IMO), affirming that it should play a greater role in promoting a common and effective application of the legal framework of rescue at sea.

Together with this resolution, the Parliamentary Assembly adopted a recommendation to the Committee of Ministers on the same issue (No. 2046). In this, the Assembly calls on the CM to instruct the Steering Committee for Human Rights (CDDH) to carry out a feasibility study on a common approach to fill crucial legal gaps with regard to search and rescue in the Mediterranean Sea and, on the basis of this feasibility study, hold a thematic debate, to exchange best practices, offer solutions and find ways to facilitate agreements between States facing regular disputes on the co-ordination of rescue at sea and disembarkation. The Assembly also calls on the CM to adopt guidelines on how to comply with the *Hirsi Jamaa v. Italy* judgment of the ECtHR (see *2013 Yearbook*, p. 243) and to urge member States to refrain from using push-back practices (see *2013 Yearbook*, pp. 235–236).

Resolution 2000 entitled *The large-scale arrival of mixed migratory flows on Italian shores* was also adopted on June 24 following a report presented to the Committee on Migrants, Refugees and Displaced Persons (*Rapporteur*: Chope). Therein, the Parliamentary Assembly commends the efforts by the Italian authorities to respond to the emergencies, in recent years, in particular through the *Mare Nostrum* operation. However, the Assembly feels there is still a dire need to meet the structural challenges to make the Italian and European systems fit for purpose. On the one hand, adequate reception capacities, proper identification and subsequent control of the movements of the identified people, and swift and transparent processing of mixed migration flow data are requirements that need to be fully met by the Italian authorities. On the other hand, European authorities have to redefine their current immigration policies and regulations and support them with adequate financial and operational means. Recalling its *resolution 1820* from 2011 (see *2012 Yearbook*, p. 229), the Assembly stresses that all Council of Europe Member States and the European Union should display more solidarity with Italy and other European front-line Countries currently faced with arrivals of migrants from the southern Mediterranean. In return, Italy and the other European front-line Countries need to assure their partners that they will take all necessary measures to ensure that people who enter the Country irregularly do not continue their journey into other Member States of the Council of Europe. The Assembly then recommends that the Italian authorities implement a series of measures to deal with mixed migratory arrivals in Italy, including continuing to carry out their search and rescue operations in cooperation with other Member States and with

Frontex. The Assembly feels, moreover, that Italy should step up their efforts to arrest traffickers of migrants, and ensure that those arrested are brought to justice; set up a transparent system to identify migrants immediately after their arrival on shore and to establish swiftly who is entitled to asylum and international protection; ensure respect of the principles and provisions of the so-called "Dublin Regulation" as applicable to the Country of first arrival. In addition, as concerns the reception and detention centres, the Assembly asks Italy to ensure adequate reception conditions and medical assistance in accordance with relevant human rights and humanitarian standards, to set up an independent monitoring body to check that conditions and standards in reception and detention facilities are in compliance with international standards; to reduce the eighteen-month maximum period of time allowed for the detention of foreign nationals without any legal permit to stay, to step up the exchange of best practices; provide training courses for operating staff in the field of migration; facilitate access to the reception and detention centres by international organisations and non-governmental organisations (NGOs); and properly inform irregular migrants, asylum seekers and refugees of their rights and obligations. The Assembly welcomes the announcement by the Italian authorities of the priority to be given to the development of a common European response to arrivals of mixed migratory flows on Europe's southern shores during the upcoming Italian presidency of the Council of the European Union (July-December 2014). Finally, the Assembly calls on CoE Member States to provide financial and operational assistance to the *Mare Nostrum* operation in order to allow it to continue; to promote changes in the Eurodac regulations to facilitate the identification of migrants and asylum seekers through the use of DNA; to implement measures to make border control more effective and respond positively to the suggestion of the Italian Minister of the Interior that camps should be set up in North African Countries to process applications for international protection and thus intercept migrants before they set sail. The UNHCR should be given access to these camps to ensure that human rights are protected. CoE Member States should also take action to arrest and bring to justice those engaged in trafficking migrants and should contribute to strengthening the capacity of the Libyan coastguard, as requested by them.

In this case too, together with the resolution, the Parliamentary Assembly adopted a *recommendation* to the Committee of Ministers on the same subject (No. 2047), in which the Parliamentary Assembly recommends the CM make use of the expertise of the Council of Europe to help Member States to tackle the human rights challenges arising from the increase in mixed migration flows. In particular, the Assembly asks the CM to launch a reflection on how best to introduce a new international crime, whether or not defined as a crime against humanity, concerning instances where a person receives a financial benefit, directly or indirectly, for transporting people in a vessel which is unsafe for the purpose and which may endanger life or cause death or injury at sea. Furthermore, the CM should make it a priority to find solutions to the issues raised by the judgment of the ECtHR in the case of *Hirsi Jamaa* and make this judgment compatible with the established principle that each Member State of the CoE is entitled to maintain control over its own borders and to grant asylum or other forms of international protection to those who meet the necessary requirements to qualify. The Assembly concludes its recommendation with a request that the CM consider the need for an extensive review of the Dublin Regulation and its implementation.

As concerns the actions of the Italian members of the Parliamentary Assembly during 2014, two reports are highlighted which were submitted to the appropriate commissions and on the basis of which the PACE will adopt resolutions or recommendations in 2015: Paolo Corsini's report to the Culture, Science, Education and Media Committee on *Good governance and enhanced quality in education*, and the report by Andrea Rigoni to the Committee on Migration, Refugees and Displaced Persons (11 December) on *Democratic participation for migrant diasporas*.

II. Committee of Ministers

On the subject of human rights, the Committee of Ministers (CM) relies on the work of the Steering Committee for Human Rights, an intergovernmental body composed of representatives of the 47 Member States which performs, among other things, standard-setting and follow-up.

The CM adopts recommendations regarding the Member States and on matters for which a common policy is agreed upon – in accordance with its role in the implementation of the European Social Charter (art. 29) – with the aim of asking some States to adapt their laws and public policies with the provisions contained in the Charter. In addition, it is ultimately responsible for monitoring the Framework Convention on National Minorities (art. 26). In this context, it adopts specific resolutions by Country based on the opinions of the Advisory Committee of the Framework Convention.

With regard to its role in relation to the European Court of Human Rights, the CM has the function of supervising the execution of judgments of the Court, ensuring that Member States act in accordance with the rulings issued by the same. The Committee terminates each case by adopting a final resolution. Finally, the CM may apply to the Court for a ruling on issues related to difficulties of interpretation of the judgments of the Court itself which would impede their implementation and if it believes that a Member State is refusing to comply with a final judgment, it may refer the issue to the Court.

In 2014, the CM adopted 11 conclusive resolutions on the implementation of ECtHR judgments by Italy: CM/ResDH(2014)40 on the case *Šneersone and Kampanella* (v. Italy), CM/ResDH(2014)65 on the *Hamidovic* case, CM/ResDH(2014)71 on *Buffalo S.r.l. in Liquidation v. Italy*, CM/ResDH(2014)80 on the *Villa* case, CM/ResDH(2014)102 on the *Bracci and Majadallah* case, CM/ResDH(2014)116 on the *Errico* case, CM/ResDH(2014)214 on the *Giacomelli* case, CM/ResDH(2014)215 on *Saadi and 9 other cases*, CM/ResDH(2014)213 on *Attenà and 2 other cases*, CM/ResDH(2014)278 on the *Sarigiannis* case and CM/ResDH(2014)283 on the *Toniolo* case (v. San Marino and Italy).

With reference to monitoring the implementation of ECtHR judgments against Italy which are still ongoing, the Committee of Ministers adopted nine decisions in 2014.

On 7 March, during the 1193rd session, the CM adopted a decision on the *Sneersone and Kampanella* case (CM/Del/OJ/DH(2014)1193/10) (see *2012 Yearbook*, p. 356). Therein, the CM notes with satisfaction that the Rome Youth Court set aside the order for the return of the child in question to Italy. Furthermore, it welcomes the answer provided by the Italian authorities on the urgent individual measures requested by the ECtHR. On the basis of the information Italy provided in a December 2013 report on general measures, the Committee considered that these are capable of preventing violations similar to the one found in the present case and decided therefore to close their supervision of this case.

On 7 March 2014, during the 1193rd session, the CM also adopted a decision on the case *M.C. and others* (CM/Del/OJ/DH(2014)1193/12) (see *2014 Yearbook*, pp. 322–323). In this, the CM noted that this judgment highlighted a systemic problem stemming from the failure to pay the annual adjustment of the supplementary part of the allowance granted under law No. 201/1992 to victims of contamination during blood transfusions. The CM pointed out that the ECtHR had requested the Italian authorities to set a binding time limit, prior to 3 June 2014, by which the authorities undertook to ensure that all the persons subject to the violation found by the ECtHR received a rapid and effective satisfaction of their right to the adjustment of their annual allowance, and therefore called upon the authorities to urgently submit an action plan on the general measures envisaged for the implementation of the judgment and a schedule for their adoption. On 25 September, during the 1208th session, the CM adopted a further decision on this case (CM/Del/OJ/DH(2014)1208/8). In this, the Committee noted that, despite the Italian authorities having provided information on the steps taken to address the requests in the previous decision, the information did not include all the general measures required to settle the problem at the origin of the judgment and on the time-frame proposed for their adoption. In particular, the CM invited the Italian authorities to provide, before the next session, a time-frame for the adoption of an adequate legal framework to guarantee that the financing required for the annual adjustment of the allowance is automatically provided for in budget laws; and for the adoption and implementation of an action plan for liquidating the arrears corresponding to the adjustment of the allowances at the regional level. On 5 December, during the 1214th session, the CM adopted a further decision on this case (CM/Del/OJ/DH(2014)1214/10). In this, the Committee recalled that, following budget allocations provided to this end, the arrears due for the adjustment of the allowances to the beneficiaries were to be paid by the proposed date of 31 December 2014. Therefore it called on the Italian authorities to confirm to the CM, immediately after this deadline, that the payments have been made according to the time-frame indicated. The CM noted that the draft budget law for 2015 included the allocation at the regional level of the funds needed to pay the arrears due to beneficiaries and invited the authorities to provide details on the measures and the final time-frame for the payments as soon as the law was approved. In this respect, due also to some differences noted at the regional level as concerns the implementation of the right to adjustment of the allowance, the Committee underlined that in order to resolve the problem at source, it is necessary to put in place an adequate legal framework to guarantee the automatic annual adjustments, and hence called upon the Italian authorities to provide, by 1 April 2015, information on the concrete measures envisaged in connection with this, together with a time-frame for their adoption. The case will be examined again during the 1242nd session in December 2015.

Again on 7 March, the CM adopted a decision on the *Torreggiani and others* case and on the *Sulejmanovic* case (CM/Del/OJ/DH(2014)1193/11). In this, the CM recalled that in response to the pilot judgment of the ECtHR, in the *Torreggiani* case (see *2014 Yearbook*, pp. 319–322), by 27 May 2014 the Italian authorities were to put in place a remedy or a combination of remedies with preventive and compensatory effect affording adequate and sufficient redress in respect of violations of the ECHR stemming from overcrowding in Italian prisons. On this issue, the CM expressed concern that the remedy contemplated by the Italian authorities is only compensatory and only available in limited circumstances. Consequently, it strongly urged the Italian authorities to take concrete steps to satisfy the requirements of the above-mentioned pilot sentence by the established deadline, and to provide the CM with information on all developments in this area. The CM reiterated that this remedy will be effective only if underpinned by substantive measures to address overcrowding, and in this respect welcomes the measures recently adopted by Italy, including l.d. 78/2013 (converted into law 9 August 2013, No. 94) which increases eligibility for early release, maximises the use of house arrest, at the same time reducing the use of pre-trial detention and increasing eligibility for release on licence. However, the CM noted that further information is needed in order to fully understand the scale of overcrowding in Italian prisons and to assess the effectiveness of the measures adopted, in particular with reference to how the calculation of total prison capacity is made, how detention conditions are monitored, updated statistics on reduction of overcrowding and a breakdown of the impact of the various measures adopted to date, together with a timetable for measures planned. The monitoring of the execution of these judgments was continued in the 1201st session. On this occasion, on 6 June the CM adopted decision CM/Del/OJ/DH(2014)1201/10. In this, the Committee welcomed both the Italian authorities' commitment to resolving the problem of overcrowding in prisons, as confirmed by the continuing drop in the prison population in Italy and the average increase in living space per detainee and the establishment of a preventive remedy within the deadline set by the *Torreggiani* pilot judgment. In order to allow a full assessment of this remedy, the CM invited the authorities to provide further information on its implementation and monitoring. The Committee noted with interest the information on steps taken to establish a compensatory remedy, also required by the ECtHR judgment, which will provide for the possibility of a reduction of detainees' sentences, or pecuniary compensation for those who have already been released. On 5 December, in the course of the 1214th session, the CM adopted a further decision on these cases (CM/Del/OJ/DH(2014)1214/11). In it, the Committee noted the further progress made by the Italian authorities, considering also the conclusion of the ECtHR stating that, although the problem remains, the situation of prison overcrowding in Italy is less dramatic than before. Consequently, the CM recalled their request to provide updated information by 1st December 2015 in a consolidated action plan, with particular reference to the functioning of existing remedies, to the statistics proving a consolidation of the positive trend achieved and to the measures aimed at improving conditions of detention.

On 6 June 2014, in the course of its 1201st session, the CM adopted a decision on the *Centro Europa 7 s.r.l. and Di Stefano* case (CM/Del/OJ/DH(2014)1201/11) (see *2013 Yearbook*, pp. 361–363). In it the CM noted that this case concerns deficiencies in the legislative framework approved by Italy to reallocate frequencies in the television-broadcasting sector, which prevented the applicant company from operating in this sector between 1999 and 2009. The Committee noted with concern that the Italian authorities had not yet provided information on the measures adopted or envisaged for the execution of the judgment at hand, and urged them to provide it by 1 September 2014.

On 26 September, during the 1208th session, the CM adopted a decision on the *Hirsi Jamaa* case (CM/Del/OJ/DH(2014)1208/9) (see *2013 Yearbook*, p. 243). In it, the Committee noted with interest the efforts of the Italian authorities to obtain assurances that the applicants will not be subjected to treatment incompatible with article 3 of the ECHR in Libya, and they will not be arbitrarily repatriated to Somalia or Eritrea. They then invited the Italian Government to continue to ensure that these assurances are respected in practice. Furthermore, the Committee remarked on the firm assurances received from the Italian authorities that the clarifications provided by the ECtHR in the judgment at hand would be incorporated into Italian law and policy, to prevent there being any pushback operations in future, and expressed its interest in receiving information on the practical implementation measures taken, including instructions, guidelines and training, by 1 December 2014 so that the case could be closed.

On 30 April 2014, the CM adopted a resolution (CM/ResChS(2014)6) on the decision of the European Committee of Social Rights on the collective complaint lodged against Italy by the *International Planned Parenthood Federation – European Network* (IPPF EN) (87/2012), in which Italy was found to have violated art. 11 ESC-R and art. E ESC-R read in conjunction with art. 11(1) ESC-R (see this Part, Council of Europe, V). In this resolution, the CM takes note of the decision by the European Committee of Social Rights and of the information provided by the Italian Government on the issue during the follow-up stage after the decision; it also welcomed the commitment of the Italian authorities to bring the situation in question into conformity with the provisions of the European Social Charter (revised).

Finally, on 8 October, the CM adopted resolution CM/ResCSS(2014)10 on the application of the European Code of Social Security by Italy (period from 1 July 2012 to 30 June 2013). The Committee found that overall the law and practice in Italy continue to give full effect to the parts of the Code accepted by Italy. The Committee expressed concern, however, over the impact that austerity measures are having, with the reduction of social expenditure and of the capacity of the benefits provided by the social security system to stop the spread of poverty. Indeed, this system would not fulfil its role if it were not able to keep workers above the poverty line. On this issue, the CM invited the Italian Government to provide, in its next report, updated statistics on the dynamics of poverty in Italy, taking into account the active population, pensioners and children, and the minimum amount of social benefits in comparison with the established poverty line.

III. European Court of Human Rights

The European Court of Human Rights (ECtHR), the first international court specifically designed for the protection of human rights in a particular region of the world, guarantees the respect of the commitments laid down in the ECHR and its protocols by Member States of the CoE.

The Italian judge who now sits at the Court, specifically in the II Section, is Guido Raimondi, elected by the PACE in January 2010. Of the 708 members of the Registry, which provides legal and administrative support to the Court in exercising its functions, 25 are Italian.

The statistical data provided by the Court and updated to January 2015 shows that the total number of complaints pending against Italy amounts to 10,079, equivalent to about 14.4% of the total (only Ukraine has a worse record, with 13,350 pending complaints (19.1% of all cases). In 2014, the Court received 5,476 valid applications by individuals who complained of a violation of the rights enshrined in the ECHR by Italy (against 3,184 in 2013 and 3,249 in 2012). Over the same period, 9,625 applications were declared inadmissible or struck from the register; 44 led to a decision on the merits (relative to 144 applications), 39 of which identified at least one violation of the Convention; 1,762 applications were communicated to the State in view of a hearing on their merits. The ECtHR also received 31 requests for temporary measures pursuant to article 39 of the rules of Court, mostly regarding the suspension of deportation proceedings for as many applicants, of which only 1 was granted by the ECtHR.

An analysis of the Court's 2014 judgments concerning Italy is given in Part IV, Italy in the Case-law of the European Court of Human Rights.

IV. Committee for the Prevention of Torture

The European Committee for the Prevention of Torture and Inhuman or Degrading Treatment or Punishment (CPT) was established by the 1987 Convention of the same name, conceived as complementary to the regulations under art. 3 ECHR which sets forth an absolute ban on torture. The CPT is a body composed of independent experts and has one member for each State Party to the Convention for the Prevention of Torture. The members of the Committee are elected by the Committee of Ministers. The independent expert for Italy is Ms Andreana Esposito, who has held the position since 20 December 2011 and whose term expires in December 2015.

During 2014, the CPT visited 16 Countries: Albania, Armenia, Austria, Bulgaria, Denmark, the former Yugoslav Republic of Macedonia, the Russian Federation, Finland, Georgia, Ireland, the Netherlands (Caribbean part), the United Kingdom, the Czech Republic, Romania, Spain, Ukraine (2 visits). It published 16 reports concerning previous visits to the following member States: Cyprus, Croatia, Denmark, Estonia, Germany, Greece, Latvia, Lithuania, Montenegro, Poland, the United Kingdom, the Czech Republic, the Slovak Republic, San Marino, Ukraine and Hungary.

The CPT has visited Italy ten times overall, most recently being in 2012. A request for publication of the two most recent reports, concerning the ninth and tenth visits, was made by the Italian authorities on 19 November 2013. Each report was then published, together with the relevant observations made by the Italian Government on the issues raised therein (see *2014 Yearbook*, pp. 227–235).

V. European Committee of Social Rights

The European Committee of Social Rights (ECSR) was established pursuant to art. 25 of the European Social Charter of 1961 in order to determine whether the legislation and practice of States Parties comply with the provisions of the European Social Charter, its Protocols and the European Social Charter (revised) (ESC-R). Currently, the Committee is composed of 15 independent experts elected by the Committee of Ministers for a period of six years, renewable only once. Since 10 November 2010 Giuseppe Palmisano has been a part of the Committee, and will remain in office until 31 December 2016.

Italy ratified the European Social Charter in 1965 and the revised European Social Charter in 1999, accepting 97 of its 98 numbered paragraphs. The only provision not accepted is article 25 ESC-R, which protects the right of workers in the event of the insolvency of their employer. As of 2014, Italy has not presented the Committee with the first report on this provision of the revised Charter (and therefore only on art. 25). Between 1967 and 2014, the Government submitted 21 reports on the application of the Charter of 1961 and 13 on the application of the revised Charter.

The latest *conclusions* on Italy were published in January 2015. The document refers to the thirteenth report, requested by the Committee by 31 October 2013, but submitted on 19 December 2013. The 2014 *Conclusions* refer to the provisions of the Charter accepted by Italy in relation to the thematic group "labour rights" (arts. 2, 4, 5, 6, 21, 22, 26, 28 and 29 ESC-R). The reference period for the Committee's analysis goes from 1 January 2009 to 31 December 2013.

Overall, the final document of the Committee refers to the Italian situation in relation to 23 articles and numbered paragraphs of the revised Charter, providing 12 conclusions on compliance (occasionally requesting additional information to be submitted) and 7 on non-compliance. In relation to 4 provisions (arts. 2(2), 4(1), 4(3) and 6(3) ESC-R) the Committee postponed its assessment to the next report on this thematic group of articles, asking the Italian Government for the specific data needed to assess the status of implementation of the provisions examined. During the previous monitoring cycle on the "labour rights" thematic group (*2010 Conclusions*, see *2011 Yearbook*, pp. 216–220), the

Committee analysed 22 articles and paragraphs of the revised Charter (on that occasion, art. 4(3) ESC-R was analysed jointly with art. 20 ESC-R in the *2012 Conclusions*), identifying 12 instances of compliance and 10 of non-compliance.

Outline by paragraph of the 2014 Conclusions on Italy

Article of the ESC-R	Conclusions of conformity	Conclusions of non-conformity	Request for further information
Art. 2 (the right to just conditions of work)	para. 3 (annual holiday with pay) 5 (weekly rest period) 6 (written information on labour contract) 7 (night work)	para. 1 (reasonable working hours) 4 (elimination of risks in inherently dangerous or unhealthy occupations)	para. 2 (public holidays with pay)
art. 4 (the right to a fair remuneration)	para. 2 (overtime)	para. 4 (reasonable period of notice for termination of employment) 5 (limits to deductions from wages)	para. 1 (remuneration sufficient for a decent standard of living) 3 (non-discrimination in remuneration between men and women)
art. 5 (the right to organise)	*The whole article (just one paragraph long)*		
art. 6 (the right to bargain collectively)	Para. 1 (joint worker/ employer consultations) 2 (voluntary negotiations procedures)	para. 4 (collective action)	para. 3 (conciliation and arbitration)
art. 21 (the right to information and consultation)		*The whole article (just one paragraph long)*	
art. 22 (the right to take part in the determination and improvement of working conditions and working environment)		*The whole article (just one paragraph long)*	

Article of the ESC-R	Conclusions of conformity	Conclusions of non-conformity	Request for further information
art. 26 (the right to dignity at work)	para. 1 (sexual harassment) 2 (moral harassment)		
art. 28 (the right of workers' representatives to protection in the workplace and facilities to be accorded to them)	*The whole article (just one paragraph long)*		
art. 29 (the right to information and consultation in collective redundancy procedures)	*The whole article (just one paragraph long)*		

With reference to art. 2 ESC-R (the right to just conditions of work), the Committee concludes that the situation in Italy is in conformity with paras. 3 (annual holiday with pay) and 6 (information on the employment contract). The Committee also finds a situation of conformity as regards para. 5 (weekly rest period). However, it requests that the Italian Government submit full and detailed information in its next report on this group of rights, clarifying, in particular, whether there are circumstances under which a worker can be asked to work more than 12 consecutive days before enjoying two days of rest. Further information is also requested with reference to the situation of conformity identified relative to para. 7 (night work). In this area, the Committee requests clarification as to whether forms of regular consultation with workers' representatives on issues connected with night work are envisaged. On the other hand, the Italian situation is considered not compliant with para. 1 (reasonable working hours), considering that current legislation allows for a working week of up to 72 hours for workers aboard seagoing vessels, and with para. 4 (elimination of risks in inherently dangerous or unhealthy occupations). The Committee explains its conclusion stating that in Italy there is no adequate prevention policy regarding the risks in inherently dangerous or unhealthy occupations and that it has not been established that the right to just conditions of work with regard to the risks present in such occupations is guaranteed. With reference to para. 2 (public holidays with pay), the Committee expresses regret over the absence of data needed for a proper assessment of the situation and therefore requests the Italian authorities to submit more detailed information in their next report.

With reference to art. 4 ESC-R (the right to a fair remuneration), the Committee finds a situation of compliancy only as regards para. 2 (overtime). With reference to para. 4 (reasonable period of notice for termination of employment), the Italian situation is not considered compliant with the provisions of the Charter, because the notice period appears insufficient in the mechanical and food industry sectors and in some categories of the textiles sector. A conclusion of non-conformity is also expressed with reference to para. 5 (limits to deductions from wages), considering that once all the authorised tax deductions are made, the remuneration of the lowest-paid workers is insufficient to support them and their dependents. With reference to paras. 1 (remuneration sufficient for a decent standard of living) and 3 (non-discrimination in remuneration between men and women), the Committee decides to defer its assessment and to ask for more detailed information from the Italian Government. As concerns the former paragraph, updated data are requested on both the gross amounts of minimum salaries in low-paid sectors and the same salaries, net of social security and tax deductions; on the "pay guarantee component" for workers whose pay depends exclusively on national wage rates; and the coverage rate of national collective agreements in the private sector. Furthermore, the Committee requests information on the minimum wages paid in sectors which are not covered by such agreements, and in particular, in the informal economy. The next report from the Italian authorities is also to include more information on the use of the option offered by the Interconfederal Agreement of 28 June 2011 to derogate from the minimum wages provided for in national collective agreements by means of local or company-wide agreements and on the level of wages thus agreed upon. Finally, the Committee requests up-to-date information on the minimum wages paid to tenured civil servants and contractual staff in the civil service.

As concerns art. 5 ESC-R (the right to organise), the Committee concludes that the situation in Italy is compliant with the provisions of the revised Charter.

With reference to art. 6 ESC-R (the right to bargain collectively), the Committee considers that the situation in Italy is in conformity with para. 1 (joint consultation) and para. 2 (negotiation procedures). However, with reference to the first paragraph, the Committee requests that in its next report the Italian Government provide a detailed description of the legal framework concerning joint consultation and its implementation. As concerns para. 3 (conciliation and arbitration), the Committee decides to defer its conclusions while awaiting detailed information on conflicts of interest that generally concern the conclusion of a collective agreement or the modification, through collective bargaining, of conditions of work contained in existing collective agreements. On this point, the Committee adds that, in the absence of such information, there would be insufficient reason to conclude that the situation in Italy is in conformity with the provisions of the Charter in this regard. With reference to para. 4 (collective action), the Committee's conclusion is one of non-conformity because it was not established that the Government's power to issue injunctions which restrict strikes in essential public services falls within the limits of art. G ESC-R (restrictions) and because the requirement to notify employers of the duration of strikes in essential public services is considered excessive.

As concerns art. 21 ESC-R (the right of workers to be informed and consulted), the Committee finds there was a situation of non-conformity with the provisions of the revised Social Charter, since the rules on information and consultation of workers do not appear to apply to all categories of employees and there are no appropriate remedies for the employees themselves or their representatives.

The situation of Italy with regards to art. 22 ESC-R (the right of workers to take part in the determination and improvement of working conditions and working environment) is also considered one of non-conformity. According to the Committee, from their evaluation of the report, it does not appear that workers and their representatives have an effective right to take part in the decision-making process in activities concerning working conditions, work organisation and the working environment. Moreover, there appears to be no legal remedies for workers in the event of violation of their right to take part in the determination and improvement of their working conditions and working environment.

With reference to art. 26 ESC-R (right to dignity in the workplace), the Committee concludes that there is a situation of conformity with both para. 1 (sexual harassment), and para. 2 (moral harassment). However, on both counts the Committee requests the Italian Government to provide further information. On the former, Italy's next report should provide information on any specific preventive and awareness-raising measures, apart from those of a legislative nature, adopted by the national authorities to inform workers about sexual harassment and the remedies available, as well as information on the level of their social partners' involvement in the development of any such measures. The report is also to contain detailed information as to the amounts of compensation awarded in sexual harassment proceedings. Similarly, as concerns para. 2, the additional information requested is about the adoption of tangible measures to prevent moral harassment, the extent of involvement of social partners in them and the amounts of compensation awarded in proceedings for moral harassment.

The Committee concludes there is a situation of conformity with reference to art. 28 ESC-R (the right of workers' representatives to protection in the workplace and facilities to be accorded to them), but they still request an updated description be provided on the facilities granted to members of the Unitarian Trade Unions (RSU) in the light of the Committee's case law in this respect.

Finally, with reference to art. 29 ESC-R (the right to information and consultation in procedures of collective redundancy), the Committee concludes that the Italian situation is in conformity with the provisions of the Charter, although it asks the Government to provide further information on any existing sanctions if the employer fails to notify the workers' representatives about planned redundancies. They also ask whether there are any preventive measures to ensure that redundancies do not take effect before the obligation of the employer to inform and consult the workers' representatives has been fulfilled.

The next report to be submitted by Italy will be a simplified document dealing with the follow up given to decisions on the merit of collective complaints in which Italy was found to be in violation of the European Social Charter (revised). The report shall also contain the input requested by the Committee in its 2013 *Conclusions* (see *2014 Yearbook*, pp. 236–240) in respect of findings of non-conformity due to a repeated lack of information in the Government's reports.

As regards the collective complaints procedure established with the Additional Protocol of 1995, two complaints were lodged against Italy in 2014. The Committee has not yet made a decision as to whether they are admissible. The first one, (No. 105/2014), submitted by the trade union association (*Associazione Sindacale*) "*La Voce dei Giusti*", claims that Italian legislation prevents supply teachers falling into the so-called "third category" from having free access to specialised training courses to qualify as "support teachers for pupils with disabilities".

The second complaint (No. 113/2014) was lodged by the *Unione Italiana del Lavoro U.I.L. Scuola-Sicilia*. In it, the complainant trade union alleges that Italy is in violation of art. 12 ESC-R (the right to social security) and 25 ESC-R (the right of workers to the protection of their claims in the event of insolvency of their employer) in combination with the general clause of non-discrimination cited in art. E, because the Regulation on social protection (inter-ministerial decree 1 August 2014, No. 83473 excludes employees in the training sector in Sicily from the redundancy fund system (*Cassa integrazione guadagni in deroga*).

On 2 December 2014, the Committee declared the collective complaint lodged on 2 August 2013 (No. 102) by the *Associazione nazionale giudici di pace* (see *2014 Yearbook*, p. 242) admissible.

Furthermore, on 10 March 2014, the Committee published its decision on the merit (adopted on 10 September 2013) of the collective complaint lodged against Italy by the international NGO *International Planned Parenthood Federation European Network* (IPPF EN) (complaint No. 87/2012). In its complaint, the NGO requested the ECSR to declare art. 9 of law 194/1978, which governs the right of medical practitioners to conscientious objection in relation to terminations of pregnancy in violation of articles 11 ESC-R (the right to health) and E (non-discrimination) (see *2013 Yearbook*, p. 255). The Committee's decision recognised the violation of both the articles cited by the NGO in its complaint.

With reference to the violation of art. 11 ESC-R, the Committee concludes its evaluation with the observation that the appropriate authorities had failed to adopt the measures necessary to remove the potential causes of deterioration in the health of women who decide to terminate a pregnancy, specifically, by ensuring that, as per the provisions of para. 4, art. 9 of law 194/1978, abortions requested in accordance with the applicable regulations are always to be performed, even if there is a high number of doctors and other medical staff who practise conscientious objection.

As regards the violation of art. E, read in conjunction with art. 11, the Committee notes, as claimed by the complainant NGO, that as a result of the lack of non-objecting medical practitioners in a number of health facilities in Italy, women who choose to terminate their pregnancy are in some cases forced to move from one hospital to another or to travel abroad, in some cases with detriment to their health. Considering this, the fact that, as maintained by the Italian Government, abortion is a service the cost of which is fully covered by the National Health Service, is not a satisfactory answer. Indeed, the Committee considers that if a service is not available in practice, it is irrelevant whether it is free of charge or has to be paid for. Furthermore, women denied access to the service may incur substantial economic costs if they are obliged to travel in order to receive the treatment and care they require. In this context, the time factor is also crucial. Women who are denied access to abortion facilities in their home region might in effect be deprived of any chance to avail themselves of their legal right to access such services, as the limited timeframe for it could prevent their organising alternative solutions.

VI. Commissioner for Human Rights

The Commissioner for Human Rights is an independent non-judicial institution created by the Committee of Ministers' resolution (99)50 of 7 May 1999. Nils Muižnieks (Latvia) is the present Commissioner for Human Rights of the Council of Europe (in office since 1st April 2012).

In 2014 the Commissioner published reports concerning country visits carried out in: Albania, Denmark, Georgia, Montenegro, the Netherlands, Romania, Spain, Ukraine and Hungary, as well as that on a visit to Kiev, Moscow and Crimea in September 2014.

The Commissioner has visited Italy five times. The most recent visit was from 3–6 July 2012 and its purpose was to re-examine a series of critical issues, relating in particular to the excessive length of legal proceedings and to the protection of the rights of Roma, Sinti, migrants and asylum-seekers. The resulting report was published on 18 September 2012 (CommDH (2012)26) (see *2013 Yearbook*, pp. 256–260).

Among the other activities carried out by the Commissioner for Human Rights in 2014, it is worth mentioning the online publication of several *Human Rights Comments,* short articles from a blog where the Commissioner examines and briefly comments on the major current human rights issues in Europe. Over the year in question, 14 Comments were published (against 13 in 2012 and 10 in 2013). Five of these make explicit mention of the human rights situation in Italy:

Hate speech against women should be specifically tackled (6 March 2014); the Commissioner wrote of the proliferation of hate speech, particularly on the Internet, where there are daily calls for violence against women, sexual assault or rape and threats of murder. Among the examples given in the Comment, the Commissioner refers to the Speaker of the Italian Chamber of Deputies, Laura Boldrini, who has been the target of repeated incidents of hate speech since she was sworn in. The Commissioner mentions, for example, the recent occasion on which the leader of the Movimento 5 Stelle (5-Star Movement) posted a misogynistic comment against the Speaker on his blog, which was then used by their members of Parliament, generating violent comments and insults against her.

Youth human rights at risk during the crisis (6 March 2014); the Commissioner examines the issue of the impact of the economic crisis on youth unemployment, which is considered the most common pathology in many of the Countries implementing austerity measures. Not only are the social and economic rights of young people undermined, but so are their right to equal treatment, their right to participation and to a place in society. Suggesting a human rights-based approach instead of the current neglect of young people in discussions about the crisis, the Commissioner quotes some statistics on youth unemployment in Europe and on its socio-economic consequences. Specifically, the Commissioner mentions the increase in the number of so-called "NEETs" (young people who are not in employment, education or training), who make up over 20% of the population in Bulgaria, Ireland, Italy and Spain (and 15.4% in Europe as a whole), according to a report published by Eurofound in 2011.

Fighting violence against women must become a top priority (27 July 2014): Prompted by the imminent entry into force of the Istanbul Convention (1 August 2014), the Commissioner reflects on the urgency of solving the problem of violence against women, one of the most widespread human rights violations which takes place in Europe on a daily basis. The Commissioner backs up his reflections with some publicly available data: it is estimated that at least 12 women are killed daily in Europe through some form of gender-based violence. In 2013, available statistics showed that domestic violence caused the death of 121 women in France, 134 in Italy, 37 in Portugal and 54 in Spain. In the United Kingdom, between April 2012 and March 2013, 84 women were killed by their partner or ex-partner; in Azerbaijan, 83 women were killed and 98 committed suicide following domestic violence; according to the Turkish media, 214 women were killed in Turkey in 2013. The data available for the first six months of 2014 show that this alarming trend continues.

Preserving Europe's social model (13 October 2014); after remarking on the tragic situation of millions of people in Europe due to the continuing economic crisis, the Commissioner states that there is growing empirical evidence that economic development is more sustainable and societies are more resilient when social rights are protected. In this context, the Commissioner recommends renewed interest in the European Social Charter, through three steps: accepting all the provisions of the Charter, increasing the application of the collective complaints procedure through the European Committee on Social Rights, and an increased use of the Committee's jurisprudence by national courts. Italy is mentioned with reference to two judgments made in 2013 by the Court of Cassation and by the Lazio Regional Administrative Tribunal (TAR) which highlighted the normative obligations deriving from the European Social Charter. Italy is also mentioned with reference to some of the most significant results achieved by the Charter since its adoption in 1961. These include the introduction of legislation prohibiting children under 15 from working and strictly regulating the work of older children, increased protection for women as concerns maternity leave, work safety, access to health services and equal pay.

Protecting Children's Rights: Europe should do more (18 November 2014); on the 25th anniversary of the adoption of the United Nations Convention on the Rights of the Child, the Commissioner identified four key areas regarding the protection of children's rights in Europe where CoE member States could and should do more: 1) cease to detain migrant children, whether they are with their families or unaccompanied; 2) facilitate access to education for all children, especially those of Roma origin and children with disabilities, within mainstream schools; 3) resolve the persisting problem of statelessness among children; 4) solve the problem of poverty and the consequent reduction of opportunities to access health and social services, adequate housing and quality education. On the second point, the Commissioner mentions Italy as one of the Countries where the subject was raised and discussed during earlier visits.

Finally, the Commissioner's office published an *issue paper* worth mentioning, on *The rule of law on the Internet and in the wider digital world* (8 December 2014).

VII. European Commission against Racism and Intolerance

The European Commission against Racism and Intolerance (ECRI), established in 1993, is a monitoring body of the Council of Europe specialised in combating any form of racism, xenophobia, anti-semitism and intolerance in a human rights perspective. The members of ECRI remain in office for five years. They are selected for their moral authority and their recognised experience in the field of combating racism, xenophobia, anti-semitism and intolerance; they act on an individual basis and independently. The Commission is composed by a member and, if a Government so wishes, a deputy member for each State of the Council of Europe. The expert in respect of Italy during 2014 has been Vitaliano Esposito. The External Relations Officers of the Commission Secretariat, part of the Directorate-general Human Rights and the Rule of Law of the Council of Europe, is Stefano Valenti.

In the course of 2014, the Commission published the reports relative to the fifth monitoring cycle concerning Belgium, Bulgaria, Germany, Romania, Slovakia, Slovenia and Switzerland. In addition, the ECRI presented conclusions on its priority recommendations addressed to the following Countries in connection with reports from the fourth cycle which had already been published: Armenia, Azerbaijan, Bosnia and Herzegovina, Cyprus, Lithuania, Monaco, Serbia, Spain and Turkey. The ECRI also visited the following Countries in 2014 as part of the fifth monitoring cycle: Albania, Austria, Estonia, Greece, Poland, Norway, the Czech Republic and Hungary.

As concerns Italy specifically, the fourth monitoring cycle finished in February 2012, with the publication of report (CRI(2012)2), concerning the visit made by the Commission during the month of November 2010 (see *2012 Yearbook*, pp. 253–262). On 9 December 2014, the ECRI adopted conclusions on the implementation of the three recommendations subject to interim follow-up, selected from those made to Italy in connection with the fourth monitoring cycle.

The first recommendation requested the Italian authorities to take steps to enhance the role of the *Ufficio Nazionale Antidiscriminazione Razziale* (UNAR), in particular by a) formally extending its powers so that relevant legislation clearly covers cases of discrimination based on colour, language, religion, nationality and national origin in addition to ethnic origin and race; b) granting UNAR the right to bring legal proceedings; and c) ensuring that its full independence is secured both in law and in fact. In this regard, moreover, the ECRI requested that UNAR be provided with all the necessary human and financial resources, in the light of its workload.

The Commission concludes that the part of its recommendation that concerns the formal extension by law of UNAR's powers has not been implemented because, although on the one hand its work has continued to cover grounds of discrimination such as age, religion, disability, sexual orientation and gender identity, no legislation has been enacted to formally extend UNAR's powers. In addition, although the number of NGOs and trade unions entitled to represent victims of discrimination or bring cases has increased, the intervention of UNAR in discrimination cases remains limited to *amicus curiae* briefs. Again, according to the Commission, the placing of UNAR under the Department for Equal Opportunities, which is part of the Prime Minister's Office, the appointment of its Director by the Government and the fact that part of the staff is made up of people seconded from various Ministries make UNAR not compliant with the principle of independence from "equality bodies" as recommended by ECRI's General Policy recommendations Nos. 2 and 7. Concerning the last part of its request, the Commission concluded that UNAR does have sufficient manpower (25 members of staff) and financial resources (2 million euro from the ordinary budget and European funds) to meet its workload. Consequently, the ECRI concludes that this recommendation has been only partially implemented.

The second recommendation urged the Italian authorities to ensure that all Roma who may be evicted from their homes enjoy the full protection of the guarantees of international law in such matters. The Commission underlined that the persons concerned must be notified of any planned eviction and benefit from appropriate legal protection. Further, Roma must not be evicted without the possibility of being rehoused in decent accommodation, even if they may stay in the Country only for limited periods of time.

After recalling that the case law of the Council of State had in 2011 judged unlawful the "state of emergency in relation to nomad settlements" declared in three Italian regions, the Commission took note of the positive developments since the publication of its last report. In particular, the ECRI recognises the importance of the adoption, in February 2012, of the *National Strategy for the Inclusion of Roma, Sinti and Traveller Communities*, of which one area is specifically devoted to the issue of access to housing; the publication in Italian of a summary of the *UN Basic Principles and Guidelines on Development-based Evictions and Displacement*, and the introduction into the Senate in June 2013 of bill (d.d.l) No. 770 (Norms for the protection of and equal opportunities for Roma and Sinti minorities), which contains important guarantees concerning evictions and social housing for Roma, in line with international standards. However, the Commission underlines the difficulty it has in gauging the impact of recent developments, in the absence of updated information as to the overall level of their implementation. Moreover, the aforementioned bill is still at the initial stage of the legislative process. ECRI has also been informed by some NGOs that evictions of Roma and Sinti continued in 2012, 2013 and 2014, often without respecting the necessary protective measures and without supplying alternative accommodation. The Commission concludes, therefore, that the policy and legislative developments constitute the beginning of a positive but slow process, aimed at changing the way in which the Italian authorities interact with the Roma communities and in particular, with how the issue of evictions is approached. Consequently, the ECRI considers its recommendation partly implemented.

The third and last recommendation asked the Italian authorities to take all necessary steps to ensure that the principle of *non-refoulement* is fully respected. In particular, the Commission urged the Government to bring their pushback policy, adopted in 2009, to an immediate and permanent end, emphasising the need to guarantee access to international protection procedures in full accordance with the 1951 Geneva Convention, the ECHR and the relevant European Union directives.

In this area, the ECRI recognises and welcomes the positive developments which have taken place, showing a significant change from the previous practice of pushing back all boats of migrants intercepted on the open sea between Italy and Libya. The Commission highlights the fact that the Italian authorities have on several occasions officially stated that this policy has been abandoned and recognised the assistance given by the Italian navy patrols through operation *Mare Nostrum*, which is credited with the rescue of about 70,000 migrants between October 2013 and July 2014. The *Praesidium* project is also mentioned as an effective example of co-operation between Government authorities, NGOs and international organisations for the identification of the different needs of migrants and asylum seekers. However, some NGOs have reported to the ECRI that information on the possibility of presenting asylum requests is still not provided systematically to all migrants: the prompt identification of migrants in need of international protection, and issues concerning legal counselling are still specific problem areas around access to asylum procedures, with particular reference to implementation procedures for the readmission agreements signed by Italy with Greece, Libya, Egypt, Tunisia and Algeria. The Commission acknowledges, however, that the Italian authorities have made significant efforts to align domestic legislation with European standards on asylum-related matters. With this in mind, it recalls that by July 2015, Italy will have to further adapt current legislation to recent EU directives on a common system of reception and procedures for granting international protection (Nos. 2013/32/EU e 2013/33/EU). According to the ECRI, the reforms required by the EU could constitute an opportunity to draft a consolidated text comprising all existing provisions on asylum, which continue to remain spread across different national laws, making some of the main rules unclear and thus hindering their application, and finally, affecting access to asylum procedures in full accordance with international standards. Consequently, in this case too, ECRI considers its recommendation partly implemented.

ECRI's next contact visit to Italy, to prepare for the fifth monitoring cycle report, will take place from 14–18 September 2015.

VIII. Advisory Committee on the Framework Convention for the Protection of National Minorities

The Committee is a monitoring body instituted pursuant to art. 26 of the Council of Europe Framework Convention for the Protection of National Minorities. It is composed of 18 independent experts with recognised expertise in the field of the protection of national minorities. They shall serve on the Committee in their individual capacity, for a period of four years. Since 2012 Italian expert, Francesco Palermo, has been a member of the Advisory Committee.

The Advisory Committee serves to assist the CM in evaluating the implementation of the Framework-Convention in States Parties, through the examination of periodic State Reports. The results of this evaluation are expressed in a detailed opinion which serves as a basis for the preparation of the CMs conclusive resolutions on the Country in question. Follow-up meetings are generally organised by the Advisory Committee with a view to bringing together all actors – governmental and non-governmental – interested in the implementation of the Convention and to examine ways of implementing the results of the monitoring procedure.

In 2014, as part of the respective monitoring cycles, the Advisory Committee of the Framework Convention carried out visits to the following Countries: Cyprus, Denmark, Estonia, the Slovak Republic, Spain and Ukraine; it adopted, but has not yet published, in line with the principle of confidentiality, opinions on Portugal, the Slovak Republic and Spain and published opinions on Bulgaria, Denmark and Liechtenstein.

Italy has participated in three full monitoring cycles of the Framework-Convention (see *2013 Yearbook*, p. 264). On 12 March 2014, the Italian Government submitted a new report to the Consultative Committee on measures adopted to protect national minorities, with special attention devoted to the priority recommendations received during the third cycle (see *2012 Yearbook*, pp. 264–268 for the opinion of the Consultative

Committee and *2013 Yearbook*, pp. 244–246 for the final resolution of the CM). The new report begins the fourth monitoring cycle of the Framework Convention for Italy.

The information provided in the new report provides an update on the Italian situation in the light of the articles of the Framework Convention. In general, the Italian authorities highlight the fact that the domestic legal framework includes in the criminal code a specific form of protection to counter racist and xenophobic behaviour, including expressing thoughts aiming to disseminate ideas based on racial or ethnic superiority or hate, as well as inciting others to commit acts of discrimination or violence on grounds of race, ethnic origin or religion. Furthermore, under current law, all cases of racial discrimination or hate are considered aggravating circumstances. There are also awareness-raising measures involving all layers of society to prevent cases of discrimination, intolerance, racism and xenophobia.

The report highlights the many initiatives ongoing in Italy to enhance the protection and promotion of the rights of linguistic minorities, particularly as concerns regional legislation for the promotion of local languages and cultures, which have developed considerably. In this respect, the report mentions that the Department of Regional Affairs, Self-government and Sports under the Prime Minister's Office has recently approved the proposal of the Technical Advisory Committee for the Protection of Historic Linguistic Minorities and consequently allocated the resources required to set up or continue the operations of the linguistic help desks, which are a tangible point of contact between the minority language speakers and the Public Administration.

As concerns the protection of linguistic minorities, especially the Slovenian ones, one of the issues on which the previous monitoring cycle had focused particularly, the report highlights the fact that despite the economic crisis and consequent budget cuts, the allocations in favour of linguistic minorities have gradually increased, to support the activities prescribed by law 15 December 1999, No. 482 (Regulations for the protection of historic linguistic minorities) and law 23 February 2001, No. 38 (Regulations for the protection of the Slovenian linguistic minority in Friuli-Venezia Giulia). With reference to the cooperation provided for in the latter law, a permanent institutional panel has been set up at the Ministry of the Interior (ministerial decree dated 4 July 2012) charged with studying the details of the issues which are most important to the Slovenian minority. The authorities also emphasise in their report that the existing *ad hoc* legislative instruments in favour of the linguistic minorities in the Valle d'Aosta/Vallée d'Aoste, Friuli Venezia Giulia, Sardinia and Trentino Alto Adige/Südtirol regions continue to provide significant supplements to the State funds for linguistic minorities and encourage comprehensive promotion of the languages and cultures of their respective minorities. As concerns the implementation of the aforementioned laws, the Italian Government's assessment in the report is positive and is based particularly on the data relative to the increased demand for the use of the minority languages, the greater awareness of their value and the many initiatives taken to preserve their written linguistic heritage.

As to the protection of the Roma and Sinti minorities, which were also the object of a number of recommendations during the previous monitoring cycle, the Italian authorities reaffirm that there are no specific laws recognising and protecting the members of these communities living in Italy as belonging to linguistic minorities, since they do not have a stable connection with the territory and Italian legislation only recognises and protects the linguistic minorities which have historically established themselves in a certain, identifiable area. Despite the absence of this requirement, the Italian authorities do however support the Roma and Sinti communities with *ad hoc* programmes concerning education, housing, employment opportunities and healthcare services. On this subject, the report gives an update on the current stage of implementation of the National Strategy for the inclusion of the members of these communities in the four areas of intervention mentioned, in particular enhancing access to schooling for children and creating employment opportunities. The report also stresses the need for concerted efforts from all European Countries in this area, in order to make actions to combat the exclusion of Roma more effective, an objective which the Italian Government has defined as a priority.

IX. European Commission for Democracy through Law

The Commission, also known as the *Venice Commission*, is the Council of Europe's advisory body on constitutional issues; it was established in 1990 and receives financial support by a law of the Region of Veneto.

> The Commission is composed of independent experts with extensive experience in the area of democratic institutions or excellence in the legal and political domains. Members are designated for four years by the participating Countries which, as well as the 47 Member States of the CoE, include Algeria, Brazil, Chile, South Korea, Israel, Kazakhstan, Kyrgyzstan, Morocco, Mexico, Peru, United States and Tunisia. Belarus is an associate member, while Argentina, Canada, Japan, the Holy See and Uruguay participate in the work of the Commission as observer Countries. The European Commission, Palestinian National Authority and South Africa have a special co-operation status.

Since 2009, Gianni Buquicchio has been the President of the *Venice Commission*. There are two further substitute members for Italy in the Commission: Sergio Bartole and Guido Neppi Modona.

One of the Commission's activities is the production of reports on topics within its mandate and promoting seminars on specific Countries and issues. Moreover, on request from the Parliamentary Assembly of the Council of Europe, it can adopt opinions on specific issues.

In the course of 2014, the *Venice Commission* adopted *36 opinions* relating to the adoption of laws or bills of constitutional importance in the following Countries: Albania, Armenia (2), Azerbaijan, the former Yugoslav Republic of Macedonia, the Russian Federation, Georgia (7), Kyrgyzstan (3), Malta, Montenegro (5), Poland, the Republic of Moldova (4), the Slovak Republic, Serbia (3), Tajikistan, and Ukraine (4).

The most recent activity concerning Italy dates from 7 December 2013, when the Commission adopted an opinion on the conformity of Italian legislation with international standards on defamation (CDL-AD(2013)038) (see *2014 Yearbook*, pp. 248–250).

X. Group of Experts on Action against Trafficking in Human Beings

The Group of Experts (GRETA) was established pursuant to art. 36 of the Council of Europe Convention on Action against Trafficking in Human Beings and is charged, together with a Committee made up of the representatives in the CM of the States Parties to the Convention (Committee of the Parties), with monitoring the implementation of the obligations contained in the Convention.

The Group is made up of 15 independent experts known for their recognised competence in the fields of human rights, assistance and protection of victims of trafficking in human beings or having professional experience in the areas covered by the Convention. The monitoring procedure is divided into 4-year rounds. The Group of Experts starts the dialogue with the Party under evaluation by sending out a questionnaire, which may be followed by requests for further information. If the Group of Experts deems it necessary, additional information may be requested from civil society organisations or gathered by organising a visit to the Country concerned. The draft report is sent to the relevant government for comments. On receiving them, GRETA prepares its final report and conclusions and transmits it to the Country concerned and to the Committee of the Parties, which can adopt recommendations on the basis of the contents of the document. Each Party to the Convention appoints a contact person to co-operate with the Group of Experts. The contact person for Italy is Michele Palma from the Equal Opportunities Department under the Prime Minister's Office.

During the year under review, the Group of Experts published its first reports assessing the state of implementation of the Istanbul Convention in Andorra,

Azerbaijan, Iceland, Italy, Luxemburg, the Netherlands, San Marino, Serbia, Slovenia, Sweden, the former Yugoslav Republic of Macedonia and Ukraine.

The Group of Experts' first report on Italy (GRETA(2014)18) was adopted in its final version on 4 July 2014, together with the comments the Italian authorities submitted in response to the initial recommendations made by GRETA. The first evaluation round on the implementation of the Convention by Italy was concluded by the recommendation of the Committee of Parties (CP(2014)16), adopted on 5 December, which substantially confirmed the Group of Experts' observations.

GRETA's report is based on an analysis of the replies to the initial questionnaire, submitted by the Italian Government on 4 June 2013 and on the information collected during the Group of Experts' visit to Italy from 2 to 6 December of that same year. In the course of their visit, the delegation held meetings with officials from the Department for Equal Opportunities and other Ministries (of the Interior, Justice, Labour and Social Policies, Foreign Affairs), and also visited four regions (Abruzzi, Apulia, Campania and Veneto). The delegation met with NGOs, religious organisations, trade unions and lawyers. It also held meetings with representatives of the International Organisation for Migration (IOM) and of the UNHCR. During their visit, GRETA visited shelters for victims of trafficking in Adelfia, Martinsicuro (TE) and Padua, a drop-in centre in Lecce and the CIE in Ponte Galeria.

In its evaluation, GRETA recognises that Italy has adopted a number of measures to combat human trafficking, dating back to the lgs.d. 286 from 1998 and including the recent adoption of lgs.d. 24/2014 which incorporates directive 2011/36/EU and amends Italian criminal law on trafficking and slavery, and provides for the adoption of a national anti-trafficking action plan and setting up a State compensation fund for victims of these crimes. Despite recognising the role played by the Department for Equal Opportunities in the implementation of anti-trafficking policies, GRETA expresses concern over the absence of a national coordination structure involving all relevant public bodies and NGOs, and consequently urges the Italian authorities to strengthen the institutional framework dealing with these issues, with particular emphasis on the involvement of civil society when adopting public policies against trafficking.

The Group of Experts notes that despite the provisions of the aforementioned legislative degree, no national plan has yet been adopted and therefore requested the authorities to take urgent steps for its approval. Moreover, it notes that although Italy has longstanding experience in tackling trafficking for the purpose of sexual exploitation, more attention should be paid to trafficking for labour exploitation, which has been on the rise. In this respect, the criminalisation of irregular migration has had negative consequences for victims of trafficking. The Group of Experts expresses concern over reports showing that victims of trafficking are sometimes found guilty of other criminal offences, particularly in connection with illegal immigration. GRETA also focuses on the trafficking of children and called upon the Italian authorities to increase prevention and protection measures addressing the particular vulnerability of children, as well as reducing the vulnerability of migrants to trafficking. As concerns information, the Group of Experts recognises the importance of awareness-raising campaigns run at the local level, but laments the absence of initiatives at the national level which include education in schools.

Another issue on which GRETA urges the Italian authorities to act is that of increasing their efforts to discourage demand as a root cause of human trafficking, bearing in mind that measures adopted should be balanced and not lead to the criminalisation of victims. Vulnerable groups, particularly people of Roma and Sinti origin, migrants without proper papers and asylum seekers can be helped by strengthening the aspect of prevention through socio-economic empowerment measures in their favour.

A further aspect on which the Group of Experts makes critical observations is the absence of guidelines or procedures at the national level for the identification of victims of trafficking in Italy, in addition to the memoranda of understanding which exist at the local level. Consequently, the Italian authorities are urged to ensure that all victims of trafficking are identified and can enjoy the support and protection provided for in the CoE Convention. Hence, Italy should strengthen multi-agency involvement in victim identification by introducing a clear national referral mechanism, to provide front-line staff in the combating of trafficking (immigration bureau officials, police, social workers, lawyers, NGO members, etc.) appropriate training to ensure the adoption of a proactive and harmonised approach to detecting and identifying victims, particularly unaccompanied minors, irregular migrants and asylum seekers.

GRETA notes that the provision of assistance to victims of trafficking is organised at the local level by civil society organisations, in co-operation with local or regional authorities, using funds mainly from the national budget. Although GRETA praises the work carried out by these organisations highly, it calls upon the Italian authorities to make sure that assistance is not made conditional on the victims' co-operating in investigations and criminal proceedings. Moreover, the Group of Experts recommends assistance projects be implemented and shelters for child victims of trafficking be established, taking into account the special needs and the best interests of the child, and asks the authorities to ensure that there is room in the shelters for male victims too.

On the legislative aspect, GRETA observes that the recovery and reflection period covered in art. 13 of the Convention is not expressly contemplated in Italian law and therefore requests the authorities to amend the law on this point, emphasising that this period must not be conditional on victims' cooperation with the police, and that victims cannot be expelled during this period. The Group of Experts welcomes the possibility for victims of trafficking to be granted a residence permit both on the basis of their personal situation and on their cooperation with the authorities. To this end, the authorities are requested to ensure that victims can actually benefit from the right to obtain a renewable residence permit regardless of the type of exploitation to which they have been subjected.

GRETA urges the Italian authorities to take steps to facilitate and ensure effective access to compensation and legal assistance for victims of trafficking, in particular by informing them of this right in a language they understand. In this area, the Italian authorities are also invited to reconsider whether the maximum compensation provided for by the State fund (euro 1,500) is proportionate to the serious violations of human rights suffered by victims of trafficking and the complex bureaucratic procedures they have to follow in order to obtain compensation.

As concerns the return of trafficked persons to their Country of origin, GRETA urges the Italian authorities to adopt a clear legal and policy framework protecting the rights, safety and dignity of the people involved. This implies informing victims about available "return/repatriation" programmes, protecting them from the risk of becoming victims of trafficking again and ensuring compliance with their *non-refoulement* obligation.

Further causes of concern to the Group of Experts are the low conviction rates for trafficking in Italy. On this issue, they urge the Italian authorities to increase their efforts to ensure that crimes connected with trafficking for all types of exploitation are investigated and prosecuted promptly and effectively, with sentences that are both proportionate and act as deterrents. Full use of all available measures should be made to protect victims and witnesses of trafficking and to prevent their intimidation during the investigation and during and after court proceedings.

Out of the recommendations made by GRETA to bring the actions against trafficking in Italy in fully line with the standards of the Convention, the following are highlighted:

- ensure that the definition of trafficking of human beings in the criminal code includes "receipt" of persons as one of the material behaviours which constitute the crime of trafficking and "abduction" as one of the possible means of procuring victims;
- establish an independent National Rapporteur to monitor the anti-trafficking activities carried out by State institutions;

- state clearly that the consent of a victim to being exploited is irrelevant; GRETA considers that this could improve the effectiveness of anti-trafficking measures and give the victims greater confidence in making reports to NGOs and public authorities;
- further develop a comprehensive and coherent statistical system on trafficking of human beings based on reliable information provided by the main actors combating trafficking and constructed in line with international standards on the protection of personal data;
- continue research on issues connected with trafficking, both as a source of information on the impact of current public policies and with a view to the future, particularly as regards trafficking for labour exploitation, internal trafficking, domestic slavery and child trafficking;
- continue efforts to promote international co-operation in combating trafficking, with particular reference to further opportunities for co-operation with governmental and non-governmental actors in the Countries of origin and transit with a view to prosecuting offenders, assisting victims and preventing the trafficking of human beings, and to awareness-raising and prevention activities in the main Countries of origin of the victims of trafficking found in Italy;
- consider adopting legislative and other measures to criminalise the use of services provided by victims of trafficking with the knowledge that the person providing them is a victim;
- make further efforts to detect and prevent the trafficking of human beings through border control measures.

XI. Group of States against Corruption

The Group of States against Corruption (GRECO) was established in 1999 in order to monitor the compliance of CoE Member States with the anti-corruption standards and rules of the Organisation. These benchmarks are contained in the legal instruments adopted by the Council of Europe on actions against corruption – the Criminal Law Convention on Corruption with its Additional Protocol and the Civil Law Convention on Corruption – as well as the recommendations and resolutions adopted by the Committee of Ministers (in particular resolution (97)24 on the 20 Guiding Principles for the Fight against Corruption).

The Group comprises 49 States (47 Member States of the CoE plus Belarus and the United States). GRECO's main objective is to improve the capacity of its members to fight corruption by monitoring their compliance with Council of Europe anti-corruption standards through a dynamic process of mutual evaluation and peer pressure. It helps to identify shortcomings in national anti-corruption policies, prompting the necessary legislative, institutional and practical reforms. GRECO also provides a platform for sharing best practices in the prevention and detection of corruption. GRECO's monitoring system occurs in periodical cycles and involves: a "horizontal" evaluation procedure in which all members are active and ends with the preparation of recommendations on the legislative and institutional reforms required; there is then a separate "compliance" procedure to assess the measures taken by the Member States to implement these recommendations.

Italy has been a member of GRECO since 30 June 2007 and has undergone three evaluation rounds to date. The first two rounds were dealt with jointly and concluded in 2013 with the adoption by the Group of States of an addendum to the compliance report (see *2014 Yearbook*, p. 253).

On 23 June 2014, on the basis of information previously provided by the Italian Government, GRECO adopted the compliance report (Greco RC-III (2014) 9E) on the measures adopted by the Italian authorities to implement the 16 recommendations received in the course of the third monitoring round regarding two themes: I) incriminations for corruption and II) transparency of party funding. Specifically, GRECO had made 9 recommendations on the first theme and 7 on the second (see *2013 Yearbook*, pp. 267–271).

The Group of States concludes that Italy has implemented or dealt in a satisfactory manner with only 4 out of the 16 recommendations contained in the evaluation report of the third round. Of the others, 10 have been implemented in part, whereas 2 have not been implemented. Referring specifically to the theme of incriminations, 1 recommendation has been satisfactorily implemented, 6 partially implemented and 2 not implemented; on the theme of transparency of party funding, 3 recommendations have been satisfactorily implemented and 4 partially implemented.

With regard to incriminations, the Group of States welcomes Italy's ratification of the Council of Europe's Criminal Law Convention (in June 2013) and its entry into force in Italy as of 1st October 2013. This result, achieved as a consequence of sweeping anti-corruption legal reforms, is however considered only partial, since Italy submitted the maximum allowable number of reservations when depositing the instrument of ratification and has not yet begun the approval process for the Optional Protocol to this Convention, as recommended by GRECO in its 2013 report. The ongoing legislative reforms have brought Italian legislation closer to the requirements of the aforementioned Convention. At the same time, however, GRECO finds it disappointing and difficult to understand the fact that these efforts have not brought the Italian situation to a higher degree of compliance with the provisions of said Convention. For example, according to the evaluation made in the report in question, further measures are required to enlarge the scope of jurisdiction for corruption offences and to broaden the legislation criminalising bribery of foreign and international officials. Further measures are also required on incrimination for bribery in the private sector and on trading in influence.

GRECO notes that some obligations under the Convention to deal with shortcomings of domestic legislation are reduced by the reservations made by the Italian Government at the time the instrument of ratification of the Criminal Law Convention on Corruption was deposited. Nonetheless, in line with GRECO's established practice in respect of member States which have deposited reservations, the Italian authorities are asked to reconsider the recommendations they have not implemented on the first theme and to amend the relevant legislation so as to make it fully compliant with the pertinent provisions of the Convention, that is, withdrawing or not renewing the reservations deposited at the time of ratification (arts. 5–8, 12 and 17 of the Convention).

As concerns the second theme (transparency of party funding), GRECO recognises that Italy has undertaken reforms mainly through two laws: l. 6 July 2012, No. 96 and l. 21 February 2014, No. 13, which amended a number of laws and regulations in the area of combating corruption. For example, Italy has put in place regulations concerning the legal status of political parties, defined election periods and aligned the transparency of elections to the European Parliament with the regulations governing domestic elections. Moreover, Italy has plans to gradually move away from public financing of parties, towards a funding system based on voluntary contributions from private citizens. Thresholds of donations above which the identity of donors must be disclosed have been considerably lowered and the parties with a certain level of support will have to be inspected by independent auditing bodies. In addition, pursuant to l. 13/2014, a new independent auditing body has been established to monitor the annual accounts of political parties: the Committee for the Transparency and Control of Financial Statements of Parties and Political Movements. Italy has also improved the range of sanctions available for offences in this area.

GRECO recognises that the effectiveness of these measures will have to be ascertained once the system has been in place for some time. In this area, GRECO observes that a number of important issues have not yet been resolved, including those relative to the overall co-ordination of the monitoring, the banning of donations from donors whose identity is not known and increased transparency of the financing of candidates in election campaigns.

To sum up, GRECO recognises that Italy had to some degree addressed a majority of the recommendations made on Theme I in the third evaluation round (incriminations), attaining a greater level of compliance with the provisions of the Criminal Law Convention on Corruption than that found at the time the evaluation report was adopted in 2012. Nonetheless, a significant number of recommendations have been only partly implemented, reflecting the many reservations Italy made on the Convention at the time of ratifying it. The amendments to legislation concerning transparency of party funding (Theme II of the third round of evaluation) have, on the other hand, improved the level of compliance of the Italian legislative framework with the principles of the recommendation of the Committee of Ministers on common rules against corruption in the funding of political parties and election campaigns (Rec(2003)4). In the light of its analysis, GRECO concludes that Italy's current low level of conformity with the recommendations received during the third evaluation round cannot be considered "globally unsatisfactory". Consequently, the Italian Delegation at GRECO is invited to submit additional information, by 31 December 2015, regarding the implementation of the most important recommendations to date not implemented or partly implemented.

European Union

I. European Parliament

The European Parliament (EP), together with the Commission and the Council of the European Union, exercises a fundamental role in the promotion and protection of human rights within the overall framework of EU activities.

Among the permanent EP Committees prominent in human rights issues the following are highlighted: the Subcommittee on Human Rights (Italian members: Ignazio Corrao and Pier Antonio Panzeri) within the Committee on Foreign Affairs (Italian members: Goffredo Maria Bettini, Mario Borghezio, Fabio Massimo Castaldo, Lorenzo Cesa and Pier Antonio Panzeri).

Other Committees with significant involvement in human rights issues are the Committee on Civil Liberties, Justice and Home Affairs (Italian members: Caterina Chinnici, Ignazio Corrao, Laura Ferrara, Lorenzo Fontana, Kashetu Kyenge, Barbara Matera and Alessandra Mussolini); the Committee on Constitutional Affairs (Vice Chair: Barbara Spinelli; other Italian members: Mercedes Bresso and Fabio Massimo Castaldo); the Committee on Legal Affairs (Italian member: Laura Ferrara), the Committee on Employment and Social Affairs (Italian members: Laura Agea, Tiziana Beghin, Brando Benifei, Mara Bizzotto and Elena Gentile), the Committee on the Environment, Public Health and Food Safety (Chair: Giovanni La Via; other Italian members: Marco Affronte, Simona Bonafè, Alberto Cirio, Eleonora Evi, Elisabetta Gardini, Enrico Gasbarra, Massimo Paolucci and Piernicola Pedicini); the Committee on Development (Italian members: Ignazio Corrao and Elly Schlein); the Committee on Women's Rights and Gender Equality (Vice-Chair: Barbara Matera; other Italian members: Daniela Aiuto) and the Committee on Petitions, of which more below (all names reported are relevant to the VIII legislature, 2014–2019).

In 2014, the Sacharov Prize for Freedom of Thought was awarded to Denis Mukwege, a doctor from the Democratic Republic of Congo in recognition of his fight to defend rights, in particular those of women.

Among the European Parliament acts adopted in 2014 containing specific references to Italy, the following are recalled: the 12 March 2014 resolution on the 2013 EU Citizenship Report, in which the Parliament calls upon all Member States which have not yet a national Ombudsman (Italy and Germany) to meet the expectations of all European citizens by proceeding to appoint an incumbent to this post (P7_TA(2014)0233);

the resolution of 18 September 2014 on the situation in Libya, in which the European Parliament expresses deep concern at the arrival on the Italian and Maltese shores of an unprecedented number of asylum seekers and irregular migrants, many of whom departed from Libya and calls upon the EU and member States to effectively help and support Italy in its laudable efforts to save lives and to tackle the spiralling migration flows from North Africa, particularly from Libya (P8_TA(2014)0028); and the resolution dated 17 December 2014 on the situation in the Mediterranean and the need for a holistic EU approach to migration, in which the Parliament recalls that the *Mare Nostrum* patrolling, rescue and surveillance operation launched by Italy to enhance the humanitarian rescue activities in the Mediterranean, aided 150,810 migrants in 364 days (P8_TA(2014)0105).

Committee on Petitions

The Committee on Petitions' task is to examine petitions presented by citizens (a right enshrined in art. 44 of the CFREU, as well as in articles 24 and 227 TFEU) and to work to resolve possible infringements of the rights conferred on them by EU law. The Italian members of the Committee are Alberto Cirio, Andrea Cozzolino and Eleonora Evi.

II. European Commission

The European Commission plays a central role in the development and implementation of European Union policies on human rights both within the Union and as regards third Countries.

Of the 28 Commissioners, particularly important are: Frans Timmermans, First Vice-President responsible for the quality of legislation, inter-institutional relations, the rule of law and the Charter of Fundamental Rights; Dimitris Avramopoulos, Commissioner for Migration, Home Affairs and Citizenship; Marianne Thyssen, Commissioner for Employment, Social Affairs, Skills and Labour Mobility; Christos Stylianides, Commissioner for Humanitarian Aid and Crisis Management; and Věra Jourová, Commissioner for Justice, Consumers and Gender Equality.

A vital financial resource for European Union human rights activities is the European Instrument for the Promotion of Democracy and Human Rights (EIDHR) which supports, among other things, the activities of the European Inter-university Centre for Rights and Democratisation (EIUC) and the European Master in Human Rights and Democratisation (E.MA).

Further details on the Commission's activities are provided in the section on EU Legislation in 2014 (see Part I, International Human Rights Law, IV, B).

III. Council of the European Union

Within the Council there are the Human Rights Working Group (COHOM), the Working Party on Fundamental Rights, Citizens' Rights and Free Movement of Persons (FREMP) and the Working Group of Public International Law (COJUR), within which a sub-group devoted to the International Criminal Court operates (COJUR-ICC).

On 12 May 2014, the EU Council adopted the new Guidelines on Freedom of Expression Online and Offline. The general purpose of the Guidelines is to tackle unjustified restrictions to freedom of expression, to promote freedom of the media and provide valuable guidance to European Union officials and staff all over the world. In particular, the Guidelines provide a series of definitions covering all aspects of fundamental rights, including the right to hold opinions without interference, the right to seek and receive information and the right to impart information and ideas of all kinds through any media and regardless of frontiers. Particular attention is devoted to the challenges that innovations in ICT (Information and Communication Technology) have brought with them. In this area, the EU is firmly opposed to all unjustified restrictions on Internet and other new media, so that all human rights which exist offline be protected online as well.

Italy held the Presidency of the Council of the European Union from 1st July to 31 December 2014. As regards specifically the issues of human rights and fundamental freedoms, the Programme presented by the Italian Government on the eve of taking up this institutional position, emphasised their central role and importance in the overall strategic framework the document outlines. In addition to defining them as "the cornerstone of the European construction and the defining element of our shared identity", human rights and fundamental freedoms are mentioned in the following individual chapters of the Programme:

– "Institutional Issues": the Italian Presidency committed to promoting the process for the European Union's accession to the ECHR and continue work on the Commission's proposal to establish a mechanism for monitoring respect of the fundamental rights within the European Union.

– "Foreign Affairs": the Italian Presidency assured that it would contribute to the shaping of a more coherent and effective EU foreign policy, with a specific focus on furthering the respect of human rights; as well as the support, in view of the LXIX session of the UN General Assembly, of EU initiatives: for a moratorium on capital punishment; promoting women's rights and combating gender-based violence; combating underage and forced marriages; on sectarian violence and discrimination, freedom of religion or belief and the protection of minorities, genocide prevention and resuming the human rights dialogue with Iran.

– "Justice and Home Affairs": on the issue of migration, the Presidency commits to supporting the design of comprehensive actions to combat human trafficking, the adoption of policies in favour of foreign unaccompanied minors, the implementation of the Common European Asylum System, and developing the integrated management of border control in full compliance with the EU Charter of Fundamental Rights.

– "Employment, Social Policy, Health and Consumer Affairs": alongside a focus on youth employment and combating undeclared labour, the development of the social dimension of the Economic and Monetary Union (EMU) is identified as one of the priority themes of the Italian presidency; on gender equality, the Presidency commits to making a thorough assessment of the implementation of the objectives of the Beijing Platform for Action; on the issue of non-discrimination, the Presidency commits to promoting a high-level conference with the aim of reaching a broad consensus on completing the existing legislative framework which outlaws discrimination on any grounds whatsoever.

– "Education, Youth, Culture and Sport": the Presidency commits to promoting young people's access to rights in order to foster their autonomy and social participation, and to complete discussions on the adoption of the Council's new Work Plan for Culture 2015/2018.

Below are some of the material achievements specifically relating to human rights that the Italian Government claimed at the close of its semester: the signing of an agreement to start an annual dialogue between Member States in the Council to promote and protect the respect of the rule of law within the Union, of legality and respect for human rights within Europe and in all Member States; fostering, within the Common European Asylum System, a reflection on the need to develop a mechanism of reciprocal recognition of decisions on asylum issues; starting negotiations on the regulations for the identification of the Member State responsible for examining a request for international protection presented by an unaccompanied minor whose family are not legally present in a member State; the organisation, together with the Fundamental Rights Agency, of a series of high level conferences on the integration of migrants and the management of asylum flows; having made progress in negotiations on the anti-discrimination directive; organising the meeting of the national contact points for the Roma inclusion Strategies; reopening the debate on combating discrimination on grounds of sexual orientation and gender identity at the European level.

IV. Court of Justice of the European Union

Following the entry into force of the Treaty of Lisbon, which made the Charter of Nice legally binding, the Court of Justice plays an ever more vital role for the promotion of human rights within the scope of EU law.

Italian members of the Court are currently Antonio Tizzano, as a judge, and Paolo Mengozzi, as an Advocate-General.

According to data provided by the CJEU, in 2014 Italy was ranked second for the number of requests for a preliminary ruling (art. 267 TFEU) submitted to the Court (52 out of 428), preceded only by Germany.

For a selection of the CJEU case-law regarding Italy in 2014, see Part IV, Italy in the Case-law of the Court of Justice of the European Union.

V. European External Action Service

The European External Action Service (EEAS) assists the High Representative of the Union for Foreign Affairs and Security Policy in upholding the CFSP/CSDP and ensuring the consistency of EU external actions in her functions both as President of the Foreign Affairs Council and as Vice-President of the Commission. In November 2014, Federica Mogherini was appointed to the position of High Representative.

One of the actions of particular interest to Italy was the statement by the High Representative on 16 December 2014 on the case of two Italian Navy riflemen held in India. Federica Mogherini, after pointing out that this dispute could damage the overall relationship between the European Union and India, as well as the global battle against piracy, affirmed that the European Union will continue to monitor the developments of the dispute, alongside the Italian Government, and also reiterated her call for a swift solution to the matter.

VI. Special Representative for Human Rights

Appointed by EU Council decision 2012/440/CFSP of 25 July 2012, the mandate of the European Union Special Representative for Human Rights involves enhancing dialogue with all relevant stakeholders concerning EU human rights policy, including international organisations, States as well as civil society organisations. Stavros Lambrinidis was appointed on 1 September 2012 as the first incumbent. His first mandate, expired in June 2014, has been extended until 28 February 2015.

No significant activities concerning Italy in 2014.

VII. Fundamental Rights Agency

The European Union Agency for Fundamental Rights (FRA), an advisory body set up in 2007, is the main technical instrument for the EU, charged with supporting European and national institutions in the promotion and protection of human rights. Director of the Agency is Morten

Kjaerum (Denmark). Since July 2012 Lorenza Violini has represented Italy in the Management Board of the FRA.

The Annual Fundamental Rights Conference was held in Rome on 10 and 11 November 2014, in conjunction with the Italian Presidency of the Council of the European Union, dedicated to migration to the EU. The main recommendations which emerged at the end of the Conference concerned: the commitment by the EU and its Member States to adopt a human rights-based approach to managing its external borders and in combating trafficking of human beings; the possibility of offering legal ways to access the EU for people in need of humanitarian protection; protection of children in the context of migration; respect of human rights in migrant integration and social inclusion policies; overcoming the negative narrative associated with migration to build more inclusive and plural societies.

The FRA's research work is done mainly by collecting and making comparative analyses of data on the situation of fundamental rights in the 28 Member States of the EU, including Italy. In this respect, below is a summary of some of the FRA reports made in 2014. After an introduction to each report, there are some remarks on the most significant data which emerged concerning Italy:

Violence against women (March 2014): the survey results are based on face-to-face interviews with 42,000 women aged between 18 and 74 in all 28 EU member States on issues such as physical, sexual and psychological violence, child abuse, sexual harassment and stalking, including new means of abuse such as the Internet. The survey results showed that: one in three women has suffered physical and/or sexual violence since age 15; one in three women has suffered psychological abuse at the hands of a current or previous partner; 18% of women have been subjected to stalking; between 45–55% of women had suffered sexual harassment.

With specific reference to Italy, the survey shows that: 29% of women have suffered physical and/or sexual violence since age 15; 91% of Italians think that violence against women is very widespread; 48% of women are not aware of the laws protecting the victims of domestic violence (against an EU average of 59%); 58% are not aware of policies or measures aimed at preventing domestic violence (against an EU average of 36%).

The right to political participation of persons with disabilities (May 2014): the report provides detailed information on how the right to political participation of persons with disabilities is respected, protected, promoted and implemented in the 28 Member States of the EU. Five key requirements emerge from the survey report: lift legal and administrative barriers to political participation; make voting procedures, facilities and election materials more accessible; expand opportunities for participation in political and public life; increase public awareness of the right to political participation of persons with disabilities; and collect data to measure the political participation of persons with disabilities.

According to the report, Italy is one of the 7 EU Countries which recognise the right to vote to all persons with disabilities, including those who are deprived of some legal capacity. However, as happens in other European Countries, there are certain additional burdens for persons with disabilities who intend to exercise their right to vote, such as, for example, the need for seriously impaired voters to apply to the town hall on whose electoral roll they are registered for a permanent permit to be supported or assisted to vote. In common with Poland, Slovakia and Sweden, in Italy the rules on accessibility of Internet sites are only applicable to public administration services. Similarly, only the public television networks are legally required to make their broadcasts accessible to persons with disabilities. Finally, the report notes that during the most recent election campaigns, no political party produced campaign material in accessible format for persons with disabilities.

– *Fundamental rights at airports: border checks at 5 international airports in the EU* (November 2014): the report examines the procedures and practices relative to border control officers' treatment of third-country nationals entering the EU via one of the five international airports surveyed. The objective of the report is to assess the compliance of border control checks with the respect of fundamental rights such as the respect of human dignity, the principle of non-discrimination, the ban on human trafficking, asylum rights, the rights of the child, the right to effective remedy and the right to protection of personal data.

With reference to Fiumicino (Rome) airport, the FRA report highlights as a promising practice that of providing a special help desk in the transit area run by an NGO, which provides useful information on international protection and reports asylum seekers to the Prefecture and the Ministry of the Interior. Also welcomed is the presence inside the airport of an immigration office run by officers from the Rome National Police. Some of the critical areas identified are: inadequate facilities for those who have to spend the night in the transit zone, particularly for families; lack of language knowledge among border authorities; lack of specific protocols for identifying victims of trafficking or for interviewing children; lack of information on the procedures for presenting complaints or appeals against decisions to refuse entry.

VIII. European Ombudsman

The European Ombudsman, an institution established in 1992 by the Treaty of Maastricht and provided for in art. 24 and 228 TFEU, examines the complaints lodged by European citizens about maladministration in the institutions and bodies of the European Union. Elected by the EP, the Ombudsman performs his duties with complete independence. Emily O'Reilly, previously the National Ombudsperson of the Republic of Ireland, has held this position since 1 October 2013, having succeeded to Nikiforos Diamandouros, European Ombudsman for the previous ten years. On 16 December 2014 O'Reilly was re-elected by the European Parliament for another five years.

According to the report on the European Ombudsman's activities in 2013, published on 23 September 2014, over the time frame in question, the Ombudsman's office received 2,420 complaints, of which 108 from Italy. In 2013 it also opened 341 enquiries (of which 39 relative to complaints from Italy), and closed 441. In that same year, 9 investigations were opened by the Ombudsman of its own initiative.

IX. European Data Protection Supervisor

Established by regulation 45/2001, the European Data Protection Supervisor (EDPS) is responsible for ensuring the right to the protection of individual privacy in the handling of personal data by EU institutions and bodies, as laid out in articles 7–8 of the Nice Charter. The EDPS is an independent supervisory authority elected by the Parliament and the Council of the EU. The current Supervisor is Peter Hustnix, whose mandate was renewed for a further five years in 2009. Giovanni Buttarelli, previously Secretary General to the Italian Data Protection Authority, is Assistant Supervisor.

Organization for Security and Cooperation in Europe (OSCE)

Through a multi-dimensional approach to security, the OSCE (57 participating States) operates in the fields of conflict prevention, crisis management and post-conflict rehabilitation. Among its specific bodies and mechanisms worth noting are the Office for Democratic Institutions and Human Rights (ODIHR), the High Commissioner on National Minorities, the Representative on Freedom of the Media and the Special Representative and Co-ordinator for Combating Trafficking in Human Beings. Lamberto Zannier from the Italian diplomatic service has been the Secretary General of the OSCE since 1 July 2011.

Head of the Italian mission to the OSCE is H.E. Filippo Formica. 13 members of the Italian Chamber of Deputies and Senate sit in the OSCE Parliamentary Assembly. The head of the Italian parliamentary delegation in 2014 was Paolo Romani.

Italy is one of the main contributors to the OSCE. In 2014, the Italian contribution to the budget was approximately 14 million euro (about 9% of the budget), the same as those of France, Germany and the United Kingdom.

I. Office for Democratic Institutions and Human Rights (ODIHR)

The ODIHR is the OSCE's main body charged with assisting Member States in the implementation of their human dimension commitments. On 1 July 2014, Michael Georg Link (Germany) was appointed Director of the Office, replacing Janez Lenarčič (Slovenia), who had held the post since 2008.

In 2014, ODIHR activities in Italy concerned mainly training and awareness-raising initiatives to combat hate crimes. Of particular interest was the first edition of the TAHCLE workshop, held in Rome on 11 and 12 February 2014, the purpose of which was to train Italian law enforcement officers in preventing and repressing hate crimes.

II. High Commissioner on National Minorities

The Office of the High Commissioner on National Minorities is the OSCE institution which is charged with identifying and seeking to resolve situations of ethnic tension in the OSCE region. In addition to serving as an instrument for preventing conflict, it can also promote rapid solutions which can halt processes of escalating violence. Astrid Thors (Finland) has held the position of High Commissioner since 20 August 2013. None of the 2014 initiatives were linked to or directly concerned Italy.

III. OSCE Representative on Freedom of the Media

Established in 1997 with a view to ensuring a high level of compliance with the rules and standards on freedom of expression and freedom of the Freedom of the Media accepted by the States Party to OSCE, the Representative on Freedom of the Media acts as an early warning instrument in cases of violation of freedom of expression, with particular attention to any obstacles or impediments to the activities of journalists. This position has been held since March 2010 by Dunja Mijatovic (Bosnia and Herzegovina).

On 23 July 2014 the Representative on Freedom of the Media attended the convention in Rome entitled "Defamation in the press. The scenario in Europe and in Italy while awaiting reforms", organised by Rome Bar Association and the National Council of the Association of Journalists, following approval by the Justice Committee of the Italian Senate of Bill No. 925 on defamation. The Representative on Freedom of the Media highlighted the shortcomings of the bill and once again called on the authorities to consider fully decriminalising defamation.

IV. Special Representative and Co-ordinator for Combating Trafficking in Human Beings

The Office of the Special Representative and Co-ordinator for Combating Trafficking in Human Beings is responsible for assisting OSCE States to progressively fulfil their commitments in this area under the 2003 Action Plan. It also serves as the body co-ordinating all OSCE activities combating trafficking. Madina Jarbussynova (Kazakhstan) was appointed Special Representative and Co-ordinator in September 2014, in succession to Maria Grazia Giammarinaro.

In July 2014 the Report on the Special Representative's official visits to Italy (17–18 June and 15–19 July 2013) was published (see *2014 Yearbook* pp. 266–267).

Humanitarian and Criminal Law

I. Adapting to International Humanitarian and Criminal Law

Italy is party to all the main international conventions on the law of armed conflict and international criminal law.

In terms of its commitments to disarmament and non-proliferation, on 2 April 2014, Italy deposited the ratification instrument of the Arms Trade Treaty.

Still linked to the arms sector, the obligation to present regular reports on the state of implementation of the provisions of the various conventions becomes particularly significant. In this respect, during 2014 Italy presented the annual report established by the Convention against Anti-personnel Mines; the report required by the Convention on Prohibitions or Restrictions on the Use of Certain Conventional Weapons (2 April 2014), that pertaining to the relative Protocol on Landmines, Booby Traps and Other Devices and that of the Protocol on Explosive Remnants of War; and the annual report required by the Oslo Convention banning cluster mines (April 2014).

II. The Italian Contribution to Peace-keeping and Other International Missions

In 2014, with two legislative degrees converted into law by Parliament (l.d. 16 January 2014, No. 2, converted by law 14 March 2014, No. 28 and l.d. 1 August 2014, No. 109, converted by law 1 October 2014, No. 141), Italy financed the extension of the participation of Italian military and civilian personnel in international missions. Changes from 2013 are that Italy began operations in India/Pakistan, Morocco and Egypt. The list below shows the military and police missions in which Italy participated with its own forces in the course of 2014.

Country/geographic Area of Intervention	**Italy's Mission and Activities**
Afghanistan	*International Security Assistance Force* (ISAF) (military, police and financial police component)
	EUPOL AFGHANISTAN (military and police component)

Country/geographic Area of Intervention	Italy's Mission and Activities
Albania	Activity in support of the Albanian armed forces
Bosnia and Herzegovina	European Union Mission named ALTHEA, within which the Integrated Police Unit (IPU) operates
	Participation of officers from the *Arma dei Carabinieri*, the State Police and one member of the judiciary in the European Union Police Mission (EUPM)
Cyprus	United Nations Peacekeeping Force in Cyprus (UNFICYP)
Egypt	MFO (Multinational Force & Observers): overseeing the respect of the Camp David Accords between Israel and Egypt and ensuring freedom of passage in the Straits of Tiran.
United Arab Emirates/Bahrain/ Qatar/ Tampa, USA	Deployment of military personnel in support of the missions in Afghanistan
Georgia	European Union Monitoring Mission in Georgia – EUMM Georgia
India/Pakistan	Supervising the ceasefire between India and Pakistan in the State of Jammu and Kashmir, as part of the UNMOGIP mission (*UN Military Observer Group in India and Pakistan*)
Iraq	TF AIR KUWAIT (a NATO operation): Organising and participating in operative duties against ISIS forces.
Kosovo/Balkans	Multinational Specialized Unit (MSU), *European Union Rule of Law Mission in Kosovo* (EULEX Kosovo) (military, police and financial police component), Security Force Training Plan in Kosovo
	Operation Joint Enterprise (NATO)
Lebanon	*United Nations Interim Force in Lebanon* (UNIFIL), which includes the use of naval units in the UNIFIL Maritime Task Force
Lebanon/Israel/Syria	UNTSO (*UN Truce Supervision Organisation*): assist Lebanon, Israel and Syria in respecting the "Agreement on disengagement" with the aim of reaching a stable condition of peace.

Country/geographic Area of Intervention	**Italy's Mission and Activities**
Libya	Participation in the European Union mission in Libya *European Union Border Assistance Mission in Libya* (EUBAM Libya) (military and police component)
Mali	Participation in the European Union mission EUTM Mali
	Participation in the *United Nations Multidimensional Integrated Stabilization Mission in Mali* (MINUSMA), pursuant to United Nations Security Council resolution 2100 (2013)
Morocco/Western Sahara	Supervision of the ceasefire between the self-proclaimed Sahrawi Arab Democratic Republic and Morocco while awaiting holding of the referendum on the definitive status of the western Sahara, as part of the MINURSO (*UN Mission for the referendum in western Sahara*) operation
Eastern Mediterranean	Participation of military personnel in the mission *Active Endeavour* in the Mediterranean (NATO)
Niger	Participation in the European Union mission EUCAP Sahel Niger
Somalia/Indian Ocean	European Union military mission *Operation Atalanta*
	Italian training mission with the Somali Armed Forces to bring their structures in line with NATO models, through conceptual, training and logistics activities (MIADIT).
	NATO *Ocean Shield* operation combating piracy
	Participation in the European Union Training Mission (EUTM SOMALIA) and EUCAP Nestor as well as the other European Union initiatives for regional maritime capacity building in the Horn of Africa and western Indian Ocean
South Sudan	Participation of military personnel in the *United Nations Mission in South Sudan* (UNMISS), pursuant to United Nations Security Council resolution 1996 (2011), adopted on 8 July 2011

Country/geographic Area of Intervention	**Italy's Mission and Activities**
Sudan	*United Nations/African Union Mission in Darfur* (UNAMID)
Occupied Palestinian Territories	Participation of military personnel in the mission *Temporary International Presence in Hebron* (TIPH2)
Occupied Palestinian Territories/Egypt	*European Union Border Assistance Mission in Rafah* (EUBAM Rafah)

Part IV

National and International Case-law

Human Rights in Italian Case-law

As in the previous editions of this Yearbook, this section presents some examples taken from the jurisprudence of the Italian courts in 2014 in which human rights as articulated in the main international sources have been given a special place. Emphasis has been put on the case-law of the Constitutional Court and of the Court of Cassation. The aim, as always, is to not to provide a comprehensive survey of the court's practice, rather to help identifying trends and patterns in the practice of Italian courts as regards human rights issues.

I. Dignity of the Person and Principles of Biolaw

A. Immunity of Foreign States and Crimes Against the Dignity of the Person

In a decision likely to spark the debate also at the international level, the Constitutional Court – judgment 238/2014 – pronounced the unconstitutionality of some provisions of the law 14 January 2013, No. 5, giving execution to the judgment of the International Court of Justice (ICJ) that adjudicated the dispute between Italy and Germany on State immunity in foreign courts.

The issue of constitutionality (see *2013 Yearbook*, pp. 310 and 374) was raised in connection with a number of judgments of Italian courts that ordered Germany to pay compensation to Italian military internees who survived imprisonment and forced labour in Nazi concentration camps during the Second World War. In 2008 Germany sued the Italian State before the ICJ, maintaining that such decisions were in breach of the principle of State immunity from proceedings in foreign courts. The ICJ, in a ruling published on 3 February 2012, backed the position taken by Germany, hence the adoption by the Italian Parliament of an act that *inter alia* explicitly prohibited courts to hear similar claims against Germany in the future. Questioned on the constitutionality of such norms (as well as of other provisions, including the alleged international customary norm on the absolute immunity of States, and the law disposing Italy's adhesion to the United Nations and acceptance of the ICJ Statute – see order of the Tribunal of Florence, 21 January 2014), the Constitutional Court refused to admit that, through the mechanism of automatic implementation in the Italian legal system of general (customary) international law set forth in art. 10(1) Const., the principle of the absolute immunity of foreign States from any civil proceedings could be in force in Italy, when acts attributable to a foreign State amounted to crimes against humanity and violations of fundamental human rights. This was the outcome of the ICJ ruling. However, even admitting that such was the rule under international customary law, the Constitutional Courts stated it would not be enforced in Italy as it contravened fundamental principles and inalienable rights of the Italian legal system – the kernel indeed of the Italian Constitution. Among these principles and rights stands the right to access a court, granted by art. 24 of the Constitution, strictly linked to art. 2 (general recognition of the inviolable rights of individuals). The combination of these normative values reflects the irreducible dignity of the person. According to the Court, "the international customary norm on State immunity from the jurisdiction of foreign States, in so far as it excludes the court jurisdiction on any damages suffered by individuals who were victim of crimes against humanity and serious violations of fundamental human rights, imposes the sacrifice of the victims' right to judicial protection, without it being possible to identify an overriding public interest that must prevail. Common sense, rather than legal considerations, suggests that the granting of immunity of a foreign State from the jurisdiction of the Italian courts may justify the sacrifice of the principle of judicial protection of the inalienable rights of the individual under articles 2 and 24 of the Italian Constitution, only as much as it safeguards, substantially and not just formally, the sovereign functions of the foreign State, the exercise of its core governmental functions. Crimes against humanity, such as deportation, forced labour and mass killings, do not worth the blanket sacrifice of the inviolable rights of the victims. In an institutional context characterised by the centrality of human rights, as enhanced by the opening of the domestic constitutional system to international sources, to preclude courts from adjudicating on the fundamental rights of the victims of the mentioned crimes would imply an utterly disproportionate sacrifice of two supreme constitutional principles for the sake of honouring State sovereignty, even more so as the behaviour of a sovereign State amounted to appalling crimes that in no way could be assimilated to legitimate governmental functions." Thus, "the part of the international norm that conflicts with the above mentioned fundamental principles has not entered the Italian legal system and does not produce any effects"; law provisions regulating such matter are therefore unconstitutional.

Thematically cognate to the mentioned Constitutional Court judgment are some rulings of the Court of Cassation that have refined the notion of "restricted immunity" of States in proceedings before foreign courts. In a number of litigations about labour issues involving employees of foreign State embassies and Government agencies, the Supreme Court reiterated that art. 11 of the UN Convention on Jurisdictional Immunity of States and Their Property, done in New York on 2 December 2004, ratified by Italy through law 14 January 2013, No. 5, reflected international customary law and allowed to submit to the territorial courts any labour disputes between the foreign State and its employee provided that the employee's assignments do not relate to official functions of the sovereign State or do not impact on the organisation of the institution. The territorial court cannot therefore adjudicate on matters such as recruitment, renewal of employment or reintegration of the employee (including applications for reintegration into the workplace for unfair dismissal), but may take cases concerning wages and other economic aspects of the labour contract, and applications for a compensatory allowance for unfair dismissal (Court of Cassation, civil division, Joint. Sec., orders 18 April 2014, No. 9034; 18 September 2014, No. 19674).

It is worth reminding in this connection that in 2014 the Supreme Court finally adjudicated a criminal case about a series of massacres committed by the German army in Spring 1944. The trial was held before the Verona Military Tribunal in 2011 and the Tribunal's decision was largely reformed on appeal in 2012 (Court of Cassation, criminal division, Sec. I, judg. 19 March 2014, No. 23288).

The criminal charges concerned the killings occurred on 18 March 1944 in the villages of Monchio, Susano and Costrignano (now the town of Palagano), and on 20 March 1944 in Civago, Cevarolo and Villa Minozzo (all localities are in the territory of Emilia), which caused 156 casualties; the massacre committed in the Province of Florence, on 10 April 1944, around Monte Morello, in the villages of Ceppeto and Cerreto, the same year in May, in which 14 non-combatant civilians, including some children, were killed; the killings occurred between 13 and 18 April 1944, in the area of Monte Falterona, causing about 200 civilian casualties, including women and children, and the massacre in Monnio and Fivizzano, in the Province of Massa, committed between 4 and 5 May 1944, in which twenty non-combatants died. Many convictions decided by the trial court in 2011 were overturned on appeal, leading to the acquittal of the Nazi officers who participated in such criminal actions. The Supreme Court's final judgment eventually upheld the prosecutors' case against the acquittals. In particular, the Court of Cassation maintained, according to the military prosecutors and in line with the conclusions of the trial court, that all military officers and non-commissioned officers who performed command functions and that participated in the operations of "annihilation", were liable of war crimes because there was factual evidence of a prior order of indiscriminate killing of civilians. Direct evidence of the defendants' actual participation to the killings was not necessary, since their involvement in the chain of command that enabled the planning and execution of the mass murders was already demonstrated. As a result, the judgment of the Supreme Court ordered to try again some of the defendants. Most of them are over ninety years old; no restrictive measures have never been taken against them by the German judiciary. The Supreme Court also confirmed as legitimate the claim for damages submitted by ANPI – National Association of Italian Partisans –, an association founded in 1945 (then after the alleged facts), but which has operated in continuity with the groups and armed units of partisans that were the target of the attacks that constituted war crimes.

B. Heterologous Fertilisation; Exchange of Embryos, and "Involuntary" Heterologous Fertilisation

Also in 2014 the Constitutional Court ruled on a number of provisions of the law 19 February 2004, No. 40 (Rules on medically assisted procreation), finding it partially unconstitutional. In its judgment No. 162, 10 June 2014, the Court took position on the prohibition of heterologous fertilisation. The target provision was essentially art. 4(3) of the law: "It is forbidden the use of techniques of medically assisted procreation of heterologous type." The Court in this judgment resumed a reasoning undertaken in 2012 and postponed to a future occasion, pending the conclusions expected from the ECtHR Grand Chamber (case *S.H. v. Austria*). Eventually, the ban on heterologous fertilisation was found by the Constitutional Court in breach of articles 2, 3, 29, 31 and 32 of the Italian Constitution, taken into account their respective normative contents and in connection with other rights and values, including the embryo protection principle. The main discrepancy is that the prohibition, in its starkness, prevents sterile or infertile couples (thus those carrying a severe disease and arguably most eager to access medically assisted reproductive methods) to use heterologous fertilisation, the sole technique of assisted reproduction that could suit them, thereby establishing a harsh discrimination against them. The ban also undermines the right to health of members of the couple, where "health" means "a state of complete physical, mental and social well-being [that] is one of the fundamental rights of every human being" (Constitution of the World Health Organisation, signed in New York, 22 July 1946). The restriction of these rights could be justified only in order to safeguard the rights of individuals born from a practice of heterologous fertilisation, in particular the right not to have their genetic identity challenged. The latter, incidentally, has been limited, among other things, by the possibility, recently admitted by the Constitutional Court, to break the secrecy of the adoptee's biological parents' identity: the law provision imposing the secrecy was found unconstitutional by the Constitutional Court with judgment 278/2013 – see *2014 Yearbook*, p. 278). Moreover, the ban was also unreasonable since the law, while prohibiting any kind of heterologous fertilisation, still regulated the recognition of the legal effects of an heterologous fertilisation performed abroad, in the Countries (not rare) where this practice is lawful; thereby introducing a further ground of discrimination among couples who aspire to have children: not only between those who are suffering from mild or severe diseases (to the detriment of the latter), but also between those who have the means to undergo a lawful practice of heterologous artificial insemination abroad and those who cannot afford the costs associated with it.

The Tribunal of Rome (ord. 8 August 2014) had to rule on a dramatic case of involuntary exchange of embryos in the course of medically assisted reproduction practices. The case can be approached to an heterologous procreation, but the conditions are obviously different, since both couples involved intended to undergo an homologous (not by donor) insemination; the outcome though, because of the serious negligence of the health personnel, was akin to an "involuntary" heterologous insemination. The case cannot be regulated as a surrogate maternity – see next paragraph –, since there was not agreement between the involved couples in this regard.

The case stemmed from an exchange of genetic material, thereby the embryos genetically pertaining to the first couple had been transferred to the woman of a second couple being treated in the same clinic for the same problem (the implantation of the second couple's embryos in the first couple's woman was unsuccessful). After giving birth (it was a twin childbirth), under article 269 civil code the babies were the offsprings of the second couple. The genetic parents asked the tribunal to issue an injunction to remove the twins from their legal parent couple (the one of the gestational mother). The court rejected the request to adopt an interim protective measure, in view of the fact that the law did not contemplate and did not deal expressly with a situation like the present one. The court also decided not to raise the issue of constitutionality with respect to article 269 civil code and related norms (which were just amended in 2013), based on the presumption that the child's mother is the woman who bore him. Indeed, to start such a procedure would put in jeopardy the interest of the two newborn children to the stability of their status and to live in the family where they were born in – and that is apparently the only one to which they belong, according to the law in force. The court noted, among other things, that according to domestic legislation and international law (recent decisions of the ECtHR are mentioned), the right to personal identity is increasingly detached from the genetic inheritance of the individual and increasingly tied to the affective environment and the family lived experiences of the individual. This trend is deemed to be consistent with the best interests of the child, as set forth in the New York Convention on the Rights of the Child. Moreover, in this case, arguing in favour of the genetic mother, and therefore to raise the issue of constitutionality, would have endorsed a case of surrogated maternity and potentially imposed the biological mother to give up the children she had borne in her womb and given birth to, causing indeed a harm to her human dignity.

C. Surrogate Maternity

The ruling of the Supreme Court, civil division, Sec. I, 11 November 2014, No. 24001, deals with a case of surrogate materhood (sometimes referred to as "rent-a-womb" practice). The Court set some points claiming to be inspired by the principles of human dignity and the best interests of the child derived from both domestic law provisions and the international law of human rights. The surrogacy case was addressed as separate from the issue – dealt with by the Constitutional Court – of the heterologous fertilisation practice as prohibited by l. 40/2004 (see the previous paragraph). The Supreme Court reviewed a judgment of the Juvenile Court of Brescia – upheld by the Court of Appeals of the same city – that placed for adoption a child born in Ukraine to an Italian couple who had resorted to heterologous insemination with a surrogate mother. The judges had found that not only the couple had turned to a practice forbidden in Italy (l. 40/2004, article 12(6))), but also that they had infringed Ukrainian law, which forbade artificial insemination with an egg donor if less than 50% of the genetic heritage of the child comes from a donor outside the couple (that is, if the father is not the husband/partner of the woman). In the case at hand indeed, the child came to Italy as the son of two Italian citizens, but in fact neither of them was either the genetic or biological parent of the baby. The two were therefore charged with forgery of the child's documents, and the child was declared abandoned. This decision was appealed before the Court of Cassation on the basis of various considerations including, in particular, its opposing the principle of the best interest of the child. The couple maintained that once the contract of surrogacy was executed – and irrespective of its lawfulness under the Italian or the Ukrainian law – since the newborn child was welcomed in the Italian family, what mattered was to grant him to keep the relationship he had established with the only parents he had had. The Supreme Court, however, dismissed such arguments on the ground that the ban of surrogacy – accompanied by a criminal sanction – is a public order principle protecting the mother's human dignity and adoption as a social institution. Italian law has set a balance between, on one hand, the interest of the child and, on the other hand, any potentially competing interests, establishing that the child's mother is the woman who gave birth to the baby, and regulating as adoption cases any filiations disconnected from biological ties; not only any forms of selling a child by a private contract was prohibited, but also courts were prevented from taking any discretionary measures on the matter. The Supreme Court also discussed the possible conflict of its conclusions with the case-law of the ECtHR, looking in particular to cases such as *Mennesson v. France*, No. 65192/11, 26 June 2014 and *Labassee v. France*, No. 65941/11, 26 June 2014. However it noticed that in those cases (dealing with surrogate motherhood practices carried out in the United States according to the local law but in contravention to the French legislation, the parents' State), a member of the couple that set the surrogacy was also the genetic father of the baby; the situations were therefore not comparable.

The Court of Cassation, of course, could not refer to the conclusions reached by the ECtHR in the case *Paradiso and Campanelli v. Italy*, No. 25358/12, 27 January 2015, relating to a situation very close to that dealt with by the Court in the present case. The Strasbourg judges found Italy to be in breach of article 8 ECHR, on the grounds that to have made considerations of public order prevail over the interest of the child to remain with the couple who had welcomed him – and then to have declared a state of neglect and the opening of the adoption of the child who had born in Russia through surrogacy circumventing national law.

D. Right to a Name, Gender Reassignment

The Supreme Court stated that, in light of the reformed article 262 civil code (last name of the child born out of wedlock), it is up to the court to decide whether or not to add the father's name to a child who had previously been given the mother's surname only (Court of Cassation, civil division, Sec. I, judg. 10 December 2014, No. 26062). In this situation, no automatism favouring the addition of the father's name applies. The Court clarified that the right to a name is a fundamental human right, guaranteed by the Constitution in an absolute way by reason of its importance in relation to the identity of the individual. In this case, despite the recognition of paternity by the father took place ten years after the child's birth, the court had properly ordered to add the second surname. On the one hand, the court had considered that the father was not a person of bad reputation and that he had actually significant relationships with the child. On the other hand, the court noted that the latter, in the community of reference, had not yet consolidated an identity solely linked to the mother's surname. From the Supreme Court's reasoning, however, it is clear that if the mother's surname alone is sufficient to identify the child and it has become an autonomous feature of the child identity in the social context, there is no obligation for the judge to grant the request to add the father's surname. Indeed, the issue does not concern the protection of a right or an interest of the parents, but to guarantee to the maximum extent the child's right to acquire and preserve his or her personal and social identity. For a similar case, see Court of Cassation, civil division, Sec. VI, judg. 28 January 2014, No. 1808: adding the surname of father (who had not immediately recognised the paternity) to that of the (non-Italian) mother was considered to be the solution that better protected the identity of the child and that had to be preferred to the complete replacement of the mother's surname. The Supreme Court rejected the argument of the trial court according to which the double surname would have been harmful for the child as it would have immediately drawn the attention to the "critical" situation experienced by a child born out of wedlock. Indeed, the stigma associated with that condition is no longer present in the current socio-anthropological context.

E. Condition of Transgender

According to the Tribunal of Messina (judg. 4 November 2014), under certain circumstances, the amendment of the records relating to a person gender in civil registers must be ordered by the court even if the applicant has not undergone a genital reassignment surgery. For the court, indeed, it is sufficient to establish the existence of an actual change in the applicant's psychological self-perception of his or her gender (transgender condition, as distinct from that of transexual). In the present case, the individual concerned had undergone a hormonal therapy and undoubtedly felt he was a woman and not man. The sex reassignment surgery, which had not been recommended for him, was in all cases not necessary for the attainment of a mental, physical and emotional equilibrium. Therefore, the Tribunal ordered the requested gender reassignment and the related name change.

F. Right to Privacy and Freedom of the Press; Right to be Forgotten

The practice adopted by the Region of Campania to include, in the causal of wire transfers in favour of the applicant, a reference to l. 210/1992 (a norm which recognises the right to compensation to individuals affected, among other things, by HIV by reason of compulsory vaccinations) was declared unlawful by the Supreme Court as it violated the fundamental right to privacy concerning sensitive data. The fact that such data was managed without due caution by both the public body and the bank constituted a violation of the right to privacy. The contested practice was found to be in contrast to, in particular, article 22 of lgs.d. 196/2003 (the so-called "Privacy code"), under which public bodies are required, on the one hand, to process sensitive data safeguarding the rights, the fundamental freedoms and the dignity of concerned individuals and, on the other hand, to use them only when it is indispensable to carry out institutional activities that cannot be fulfilled by processing anonymous or different personal data. In any case, personal data concerning the state of health may not be disseminated. The same article, in its sixth comma, states that health data should be processed with encryption techniques or identification codes that temporarily render them unintelligible to those who are authorised to access them (Court of Cassation, civil division, Sec. I, judg. 19 May 2014, No. 10947).

The Supreme Court also adjudicated cases involving the publication in newspapers of photos of people who had been arrested. A case dealt with by the Supreme Court concerned the publication in newspapers of the applicant's passport photo, perhaps obtained from the mug shot, in the context of news articles reporting his arrest. The Court, ruling on the right to the protection of one's image, stated that, in order to be legitimate, the publication in a newspaper of the photo of a person immediately after his arrest must not only be essential to illustrate the content of the article and constitute a lawful exercise of freedom of the press (article 137 of the Privacy code). It also has to comply with specific safeguards imposed to protect the dignity of the person as prescribed by the Code of conduct and professional practice of journalists and article 8 ECHR. This additional restriction is justified on account of "the potential detrimental effect to the dignity of the person connected to the emphatic nature of the visual tool through which, more easily than other communication means, information may be disseminated out of context and with no possibility of control by the concerned person" (see, among others: Court of Cassation, civil division, Sec. III, judgments 10 January 2014, No. 194; 6 June 2014, No. 12834).

In another decision concerning the right to privacy (Court of Cassation, civil division, Sec. III, judg. 25 November 2014, No. 24986), the Supreme Court upheld the decision of the lower courts which had condemned the managing editor of a municipality newspaper for having published, next to the article reporting the allocation of a contribution to a couple whose daughter suffered from a disability, the photo the little girl, provoking an unwelcome curiosity on the family. The exonerating circumstance set forth in article 137 of the Privacy code (lgs.d. 196/2003) according to which "personal data relating to circumstances or facts directly disclosed by the individuals concerned through their behaviour in public may be processed", does not apply in the present case. Indeed, the fact that a person is identifiable for the general public by reason of obvious external characters, as a person with a disability may be, is not sufficient: in order to publish the photo, there is still the need to obtain the explicit consent of the person concerned or the consent of his legal representatives, especially if the case concerns a minor. The Court also recalled its previous case-law on the issue (see *2014 Yearbook*, p. 301).

Worth mentioning, even if delivered in 2013, is the Supreme Court judgment concerning the so-called right to be forgotten. The case concerned the publication in a local newspaper, in 1998, of the news of the discovery of an arsenal allegedly belonging to terrorist groups active in Italy in the 1970s. The article was integrated by an interview and a photo of a former member of the terrorist group Prima Linea, in the context of which the interviewee expressed the wish to be no longer associated with this type of events. Having served the sentence he was convicted of, he wanted to cut all ties with such experience. The Supreme Court upheld the appeal court judgment noting that the dissemination of the interview and the picture of the applicant in connection to a news linked to events occurred in the past and connected to a phase of the interviewee's life that he now considered to be closed, constituted a violation of the right to privacy. The freedom of the press prevails over the right of the person that data on his personal history no longer appear ("right to be forgotten") only when there is an actual and current interest to present them again on the ground that they are closely connected with current events. The fact that the concerned individual had been a member of groups that had historically characterised the so-called "years of lead" is without prejudice to the arbitrariness of the association and to the violation of the right to privacy. The former terrorist received a compensation of 30,000 euro (Court of Cassation, civil division, Sec. III, judg. 26 June 2013, No. 16111).

On a similar issue, worth mentioning is the judgment of the Court of Appeal of Milan (27 January 2014), which affirmed the right of every person to have their publicly available personal data updated, with particular reference to data available on databases accessible via the Internet by newspapers. This right is grounded on the constitutionally relevant interest of the protection of the personal and moral identity of the individual in the social dimension. This is all the more true when obsolete data concerns information for the disclosure of which journalists had been convicted for defamation.

II. Political Rights and Electoral System

2014 began with the adoption of a significant and awaited ruling of the Constitutional Court. In its judgment 1/2014, the Court declared that some key provisions of the law for the election of both Houses of Parliament were unconstitutional as contrary to articles 3, 48(2), 49, 56(1), 58(1) Const. as well as to article 117(1) Const. in connection to article 3 Protocol I ECHR on the right to free elections. The issue of constitutionality had been raised by the Supreme Court in connection to some articles of the d.p.r. 30 March 1957, No. 361 (Consolidated law for the election of the Chamber of Deputies) and of the lgs.d. 20 December 1993, No. 533 (Consolidated law for the election of the Senate), as amended by

l. 21 December 2005, No. 270 (Amendments to the rules for the election of the Chamber of Deputies and the Senate).

The Constitutional Court held that the system of "majority weighting" in the two Chambers of Parliament (a number of seats are reserved for the coalition which obtain the most votes), having no minimum threshold, disproportionally limited the Parliament function of representation and the equality of voters with respect to the purpose of strengthening Governments stability. The issue of constitutionality was also raised with concern to the rules establishing a system of "blocked lists" (in which the order of candidates is determined by the party itself) by reason that it rendered the vote of the citizens substantially "indirect", leaving to the parties the responsibility to "appoint" deputies. Although in 2012 the ECtHR had dismissed as manifestly ill-founded the case brought by some Italian citizens dealing with the same provisions of the electoral law now been quashed, that ruling did not bind the Constitutional Court in that the ECtHR decision was based precisely on the margin of discretion that States authorities – including their constitutional courts – enjoy in the electoral domain (see *2013 Yearbook*, p. 364).

The judgment, extremely relevant as it affects fundamental political rights, had a number of effects. Some courts have in fact raised the issue of constitutionality of a number of particularly controversial legal provisions, so far not quashed by the Constitutional Court. Among others, the issue of constitutionality was raised in connection to the provisions of the Consolidated law on immigration criminalising the illegal entry and residence in the Country as well as the violation of the order to leave the territory of the State by reason that such rules were adopted by a Parliament that was "illegitimate" in that it had been elected under an electoral law that did not respect the political rights of citizens. The issue was dismissed as inadmissible on the grounds that judgment 1/2014 carefully clarified that it was without prejudice both to the acts enacted by Parliaments elected since 2005 onwards and to the acts that Chambers will adopt pending new elections (Constitutional Court, judg. 57/2014).

III. Asylum and International Protection

A. Recognition of International Protection

The Supreme Court quashed and referred back a number of appeal courts judgments which had rejected the applications for international protection filed by some Nigerians on the ground that the applicants' statements about the threats connected to the existence of "secret societies" or otherwise related to the situation of widespread violence in some parts of Nigeria were not credible, not substantiated or "repetitive". The Supreme Court considered that in similar circumstances national courts are required to formulate their reasoning along the lines of the ECJ jurisprudence, referring in particular to the cases 2009/172 (*Elgafaji*) and 2014/285 (*Diakité*). In those judgments, the ECJ has developed the requirements for the recognition of subsidiary protection in relation to cases involving individuals coming from areas affected by armed conflicts. This form of protection, which must be recognised in the presence of a serious and individual threat to the life or person of an applicant for subsidiary protection, is not subject to the condition that that applicant adduces evidence that he is specifically targeted by reason or factors particular to his personal circumstances: "the existence of such a threat can exceptionally be considered to be established where the degree of indiscriminate violence characterising the armed conflict taking place – assessed by the competent national authorities before which an application for subsidiary protection is made (…) reaches such a high level that substantial grounds are shown for believing that a civilian, returned to the relevant Country or, as the case may be, to the relevant region, would, solely on account of his presence on the territory of that Country or region, face a real risk of being subject to that threat." National courts are therefore invited to review their decisions in light of these parameters. The fact that the situation of Nigeria in recent years could fall within this particular notion of "armed conflict" must be taken into account in dealing with applications for international protection filed by individuals coming from that Country (see Court of Cassation, civil division, judgments 7 July 2014, No. 15466; 17 October 2014, No. 22111).

Again in connection with an asylum seeker from Nigeria, the Tribunal of Bologna extensively reviewed the socio-political and humanitarian situation of the Country concerned and concluded, reversing the decision of the Asylum Territorial Commission, that the applicant's life, precisely because of his family history (Christian, a native of the northern territories of the Country with a Muslim majority, the son of a politician) and for reasons related to the events that happened in the Country of origin, had considerably worsened (events such as the killing of his father, the loss of the inheritance and the house, the injuries suffered, the flight from the Country of origin were mentioned). Moreover, the applicant had suffered assaults and abuses, including the deprivation of the house left to him by his father, and was again exposed to the risk of serious threats to his life or physical integrity. This, according to the court, justified the granting of political asylum (Tribunal of Bologna, Sec. I, judg. 3 November 2014, No. 25).

Differently, in another case involving a Nigerian citizen who claimed to come from the northern part of the Country, the Tribunal of Trieste (judg. 14 October 2014) granted the applicant humanitarian protection pursuant to article 5(6) of the Consolidated law on immigration. The applicant, who declared she had fled Nigeria because of terrorist acts carried out by groups such Boko Haram, during the interview with the Asylum Territorial Commission recalled the attack and the fire caused by Boko Haram against Christian churches, following which she had suffered severe burns.

In its judgment No. 6503 (civil division, Sec. VI, 20 March 2014) the Supreme Court, dealing with the application for international protection filed by a citizen of Bangladesh, tackled the distinction between refugee and subsidiary protection status (lgs.d. 19 November 2007, No. 251, article 14). The applicant in the present case was the youngest member of an influential political family, whose father was tortured and killed in 2012 for his involvement in a political party. Fled from Bangladesh through India, the applicant had arrived in Libya and from there to Lampedusa. The Court noted that, while the status of refugee is granted once the existence of a specific and individual risk for the person concerned has been established, subsidiary protection may be granted even if the causal link between the applicant story and the risk is less evident. Since there was no evidence of a direct involvement of the applicant in political activities, he must not be granted the status of refugee, but the status of subsidiary protection on account of the fact that in his Country of origin he would face serious risks.

Worth to mention is that, in different circumstances, the Supreme Court dismissed claims against courts decisions concerning applications for international protection, also in consideration to the recent reform of article 360 code of civil procedure. In its original formulation, that is before being reformed by the Consolidated law on immigration 83/2012, said provision provided that appeals before the Supreme Court could challenge "the lack, the inadequacy or the contradictory character of the court reasoning with respect to a crucial issue of the dispute, identified either by the parties or ex officio". The current formulation, on the other hand, limits the jurisdiction of the Supreme Court to "the omitted examination of a fact that was crucial for the judgment and that has been discussed between the parties." For an example, see Court of Cassation, civil division, Sec. VI, judg. 29 May 2014, No. 12076: the application for international protection filed by a Togolese national by reason of threats allegedly faced in his home Country was rejected on the ground that the adduced threats seemed to refer to inter-personal relationships (even if the threat to the person of an applicant by reason of private violence may be exacerbated by the alleged inefficiency of the police of the Country). Be that as it may, the Supreme Court, in light of the reformed article 360, could not review this point which, having already been identified before the trial court, could not therefore be reviewed.

B. Humanitarian Protection of Victims of Exploitation

In a case concerning the application for a resident permit filed by a Nigerian women who had been assisted for four years in the framework of the protection program for victims of trafficking set up by article 18 of the Consolidated law on immigration, the Supreme Administrative Council clarified that the confirmation of this regime – and therefore the suspension of the expulsion order – was possible only when the various conditions laid down by the law persisted. In particular, despite the fact that the applicant had been forced into prostitution and had been a victim of exploitation was undisputed, according to the judges, other conditions were no longer present. In particular, the Supreme Administrative Council referred to the lack of any "serious and current" risks for the person and to the lack of any effective contribution to investigative and judicial activities aimed at combating crime and at prosecuting offenders. Absent these conditions, the application for a residence permit under article 18 of the Consolidated law on immigration must be rejected (Supreme Administrative Council, judg. 22 December 2014, No. 6347).

IV. Discrimination

A. Burden to Qualify Discrimination

The Supreme Court dealt with the case of a retiree who complained that INPS (National Social Welfare Institution) adopted a discriminatory behaviour against him on account of the fact that he was granted a pension which was lower than that of another person with the same social security situation. The Court held that in appeals brought before the Court of Cassation relying on, in particular, articles 14 (non-discrimination) and 6 ECHR (fair trial), the plaintiff not only has the burden to clearly indicate the standards inferred from the ECHR or from the ECtHR case-law that he considers to be relevant. He also has to explain the reasons why he considers that the trial court has departed from these standards, indicating which aspects of his case are similar to cases dealt with by the Strasbourg Court (Court of Cassation, civil division, Sec. employment, judg. 7 January 2014, No. 76). The general reference to an allegedly suffered discriminatory treatment or violation of due process standards cannot be dealt with by courts.

B. Access of Foreigners to the National Voluntary Civil Service

The issue of equal status of foreign and Italian citizens in relation to the possibility to access the call for the national voluntary civil service has been dealt with since 2012 (see *2013 Yearbook*, p. 311). On the issue, however, courts rulings has been discordant. Indeed, while the Tribunal of Brescia confirmed the legitimacy of the current legislation (article 3 of lgs.d. 77/2002, implementing l. 64/2001) that restricts the access to the national civil service solely to Italian citizens, both the trial and the appeal court of Milan considered said legislation discriminatory. Meanwhile, calls for the national civil service have been delayed. The 2013/2014 call, which originally applied the restrictive rule, had been reopened after another ruling for unlawful discrimination had been issued. Some categories of non-Italian citizens legally resident in the Country were therefore subsequently admitted: EU nationals, refugees, holders of resident permit for subsidiary protection, third-Country nationals who are long-term residents. In 2014 two important rulings, which in all likelihood conclusively settled the dispute, had been issued.

In the first one, the Supreme Administrative Council (opinion 9 October 2014, No. 1091), after an extensive review of the national legislation and jurisprudence dealing with the national civil service, recognised that what initially had unquestionably been an alternative to compulsory military service, grounded solely on article 52 of the Constitution, has evolved into "a voluntary service that can be accessed thought a public competition and that has wide purposes including the mandatory duties of social solidarity and the duty to contribute to the material and spiritual progress of the society provided for in articles 2 and 4 of the Constitution, incumbent not only upon Italian citizens, but also upon foreign nationals residing in our Country." The national civil service could also be classified among the activities, such as internships, aimed at both the professional training of young people and their access to the job market. The possibility to access civil service must therefore be granted to all those who, according to EU law, have access to vocational training: EU citizens, third-country nationals who are long-term residents, and holder of international protection resident permits.

In the second judgment (Joint Sec., ord. 10 October 2014, No. 20661), the Supreme Court, invoking the special importance of the matter, raised the issue of constitutionality of article 3 of the l. 77/2002 notwithstanding the dispute at the origin of the relevant proceedings had already been settled. The contested provision, in fact, establishing that holding Italian citizenship was a necessary condition to access the call for the national civil service Italian, undoubtedly refers to a notion of formal citizenship. And it is precisely for this that, according to the Court, it is discriminatory. Indeed, the civil service, based on articles 2 and 4 of the Constitution, must be open to all those who enjoy the fundamental rights recognised in article 2 Const., and therefore also to foreigners legally residing in the Country (not only to those falling within "protected" categories under EU law). Such a conclusion is not in contraction with article 52 Const. according to which the defence of the Fatherland (which includes the activities of the civil service) is a "sacred duty of every citizen." In this regards, while the main objective of article 52 Const. is to call all citizens, without exemptions and privileges, to serve their Country as the law provides, it does not rule out that such a broad duty may be carried out, on a voluntary basis, also by foreigners. The joint sections of the Court of Cassation, therefore, concluded: "the participation of foreigners legally residing in Italy to a community of rights that is broader and more comprehensive than the one based on the notion of citizenship in its formal sense, postulates that foreigners, without discrimination on the grounds of nationality, are also entitled, on a voluntary basis, to engage in civil and social activities in favour of the community itself, experiencing the potential inclusiveness of solidarity actions on behalf of others and for the protection of the values enshrined in the Constitution". The issue has now to be examined by the Constitutional Court.

V. Rights of Persons with Disabilities

A. Right to Challenge a Marriage Contracted by a Person Allegedly Deprived of Legal Capacity

The Supreme Court dismissed as manifestly ill-founded the issue of constitutionality of articles 120 and 127 civil code raised by the relatives of a man who had married with his domestic worker. According to the plaintiffs, their relative, although neither interdicted nor placed under guardianship, had absolute no legal capacity. The Court, in particular, pointed out that marriage is a peculiar legal act: the right to challenge it on account of the fact that one of the spouses lacked legal capacity could only be invoked by the latter (a right that, in any case, extinguishes after one year of cohabitation). Such right, moreover, could not be transmitted to the spouse's heirs, who may have an interest in excluding the unexpected relative-in-law from the inheritance of the deceased. The Court therefore held that the current regulatory framework is in line with the full recognition of the dignity of the person with disability, as it is established also in the 2006 Convention on the Rights of Persons with Disabilities. Moreover, the Court noted, the legal framework allows for the possibility that, even in undertaking very personal acts such as challenging one's marriage, the individual may be assisted by a special trustee. This reflects the recognition of both the eminently free nature of the choice to marry and the inherent dignity of the person. Indeed, while in a vulnerable position because of illness or old age, the individual's legal capacity cannot, but partially, be limited. While recognising that it may occasionally give rise to abuses, the Court concluded that the choice of legislators, who had clearly opted to grant the right to challenge a marriage only to the spouses and not to the heirs, is reasonable and does not raise doubts as to its constitutionality (Court of Cassation, civil division, Sec. I judg. 30 June 2014, No. 14794).

B. Discrimination in Schools and in Public Transport

The ruling of the civil division of the Supreme Court, Joint Sec., 25 November 2014, No. 25011, innovating in the matter, recognised that the failure to assign to a girl with severe disabilities a support teacher in accordance with the individualised educational project developed by the competent institutions is not a violation of a legitimate interest of the student with disabilities, to be challenged before administrative courts, but a discriminatory act (indirect discrimination) which falls within the jurisdiction of ordinary courts. In these circumstances, indeed, the Supreme Court confirmed the possibility to file a suit for discriminatory conduct pursuant to article 3 of law 1 March 2006, No. 67 (Measures for the judicial protection of persons with disabilities victims of discrimination) according to article 702-*bis* code of civil procedure (as reformed by l. 150/2011). The case involved a girl with severe disabilities who, while having the right to a support teacher for all school hours (40) in a kindergarten, had been assigned by the school administration only a limited number of hours of educational support (afternoons were excluded). According to the Ministry of Education and to a settled case-law on the issue, the competent authority to adjudicate the dispute was the administrative court. After a detailed review of the relevant domestic and international legislation (in particular the Convention on the Rights of Persons with Disabilities), the joint sections of the Supreme Court concluded, however, that the right to education of children with disabilities is a fundamental right, the protection of which is dependent upon the action of the public administration that must guarantee the school attendance, including in kindergarten, of children with disabilities. The Court acknowledged that "the category of fundamental rights does not delimit an area that is impenetrable for public authorities". Indeed, the latter are called "not only to perform those acts that may be necessary to implement the rights guaranteed by the Constitution, but also to guarantee their systemic protection while balancing them with the needs of public services and taking into account, in order to satisfy the public interest, of the limit of available resources decided by competent authorities." Among other things, the Supreme Court reiterated that also the issue concerning the presence of the crucifix in classrooms, while affecting a fundamental right such as the right to religious freedom, in Italy had been dealt with exclusively by administrative courts. According to the Supreme Court, however, the present case concerned the failure to adopt a measure (the appointment of the support teacher for all school hours) that, once established in the individualised educational project to respond to the needs of the child with disabilities, leaves no discretion to the public body. The judgment is also important as it pointed out that the right to education of children with disabilities cannot be confined to compulsory education but must be understood to also apply to kindergarten attendance.

The judgment of the joint sections of the Court of Cassation, however, does not rule out the possibility that disputes concerning access to education of students with disabilities continue to be settled by administrative courts. As a matter of fact, also in 2014 numerous judgments issued by administrative courts recognised the right of students with disabilities to have their class assigned a support teacher, whose working hours must be determined taking into account the staffing of the school and the actual needs of integration of the student – with prevalence of the latter. In particular, according to the TAR Campania, Sec. VIII, judg. 9 January 2014, No. 51, in cases involving children with severe disabilities, the assignment of a support teacher in derogation from the regular school staffing has to be always assessed against the specific learning difficulties of the pupil, which are dependent on the type of handicap, its severity, but also on the evolution of the disease as well as on possible improvements. In the case under analysis, instead of taking into account the pre-eminent educational needs of the child with severe disabilities, school authorities had decided the assignment of educational support mainly taking into account the staffing plan for support teachers established by the Regional school office. See also, TAR Sicily, Sec. III, judgments 3 February 2014, No. 360; 3 December 2014, No. 3111; TAR Apulia, Sec. II, 27 November 2014, No. 2922; TAR Calabria, Sec. II, judg. 15 January 2014, No. 46; TAR Campania, Sec. VIII, judgments 16 March 2014, No. 1788; 16 April 2014, No. 2172; 15 May 2014, No. 2672; 12 June 2014, No. 3261; 27 June 2014, No. 3589.

Moreover, according to the Supreme Administrative Council (Sec. VI, judg. 27 October 2014, No. 5317), the non-pecuniary damage suffered by a child with a severe form of autism who, for about a month and a half, had been assisted by a support teacher for only half of the hours established by his educational project should be compensated, on the ground that the violation he suffered affected a constitutionally protected right (article 2059 civil code).

The Tribunal of Rome, Sec. II, in its judgment of 10 June 2014, ordered, pursuant to l. 67/2006, the joint-stock company managing public transport in Rome and the body public "Roma Capitale" to compensate the non-pecuniary damage suffered by a minor with physical disabilities. The latter, indeed, had been unable to access trains in some Rome metro stations because of the ineffectiveness, rather that the absence, of facilities for disabled, which were either not working properly or not equipped with staff. The Tribunal held that this was a case of indirect discrimination, which occurs when a rule, practice or other behaviour, apparently neutral, put persons with disabilities at a disadvantage if compared with other people. The Tribunal condemned both the transport company (a joint stock company), and the public body that, owing 100% of the company shares, should have monitored the non-discriminatory management of the service.

C. Compulsory Employment of Workers with Disabilities

A number of decisions of the Supreme Court clarified that the right of persons with disabilities to be employed pursuant to the quota system established by law 68/1999 (Regulations for the right to work of persons with disabilities) can be invoked also by a disabled person that is not unemployed, but rather an occasional worker. In the present case, the Autonomous Province of Trent opposed the hiring of some teachers with disabilities who, at the moment of assuming office, were working as substitute teachers. The Court recognised that the purpose of the provision on compulsory employment is to be found also taking into consideration the principles established by the United Nations Convention on the Rights of Persons with Disabilities, ratified and implemented by Italy with l. 3 March 2009, No. 18, whose article 27, in particular, provides that "States Parties recognise the right of persons with disabilities to work, on an equal basis with others; this includes the right to the opportunity to gain a living by work freely chosen or accepted in a labour market and work environment that is open, inclusive and accessible to persons with disabilities". It was therefore correct, according to the Court, to interpret the 1999 law, whose purpose is precisely the inclusion of people with disabilities, in the sense that a fixed-term contract could not exclude a person with disabilities from the benefits established by that law (see Court of Cassation, civil division, Sec. employment, judgments 20 November 2014, No. 24723; 9 December 2014, Nos. 25897, 25898; 10 December 2014, No. 26033).

VI. Social Rights

A. Wrongful Dismissal and Reinstatement

In one of the last ruling issued pursuant to article 18 of l. 300/1970 (Workers' statute) on the obligation to reinstate the worker unfairly dismissed (the law was reformed in 2012 and is going to be radically changed with the new labour legislation adopted in late 2014), the Court of Cassation (civil division, Sec. employment, 30 July 2014, No. 17372) reiterated that the obligation for the company to reinstate the worker (and union representative) fired without just cause cannot be restricted. But this did not mean that the company may limit itself to pay the worker's salary without organising his return to work. The performance of work, indeed, is a right but also a duty for the individual, the work being an instrument of professional and personal growth at the social and individual level – as recognised by articles 1 and 4 Const. Similarly, article 18 of the Workers' statute (the version in force at the relevant time) established the obligation for the employer that was not ensuring the effective reinstatement of the employee to pay, in addition to the amount due to the employee, an amount equivalent to the latter salary and to allocate it to the fund for pensions adjustments, that is to the community.

B. Employees of Italian Diplomatic Missions Abroad

The Court of Cassation held that the provisions of d.p.r. 5 January 1967, No. 18, as amended and supplemented (Rules for the administration of foreign affairs) are legitimate and not discriminatory. The rule which had been challenged, in particular, provided that diplomatic missions, in addition to permanent staff, could employ, with contracts of indefinite duration, additional local personnel. The latter could be recruited with individual contracts partially regulated by local legislation and therefore providing for a salary indexed to the local standards which, for the plaintiff in the present case (a Russian citizen who had then acquired Italian citizenship, employed at the Italian embassy in Moscow), could also be considerably low if compared to the salary received by other employees of the embassy who, while similarly recruited, were Italian nationals (Court of Cassation, civil division, Sec. employment, judg. 26 September 2014, No. 20356). The Court, in particular, excluded that the above-mentioned provision could constitute a violation of the principle of non-discrimination on the ground of nationality enshrined in the Universal Declaration of Human Rights, the ECHR and the International Covenant on Civil and Political Rights.

C. Limits in Accessing University (Numerus Clausus)

The lawfulness of the practice of enrolling in foreign universities to circumvent the "numerous clausus" rule in order to skip the entrance examination (l. 264/1999) organised by Italian universities for some degree courses (medicine, dentistry) is controversial. In 2014, Regional Administrative Tribunals issued discordant rulings on the issue.

The TAR Lombardy (Sec. I, judg. 26 November 2014, No. 1297) dealt with a case involving the refusal of the University of Brescia to enrol to the second and subsequent years of the degree course in medicine a group of (Italian) students who had attended university courses in medicine in Spain and Romania, where no entrance test was required, on account of the fact that they had not passed the entrance test that the University considered as a condition for enrolment. The TAR held the refusal unlawful. In particular, the Tribunal examined the Italian legislation concerning the "numerous clausus" at universities in light of the principles of free movement in the EU and the rules of the 1997 Lisbon Convention on the Recognition of Qualifications concerning Higher Education in the European Region (ratified by Italy with l. 148/2002), a fundamental component of the European Higher Education Area project ("Bologna Process"). According to the Lisbon Convention, States have an obligation to recognise periods of study completed by students in another Member State, unless "substantial differences can be shown between the periods of study completed in another Party and the part of the higher education programme which they would replace in the Party in which recognition is sought." According to the TAR, passing the entrance test could not be considered a part of the education program. Indeed, it has to be intended as a measure to limit the number of students due to the financial constraints of the university system, favouring the entrance of the most prepared ones on the basis of a selection which, by the way, tests knowledge and skills that do not necessarily have to do with the content of the degree course. As for the "numerous clausus", the ECtHR considered it – albeit with some reservations – compatible with article 2 Protocol I ECHR (see *Tarantino v. Italy*, *2014 Yearbook*, p. 333). The idea that those who attend the first years of a degree course in a foreign university (and then come back to Italy skipping the entrance examination) are opportunistic is based on the presumption that the quality of higher education in Italy is higher. This misconception not only denies the value of educational programs of other Countries, but contributes to the isolation of the Italian university system from the European and international context, in contradiction with the principles of free movement and of the European Higher Education Area referred to above.

D. Sharing of Care Expenses

In 2014 the Supreme Administrative Council and TARs have reiterated the position according to which regions and – in the absence of regional regulations – municipalities with their own regulations, may require persons hospitalised in care facilities to contribute to the expenses connected with their care with amounts that are higher than what would result from the strict application of the criteria for the determination of their economic situation (ISEE – equivalent economic situation indicator). In the present case, some municipalities had decided to also take into account sources of income not considered by ISEE – such as disability pension and attendance allowance (Supreme Administrative Council, Sec. III, judgments 14 January 2014, No. 99; 8 April 2014, No. 1676; TAR Veneto, Sec. III, judg. 8 October 2014, No. 1284).

VII. Laws Affecting Individual Rights with Retroactive Effect

The Constitutional Court (judg. 191/2014) quashed a provision of l.d. 225/2010 on the ground that it had amended, with retroactive effect, the requirements that candidates had to possess in order to be appointed for the position of Government commissioner for the City of Rome. In this way, in fact, legislators had interfered – favouring the Prime Minister Office – in a legal dispute pending before the administrative court initiated by the commissioner who had been appointed on the basis of the pre-existing criteria that, after the entry into force of the new regulation, had been replaced. The legislative intervention was not only deemed unsustainable as for the content (the candidate's prior working experience in private companies was introduced as an "essential" condition), but also declared contrary to the principles of due process and of the independence of the judiciary (violation of article 6 ECHR as "interposed parameter", and article 111 Const.). Indeed, the interference of the legislative power in the administration of justice in order to influence the outcome of a judicial proceedings can only be justified by overriding public interests (absent in the present case).

The issue of the legitimacy of legislative interventions which retroactively and negatively affect the treatment of pensions holders (see *2013 Yearbook*, pp. 320–323) was addressed in 2014 in a variety of contexts. In its judgment 10/2014, the Constitutional Court dealt with the ECtHR case-law as expressed in *Maggio* (see *2012 Yearbook*, pp. 305 and 347), reiterating what it had already established in its judgment 264/2012 (see *2013 Yearbook*, p. 320) and therefore dismissing as manifestly ill-founded the issue of constitutionality of the rules that retroactively applied the contribution-based pension scheme also to those who had gained their retirement working in Switzerland. Irrespective of this, the Court of Cassation, civil division, Sec. employment, ord. 20 February 2014, No. 4048, decided to raise the issue of constitutionality of the provisions of the 2007 budget law that retroactively imposed an authentic interpretation bearing negative effects on still pending disputes involving holders of "reversibility" pensions.

A great number of decisions on a similar issue, but concerning the social security situation (INPS position) of aeronautical pilots (flight crew pension fund) were adopted in 2014. On this dispute, numerous were the judgments of the Court of Cassation: Joint Sec., judg. 28 May 2014, No. 11907; see also, among others: civil division, Sec. employment, judgments 30 October 2014, No. 23066; 18 November 2014, Nos. 24527, 24528, 24529, 24530, 24531, 24532; 19 November 2014, Nos. 24672, 24673, 24674; 20 November 2014, Nos. 24732, 24733; 24 November 2014, Nos. 24951, 24957; 25 November 2014, Nos. 25024, 25025, 25026, 25027; 26 November 2014, Nos. 25165, 25166, 25167, 25168; 28 November 2014, Nos. 25346, 25347; 1 December 2014, Nos. 25381, 25385; 3 December 2014, No. 25596; 4 December 2014, Nos. 25675, 25681; 15 December 2014, Nos. 26309, 26310, 26311, 26312, 26313, 23614, 23616, 23617, 23618; 16 December 2014, Nos. 26405, 26406, 26407, 26408, 26409, 26410; 17 December 2014, Nos. 26603, 26604; 18 December 2014, Nos. 26734, 26736; 22 December 2014, No. 27230;

23 December 2014, Nos. 27365, 27366, 27367; 29 December 2014, Nos. 27417, 27418, 27419, 27421, 27423; 30 December 2014, Nos. 27473, 27474, 27475, 27476, 27477.

With judgments Nos. 191/2014 and 227/2014, the Constitutional Court ruled on the issue as well. In these cases, the Court reiterated that under Italian law the prohibition for the legislative power to enact retroactive law only applies to criminal matters; in other fields, and in particular on social security issues, an intervention which retroactively bears a (moderate) negative impact on the worker may be legitimate if it does nothing more than clarify (authentic interpretation) the content of a provision giving it a meaning already contained in it, especially when the legal provision had created a situation of legal uncertainty because of an unresolved conflict in jurisprudence. Moreover, according to a consolidated position of the Constitutional Court, a retroactive provision, even on social security issues, cannot be considered unreasonable if it responds to a need for systematic order imposed by the contradictory jurisprudence that from such norm has originated (see, for all: Constitutional Court, judg. 227/2014). This conclusion was considered in line with the case-law of the ECtHR, which had recognised the compatibility with the right to fair trial (article 6 ECHR) of the possibility for legislators to enact laws with retroactive effects to settle pending disputes at the advantage of social security institutions (disputes that, relying on previous case-law, could have been decided in manners favourable to pension holders) when the legislative intervention is demanded by "overriding reasons of general interest". Therefore, (not final) court and appeal court decisions that had recognised to pilots pension benefits resulting from a provision on the calculation of pension shares dating back to the 1960s, and amended by a 2007 law of authentic interpretation having retroactive effect, are quashed.

In some of the above-mentioned judgments, parties of the dispute asked the Supreme Court to submit a request for preliminary ruling to the ECJ or a request for an advisory opinion to the ECtHR pursuant to Protocol XVI ECHR. The Supreme Court, however, noted that Protocol XVI had not yet entered into force. As for the possible role of the ECJ, the Court confirmed the distinction between, on the one hand, cases involving alleged violations of human rights protected by the ECHR and falling within the competences of EU law – for which it is conceivable for Italian courts to submit a request for a preliminary ruling to the ECJ in order to receive an interpretation – and, on the other hand, cases of alleged violation of human rights recognised by the ECHR that are unrelated to EU law. Only with respect to the latter the Italian courts can raise the issue of constitutionality of the relevant Italian norm by referring to article 117(1) Const. (violation of international law or the ECHR). In the event the constitutionality review of a given provision is not favourable, the individual involved may also bring the case before the ECtHR for the determination of the State responsibility for the alleged violation of its international obligations.

The principle according to which retroactive provisions dealing with pensions are legitimate if they are enacted to respond to the need to rationalise and reform the social security system is reaffirmed also in relation to business owners who had in the past carried out activities similar to that of employees: see Court of Cassation, civil division, Sec. employment, judg. 6 October 2014, No. 21006; Sec. VI, judg. 22 December 2014, No. 27275 (see also *2012 Yearbook*, p. 305). On the elimination of the so-called "gold clause" (adjustment of pensions to wage increases of colleagues still at work) applied to the banking sector, the Court of Cassation confirmed its previous case-law (see civil division, Sec. employment, judgment 11 July 2014, No. 16022; 16 July 2014, Nos. 16257, 16258; 29 July 2014, No. 17182; 19 September 2014, No. 19781; 22 September 2014, No. 19928).

Similarly, the Supreme Court had to deal again with cases related to the transfer from the local to the national administration of public school non-teaching personnel, whose salary treatment had worsened because a provision with retroactive effect did not recognise the length of service they had completed with their first employer. Such a result, unfavourable for the worker, had to be considered incompatible with EU law on "transfer of undertaking": the appeals filed by the Ministry of Education were therefore systematically dismissed (see *2012 Yearbook*, pp. 345–348 and 363–364; *2013 Yearbook*, p. 320; for 2014, see, among others, Court of Cassation, civil division, Sec. VI, judgments 19 March 2014, Nos. 6277, 6278, 6279, 6280; 9 June 2014, Nos. 19872, 12967, 12973, 12974, 12975, 12976; 25 June 2014, No. 14488; 26 June 2014, Nos. 14588, 14589; 27 June 2014, No. 14698; 1 July 2014, No. 14982; 4 July 2014, No. 15417; Sec. employment, judgments 30 May 2014, No. 12202; 1 August 2014, No. 17547; 5 August 2014, No. 17621; 6 August 2014, No. 17703; 12 August 2014, No. 17832; Sec. VI, judgments 6 November 2014, Nos. 23714, 23775; 7 November 2014, Nos. 23771, 23772; 14 November 2014, Nos. 24270, 24271, 24272, 24273, 24274, 24275, 24276; 19 November 2014, Nos. 24577, 24578, 24579, 24580, 24581; 22 December 2014, No. 27274).

Another group of cases involving INPS employees and retirees focusing on the same issue (retroactive application of laws in the field of social security that, while producing adverse effects for workers, are considered crucial for the reform of the system) has been dealt with by the Constitutional Court in its judgment 156/2014 and by the Court of Cassation, civil division, Sec. employment, in its judgments 22 October 2014, No. 22382; 7 November 2014, No. 23803; 10 November 2014, No. 23928; 27 November 2014, Nos. 25241, 25261; 9 December 2014, No. 25870; 16 December 2014, Nos. 26442, 26443, 26444, 26445, 26446, 26447, 26448, 26449; 17 December 2014, Nos. 26579, 26580, 26581, 26582, 26583, 26584, 26585, 26586; 26587; 19 December 2014, No. 27121; 22 December 2014, Nos. 27248, 27252). In all these decisions, lawsuits brought by INPS against its former employees who had challenged the legality of a "solidarity contribution" imposed on them in 1999 were successful before the Court of Cassation.

In other cases, the Supreme Court excluded the existence of the need for a structural reform of the system justifying, for imperative reasons of a general nature, the retroactive application of laws that unfavourably affected retirees. According to the Court of Cassation, indeed, the provisions of the 2007 budget law that imposed the transition from the partially retributive pension scheme applicable for accountants and business consultants to the contribution-based pension scheme (and thus to a system less favourable for workers) are to be intended as non-retroactive (see, for example, civil division, Sec. employment, judg. 13 November 2014, No. 24221; see, also, judg. 12 August 2014, No. 17892).

Legislative interventions applying retroactively have been enacted also with respect to issues other that pension regimes. The Court of Cassation, civil division, Sec. VI, judgments 6 February 2014, No. 2760 and 10 April 2014, No. 8491, dealt with the situation created by l. 4 November 2010, No. 183, article 32(5) which provided for the closure, upon the payment of a comprehensive compensation, of a number of disputes between the Italian Post Office and a group of its workers whose employment contracts, while apparently of indefinite duration, had been converted into fixed-term contracts. While negatively affecting rights with retroactive effect, the Court confirmed the legitimacy of the above-mentioned provision. The Court, in particular, relied on the rulings of the Italian Constitutional Court which had highlighted the extent to which the ECtHR case-law recognised States a margin of appreciation regarding the use of retroactive legislation in non-criminal matters. Similarly, several judgments recognised the opportunity for regions to enact, within constitutional parameters, retroactive provisions in the social area.

VIII. Immigration

A. Right to Family Reunification

The Supreme Court (Joint Sec., 24 October 2014, No. 22612) confirmed that the right to family reunification for immigrants is a fundamental human right rooted in articles 8 ECHR and 7 CFREU (see also *2014 Yearbook*, p. 295). The case challenged before the Court concerned a delay in the administrative procedure for the recognition of the right to family unity. The applicant, a Ghanaian citizen, in 2007 had obtained the authorisation for the entry in Italy of her two minor children residing in Ghana, but it was only in 2012 that one of the two children (a DNA test ordered by the Italian embassy in Ghana excluded the applicant's maternity as for the other children) had obtained an entry visa. According to the Supreme Court, however, although the dispute ultimately concerned the effectiveness of an individual right, the competent court to hear the applicant's claim for compensation of damages resulting from a disproportionate delay in the execution of the administrative procedure is not the ordinary but the administrative court. The dispute, indeed, focused on the request for damages against the Ministry of Foreign Affairs and therefore it concerned the excessive length of administrative proceedings. Furthermore, the Court noted that administrative justice guarantees as adequately as ordinary courts the protection of fundamental rights (see, for example, Supreme Administrative Council, Sec. V, judg. 21 August 2014, No. 4273; TAR Bolzano Trentino-Alto Adige, Sec. I, judg. 30 December 2014, No. 305).

B. Expulsions, Push-backs

A number of judgments delivered by administrative courts, summarised in the decision of the Supreme Administrative Council of 12 November 2014, No. 5570, gave application to the principles established by the Constitutional Court in its judgment 202/2013 (see *2014 Yearbook*, p. 295) according to which article 5(5) of the Consolidated law on immigration has to be interpreted in the sense that the renewal of the residence permit may be granted to a non-EU citizen despite the latter had been convicted for one of the offense for which the law excludes such a possibility. For the Constitutional Court, in particular, this would be possible whether, after a careful determination, there was either no evidence of the migrant's social dangerousness or the existence of significant family ties in Italy. In above-mentioned judgment of the Supreme Administrative Council, relevant was also judgment 32/2014 of the Constitutional Court which had recognised the unconstitutionality (for violation of article 77 Const.) of the rules introduced in 2005 which had significantly increased penalties for a number of drug-related offenses by reintroducing the distinction between "soft drugs" like hashish, and "hard drugs" such as cannabis derivatives (heroin and other opiates). As a matter of fact, in the case adjudicated by the Supreme Administrative Council, the offense the applicant was found guilt of, and that therefore barred the possibility to obtain a residence permit, concerned the possession of hashish (Supreme Administrative Council, Sec. III, judg. 12 November 2014, No. 5570).

The Supreme Court (Sec. VI, ord. 30 July 2014, No. 17407) issued a ruling on the facts occurred in May and June 2014 involving a Kazakh citizen, wife of a controversial businessman and political dissident, who had been expelled to Kazakhstan together with her underage daughter in circumstances that raised several concerns. Indeed, within a few hours the woman not only had been reached by police officers in her house in Rome, but she was issued a deportation order, immediately validated by the justice of the peace on the ground that she had no valid residence permit, and then she had been forcibly boarded with her daughter on a flight to Kazakhstan, a Country ruled by a regime known for repressing political opponents (including the woman's husband). The expulsion order was challenged by the woman's Italian lawyers and, pending the proceedings, the Prefect of Rome, in July 2013, recognised the absence of the conditions for enforcing an expulsion under article 13(2)-lett. a) of the Consolidated law on immigration. As a matter of fact, as the concerned foreign citizen not only held two valid residence permits granted in two EU Countries, but she also had a diplomatic passport issued by the Central African Republic, the Prefect ordered the revocation of the expulsion order. While the applicant sought a declaration of invalidity of the expulsion order with retroactive effect, the justice of the peace simply ordered the end of the dispute. An appeal before the Court of Cassation against the latter decision was then filed. The Supreme Court recognised the relevance of the applicant's interest in the determination of the allegedly illegitimate intervention of the justice of the peace. Indeed, a finding recognising the illegitimacy of the deprivation of liberty suffered by the applicant not only implied the right to compensation but also the right of the person unlawfully expelled to return in Italy. The Supreme Court extensively criticised the system of "dual protection" existing in the Italian legal order for these cases: on the one hand, full court jurisdiction on the validity of the expulsion order and, on the other hand, legitimacy control (validation) on the same act to be performed in the immediacy of its issuance, even as a basis for the adoption of measures restricting individual freedom (detention in Identification and Expulsion Centres (CIEs), forced repatriation). The Court noted that, although theoretically capable of ensuring respect for the freedom, rights and dignity of the person, this system has a number of shortcomings, highlighted by the events under analysis. In fact, at the time of the validation decision – actually occurred a few hours from the issuance of the act – the expulsion order was formally valid and effective. However, the sequence of actions which included the issuance of the expulsion order, its forced execution (the right to voluntary return was not recognised due to the risk of absconding) and the validation decision before the justice of the peace had been so rapid that both the challenge to the expulsion order and the same validation decision had been deprived of their efficacy. In addition, given the distance from Italy, the fact that the applicant's repatriation was decided and carried out in little more than two days had hampered the initiation and the conduct of the proceedings challenging the expulsion. In conclusion, the order issued by the Supreme Court clearly condemned the conduct of State authorities. The act validating the expulsion was therefore quashed since it had not established the original manifest unlawfulness of the expulsion order, which was to be inferred from the way in which the applicant was seized: a night raid not clearly motivated; the incorrect presumption of the non-authenticity of a Central African Republic diplomatic passport and of two EU residence permits, indeed perfectly valid (and yet the ways in which the operation had been planned indicated that the authorities knew everything about the identity of the applicant); the deprivation of any opportunity to exercise the right of defence and to apply for asylum.

The above-mentioned order is connected to the decision the Supreme Court, civil division, Sec. VI, judg. 5 June 2014, No. 12609 (see also, No. 12612), which clarified that, in order to comply with articles 5.f) and 13 ECHR, and then to the Constitution (article 117 (1) Const.), article 14 of the Consolidated law on immigration, pursuant to which the justice of the peace validates the deportation and detention order in CIEs issued by the *Questore* (chief of police), must be interpreted in the sense that the judicial review should not be limited to a mere assessment of formal conditions, but has to be extended to an assessment of the lawfulness of detention in its merit.

> The issue of constitutionality raised in connection with articles 13(5)-ter and 14 of the Consolidated law on immigration on the validation of the deportation order by reason of their alleged incompatibility with articles 2, 3, 10, 13, 24, 97, 111 and 117 Const. (the latter in relation to article 5 ECHR) was dismissed by the Constitutional Court on account of the fact that the issue had been too broadly formulated. Among other things, the referral order claimed that the above-mentioned provisions give police authorities wide powers to identify the CIE in which the irregular alien should be placed pending expulsion and thus to "choose" the justice of the peace entrusted with the validation of the expulsion (ord. 93/2014).
>
> The expulsion of a Ghanaian woman is legitimate even if it was decided on the basis of documents written in British English, a language that the applicant does not speak as she only knows a local form of broken English. The Supreme Court noted that English is the official language in Ghana and therefore the legal presumption of knowledge of that language by the applicant is valid (Court of Cassation, civil division, Sec. VI, judg. 3 September 2014, No. 18610).
>
> According to the Court of Cassation, the family situation of the alien must always be taken into account when deciding upon his expulsion, even when the individual is accused of particularly serious offenses such as those related to drug trafficking. In the present case, the person who should have been expelled was married, while not cohabiting, with an Italian citizen and had a brother of Italian nationality. However, it was the fact that he had a little son in Italy that proved to be decisive. Indeed, article 19(2)-lett. d) of the Consolidated law on immigration (lgs.d. 286/1998), which prevents the expulsion of the cohabiting husband of a pregnant woman or in the six months following the birth of the child, according to a constitutionally oriented interpretation should be considered applicable, after the birth of the son, also to the father who was neither married nor cohabiting with the mother (Court of Cassation, criminal division, Sec. IV, judg. 25 November 2014, No. 50379).

Worth mentioning is also that the Supreme Court held that expulsion as an alternative to detention as per article 16(5) of the Consolidated law on immigration, as amended by l.d. 23 December 2013, No. 146, converted into l. 21 February 2014, No. 10, can be ordered also for crimes committed before the entry into force of above-mentioned reform (and therefore for crimes that previously did not contemplate such measure) since the relevant criminal provision had not substantive nature and could therefore apply regardless of the moment in which the offense was committed (Court of Cassation, criminal division, Sec. I, judg. 11 November 2014, No. 52578).

C. Status of Irregular Migrant and Damages for Failure to Regularise

The Tribunal of Rome (judg. 10 February 2014) upheld the claim brought by an Albanian immigrant whose request to regularise his stay in Italy had been rejected because he had been "reported" for reasons of public safety in the Schengen Information System (so-called "Schengen alert system"). Between 2003 and 2010 the applicant, therefore, stayed in Italy as "undocumented" migrant, a status preventing him from performing any legal job. From the second denial of the applicant's request it emerged that the mug shot on the basis of which the regularisation request was rejected and the deportation order was issued could only be considered as "compatible" with the applicant identity. In 2012, after public security concerns had been declared ill-founded as based on extremely weak elements, the applicant obtained a residence permit and entered into a formal contract for domestic workers. The judge granted the request for damages for breach of contract (article 1218 civil code) against the Italian State, whose authorities had committed an inexcusable error in confusing "identity" and "similarity". The damage to be compensated was around 100,000 euro, an amount the Court calculated considering the average monthly salary of about 600 euro for eight years in respect of lost profits, with a 50% increase due to the violation of the fundamental right to a free and independent life (article 36 Const.).

The status of irregular migrants held in CIEs is indirectly dealt with by the Court of Cassation, criminal division, Sec. II, judg. 29 May 2014, No. 24288. The Court upheld the decision of the Tribunal of Trieste which, while confirming the charge of aggravated damage against a migrant held in the CIE of Gradisca d'Isonzo, had rejected the request for pre-trial detention absent reasonable grounds to believe that the defendant would commit again similar acts. The destruction of IT staff of the CIE in Gradisca had in fact occurred during a protest organised by people held in that facility and was therefore to be considered casual. According to the Supreme Court, "it is quite clear that the criminal conduct [...] directly derives from the state of exasperation that develops in all contexts in which fundamental human rights are severely limited".

D. Social Rights of Immigrants

In its judgment of 2 September 2014, No. 18523, the Court of Cassation extensively ruled on the long-lasting restrictions for migrants as for the access to public administration employment. In accordance with current regulations, adopted to comply with EU law (lgs.d. 165/2001, in particular article 38 as amended by l. 6 August 2013, No. 97 – European Law 2013), "Citizens of EU Member States, and their family members who are not nationals of a Member State who are holders of the right of residence or the right of permanent residence, may access public administration employment which does not involve direct or indirect exercise of public powers, or do not relate to the protection of the national interest". The same applies to third-country nationals who hold a EU long-term residence permit or who are holders of refugee or subsidiary protection status. In the case brought to the attention of the Supreme Court, the request of an Albanian citizen to be employed by a public body in the quota reserved to people with disabilities had been dismissed by lower courts: the applicant had then complained about the discriminatory nature of such exclusion.

As a matter of fact, the legislation in force in Italy clearly highlights the legislators' intention to exclude from the remit of the above-mentioned provision all categories of non-EU citizens not specifically mentioned. On the other hand, article 43(2) of the Consolidated law on immigration provides that an act of discrimination is committed by "whoever unlawfully imposes more disadvantageous conditions or refuses to provide access to employment, housing, education, training, social and welfare services to foreigners legally residing in Italy only because of their status of foreigner or their belonging to a particular race, religion, ethnicity or nationality." The reference to the "unlawfulness" of such conduct means that this anti-discrimination clause cannot be used to challenge differences in treatment based on legal provisions. As for the possible unconstitutionality of such provisions, while the Constitutional Court had already declared unlawful the exclusion of third-country workers from the lists provided by l. 482/1968, article 19, on the compulsory employment of individuals belonging to protected groups (persons with disabilities and others), the complete equalisation of third-country nationals does not follow. In particular, if in the private sector the principle of equal treatment among Italian, EU and non-EU nationals is fully applicable, with regard to public employment, special consideration should be paid to the peculiar and sensitive nature of functions performed by civil servants. On the issue, international standards (including the 1975 ILO Convention on

Migrant Workers, No. 143 and the Convention on the Rights of Persons with Disabilities) grant States a certain margin of appreciation. The ECHR, for its part, does not specifically deal with the right to work.

On the issue of welfare benefits (attendance allowance, disability pension and disability allowance) that are not aimed to remedy serious emergency situations, while the State can restrict their supply to foreign nationals who provide evidence of a non-episodic residence in the Country, it cannot discriminate between holders of residence permit and holders of EU long-status residence permit. Among other things, being the latter subject to a certain level of income, it would be unreasonable to consider it as a condition for obtaining social benefits set up to help those who have insufficient incomes (as already recognised by the Constitutional Court in its judgments 306/2008, 11/2009, 187/2010 – see *2011 Yearbook*, pp. 280–281; see also Constitutional Court, judg. 40/2013 and *2014 Yearbook*, pp. 296–298). The Court of Cassation (civil division, Sec. VI, judg. 20 March 2014, No. 6587) applied the same principle to disability allowances due under l. 118/1971, which have then to be issued without discrimination to any foreigner holding a residence permit and fulfilling all conditions provided by law. An issue of constitutionality raised on the above-mentioned law on disability allowances was dismissed as manifestly inadmissible by the Constitutional Court since in its previous case-law a constitutionally oriented interpretation had already been established (ord. 252/2014).

The Constitutional Court (judg. 168/2014) declared the unconstitutionality of the provision of the law of the Region Valle d'Aosta 3/2013 on the ground that it conditioned the access to public housing of foreigners to their residence for at least eight years in the Region (and not, therefore, as a mere rule of preference). The norm, indeed, constituted an unreasonable discrimination against both EU citizens, who must be guaranteed equal treatment with nationals of the Member State in which they reside (article 24(1) of directive 2004/38/EC) and against third-country nationals who are long-term residents and who, under article 11(1)-lett. f) of directive 2003/109/EC, enjoy equal treatment with nationals also as regards access to social housing procedures.

IX. Right to Privacy, Right to Property

A. Marriage, Cohabitation

Judgment 170/2014 of the Constitutional Court, dealing with the issue of constitutionality raised by the Supreme Court in 2013 (see *2014 Yearbook*, pp. 275–276), ruled on the legal effects of the rectification of attribution of sex on a pre-existing marriage regularly contracted by an individual who had exercised his right to gender reassignment. Indeed, the current legal framework provides that, if the gender distinction between spouses disappears, the marriage automatically terminates. In the present case, however, this contradicted the will of the spouses to continue in wedlock. The referring court had raised the issue of constitutionality of articles 2 and 4 of l. 14 April 1982, No. 164 (Rules of rectification of attribution of sex) in relation to several articles of the Constitution, including articles 29 and 117(1), and invoking articles 8 and 12 ECHR as "interposed parameters". Essential for the Constitutional Court was the reference to article 2 of the Constitution. Indeed, the case under analysis highlighted the contradiction between, on the one hand, the interest of the State in maintaining the heterosexual marriage model (the wedlock should therefore terminate once the gender distinction between spouses has disappeared) and, on the other hand, the interest of spouses to preserve the marriage in the framework of which they had lived for years and which they do not consider terminated despite the sex change of one of them. As a matter of fact, the couple in the present wished their marriage to continue as a form of partnership in which to develop their individual life as well as their relationship. The Court found a violation of article 2 of the Constitution on account of the fact that the current Italian legislation by no means considers as relevant the above-mentioned couple's need. Furthermore, considering that the Constitutional Court cannot amending existing laws and that the existing gap concerned the protection of a right, it invites legislators to introduce "at the earliest" an alternative form (different from marriage) of partnership in order to avoid a "forced divorce".

> As for the issue of marriage and family life, worth to mention are also the judgments of the Court of Cassation, Joint Sec., 17 July 2014, Nos. 16379 and 16380. In these decisions, the Court held that the recognition of the judgment issued by an ecclesiastical court ruling that a concordat marriage was not valid (on account of the fact that one of the spouses had expressed a belief contrary to the indissolubility of the wedlock), although the couple had lived together as spouses for over ten years and had had a daughter, was contrary to public policy. Recalling the notion of marriage as a relationship, which is distinct from that of marriage as a formal act, the judges of the Court of Cassation noted that both internal and international rules mandate to protect the legal situations arisen from such a relationship, as well as the conditions of validity and the legal effect of said act. For these reasons, the Supreme Court concluded that the Italian legal system is precluded from recognising judgments delivered by ecclesiastical courts which had declared concordat marriages not valid for intrinsic defects of the marriage if the spouses had lived in the fullness of the marriage relationship for at least three years.

The civil division of the Court of Cassation (Sec. I, judg. 19 March 2014, No. 6289) considered a judgment issued by the appeal court which had ordered the reduction of the amount of maintenance due by the ex-spouse to his ex-wife on account of the fact that the man, with whom the child of the couple was living, had another son with his second wife. The former wife had challenged the appeal court decision before the Supreme Court asking, in particular, to bring the maintenance at its original amount claiming that the birth of a child from the new union could not limit her rights. The Supreme Court, in dismissing the claim, stated that, without prejudice to the need to assess the actual financial situation of both former spouses, the right to a family – and then the right to have a child – is a fundamental right under both constitutional and supranational law (article 12 ECHR, article 9 CFREU). Therefore, a divorce cannot be considered the limit beyond which this right becomes subordinated to maintenance obligations towards the former spouse.

B. Right to Property and Reparations to Istrian Refugees

The Supreme Court dealt with a lawsuit filed against the Italian State by a group of Italian citizens of Istrian origin seeking compensation for material and moral damages or the payment of a just satisfaction linked to the actual market value of the goods they had possessed and that, being located in the territories ceded to Yugoslavia pursuant to the 1947 Treaty of Peace, had been expropriated or nationalised by the Yugoslav Government. The plaintiffs, in particular, complained that the Italian State had unsatisfactorily compensated them.

Relying on the merits of the conclusions of the trial court and the Court of Appeal of Trieste, the Supreme Court (Joint Sec., judg. 7 April 2014, No. 8055) stated that Italian citizens victims of measures of nationalisation or expropriation have the individual right to compensation the extent to which, however, had already been determined by national legislators. The latter, which in determining the amount of compensation had considered all the constitutionally relevant elements, including the financial ones, as well as the international obligations established in the Treaty of Peace, had however not duly considered that under article 1 Protocol I ECHR the amount of compensation should be reasonably related to the value of the property concerned. Contrarily to what argued by the applicants, the Court held that the present situation was radically different from that dealt with by ECtHR in 2004 in *Broniowski v. Poland*, a case which concerned properties located beyond the river Bug in the Polish eastern border. In the present case, indeed, the allegedly illegal expropriation could not be attributed to Italy since it had been carried out by Yugoslavia, that is the State which had taken over from Italy (defeated in the Second World War) sovereignty in the areas of Istria and Dalmatia. In the case *Broniowski v. Poland*, instead, in the framework of the agreements concluded between the Polish committees of national liberation and the former Soviet Socialist Republics of Ukraine, Belarus and

Lithuania, the specific obligation incumbent on the Polish State to award compensation to its citizens forcibly expelled from the territories ceded to other Countries was explicit.

C. "Indirect Expropriation", Fair Compensation

Also in 2014 trial courts and the Supreme Court issued numerous decisions concerning the practice of "indirect expropriations" and related lawsuits for damages filed by individuals who had been expropriated. The current position of the Italian case-law, which after having endorsed such practice for a number of years had aligned with the ECtHR case-law that had systematically condemned it, is summarised in TAR Calabria, Sec. I, judg. 13 March 2014, No. 424. More specifically, courts held that, even if, due to the realisation of public works, the illegally expropriated land has undergone an irreversible transformation, what is due to the original owner is not a form of compensation. Indeed, since compensation would imply the transfer of the land to the public authorities, and therefore a violation of article 1 Protocol I ECHR, the public authority must first of all return the property to the original owner; only the impossibility of achieving this outcome justifies the award of compensation to be calculated on the basis of the property market value.

The same issue was dealt with by the Constitutional Court in its judgment 187/2014. In that decision, the Court stated that the parameters, referred to the market value of the expropriated property, used to evaluate the fairness of the compensation to be paid by the State and other entities should also be followed by the Autonomous Provinces of Trent and Bolzano – which have primary responsibility in this matter. Therefore, the norm of the Autonomous Province of Trent which provides that the compensation for the expropriation of non-development areas corresponds to that properties value as agricultural lands (which essentially depends from the most likely cultivation, without considering that the market value of the expropriated land may considerably vary according to many variants such as access to water, soil quality, exposure, etc.) was declared unconstitutional. The local authority, indeed, had violated article 117 Const. as it had disregarded the right to peaceful enjoyment of property protected by article 1 Protocol I ECHR.

The Court of Cassation, in its judgment 17 April 2014, No. 8965, reviewed the evolution in the legislation and in the jurisprudence of the practice of "indirect expropriation" concluding – in line with its previous case-law – that since legislators have indirectly endorsed such practice only as of the entry into force of l. 27 October 1988, No. 458, the statutory limitation period (five years) on the claim to compensation for damages connected this practice, now considered illegitimate, could not start before the date of entry into force of this law, that is 3 November 1988. The Court, indeed, held that it would have been unreasonable to expect that holders of the right to compensation had thought, before 1988, that the practice under analysis could have been considered legitimate in the Italian legal system (see also, Court of Cassation, civil division, Sec. I judg. 19 September 2014, No. 19793). On the unlawfulness of "indirect expropriation" in light of the case-law of the ECtHR and of the Constitutional Court as of 2007, worth to mention is the judgment delivered by TAR Piedmont, Sec. I, 26 June 2014, No. 1127.

D. *Right to Privacy and Data Bases*

For a certain period the University of Rome 3 allowed for the indiscriminate access via the Internet to documents containing data (not merely personal ones) of several thousands of students or former students, which could therefore be obtained and exploited for many purposes, also illegal. The Tribunal of Rome had condemned the University for the violation of lgs.d. 196/2003 (Privacy code) and ordered it to pay each individual involved a compensation of 3,000 euro for non-pecuniary damages linked to the "hardship suffered as a result to the (indiscriminate) personal and economic exposure" provoked by the way personal data had been managed by the public body. The Supreme Court, considering the appeal filed by the University, recalled its case-law according to which a constitutionally oriented interpretation of article 2059 civil code allows for the compensation of non-pecuniary damages suffered as a result of crimes or other illegal acts, that is when fundamental constitutional rights are violated. In this case, the Court pointed out, the right to compensation for non-pecuniary damage is recognised only if the violation of the right is serious and that the damage suffered is not trivial, merely hypothetical or imaginary. The extent of the damage and the severity of the violation, however, are in inverse relationship, in the sense that the lesser the violation of the fundamental right the higher the compensation for moral damages. The Court, however, excluded that a violation of fundamental rights is always necessarily associated with a non-pecuniary damage for which compensation is due. The judgment which had been challenged should therefore be quashed and referred back to another court because with specific reference to the case under analysis, it had adequately motivated neither the seriousness of the violation of the right to privacy as a specific expression of the dignity of the person, nor the extent of the damage suffered by the plaintiffs (Court of Cassation, civil division, Sec. III, judg. 15 July 2014, No. 16133).

Again on the issue of privacy, the Supreme Court held that trading practices such as the automatic sending of fax to private numbers found in the yellow pages are unlawful. The consultation of such telephone directory, indeed, is aimed at finding subscribers for interpersonal communications. Sending automatic commercial information to fax numbers is a way of "processing" such data, that is an activity allowed only if the recipient of the communication has expressively given his consent (Court of Cassation, civil division, Sec. II, judg. 24 June 2014, No. 14326).

X. Children's Rights

A. Detainees for Mafia Related Crimes and Minor Children

The Constitutional Court (judg. 22 October 2014, No. 239) declared the unconstitutionality of article 4-*bis* (amended several times) of the Prison act (l. 26 July 1975, No. 354) to the extent that it is applicable to female inmates with minor children. The contested provision, among other things, prevented access to alternatives to detention or other non-custodial measures, such as the special home detention provided for mothers of children under the age of ten, to female detainees convicted of Mafia related offenses, unless they cooperate with judicial authorities. According to the court which had raised the issue of constitutionality, the lack of access to the special home detention (that is to serve the first part of the sentence in special institutions for female detainees who are the caregiver of minor children or, if there is no risk of absconding or recidivism, at home with children up to the age of ten, article 47-*quinquies* of the Prison act) was not reasonably justified. In particular, according to the referring court, it disproportionately harmed children, whose rights – including that to live in a suitable environment with their parents – should enjoy primary consideration. The Constitutional Court maintained that, although justifiable as a measure to enhance "repentance" and linked to the rehabilitation aim of detention, the exclusion from the special home detention of those convicted of serious offenses related to the organised crime that are not cooperating with the judicial authorities represented a disproportionate burden on the minor child. The provisions is therefore contrary to article 31(2) Const. ("The Republic protects mothers, children and the young by adopting necessary provisions"), to the Convention on the Rights of the Child and to article 24 (2) CFREU on the best interest of the child. The exclusion of female detainees from the special home detention regime must be then decided only on a case by case basis taking into account, in particular, the risk of recidivism or absconding. The lack of cooperation with judicial authorities could not, according to the Constitutional Court, be considered as a factor that automatically precludes the access to the special regime.

B. Right to be Heard in Judicial Proceedings; Best Interest of the Child

The Supreme Court upheld the decision of the trial court not to hear the children involved in the proceedings initiated by the father to obtain their custody after that their mother had brought them along in Portugal without the consent of the other parent. While recognising the fundamental importance of national and international standards on the children's right to participate in proceedings affecting them, the Constitutional Court reiterated that children under the age of 12 must be heard by the court only if their maturity excludes that the potential benefit linked to the possibility to express their opinion before the court is not outweighed by the likely trauma of entering into contact with judicial authorities. In the present case, considering that at the time of the disputed decision children were aged between five and seven years, the Court of Cassation concluded that the trial court decision not to hear them had been appropriate (Court of Cassation, civil division, Joint Sec., 18 September 2014, No. 19664).

Against this background, the Supreme Court confirmed that "the right of the child to be heard in the case of proceedings before a judicial authority affecting him or her, already recognised in article 12 of the New York Convention on the Rights of the Child, is now recognised as a procedural requirement pursuant to article 3 and 6 of the Strasbourg Convention", unless this would be manifestly contrary to the best interest of the child (Court of Cassation, civil division, Sec. I, judg. 5 June 2014, No. 5237; see also Sec. I, judg. 5 March 2014, No. 5097). The Supreme Court, therefore, quashed a decision that, in a case of international child abduction, had ordered the return to the mother, in the United States, of a girl illegally retained by the father in Italy, despite the outright opposition she had expressed. The trial court had heard the minor only to exclude the existence of any risk associated with her return to the USA, without giving due weight to the wish expressed by the teenager to stay in Italy with her father. Concerning the right of minors to be heard, see also Court of Cassation, civil division, Sec. I, judg. 5 March 2014, No. 5097.

The Supreme Court upheld the decision of the appeal court which had denied the request of a mother of British nationality to move to her Country of origin together with the child she had in Italy. The request was motivated by better career opportunities and by the fact that the child would have had adequate chances to maintain contact with the Italian father notwithstanding the distance. In the present case, the Court of Cassation considered that the shared custody of the child was not compatible with the mother's decision to move in the UK. Indeed, the best interest of the child (under the age of five) to develop a relationship with both parents implies that, if necessary, the exercise of rights and fundamental freedoms of each parent, including the right to move and set up residence elsewhere, may suffer temporary and proportionate restrictions (Court of Cassation, civil division, Sec. I, judg. 18 September 2014, No. 19694).

C. Abandonment State and Adoptability, Adoption in Special Cases and Homosexual Couples

The Supreme Court dealt with the issue of the determination of the abandonment state of a minor as a condition for the declaration of adoptability. The case considered in the judgment of the civil division of the Court of Cassation, Sec. I, judg. 1 July 2014, No. 15861, involved two sisters who had been declared eligible for adoption because they had been neglected by their parents and grandmother. Also with reference to recent ECtHR case-law, the Supreme Court stressed the importance for the children to remain as much as possible in their family and social environment. In this connection, despite the imperfect performance of the family of origin, the Court noted that from the relevant proceedings it emerged the existence of a strong emotional bond between the parents and girls who, in any case, were not affected by any developmental delays. The stringent requirements that would justify the determination of the state of abandonment were therefore not present. Moreover, not without contradicting its conclusions, the appeal court had declared one of the girls eligible for adoption not by reason of the lack of relations with her parents and grandmother, but on the ground that her status could not be separated from that of her sister. The Court of Cassation, therefore, quashed the judgment of the appeal court, juvenile division, and referred it back to the appeal court in a different composition.

The Juvenile Court of Rome ordered the adoption of a girl by her mother's same sex partner. The latter had married the biological girl's mother in Spain and had shared the experience of medically assisted procreation from which the baby was born. The Court relied on article 44 of l. 184/1983 governing "adoptions in special cases", that is a particular form of adoption not requiring the previous declaration of the abandonment state and having limited legal effects. More specifically, the above mentioned provision provides for an exhaustive list of cases in which the best interest of the child can justify such procedure. Among these, the case (article 44(1)-lett. d) in which, lacking the conditions for the ordinary adoption, regular pre-adoptive placement is impossible. In the present case, however, pre-adoptive placement was excluded not because no foster family or structure was available but because, on the contrary, the child was very happily living with her mother and her mother's partner (therefore, she could not be consider in state of neglect). On the other hand, since the couple was not (and could not be) married under Italian law, ordinary adoption could be not be requested either. According to the Juvenile Court, moreover, article 44 does not exclude that, in the interest of the child, the latter can be adopted (through the special procedure) by the partner of his or her biological parent: in some cases, indeed, children were adopted by the unmarried partner of one of their parent. In Italy, however, this had so far occurred only within heterosexual couples. In the judge's opinion, in the case of homosexual couples, the impossibility of pre-adoptive placement is to be considered a legal, rather than a factual, impediment. In particular, the Court noted that the current legal regime preventing any form of legal qualification of the bond existing between the child and the mother's partner, is detrimental to the child. As a matter of fact, the Italian jurisprudence had already recognised that the harmfulness for a minor of a homosexual family context could not be presumed. Nor one can assume that the best interest of the child cannot be realised in the context of a homosexual couple. In the Court reasoning, therefore, interpreting article 44(1)-lett. d) as excluding the adoption by the same sex partner of the child's parent would be discriminatory (article 3 of the Constitution) and contrary to the fundamental right to family life which same-sex couples also enjoy. A very similar situation had been dealt with by the ECtHR (*X and Others v. Austria* [GC], No. 19010/07, ECHR 2013) which had condemned Austria for having precluded the adoption of a child by the same sex partner of his mother, while granting such right to heterosexual couples in the same situation. The ECtHR had found a violation of article 8 ECHR on the right to family life (applicable also to homosexuals) and of article 14 ECHR (non-discrimination) on account of the fact that the Austrian Government had not provided any evidence that the protection of the family, understood in the traditional sense, and the interests of the child, required the exclusion of same-sex couples from the so-called second-parent adoption to which, instead, heterosexuals couples (including de facto) have right to. In conclusion, despite the opposition of the Juvenile Prosecutor, the Juvenile Court, relying on article 44(1)-lett. d) of l. 184/1983, ordered that the child be adopted by the homosexual partner of her mother.

D. Foreign Children and Special Residence Permit for their Parents

In a case involving the application of article 31 of the Consolidated law on immigration (temporary residence permit for parents of non-repatriable foreign children in case of emergency or exceptional situations), the Supreme Court stated that when one of the child's parent is legally present in Italy but cannot take care of him for serious reasons (in this case, the mother had to take care of a seriously ill older son), the other parent, irregularly present in the State, may not be expelled and must be granted a temporary residence permit pursuant to article 31. The latter repatriation, indeed, would harm and put at serious risk the mental and physical development of the child and would be contrary to the duty of the State to promote the best interest of children as set forth in the Convention on the Rights of the Child (Court of Cassation, civil division, Sec. VI, ord. 2 December 2014, No. 25508).

XI. Due Process, Pinto Act, Ne Bis in Idem, Execution of ECtHR Judgments

A. Excessive Length of Proceedings

Ineffectiveness of the Reformed "Pinto Act"

In 2014 both the joint sections of the Supreme Court (civil division) and the Constitutional Court ruled on the procedure established by l. 89/2001 (the so-called "Pinto act") for the determination of damages suffered as a result of the excessive length of judicial proceedings as recently reformed by l.d. 83/2012, and converted into l. 143/2012.

The Court of Cassation (Joint Sec., judgments 19 March 2014, Nos. 6312, 6313, 6314, 6315, 6316, 6317, 6318) clarified that the Pinto procedure could not be used to challenge the excessive length of proceedings initiated to obtain the payment of the just satisfaction awarded in the main cause. In other words, the judges observed that, if there is a delay in the "realisation" of the right to compensation (and related interests) previously recognised in a proceedings initiated under the Pinto act and the applicant had requested the enforcement of debt by the State, the failure of the administration which does not pay the due amount in a timely manner cannot be the object of a proceeding under the Pinto act. And this is because – to quote the Court – "the phenomenon of these endemic delays of the public administration, criticized several times by the European Court of Human Rights, was certainly alien to the intention of law-makers in 2001". The only option at the disposal of the applicant will then be a complaint before the ECtHR. For an application of this principle, see for example, Court of Cassation, civil division, Sec. II, 27 October 2014, No. 22770; Sec. VI, judgments 3 September 2014, Nos. 18568, 18569, 18570; 10 November 2014, No. 23916.

In several decisions, the Supreme Court reiterated its case-law according to which the Pinto act, providing that compensation is only due for the period of the proceedings exceeding the reasonable length (generally fixed, for the three stages of judgment, in six years) and, therefore, not in proportion of the whole duration of the proceedings, is compatible with the margin of appreciation States enjoy according to the case-law of the ECtHR. The Pinto act, therefore, is not contrary to article 6(1) ECHR and does not infringe article 117(1) Const. (see for example, Court of

Cassation, civil division, Sec. VI, judgments 14 May 2014, No. 10592; 10 June 2014, Nos. 13075, 13082, 13105).

In its judgment 30/2014 the Constitutional Court dismissed as inadmissible the claim of unconstitutionality raised with reference to l. 134/2012, which converted l.d. 83/2012 whose article 55 amended, with no retroactive effect, the Pinto act (see Court of Cassation, civil division, Sec. II, judgments 19 September 2014, Nos. 19810, 19811, 19812, 19813, 19814, 19815, 19816, 19817; 22 September 2014, Nos. 19896, 19897, 19898, 19899, 19900, 19901, 19902, 19903, 19904, 19905). Notwithstanding this decision, the Court did not miss the opportunity to criticise in depth the 2012 reform.

The newly introduced article 4 of l. 89/2001 provides that the request for damages for the excessive length of trial can only be filed after the proceedings is concluded (and within a period of six months). Therefore, the possibility to seek reparation for the excessive length of a proceedings that is still pending, provided for by the original version of the provision, is excluded. According to the Constitutional Court, this amendment prevented the procedure from effectively ensuring the right to fair trial and its reasonable duration as required by article 6 ECHR. The Constitutional Court, after having extensively examined the 2012 Pinto act reform, concluded that the law is now incompatible with the possibility of initiating the Pinto procedure while the main proceedings is still pending. Said conclusion can be inferred, for example, reading the norms that directly link the determination of the compensation to the number of years exceeding the standard duration of a civil proceedings, with the result that the relevant sum could not be calculated if the proceedings is still pending. According to the Constitutional Court, no rule of judicial interpretation may remedy such situation – as it was suggested by the referring court. The conclusion of the Court is that "[t]he vulnus [to the effectiveness of compensation claims envisaged] and the need for the legal system to have an effective remedy against the violation of the reasonable length of the proceedings […] impose […] to stress that an excessive protracted legislative inertia in relation to the problem identified in the present ruling would not be tolerated."

Referring to the Constitutional Court judgment 30/2014, the Supreme Court dismissed a number of appeals filed after the entry into force of the 2012 reform in order to obtain the recognition of the admissibility of a number of Pinto procedures initiated in connection to proceedings that were still pending: see, for example, Court of Cassation, civil division, Sec. II judgments 16 September 2014, No. 19479; 22 October 2014, No. 22468.

The Constitutional Court, with ordinances 124/2014 and 204/2014, dismissed several claims of unconstitutionality of the new version, enacted in 2012, of article 2-*bis* (3) of the Pinto act which states that "the amount of compensation [...] cannot in any case exceed the amount in controversy or, if lower, that of the right established by the court" (see *2014 Yearbook*, p. 303). As a matter of fact, the text seems to suggest that only the party who had won the case (and not also the party who had lost it) could seek compensation for the excessive length of proceedings. If this were the case, the norm would be in clear violation of the right to a trial within a reasonable time enshrined in article 6 ECHR, which should be recognised to both disputing parties regardless the outcome of the proceedings. The judges of the Constitutional Court, however, dismissed such an interpretation and read the disputed provision as intended solely to establish a limit to the amount of compensation in those cases the right of the applicant had been established, without bearing any of the consequences envisaged by the referring courts.

More Clarifications on the Pinto Act

The Supreme Court confirmed that disputes settled by tax courts are not covered by the guarantees of the Pinto act and their excessive length cannot, therefore, be compensated. This conclusion was grounded on the fact that this category of proceedings concerns neither criminal matters (except when they impose tax penalties expressly qualified as criminal by law: see civil division, Sec. VI, judg. 13 January 2014, No. 510) nor civil matters (according to the definition provided by the ECtHR). Indeed, such proceedings concern public law obligations (civil division, Sec. II, 20 February 2014, No. 4090; 23 May 2014, No. 11554; Sec. VI, judgments 28 October 2014, No. 22872; 24 December 2014, No. 27390).

On the contrary, the excessive length of a Pinto procedure, whose "normal" duration is fixed (in line with the ECtHR case-law) in two years, including the appeal before the Court of Cassation, may be compensated under the Pinto act (see civil division, Sec. VI, judgments 15 January 2014, Nos. 726, 727, 728, 729, 730, 731, 732, 733, 734, 735, 736, 737, 738, 739, 740, 741).

When calculating the duration of the proceedings, the time required for the completion of arbitration awards, which have a private nature and are unrelated to the exercise of the judicial power, should not be taken into consideration (Court of Cassation, civil division, Sec. VI, judg. 13 February 2014, No. 3316).

Public bodies (such as provincial or municipal authorities) are not entitled to bring claims under l. 89/2001 (see for example Court of Cassation, civil division, Sec. II, judg. 20 May 2014, No. 11049; Sec. VI, judgments 7 March 2014, Nos. 5421, 5422, 5423, 5424, 5425, 5429, 5430, 5431, 5432, 5433; 23 May 2014, No. 11559).

A claim under the Pinto act may be brought by a minor, represented by a parent or a legal guardian; if during the Pinto procedure the minor under representation comes of age, he retains the right to directly receive the fair compensation without necessarily having to start an independent legal action (Court of Cassation, civil division, Sec. VI, judg. 10 April 2014, No. 8424). In several of its judgments (including civil division, Joint Sec., 7 April 2014, No. 8053; with reference to the Pinto procedure see civil division, Sec. VI, judgments 20 November 2014, No. 24772; 18 December 2014, No. 26801), the Supreme Court also reiterated that, considering the reforms introduced to the code of civil procedure by the Consolidated law on immigration 83/2012, converted into l. 7 August 2012, No. 134, the trial court decision on the amount of compensation can be challenged only in the following circumstances: when it is completely groundless; or when the motivation makes references to non-existent facts or is logically incongruous (see the newly articulated article 360 code of civil procedure). In order to challenge before the Supreme Court the amount of compensation, the applicant cannot simply assert that the decision is insufficiently reasoned, but has to demonstrate that the trial court did not consider crucial "historical facts".

Again with reference to the 2012 reform, which has profoundly amended the Pinto act, the Supreme Court concluded that the new article 2(2)-*bis* and -ter of l. 89/2001 ("the reasonable length is deemed to be respected [...] if the proceedings does not exceed three years at the trial stage, two years in appeal, one year before the Court of Cassation [...] the reasonable length is in any case considered respected if a final decision is reached in less than six years") cannot be construed to extend the ordinary duration of proceedings at first instance to six years: in this case, the amount of compensation must be calculated taking into account the period exceeding three years (Court of Cassation, civil division, Sec. VI, judgments 6 November 2014, Nos. 23745, 23746; 7 November 2014, No. 23887; see also judgments 26 September 2014, Nos. 20436, 20437. On a similar problem, see also civil division, Sec. VI, judgments 4 June 2014, No. 12606; 17 June 2014, No. 13712). On the other hand, the excessive length of a proceedings should be calculated taking into account the proceedings in its entirety, and not its single phases: see, for example, civil division, Sec. II, judgments 23 May 2014, Nos. 11555, 11556, 11557, 11558). In its judgment (civil division, Sec. VI, 24 December 2014, No. 27388) the Court of Cassation confirmed that the Pinto procedure cannot be initiated in relation to a specific stage of the trial exceeding the average duration, but only with regard to the whole duration of the proceedings: the impossibility to seek compensation for single phases of the trial does not raise issues of constitutionality (see also judgments 23 May 2014, No. 11558; 1 September 2014, No. 18464; 2 September 2014, No. 18540).

When deciding upon the existence of a violation of the reasonable duration of a proceedings, appeals court must establish the facts making use, if necessary, of their power of initiative in order to go beyond the information submitted by the applicant. In all cases, however, the applicant still bears the burden of proof concerning his position in the proceedings, the starting and concluding date of the latter, and the degrees in which the trial was articulated (Court of Cassation, civil division, Sec. VI, judg. 28 November 2014, No. 25270).

According to the Supreme Court, it was not possible to conclude that the appeal court, having imputed to the inertia of the parties the entire span of time between the establishment of the case (January 1975) and the time of initiation of the case (January 1996), had adequately adjudicated the relevant dispute. The appeal court, indeed, had concluded that a proceedings lasting for over thirty five years exceeded the reasonable length of only six years and six months, maintaining that the abnormal length of the proceedings was entirely attributable to the parties. Even assuming the uncooperative attitude of the parties, the Court of Cassation considered that the powers of initiative of the judicial authorities had been clearly disregarded by the officers in charge of the case. For this reason, the duration of the proceedings exceeding the reasonable delay should be extended (civil division, Sec. VI, judg. 19 May 2014, No. 10957).

A trial started in 1995 and still pending in 2009 cannot be reasonably considered exceeding the ordinary duration of only five years, whereas the three stages of judgment should not exceed six years: the Supreme Court ordered a new determination of the extent of the delay and of the amount of compensation for non-pecuniary damage (civil division, Sec. VI, judg. 17 June 2014, No. 13713; see also judg. 6 June 2014, No. 12866). Furthermore, in calculating the duration of proceedings, what should be taken into account is only the time during which the court was considering the case. The period during which the parties were free to decide, for example, whether or not to appeal, is excluded (Court of Cassation, civil division, Sec. VI, judg. 5 June 2014, No. 12618).

The possibility to rely on the particular complexity of the case to justify a duration of the proceedings exceeding the ordinary standard should be justified in relation to the different phases of the proceedings. As a consequence, a dispute that had been very complex in the first instance (for example due to the presence of a large number of parties) would not necessarily be the same in appeal. For this second phase, therefore, the standards set by law for the reasonable length of proceedings must be strictly complied with (Court of Cassation, civil division, Sec. VI, judg. 4 June 2014, No. 12580).

Another element clarified by the Supreme Court concerned the possibility to bring a claim under the Pinto procedure on behalf of a defendant who had not been present in the main criminal proceedings. The Court pointed out that the choice of the defendant not to be present at trial does not necessarily indicate his total lack of interest for the case and is without prejudice to the right to have one's case discussed within a reasonable time. The amount of compensation, however, must be determined taking into account that the default of appearance in court by the defendant may have been the cause of the long duration of the trial (Court of Cassation, civil division, Joint Sec., judg. 14 January 2014, No. 585; similarly see, among others, Court of

Cassation, civil division, Sec. II, judgments 28 October 2014, No. 22871; Sec. VI, 10 April 2014, No. 8426; 3 November 2014, No. 23374; Sec. VI, judg. 3 December 2014, No. 25619). Likewise, the fact of having concluded a legal dispute with a dispute settlement that met the interests of the parties (after that the proceedings went on for about 34 years!), is without prejudice to the right to seek compensation for the excessive length of the proceedings (Court of Cassation, civil division, Sec. VI, 27 May 2014, No. 11820).

The fact that the court promptly suspended the measure contested by the applicant, protecting the latter from the negative effects of such an act, is without prejudice to the right to compensation for the excessive length (15 years) of the trial: the Supreme Court was clear in pointing out that the injunction which had anticipated the final decision was not the judgment and did not relieve the applicant, if only partly, from the suffering related to the compression of the right to a prompt adjudication (Court of Cassation, civil division, Sec. VI, judg. 24 November 2014, No. 24925). In some special cases, however, trial courts – whose decisions had been subsequently upheld by the Supreme Court – considered that the issuance of a suspension measure represented a sufficient reason to exclude the existence of a non-pecuniary damage despite a delay in the resolution of the dispute (the case concerned the appeal against the denial of the application for the exemption from the military service – Court of Cassation, civil division, Sec. VI, judg. June 11, 2014, No. 13262).

If, after a jurisdictional hearing, a proceedings which had started before the ordinary court was ordered to continue before the administrative court, the periods of time accumulated before the two different jurisdictions had to be sum up. Indeed, since for the purpose of the Pinto procedure the proceeding is the same, damages should be asked both to the Ministry of Justice (responsible for the part of the delay attributable to the ordinary justice) and to the Ministry of Economy (responsible for part of the delay attributable to the administrative court) (Court of Cassation, civil division, Sec. VI, judg. 10 April 2014, No. 8417).

For the heirs of the plaintiff seeking compensation in a criminal proceedings, the term starting from which it is possible to calculate the excessive length of the proceeding is the moment in which such heirs become aware of the filing of the claim by their predecessor; if this cannot be proven, the calculation begins the moment in which the heirs bring the civil action (Court of Cassation, criminal division, Joint Sec., judg. 23 September 2014, No. 19977; civil division, Sec. VI, judgments 12 May 2014, No. 10265; 4 September 2014, No. 18652).

Ruling on the compliance by the applicant with the six-month period prescribed by the Pinto act to file the request for equitable compensation, the Supreme Court pointed out that such term runs from the moment in which the decision disposing of the proceedings has become final; in other words, after one year and forty-five days from the filing of the judgment at the court registrar, or after thirty or sixty days from its notification to the person concerned.

If the State is unable to prove that the notification was actually made, the longer term is the one to be taken into account (Court of Cassation, civil division, Sec. II, judg. 27 August 2014, No. 18388).

As for the amount of compensation, the Supreme Court confirmed that in the case of proceedings lasted over ten years before administrative courts, a sum of 500 euro for every year exceeding the "fair" duration is adequate (civil division, Sec. II, judg. 21 March 2014, No. 6791); similarly, among others, judgments Sec. II, 24 March 2014, No. 6885; 10 June 2014, No. 13042; Sec. VI, judgments 14 May 2014, No. 10595; 15 May 2014, Nos. 10689, 10729; 16 May 2014, Nos. 10891, 10892, 10893; 21 May 2014, No. 11294; 27 June 2014, Nos. 14621, 14622; 10 July 2014, No. 15869; 13 August 2014, Nos. 17930, 17931; 26 August 2014, No. 18296; 2 September 2014, Nos. 18537, 18543, 18544, 18545, 18547; 9 September 2014, Nos. 18967, 18968, 18969, 18970, 18972, 18973, 18974, 18975; 10 September 2014, Nos. 19120, 19121, 19122, 19123, 19125; 30 September 2014, Nos. 12914, 20617 – in which the Supreme Court, on the basis of considerations such as, in particular, the low value of the disputed right, reduced to 500 euro for each year of delay the previous determination of the appeal court that had rigorously applied the parameter developed by the ECtHR, that is 750 euro for each year of delay until the third, then 1,000 euro per year; 9 September 2014, Nos. 18971, 18976; 18 September 2014, Nos. 19715, 19716; 2 October 2014, Nos. 20862, 20864, 20865; 6 October 2014, Nos. 21045, 21048; 8 October 2014, Nos. 21274, 21275, 21276, 21277, 21278, 21279, 21280, 21281, 21282, 21283; 20 October 2014, Nos. 22210, 22211, 22212, 22213, 22214; 22 October 2014, No. 22355; 7 November 2014, No. 23842; 20 November 2014, Nos. 24767, 24768; 21 November 2014, No. 24909. In relation to a particularly complex case, the Supreme Court concluded that "European" parameters are to be considered fair and therefore rejected the request of the applicant to increase the amount of the compensation: Court of Cassation, civil division, Sec. VI, judg. 29 July 2014, No. 17237. In other cases, the "European" determination of the non-pecuniary damage is applied rigorously and, in the presence of a well-reasoned decision of the court of first instance, the Supreme Court had no special powers to reform the decision of the lower court (Court of Cassation, civil division, Sec. VI, judg. 23 June 2015, No. 14246). This also applies in relation to proceedings in which the individual concerned died and was replaced by the heir (civil division, Sec. VI, judgments 27 May 2014, Nos. 11817, 11818, 11819). If the judge intends to deviate from the ECtHR jurisprudence, it has the burden to justify its choice: if it doesn't, the Supreme Court may refer back the decision to the lower court for a more reasoned determination (see Court of Cassation, civil division, Sec. VI, judg. 11 June 2014, No. 13192).

In light of considerations specifically related to the main proceedings, a compensation of 800 euro for each year of delay was considered adequate (Court of Cassation, civil division, Sec. VI, 23 October 2014, No. 22563; see also civil division, Sec. VI, judg. 2 September 2014, No. 18506). Conversely, a sum of

200 or 300 euro for each year exceeding the reasonable length was considered inadequate and, therefore, the Court of Cassation directly increased it (see, for example, Court of Cassation, civil division, Sec. VI, judgments 13 May 2014, Nos. 10376, 10377, 10378; 19 May 2014, No. 10958; 11 September 2014, No. 19188; 10 October 2014, Nos. 21522, 21523; 7 November 2014, Nos. 23883, 23884, 23885, 23886, 23887; 10 November 2014, Nos. 23965, 23966, 23967, 23968, 23969; 12 December 2014, Nos. 24148, 24149, 24150, 24151).

According to the Supreme Court, the reasonable length of bankruptcy proceedings is five years for cases of moderate difficulty and seven years for those of particular complexity, to be calculated from the date in which the creditor had filed the claim in bankruptcy (see Court of Cassation, civil division, Sec. VI, judgments 15 May 2014, Nos. 10654, 10691, 10692). The determination of the sum to be paid must comply with the criteria developed by the ECtHR (thus 750 euro for each of the first three years of delay and 1,000 euro for each successive year: 26 May 2014, No. 11621; 9 July 2014, No. 15724; 24 September 2014, No. 20151; 25 September 2014, Nos. 20255, 20256; 10 October 2014, No. 21524). A deviation from those standards is however possible when a reasoned decision is provided (see, among others, Court of Cassation, civil division, Sec. VI, judgments 15 May 2014, Nos. 10657, 10658, 10659, 10693): a compensation of 500 euro for the first three years and of 600 euro for the successive years was considered reasonable (civil division, Sec. II, judg. 15 October 2014, No. 21849), as well as a compensation of 700 euro for each year exceeding the reasonable length (Court of Cassation, civil division, Sec. VI, judg. 8 October 2014, No. 21284). In other decisions, the parameter considered valid for administrative proceedings (500 euro for each year of delay) was applied to bankruptcy cases: see Court of Cassation, civil division, Sec. VI, judg. 16 July 2014, No. 16311.

Always in respect to the amount of the compensation, the Supreme Court confirmed that pecuniary damages may be compensated only to the extent that they were caused by the unreasonable delay of the proceedings: economic losses that should or could have been claimed in the main proceedings cannot be taken into consideration. Indeed, the Court concluded, not all damages that the applicants considered to be connected to the delay of the proceedings may be compensated. Only those directly caused by the delay may be compensated (Court of Cassation, civil division, Sec. VI, judg. 9 September 2014, No. 18966).

The Supreme Court also confirmed its previous case-law on the determination of the amount of compensation when the value of the controversy is particularly low. In some cases decided by the civil division of the Supreme Court (see for example, Sec. VI, judgments 4 June 2014, No. 12601; 24 November 2014, Nos. 24927 and 24928), the Court concluded that, despite the proceedings lasted well beyond the limits of reasonableness, no compensation is due when the economic value of the controversy corresponds to few hundred euro and is considered economically irrelevant by the parties. The

Court reached this conclusion also by referring to the entry into force in 2010 of an additional admissibility criterion according to which the ECtHR can declare inadmissible any individual application if it considers that the applicant has not suffered a significant disadvantage. The determination of the irrelevance of the amount in controversy should be done, however, without any automatism. In particular, even though the value of the controversy is low, the nature of the entitlements (such as welfare benefits or cases involving labour disputes) and the socio-economic situation of the applicant must be taken into account (see, Court of Cassation, civil division, Sec. VI, judgments 25 June 2014, No. 14382; 13 August 2014, No. 17944; 2 September 2014, No. 18536; 4 September 2014, No. 18657; 5 September 2014, Nos. 18725, 18726, 18727, 18728). The fact that the proceedings was not complex and that it was held in camera are elements that could justify a higher severity (not the reverse) in assessing the delays of the judiciary, taking into account the overall demand for justice that is reflected at the national level (Court of Cassation, civil division, Sec. VI, judg. 5 May 2014, No. 12616).

In the case decided by the Court of Cassation, civil division, Sec. VI, judg. 4 September 2014, No. 18659, the judges held that, since the dispute had been concluded with a settlement, the delay of the proceedings brought by Codacons dealing with the milk quota regime was due to the latter's lack of interest in the dispute. The delay, therefore, had not caused harm or suffering to the applicant and no compensation is due under the Pinto act. Moreover, when the proceedings has a "collective" nature (in the present case it was a labour dispute promoted by a high number of employees), the Court of Cassation held that the suffering of individuals linked to the unreasonable length of proceedings are mitigated (civil division, Sec. VI, judg. 27 August 2014, No. 18400).

When one of the party of a proceedings exceeding the reasonable length is an apartment building (represented by the administrator), just compensation is to be awarded to the condominium itself and not to its residents – unless they have individually become parties to the proceedings. Under the Pinto act, indeed, non-pecuniary damages, understood as moral damages, are the normal consequence of the violation of the right to a trial within reasonable time under article 6 ECHR also for legal entities and collective subjects. And this is because of the psychological discomfort that the violation of such right usually causes to people responsible for the management of such entities or to theirs members. The apartment building that was not formally a party in the main proceedings is not entitled to take action for equitable compensation under l. 89/2001 (Court of Cassation, civil division, Joint Sec., judg. 18 September 2014, No. 19663). The fact that non-pecuniary damages are the normal (but not the automatic) consequence of the unreasonable length of proceedings does not relieve the competent court to verify, case by case, the actual existence of said damages and consequently to positively test their absence (see, among others, Court of Cassation, civil division, Sec. VI, judgments 14 March 2014, No. 6004; 10 April 2014, No. 8419; 14 May 2014,

No. 10594). In particular, the Supreme Court confirmed its previous case-law according to which the fact that the Pinto procedure had been initiated by the parties who had lost a collective action does not necessarily imply the absence of damages (see Court of Cassation, civil division, Sec. VI, judg. 7 March 2014, No. 5429).

In terms of legal costs, the Supreme Court upheld the decisions issued by a number of courts that had ordered the applicants of the Pinto procedure to pay the legal costs in the circumstance their request for compensation had been rejected. The appellants, in particular, stressed the fact that the Pinto procedure is meant to "substitute" the application procedure before the ECtHR, which is free of charge. The Court dismissed the argument according to which the ECHR may be interpreted as implying a duty for the State to conform the procedure for the payment of just compensation with the rules on legal costs applied by the Strasbourg Court (Court of Cassation, civil division, Sec. VI, 26 August 2014, No. 18298). With regard to the interest due on the sums the State must pay as compensation, the Court established that not only it starts running from the lodging of the application under the Pinto act, but that it must be specifically requested. Courts, therefore, can neither calculate interest payments from the beginning of the main proceedings nor attribute them in the lack of an explicit request (see, for example, Court of Cassation, civil division, Sec. VI, judg. 17 June 2014, No. 13714).

In several decisions (see, particularly, civil division, Joint Sec., judg. 12 March 2014, No. 5700; Sec. VI, judgments 10 April 2014, No. 8421; 2 May 2014, Nos. 9558, 9559), the Court of Cassation pointed out that, under the Pinto act, the deadline set by the appeal court for the notification to the opposing party of the action brought for the excessive length of the proceedings and of the related decision setting the date of the hearing is not mandatory; therefore, if the parties spontaneously take part in the proceedings and ask for a hearing, or if the court grants a new (this time peremptory) deadline for the notification, the decision on compensation can regularly be adopted (Court of Cassation, civil division, Sec. II, judg. 11 November 2014, No. 24015).

Also in 2014, the Supreme Court reaffirmed that requests for compensation for unreasonable length of administrative proceedings may only be submitted if during the main proceedings the applicant had filed an interim drawing motion (*istanza di prelievo*), or at least, that the latter is necessary for the determination of the compensation in order to calculate the period of time elapsed before the submission of the claim (see *2013 Yearbook*, p. 336 and *2014 Yearbook*, p. 304). Several judgments (Court of Cassation, civil division, Sec. VI, 2 September 2014, No. 18505; 16 September 2014, No. 19476; 3 October 2014, No. 20935) pointed out that the filing of the interim drawing motion before the entry into force of article 54 of the Consolidated law on immigration, 25 June 2008, No. 112, converted into l. 6 August 2008, No. 133, a provision that had been qualified as "procedural requirement" under the Pinto procedure, entails that the request for compensation remains valid and there is no need to re-file it on account of the fact that the party had already expressed its interest to have the administrative proceedings quickly adjudicated. The late submission of the interim drawing motion (in the regime created after the entry into force of the 2008 Act) does not entail that the time elapsed between the entry into force of the new law and the day of the submission of the motion cannot be taken into account when calculating the total duration of the proceedings. Conversely, that time span can be considered for the calculation of the compensation (see, among others, Court of Cassation, civil division, Sec. II, judg. 10 June 2014, No. 13041; Sec. VI, judgments 10 June 2014, Nos. 13096, 13097, 13098). Furthermore, the fact that the main proceedings terminated due to a decade long inactivity of the parties does not mean that those who have submitted a request under the Pinto act lose the right to be compensated for the whole period exceeding the ordinary length, including the time elapsed between the filing of the interim drawing motion and the termination of the proceedings, even though during that period the applicant has not taken any action (Court of Cassation, civil division, Sec. II, judg. 24 March 2014, No. 6885; Sec. VI, judgments 26 May 2014, No. 11622; 2 September 2014, No. 18504).

Among the amendments introduced by the Consolidated law on immigration 83/2012, converted into l. 134/2012, which contained, among other things, a reform of the Pinto procedure, it is worth mentioning article 5-*quater* ("legal sanctions"), which gives the judge the power to order the applicant to pay a sum between 1,000 and 10,000 euro when the request for compensation is inadmissible or manifestly ill-founded. The Supreme Court interpreted this provision as also including cases in which the request for compensation was held inadmissible on account of the fact that it was filed after the expiration of the six months period following the last decision adopted by the administrative court (Court of Cassation, civil division, Sec. II, judg. 31 October 2014, No. 23302).

The notion of "final decision" in article 4 of the Pinto act shall be interpreted as including any judicial decision that formally conclude all issues related to a dispute. Therefore, the decision of the judge for the preliminary investigations to refer back the case to the public prosecutor, being a decision aiming at the prosecution of the relevant proceedings, cannot be characterised as a final decision (Court of Cassation, civil division, Sec. VI, judg. 29 August 2014, No. 18427).

Issues of unconstitutionality, systematically dismissed by the Supreme Court, were raised in connection to various aspects of l. 134/2012 (see, for example, Court of Cassation, civil division, Sec. II, judgments 22 September 2014, No. 19897 and 27 October 2014, No. 22772).

In a series of decisions issued since January 2014, the Supreme Court (see, for example, Sect. VI, judg. 15 January 2014, Nos. 714, 715, 716, 717) dealt with a problem that had emerged in connection with the ECtHR jurisprudence. The ECtHR, indeed, held that compensation for the excessive length of criminal proceedings is excluded when the latter ended up in a positive way for the applicant, including cases of acquittal by prescription (see *2013 Yearbook*, p. 335 and *2014 Yearbook*, p. 306). The Supreme Court departed from its previous case-law, and also from that of the ECtHR, by referring to specific provisions of l. 89/2001 (art. 2(2)-*quinquies*, lett. d), introduced by the Consolidated law on immigration, l. 83/2012) as well as to the ratio of the 2012 Pinto act reform. According to the Supreme Court, therefore, the just compensation for the violation of the right to have the case adjudicated within a reasonable time must be recognised even though the delay in the definition of the criminal proceedings had caused its termination by prescription, unless such result occurred due to the use, by the defendant, of dilatory tactics or of abuse of the right of defence. As it is known, in fact, delays largely depend on shortcomings of the judicial system, rather than from abusive conduct of the parties (Court of Cassation, civil division, Sec. VI, judgments 5 June 2014, No. 12744; 29 August 2014, Nos. 18426, 18428; 2 September 2014, No. 18498; 4 September 2014, No. 18653).

The Constitutional Court, for its part, dismissed as manifestly ill-founded the issue of constitutionality raised in connection with the provision of the Pinto act according to which compensation for the violation of the right to a reasonable length of trial terminated because of prescription was excluded only if prescription was "connected to the dilatory conduct of the party" (ord. 18 July 2014, No. 223). The Court, indeed, observed that while legislators are prevented from adopting norms which reduce the rights enshrined in the ECHR, they are not precluded from adopting norms which extend such rights, as in the case of the provision which admits to the Pinto procedure also those individuals whose proceedings had terminated because of prescription.

B. Ne Bis in Idem and Disciplinary Sanctions

The Supreme Court considered the case of an employee of the Italian Post Office that, after being sanctioned with a suspension from work without pay for one day for having embezzled money of savers and after being convicted in a criminal proceedings for the same facts, had been fired pursuant to a provision of the collective employment agreement. The court before which the former employee had challenged his dismissal had ordered the latter's reinstatement in the workplace and the payment of damages. The Supreme Court upheld the lower court decision stressing that the dismissal, being a penalty for acts that had already been punished with the previous disciplinary measure, had to be considered illegitimate. Reference was made to the *Grande Stevens and Others v. Italy* case, recently adjudicated by the ECtHR (see, in this Part, Italy in the Case-law of the European Court of Human Rights, II).

C. Enforcement of ECtHR Judgments

A number of administrative courts decisions dealing with claims brought by citizens who wanted to force the State to pay the compensation awarded them by the ECtHR delimited the effects on the State administration of the Strasbourg Court judgments. According to the TAR Lazio, Rome I, judg. 9564/2014, the decisions of the ECtHR cannot be considered as judicial entitlements that can be enforced by a court order against the State in order to force the latter to pay the amount due (in the present case, the sum was considerable: more than 47 million euro for the "acquisitive expropriation" carried out by the Municipality of Rome to the detriment of a real estate company). Since no provision of the European Convention provides for direct enforcement mechanisms for these measures, while judgments of the ECtHR create mutual and mandatory constraints among States, they do not give rise to civil obligations towards the victims of the violations. The appeals filed against the Italian Government (the Prime Minister's Office and Ministry of Economy) relying on ECtHR judgments must therefore be dismissed (see also TAR Sicily, Catania, judg. 424/2014).

XII. Torture, Prison Conditions, Prisoners' Rights

The criminal division of the Court of Cassation excluded that article 41-*bis* of the prison regulation, whose measures had become harsher after the entry into force of l. 15 July 2009, No. 94, could be considered a "separate punishment". Such an argument was raised in order to challenge the extradition from Spain of a notorious mafia boss on the ground that in the surrender request submitted by Italy pursuant to the European arrest warrant there was no indication that the requested person would have been subject to this special regime. The applicant, in particular, considered the issue especially relevant by reason of the fact that the regime applicable in Spain would have been radically different. The Supreme Court, however, concluded that the exceptional restrictive measures provided for in article 41-*bis* are preventive in nature and do not change the penalty imposed. In addition, the Court noted, the special restrictions imposed are justified on the ground of the actual danger that detainees maintain links with mafia organisations (criminal division, Sec. I, judg. 29 April 2014, No. 52054).

Nor should it be considered contrary to the rights of detainees subjected to article 41-*bis* regime the rule according to which, while allowing visits from family members under the age of 12, during interviews detainees and visitors have to be portioned by glass: see Court of Cassation, criminal division, Sec. I, judg. 11 June 2014, No. 28250. According to the same rules, moreover, interviews have to place without the presence of other adult family members. Detainees, indeed, have neither the right to make physical contact with their underage family members nor to meet them in the presence of other relatives (criminal division, Sec. I, judg. 4 June 2014, No. 35488; judg. 11 June 2014, No. 39966). More generally, the Supreme Court recognised that the restrictive regime regulated by article 41-*bis*, applicable to particularly dangerous persons, does not exclude such persons from interviews with family members. It may, on the contrary, impose limits on the number and duration of these interviews as well as prescribe rigid restrictions. The choice of the judge responsible for the execution of sentences to deny the meeting between a father and his son, both inmates (the latter subjected to article 41-*bis* regime) which had last met in 1996, however, constituted a surplus of requirements. Indeed, in the present case a video-conference interview, provided all security requirements were met, could have represented a valid alternative (criminal division, Sec. I, judg. 12 December 2014, No. 7654).

The Supreme Court also stated that the prohibition to an inmate subjected to article 41-*bis* regime to receive local newspapers from his area of origin, while compressing the fundamental right to information, is not unlawful since it is functional to requirements of public safety, namely to stop a possible channel of communication with the outside world and then a possibility to interact with members of the criminal group (criminal division, Sec. I, judg. 2 July 2014, No. 32904). Restrictions on the possibility to obtain books, magazines and other material functional to the right to education and information not only may be imposed by a ministerial circular, but are not subject to the judicial review of the post-sentencing judge by reason that they protect rights that are less fundamental than the one to maintain, through correspondence, contacts with family members or other people outside the prison (the complete isolation of the detainee would be instead an inhuman or degrading treatment contrary to article 3 ECHR) (see Court of Cassation, criminal division, Sec. I, judg. 29 September 2014, No. 1774). Judicial review is instead applicable to those restrictions that, while established by a ministerial decision on the special regime implementation, regulate the modalities through which detainees can purchase books or magazines or keep them at their disposal in cell (see Court of Cassation, criminal division, Sec. I, judgments 16 October 2014, No. 50156; 11 November 2014, No. 11184). According to the Supreme Court, these restrictions must be applied without disproportionately limiting the right to information: it follows that the seizure of a magazine attached to a letter received by a detainee sentenced for terrorism related crimes is illegitimate, since the latter could have obtained the same issue of the magazine through a request to the penitentiary institution (criminal division, Sec. I, judg. 16 October 2014, No. 6887).

More generally, the ruling of the criminal division of the Court of Cassation, Sec. I, 9 May 2014, No. 37231, dismissed the position according to which article 41-*bis* contains measures contrary to international standards on the rights of detainees (including the CoE Prison Rules and the UN Standard Minimum Rules for the Treatment of Prisoners). In the present case, the fact that the applicant was placed in the "high security" circuit (so-called "reserved area") of the Opera prison in Milan, together with only another detainee, did not constitute, in the Court's opinion, an inhuman treatment. All the more so that the prison organisation does not even fall within the competences of the judge responsible for the execution of sentences.

On 31 October 2014 the Rome Court of appeal issued its judgment in the case involving the suspicious death from ill-treatments of a young man, Stefano Cucchi, occurred in Rome in 2009. Cucchi was arrested (because suspected of drugs dealing) and then transferred to two police stations on the night between October 15 and 16; in the morning of October 16, he had been brought to the court located in Clodio square and held in a cell of that structure. Subsequently, he was held in the Regina Coeli detention facility, and later, on the evening of October 16, he was brought to the Fatebenefratelli hospital from which, however, he was discharged at his request, and then brought back to Regina Coeli prison. From there, in the morning of October 17, he was brought back to the Fatebenefratelli hospital; since there was no place, on the evening of the same day, Cucchi was transferred to the Sandro Pertini hospital where he was hospitalised. In the morning of October 22, Cucchi died. The suspicion that the death occurred as a result of ill-treatment by law enforcement officers under whose custody Cucchi was or as a result of inadequate medical treatments quickly emerged on account of the extreme weakness conditions of the deceased 30 years old's body, abstractly compatible with acts of torture. Both police and health personnel had been indicted for a number of criminal offenses: neglect of a care-dependent person, abuse of office, aiding and abetting, intentionally false statements, bodily harm and abuse of power. In 2013 the Court of first instance of Rome had convicted for manslaughter some of the doctors of the Pertini hospitals, while it had acquitted all prison officers for lack of evidence. In 2014, the Court of appeal had acquitted all defendants. Indeed, the cause of Stefano Cucchi's death could not be established. The latter's death, occurred while he was under arrest in a hospital, and then under the supervision of both health and law enforcement personnel, remains without explanation and without identified perpetrators. The public institutions involved in the case are negatively marked.

Again in 2014, the Court of Cassation (criminal division, Sec. I, judg. 4 March 2014, No. 18206) reiterated its case-law as well as the case-law of the Constitutional Court regarding the so-called "*ergastolo ostativo*" ("obstructive" life sentence), namely a situation whereby detainees, convicted for some serious crimes, mostly linked to the mafia, including those sentenced to life imprisonment, are not allowed to any benefit (work outside the prison, temporary licences, probation and other alternative measures), unless they cooperate with the judiciary (article 4-*bis* of the prison regulations; see *2013 Yearbook*, p. 348). Since the relevant norm is addressed to particularly dangerous offenders, according to the Supreme Court, the above-mentioned measures are not incompatible with the constitutional and international provision on human rights and on the rehabilitative purpose of the penalty.

XIII. Criminal Matters

A. Extradition and Risk of Ill-treatment

The Supreme Court struck down a ruling that had granted the request presented by Serbia for the extradition of one its citizen in order to have the latter serving there a final prison sentence. The reason was that reliable sources indicated that in Serbia prisons overcrowding was a serious issue. According to the ECtHR, whose decisions are binding for the Italian courts, when prison overcrowding reaches a certain level, the lack of space may constitute a central element to be taken into account when assessing the compatibility of a given situation with article 3 ECHR (inhuman treatment). The certainty or the real danger that the individual whose extradition is sought will be subjected to such conditions prevents a ruling granting the extradition. The case was therefore referred back to the competent appeal court which had to reconsider the extradition request taking into account these criteria (criminal division, Sec. VI, judg. 30 December 2014, No. 13823). On the other hand, the generic reference to overcrowding or lack of medical care in Romanian prisons is not sufficient to prevent extradition, unless the assertions made are not supported by evidence of the concrete level of danger or by facts relating to the specific situation (criminal division, Sec. VI, judg. 15 October 2014, No. 43537).

According to the criminal division of the Court of Cassation, Sec. VI, judg. 30 April 2014, No. 30087, Brazil, while characterised by frequent episodes of violence in prisons, could not be considered a Country where detainees are systematically subjected to inhuman treatments, all the more if one considers that it had recently ratified the Protocol to the Convention against Torture. The extradition to that Country of an individual who had to serve the remaining part of a sentence for conspiracy and trafficking in organs should therefore be granted as it does not constitute a violation of neither the extradition agreement nor article 3 ECHR. With regard to the requirement of double criminality, the Brazilian offense of trafficking in organs is punished under Italian law with the crimes of grievous bodily harms and trafficking in persons (article 601 criminal code).

Similar considerations were made by the Supreme Court (criminal division, Sec. VI, judgments 5 March 2014, No. 13095; 8 April 2014, No. 30864) in relation to a request for extradition from Ukraine: in order to be relevant, inhuman treatments or human rights violations should be based on legal or material choices of the State and not from contingent circumstances against which judicial remedies are available. The Supreme Court also reiterated the principle according to which, in order to justify the denial of an extradition request, information concerning the risk of ill-treatment for detainees in a particular Country must be based not only on NGOs reports, but also on concordant observations of inter-governmental organisations. The same conclusion was reached by the criminal division of the Court of Cassation, Sec. VI, judg. 8 October 2014, No. 53130, in relation to an extradition request from Turkey. Among the elements that the Court referred to in order to demonstrate the absence of a policy of tolerance of that State towards the practice of inhuman treatment in prison, worth to mention are the establishment by the Turkish Parliament, in 2012, of the National Ombudsman as an independent institution for human rights, and the authorisation to ratify the Optional Protocol to the Convention against Torture.

An extradition to Macedonia did not raise any problems as well: the Supreme Court, criminal division, Sec. VI, judgments 23 January 2014, No. 5088 and 9 July 2014, No. 34209, noted that the applicants had only demonstrated the existence in Macedonia of certain specific cases, occurred in some specific prisons, of violations of the right of detainees not to be subject to inhuman or degrading treatments, without providing any evidence of the existence in that Country of a systematic and legally accepted pattern of violation of human rights, including in the form of ethnic persecution against citizens of Albanian origin.

The Italian court had refused the extradition of an Italian citizen convicted in Romania for aggravated embezzlement, ordering the sentence to be served in Italy. The individual whose extradition was sought appealed said decision before the Supreme Court arguing that the extradition should have been refused – and therefore that he should have been set free – on account of the fact that his rights to defence during the trial in Romania had been violated. The Supreme Court (criminal division, Sec. VI, judg. 15 May 2014, No. 21322) dismissed the appeal and stated, among other things, that the failure to deliver to the defendant the Italian translation of some documents, provided that the latter was assisted by an interpreter, was not enough to constitute a violation of fair trial standards. The fact that a recent EU directive prescribes additional rights in connection to language assistance during trial was not relevant in the present case.

With two judgments delivered in the same day (17 July 2014) the Supreme Court refused the extradition to Argentina of individuals accused of serious crimes related to the 1976–83 dictatorship.

In the first case (criminal division, Sec. VI, judg. 17 July 2014, No. 43170) the Court held that the lack in the bilateral extradition treaty between Italy and Argentina of any reference to the obligation for the requested court to determine the existence of evidence of the extraditee's guilt did not exempt Italian courts from carrying out this assessment, in particular in the case the person sought has dual (Argentine and Italian) citizenship. In this case, the extraditee, resident in Italy, was accused of having participated, as official of the Mountain Infantry Regiment No. 22, to the commission of three murders as well as to the crimes of criminal conspiracy, aggravated injury, burglary and kidnapping. The Argentinean judges, however, specified that the extraditee was accused of having acted under a system in which "working groups" made up of officers of the Argentinean army had operated with criminal methods against organisations of political dissidents, always guaranteeing "the anonymity of the material perpetrators of the crimes as well as their interchangeability". According to the Supreme Court, however, this form of participation was very similar to a form of objective liability linked to the mere fact of belonging to the armed forces of Argentina. The extradition request was therefore denied.

In the second case (criminal division, Sec. VI, judg. 17 July 2014, No. 46634), the Supreme Court denied the extradition to Argentina of an individual accused of torture on the ground that the offences that under Italian law may have been used to punish the corresponding material conduct, namely grievous bodily harm and aggravated kidnapping, were time-barred as the fact allegedly committed had taken place in the 1970s. The fact that under Argentinean law the crime of torture is not subject to any statute of limitation, or that the Italian failure to incorporate the crime of torture under domestic law constitutes a violation of an explicit obligation enshrined in the Convention against Torture, ratified by Italy in 1987, had no relevance. Significantly, the Court added: "One cannot but observe that the failure of Italy to implement the UN Convention creates a paradoxical situation in which a crime as torture, internationally considered a *delictum juris gentium* and which under certain conditions can also constitute a crime against humanity, does not constitute a specific offense under Italian law. However, since the crime of torture does not exist, the applicant' claim as to its imprescriptibility has to be dismissed."

B. Crime of Apology of Fascism, Propaganda of Racist Ideas, Negationism

The Court of Cassation (criminal division, Sec. I, judg. 25 March 2014, No. 37577) upheld the conviction of the two applicants who, during a commemoration of the victims of *foibe* (sinkholes) killings had made the Roman salute and sang fascists songs. The applicants' request to recognise the illegitimacy of l. 30 June 1952, No. 645 because of its incompatibility with the right to freedom of expression was dismissed. According to the Supreme Court, the relevant offense occurred even if most of the participants to the event were members of the far-right association "Casapound" and therefore the "propaganda" effect was missing. Indeed, even though the Italian norm only punishes those acts aiming at the reorganisation of the fascist party, the fact that the other participants to the event shared the applicants' fascist ideology as well as the use of symbolic acts characterising such ideology such as the Roman salute does not alter, yet confirm, the concrete dangerousness of the conduct. The fact that during the event no violent act has occurred was irrelevant.

C. Defamation and Right to Criticise; Aggravating Circumstance of Ethnic, National, Racial or Religious Discrimination

The Supreme Court (criminal division, Sec. V, 4 November 2014, No. 7715) upheld the decisions of the court of first instance and the court of appeal which had both found that the crime of libel had been committed in the case of a newspaper article which had attributed anti-Semitic feelings to the author of a cartoon published in another newspaper. The latter, indeed, had drawn the caricature of a well-known journalist and political leader of Jewish origin with features that highlighted the alleged contradiction between being Jewish and member of a right-wing party. The article, without apparently grasping the references to the current political scenario that were at the basis of satirical cartoon, had manipulated the latter's contents and accused its author of anti-Semitism. The Supreme Court observed that the exercise of the right to criticise the author of the cartoon cannot exclude the defamatory character of the article in question, since the anti-Semitic interpretation of the cartoon was clearly unfounded both in subjective and (what is more important) in objective terms. Therefore, the right to criticise cannot be invoked as exonerating circumstance.

The crime of defamation with the aggravating circumstance of ethnic discrimination and hatred occurs when someone use his own public Facebook page to publish insults ("let them return to the jungle") addressed to a minister of African descent (Tribunal of Trent, judg. 14 July 2014, No. 508). The judge, among other things, excluded any pertinence to unconstitutionality grounds raised in connection to the aggravating circumstance of ethnic, national, racial or religious discrimination and hatred (introduced by l.d. 122/1993, converted into l. 25 June 1993 No. 205) on the ground that there no uncertainties concerning the interpretation of the notions of discrimination, hate and race relevant to the present case. The judge, therefore, supported by a number of quotations from recent judgments of the Supreme Court, concluded that the right to criticise cannot be interpreted as to legitimate expressions that impinge on human dignity. Some associations were admitted as civil parties in the proceedings. The author of the defamation via Facebook was sentenced to pay a fine of 2,500 euro, as well as to pay compensation to the civil parties and the costs.

D. *Immunity of Diplomatic Agents; State Secret and Extraordinary Renditions*

Once again, the criminal division of the Court of Cassation (Sec. V, judg. 11 March 2014, No. 39788) has dealt with the case of the abduction of the imam Abu Omar carried out by American agents, occurred in Milan in 2003, and following which the Muslim cleric was subject to inhuman treatment in Egypt (see *2013 Yearbook*, pp. 342–344; *2014 Yearbook*, p. 245). Relevant for the issue is also a ruling by the Constitutional Court regarding State secret.

Indeed, in a 2014 judgment, the Constitutional Court essentially overturned the decision adopted by the Supreme Court in 2012 (see *2013 Yearbook*, pp. 264–265) which, circumscribing the scope of the rules on State secret, had confirmed a number of criminal convictions inflicted on top officers of the Italian intelligence for the support they provided to their American counterparts in the kidnapping of Abu Omar. More specifically, in its judgment 24/2014, the Constitutional Court endorsed a notion of State secret according to which judicial authorities are prevented from performing acts that could affect – removing it – the contours of the domain covered by State secret as this is defined by the President of the Council of Ministers. A domain, according to the Constitutional Court, that only the President of the Council of Ministers has the power to define. The scope of State secret, therefore, cannot be redefined by other organs or authorities through actions that, however elusive, in the substance circumvent the limits imposed by it, even when such actions are aimed at prosecuting criminal offences. In short, the Constitutional Court endorsed a concept of State secret as a "black curtain" over the disputed facts. An understanding, however, that the Supreme Court in 2012 had rejected. The latter, indeed, had highlighted the fact that, in the present case, not only the domain covered by State secret was not clearly specified, but that many of the (often late) classified information were already public and known by judicial authorities. According to this reasoning, the Court of Cassation had therefore tried to limit in a logical way the contours of what could qualify as covered by secret from what could be relevant for the proceedings. In the opinion of the Court of Cassation, moreover, qualifying as "classified domain" the commission of acts that, according to other reliable sources, were clearly criminal under Italian law was at the very least problematic. In fact, the full protection against any investigation guaranteed by various Governments to Italian officials that had cooperated in the extraordinary rendition of Abu Omar would seem to imply the responsibility of Italian political authorities for the alleged human rights violations (articles 3, 5, 6, 13 ECHR) suffered by the victim of the illegal operation. On this particular aspect, an application has been lodged before the ECtHR.

Bound by the above-mentioned judgment of the Constitutional Court, few days later its delivery, the Supreme Court (criminal division, Sec. I, judg. 24 February 2014, No. 20447) struck down the conviction against Italian intelligence officials involved in the Abu Omar extraordinary rendition, who were therefore definitively acquitted, on account of the fact that the criminal prosecution could not continue due to the existence of State secret (article 41 (3), l. 3 August 2007, No. 124). Significantly, with regard to the ruling of the Constitutional Court, the judges of the Supreme Court observed that "it seems to break down at its roots the very possibility of a test of legitimacy, continence and reasonableness of the exercise of the power of classification of the competent administrative authority, and therefore significantly affecting the duty of criminal investigation of the judicial authority, which inevitably ends up being left to the discretion of the political authority – a scenario that cannot but stimulate broad and deep reflections that go beyond the individual case."

Finally, it is interesting to note that in a subsequent decision (criminal division, Sec. VI, judg. 13 November 2014, No. 1198), the Supreme Court partially addressed again the abovementioned issue. In this case, the Supreme Court decided, despite State secret, the continuation of the proceedings for the crime of embezzlement against some of the Italian intelligence officials involved in the Abu Omar case. The Court, in fact, reiterated that "if the invocation by the defendant of State secret, confirmed by the President of the Council of Ministers, prevents the use of classified information in the proceedings, the competent judge has to issue a judgment not to proceed in accordance with article 41 (3), l. 3 August 2007, No. 124, only when the acquisition of such information is considered essential for the outcome of the proceedings."

The Supreme Court dealt with the appeal against the conviction of 23 American CIA agents for complicity in aggravated kidnapping brought by three officials of the US embassy in Italy. Among others grounds of appeal, the applicants had invoked diplomatic immunity. According to the 1961 Vienna Convention on Diplomatic Relations, in fact, there is immunity in respect of acts performed by an individual in the exercise of his functions as a member of the mission. In the view of Italian courts, however, the three officials, when planning and implementing the "extraordinary rendition" of the Muslim cleric suspected of ties to al Qaeda, were not acting as members of the diplomatic mission, but in their capacity as CIA agents, that is the organisation that has materially carried out the operation. Moreover, the three defendants, having left the Italian territory and having their diplomatic functions in Italy expired, cannot invoke immunity from the jurisdiction of a foreign State pursuant to the Vienna Convention. The Italian judge also dismissed the defence of superior orders. Even though this exonerating circumstance could be accepted in the framework of US law, under Italian law (article 51 criminal code), the only relevant in the present case, it is undisputed that there can be no institutional duty or specific order issued by authorities other than the judicial ones, that can legitimately impose on anyone the obligation to deprive a person of his liberty. If the action put in place amounts to the criminal offense of kidnapping, the agent cannot invoke as a cause of justification the fact of having acted under the compulsion of an order and therefore has be to held criminally accountable.

E. Procedural Issues: Resumption of the Hearing to Reform a Judgment in Peius

The Constitutional Court pronounced the unconstitutionality, also on account of their incompatibility with the ECHR, of certain provisions of the code of criminal procedure providing for closed doors session, and thus not a public hearing, for cases concerning the application of security measures, namely procedures intended to establish the social dangerousness of an individual. The incompatibility with the ECHR of national provisions allowing some court decisions to be adopted in closed doors, such those concerning the application of security measures or reparation for wrongful detention had been addressed on several occasions by the ECtHR (for similar issues, see *2014 Yearbook*, p. 318; *2013 Yearbook*, p. 354; *2012 Yearbook*, p. 294). In its judgment 135/2014, the Constitutional Court held that procedures concerning the application of security measures do not have the purely and highly "technical" character that would justify to hold them in closed session. Moreover, the impact such procedures may have on the individual, both in the personal and economic domain, can be very significant. The Constitutional Court therefore concluded that the articles of the code criminal procedural under analysis are unconstitutional, on the grounds that they do not envisage the possibility to hold, upon request of the individual concerned, public hearings in the context of proceedings concerning the application of security measures held before post-sentencing courts.

In a number of cases decided by the Court of Cassation (criminal division, Sec. I, judg. 4 July 2014, No. 52965; Sec. VI, judgments 29 May 2014, No. 39925; 23 September 2014, No. 46067), the Court had the opportunity to clarify that "pilot judgments" issued by the ECtHR have consequences only in the legal system of the State in respect of which they are adopted. The case originated from the request made by a prisoner subjected to article 41-*bis* detention regime. The latter complained that the outcome of the criminal proceedings that ended up with his conviction had been conditioned by the limitations imposed by article 41-*bis* on the possibility he had to interact his lawyer. In addition, in a case involving similar restrictions in force in Turkey, the ECtHR had issued a judgment that could be interpreted as pilot judgment (case *Öcalan v. Turkey* [GC], No. 46221/99, ECHR 2005-IV). Also the Italian Constitutional Court has recently recognised that restrictions on external contacts provided for in article 41-*bis* are partly unconstitutional (judg. 143/2013, see *2014 Yearbook*, p. 318) and that a special form of review should be allowed if the ECtHR found the proceedings to be tainted by a breach of fair trial principles enshrined in article 6 ECHR (Constitutional Court, judg. 113/2011, see *2012 Yearbook*, pp. 312–313). The Supreme Court stated, however, that the remedy sought – namely the reopening of the proceedings allegedly vitiated by restrictions of the right to defence applicable under article 41-*bis* – could not be granted. As a matter of fact, the Supreme Court noted that no ruling specifically concerning the case under analysis had been issued by ECtHR against Italy. In this connection, even though the *Ocalan* case could be considered as a pilot judgment requiring structural interventions in the legal order of the State, it concerned Turkey and certainly not Italy. Moreover, the judgment of July 2014 indicated that, differently from the case under examination of the Supreme Court, in the *Ocalan* case the violation of the right to defence was connected not only to a limitation on the talks between the defendant and his lawyer, but also to a series of circumstances that markedly prevented the effective exercise of the right to defence.

In a number of decisions, the Supreme Court, relying on the principle of fair trial as interpreted by the ECtHR, concluded that in order to reform *in peius* an acquittal, courts cannot limit themselves in providing a reasoning which is different from the one developed at first instance but it has to hear again the key witnesses of the case. In particular, the Supreme Court, criminal division, judg. 11 September 2014, No. 53562, struck down and referred back to the lower court for further consideration a conviction on appeal decided after that at first instance the accused was acquitted of rape: the appeal court had delivered the judgment without having re-examined the victim, considered unreliable at first instance, in order to assess her credibility (see also Court of Cassation, criminal division, Sec. II, judgments 12 June 2014, No. 40254; 18 July 2014, No. 38049). The principle does not apply, however, in the event of an abbreviated "unconditional" criminal proceedings: Court of Cassation, criminal division, Sec. II, judg. 23 May 2014, No. 33690; Sec. III, judg. 30 September 2014, No. 45456. The principle, moreover, applies only to the examination of witnesses and not to the production of documents (Court of Cassation, criminal division, Sec. VI, judg. 15 April 2014, No. 36179). The principle according to which fundamental testimonies heard at trial have to be reproduced in appeal in order to deviate from the decision of the court of first instance is valid not only when the new judgment revises *in peius* the position of the defendant, but also when in appeal the judge opts for an acquittal instead of confirming the conviction: see Court of Cassation, criminal division, Sec. II, judg. 24 April 2014, No. 32619.

Italy in the Case-law of the European Court of Human Rights

I. Prison Conditions, Torture, Collective Expulsion

On 21 October 2014, the European Court of Human Rights (ECtHR) deliberated on the case *Sharifi and Others v. Italy and Greece* (No. 16643/09). The case concerned the return carried out by Italian border authorities of a group of migrants, 32 Afghans, two Sudanese nationals and one Eritrean, arrived in Italy in the ports of Bari, Ancona, Venice from Greece between 2008 and 2009. The applicants submitted, in particular, that they had entered Italy illegally from Greece and they had been immediately returned back to this Country, with the fear of subsequent deportation to their respective Countries of origin, where they faced the risk of death, torture or inhuman or degrading treatment (articles 2 and 3 ECHR). They complained, moreover, of having had no access to the domestic courts in order to assert their grievances (art. 13 ECHR) and had been ill-treated by both the Italian and Greek police, as well as by the crews of the ships on board of which they were brought to Greece (art. 3 ECHR). In respect of Italy, moreover, the applicants claimed to have been victims of indiscriminate collective expulsion (art. 4 Protocol IV ECHR) and that they had been deprived of the right to bring their case before the Strasbourg Court due to the impossibility to contact an interpreter and a lawyer (art. 34 ECHR).

Having decided to continue the examination of the application only with regards to four Afghans nationals, the ECtHR examined the applicants' complaints against Italy. With respect to the alleged breach of article 4 Protocol IV ECHR (prohibition of collective expulsion of aliens), the Court firstly rejected the admissibility exception put forward by the Italian Government according to which such provision would not apply to returns or refusals to allow entry to the national territory, but only to persons whose stay in the territory was legal. On the merit, the Court was not persuaded by the Italian position according to which the procedure of identification of undocumented people in the Italian Adriatic ports carried out by police officers had offered sufficient guarantees that the situation of each individual was individually and properly considered. Moreover, contrary to what the Italian Government maintained, the judges in Strasbourg considered that the application of the Dublin II regulation did not exempt Italy from the duty to undertake an evaluation of the individual circumstances of each applicant. Having failed to do so, the Court concluded that the measure the applicants had been subjected to amounted to a breach of article 4 Protocol IV ECHR. On the alleged violation of article 3 ECHR connected to the risk of arbitrary repatriation to Afghanistan as a result of the applicants' removal to Greece, the ECtHR reaffirmed that it was for the State carrying out the return to ensure, even in the context of the Dublin system, that the asylum policy of the destination Country offered sufficient guarantees to prevent the person concerned from being removed to his Country of origin without an assessment of the risks faced. Having found in this case a violation by Greece of article 13 ECHR, taken together with article 3 ECHR, on account of the lack of access to the asylum procedure and the risk that the applicants would be deported to Afghanistan, where they were likely to be subjected to inhuman and degrading treatment, the ECtHR concluded that Italy had violated art. 3 ECHR because of the indirect *refoulement* in Afghanistan of the applicants. The Court, finally, found also a violation of art. 13 ECHR (right to an effective remedy) taken together with articles 3 ECHR and 4 Protocol IV ECHR, for the impossibility of the applicants to access asylum procedures in the port of Ancona.

On 4 November 2014, the Grand Chamber of the ECtHR decided the case *Tarakhel v. Switzerland*, concerning the application of the Dublin III regulation by Swiss authorities. The applicants in the present case were the members of the Tarakhel family (mother, father and six minor children) who, after a long journey from Afghanistan to Pakistan, from Iran to Turkey, had reached Italy by sea and were then placed to the Reception Centre for Asylum Seekers (CARA) in Bari. After a short period, family members decided to leave the Centre to reach Austria, from where they were sent back to Italy. Subsequently, the family entered Switzerland where, according to the Dublin regulation, the authorities refused to consider the applicants' asylum claim and arranged their transfer to Italy, Country of first entry.

According to the ECtHR, the transfer of the family to Italy, decided by the Swiss authorities in accordance with the Dublin regulation, would have resulted, in the absence of specific guarantees from the Italian authorities on assistance measures suitable for minors and for the family unit, in a breach of article 3 ECHR (prohibition on inhuman and degrading treatment). In particular, the Court found that, given the current state of the reception system in Italy and in the absence of detailed information about the specific reception facility, the Swiss authorities were not in possession of the necessary guarantees that once repatriated in Italy the applicants could have access to forms of international protection consistent with the needs of children and the preservation of the family unit.

The Court, more specifically, noted that "without entering into the debate as to the accuracy of the available figures, it is sufficient for the Court to note the glaring discrepancy between the number of asylum applications made in 2013, which according to the Italian Government totalled 14,184 by 15 June 2013, and the number of places available in the facilities belonging to the SPRAR network (9,630 places), where – again according to the Italian Government – the applicants would be accommodated. Moreover, given that the figure for the number of applications relates only to the first six months of 2013, the figure for the year as a whole is likely to be considerably higher, further weakening the reception capacity of the SPRAR system."

In a judgment delivered on 11 February 2014 in the case *Contrada (No. 2) v. Italy* (No. 7509/08), the ECtHR found again a violation of article 3 ECHR by Italy in connection to conditions of detention of people affected by serious diseases. The applicant, a former police officer sentenced to imprisonment for aiding and abetting a Mafia-type organisation, brought a complained before the Strasbourg Court on the grounds that, although his serious health conditions were manifestly incompatible with the penalty imposed, he had to stay in prison for a period of almost a year before he was granted the possibility to serve the sentence on house arrest.

The Court, having considered that the applicant's severe health conditions were known by the Italian judicial authorities even at the time of the proceedings against him, found a violation of art. 3 ECHR on account of the fact that the applicant's permanence in prison was actually incompatible with the state of his health and amounted to inhuman and degrading treatment. The part of the application claiming a violation of article 6 ECHR (right to a fair trial) was declared inadmissible as being manifestly ill-founded.

A case dealing with similar issues is *G.C. v. Italy* (No. 73869/10) decided on 22 April 2014. The applicant, an inmate of the Bellizzi Irpino (Avellino) prison suffering from severe incontinence problems, claimed a violation of article 3 ECHR. In deciding the case, the ECtHR concluded that in the light of the applicant's specific conditions of health (he had twice attempted to commit suicide), the late administration of medical care by prison authorities had caused him a state of embarrassment and anguish amounting to a degrading treatment contrary to article 3 ECHR.

The case *Riina v. Italy*, No. 43575/09, in which the Strasbourg Court had to assess the compatibility with articles 3 ECHR (prohibition on inhuman and degrading treatment) and 8 ECHR (right to respect for private and family life) of the constant surveillance in the cell and in the toilet of the applicant was declared inadmissible for non-exhaustion of domestic remedies. Indeed, after his application had been rejected by the competent court, the applicant did not lodge an appeal before the Court of Cassation.

In the case *Alberti v. Italy* (No. 15397/11), decided on 24 June 2014, the applicant alleged a violation of the material limb of article 3 ECHR on the ground that he had been struck by the *carabinieri* during his arrest, and a violation of the procedural limb of the same provision due to the failure of Italian authorities to carry out a thorough, prompt and independent investigation into his allegations. Unable to determine with certainty the precise cause of the injuries suffered by the applicant (three broken ribs and an haematoma on the right testicle), the ECtHR could not but find that such injuries had occurred while the applicant was under the total control of the police. The absence of any plausible justification by the Italian Government was sufficient for the Strasbourg Court to establish Italy's responsibility for the violation of the material limb of article 3 ECHR. The Court also found the violation of the procedural limb of the invoked provision, emphasising the superficiality of the investigation carried out at the national level. Not only the victim had not been heard by the judicial authorities, but the latter had not tried to determine the facts or to identify those allegedly responsible for the injuries suffered by him. Moreover, according to the Court, if on the one hand, the credibility of the applicant had been undermined from the outset by the excessive weight the prosecutor gave to his criminal record, on the other hand, the effect of medicines taken by the applicant on his ability to make a detailed and accurate account of the violence was not taken into account. The applicant was granted a compensation of 15,000 euro for moral damages.

In *Saba v. Italy* (No. 36629/10), the applicant, detained for a period of time in the Sassari prison, alleged a violation of both the procedural and the substantive limbs of article 3 ECHR by reason of mistreatments committed against him by some prison officers who, because of the length of the judicial procedure, had benefited from the intervention of the statute of limitations, thus avoiding punishment. Specifically, the applicant declared he was forced by prison officers to strip naked, to stay in front of his cell with his head against the wall and to pass between two lines of officers with his head bowed as he was insulted and threatened, and searched without justification. Cells were devastated and detainees' personal belongings were destroyed. Having determined that the purpose of the treatment the applicant was subject to was to degrade and humiliate in a context of strong emotional tension that may have led detainees to legitimately fear for their fate, the ECtHR concluded that the treatment in question qualified as "degrading", thus finding that there had been a violation of the substantial aspect of article 3 ECHR.

With regard to the substantive limb of the invoked provision, the Court considered that the various measures adopted by national authorities had not fully complied with the standards of a thorough and effective investigation identified in its previous case-law. The Court referred, first and foremost, to the excessive length of the proceedings which led to a decision not to prosecute due to prescription, as well as the tenuous nature of the penal and disciplinary sanctions in respect of the gravity of the facts and the status of State officials of the defendants.

In the case *Carrella v. Italy* (No. 33955/07) the applicant, who had since died, relying in particular on article 3 ECHR (prohibition of inhuman or degrading treatment), complained about the conditions of his detention, alleging in particular that he had not received adequate medical treatment in prison and that as a result of various errors and omissions, the operation he had needed to undergo had been delayed. He also complained that the authorities had not considered, in view of his state of health, alternative measure to detention, and that they had taken no action on his complaint. The Court dismissed the applicant's case. Indeed, despite some delays, the Italian authorities had complied with their obligation to protect the physical integrity of the applicant through the administration of appropriate medical checks. In the Court's opinion, therefore, the treatment the applicant was subject to did not reach the minimum threshold of severity necessary to fall within the scope of article 3 ECHR and thus it did not constitute a violation of its material limb. As for the effectiveness of the investigation conducted at the national level following the applicant's complaint, the Court concluded that nothing suggested that the investigative efforts were manifestly inappropriate or ineffective. The fact that such efforts had not led to the conviction of the prison authorities did not mean they were ineffective. A violation of the procedural limb of article 3 ECHR is then also excluded.

The case *Rumor v. Italy* (No. 72964/10) concerned the alleged violation of the positive obligations under article 3 ECHR (prohibition on torture, cruel, inhuman and degrading treatment) in connection with domestic violence. Invoking article 3 ECHR alone and in conjunction with article 14 ECHR (prohibition of discrimination), the applicant complained about the inaction of the Italian authorities, which had allegedly failed to protect and support her after the violence she had suffered. Having determined that the applicant was subjected to ill-treatment within the meaning of article 3 of the Convention, the Court however excluded that the Italian authorities had not complied with their positive obligations under the invoked provision. The elements considered by the Court to reach such conclusion were, among others: the criminal proceedings against the offender held with due expedition and concluded with a three years and four months prison sentence; the effective response in relation to the custody of the couple's children; the diligence of the post-sentencing judge in the proceedings concerning the application for house arrest of the applicant's former partner. In the light of the above considerations, the Court concluded that the authorities had put in place a legislative framework allowing them to take measures against persons accused of domestic violence and that the framework had been effective in punishing the perpetrator of the crime of which the applicant was victim and preventing the recurrence of violent attacks against her physical integrity. There has accordingly been no violation of article 3 of the Convention.

In the case *Placì v. Italy*, No. 48754/11, the applicant, conscripted to compulsory military service at the age of 18, complained of having being victim of inhuman and degrading treatment as he was called to undertake the military service despite his physical and mental vulnerability. According to the applicant, moreover, his right to a fair trial had been denied to the extent that the medical boards in charge of checking his fitness for military service were dependent on the Ministry of Defence, a part in the proceedings initiated by the applicant in order to receive compensation. The Court endorsed the applicant's claim and ordered Italy to pay him 40,000 euro in respect of non-pecuniary damages.

In *Stella and Others v. Italy*, the applicants, all (current or past) detainees of various prisons in Italy, invoked article 3 ECHR and claimed that they were kept in overpopulated cells which had insufficient ventilation, lighting and heating. In contesting the admissibility of the case, the Italian Government observed that following the application of the pilot judgment procedure in the case *Torreggiani and Others* (see *2014 Yearbook*, pp. 307–308), Italy had enacted a number of legislative measures aimed at resolving the structural problem of overcrowding in prisons, had reformed the law to allow detainees to complain before a judicial authority about the material conditions of detention and had introduced a compensatory remedy providing for damages to be paid to persons who had been subjected to detention contrary to the Convention. Despite the applications in the present case had been lodged before the entry into force of the new legislative provisions, the ECtHR considered that there were grounds for departing from the general principle that the exhaustion requirement should be assessed with reference to the time at which the application was lodged. In accordance with its subsidiary character, then, the Court opted for examining the Government exception on the basis of the current state of the national legal system. Having no evidence on which to find that the remedies in question did not offer, in principle, prospects of appropriate relief for the complaints submitted under article 3 ECHR, the Court, while not excluding a possible re-examination of the remedy's effectiveness, declared the complaint inadmissible for non-exhaustion of domestic remedies. The same conclusion was reached in the case *Rexhepi and Others v. Italy* of 19 September 2014.

The ECtHR declared inadmissible as manifestly ill-founded the application of a prisoner (case *Vindice v. Italy*, No. 46925/09) who complained that his right under the ECHR had been violated on account of the fact that he was placed in a cell with smokers; that he was transported in vehicles unsuited to his claustrophobia; and that he was not assigned a single cell.

II. Fair Trial, Excessive Length of Proceedings

The judgment delivered by the ECtHR on 4 March 2014 in the case *Grande Stevens and Others* (Nos. 18640/10, 18647/10, 18663/10, 18668/10 and 18698/10) concerned two companies and three Italian citizens that, after having received an administrative penalty (later become final) by the Italian Companies and Stock Exchange Commission (Consob) for acts of market manipulation, had to undergo a criminal proceedings in respect of the same facts. The applicants complained a violation of their right not to be tried or punished twice for the same acts (article 4 Protocol VII ECHR) arguing that the penalty imposed by Consob could be classified as "criminal"; of their right to a fair trial (article 6 ECHR) on account of the lack of independence and impartiality of the proceedings before the Consob; and of their right to peaceful enjoyment of property (article 1 Protocol I ECHR).

In examining the case, the ECtHR had first and foremost to settle the issue of the reservation made by Italy with regard to the application of article 4 Protocol VII ECHR according to which this provision would apply only to offenses, proceedings and decisions classified as "criminal" by Italian law. Relied upon by the Italian Government to exclude the admissibility of the case on the basis of the fact that the offences proscribed by Consob are not qualified by law as "criminal", the Italian reservation was nonetheless declared invalid by the ECtHR because of its general character.

On the question whether the applicants had been "convicted of a crime by a final judgment" in the meaning of article 4 Protocol VII ECHR, the Court relied on its established case-law according to which, in order to establish the existence of a criminal charge, three are the relevant criteria: the legal classification of the offence under national law, the very nature of the offence, and the degree of severity of the penalty that the person concerned is liable to incur. In the present case, having the Consob imposed to the applicants fines of undeniable severity, the Court concluded that the penalties imposed were criminal in nature. Consequently, the Court established that the criminal proceedings against the applicants were based on facts which were substantially the same as those which had been sanctioned by Consob and thus found a violation of article 4 Protocol VII ECHR. With regard to the fairness of the proceedings before the Consob, the ECtHR concluded that, although the latter did not meet the requirements of fairness and objective impartiality set out in article 6 ECHR, the applicants had then had access to a court with full jurisdiction such as the Turin Court of Appeal. However, as the latter did not hold a public hearing, the Court found a violation of article 6 of the Convention. On the contrary, no violation of article 1 Protocol I ECHR was found.

Each applicant was granted 10,000 euro in respect of non-pecuniary damages and 40,000 euro of expenses.

The applicants in the cases *Mottola and Others* (No. 29932/07) and *Staibano and Others* (No. 29907/07), decided by the ECtHR on 4 February 2014, are some doctors that in 2004 sought before the Italian administrative courts the recognition of a contract of indefinite duration with the University Hospital "Federico II" of Naples in relation to the period 1983-1997 and, consequently, the payment of the corresponding social security contributions. During that period, the doctors had worked in the aforesaid Hospital with job on call contracts. After the applicants' claim had been successful before the TAR Campania, it was dismissed by the Supreme Administrative Council according to the rules on the repartition of competences between ordinary and administrative courts in the area of public employment (Consolidated law on civil service, lgs.d. 30 March 2001, No. 165, article 69(7)). Indeed, if in the first period of its application the abovementioned norm had been interpreted in the sense that all claims brought subsequent to 15 September 2000 could be re-assigned to ordinary courts, after a jurisprudential *revirement* that date was interpreted as the final and mandatory term to introduce any claim related to employment relationships started prior to June 30, 1998. Relying on article 6 ECHR (access to a court) and on article 1 Protocol I ECHR, the applicants claimed that the decision of the Supreme Administrative Council had deprived them of any opportunity to submit their claim before a national court and to then obtain the recognition, for pension purposes, of the period they had worked with on-call contracts.

While acknowledging that the norm whose application was contested pursued an aim of general interest, namely a coherent and rational jurisdictional repartition between administrative and ordinary courts in the area of public employment, the ECtHR considered that the applicants' right to access to a court (article 6 ECHR) has been violated. The applicants, indeed, who had in good faith seized the administrative court relying on a legal framework that could have given rise to a number of plausible interpretations, have been deprived of the possibility to re-present their claims before the courts definitively identified as competent. In respect of the alleged violation of article 1 Protocol I ECHR, the Court first of all established that the legitimate expectations of the applicants in connection to the payment of pension contributions by the University of Naples were sufficient to qualify as "goods". The Court then found that Italy failed in guaranteeing a fair balance between the public and private interests at stake and that the decision of the Supreme Administrative Council constituted an unreasonable and exorbitant burden on the applicants in violation of the provision of the Convention.

The incompatibility with the principles of due process of legislative initiatives that, despite being presented as "interpretative laws" of existing provisions, as a matter of fact interfered retroactively with legal positions that people thought they had gained on the basis of settled case-law, is the basis of two judgments issued by the ECtHR in 2014: *Silverfunghi and Others* (24 June) and *Guadagno and Others* (1 July). The applicants in the first case are a group of agricultural firms that in a number of judgments (at first instance and in appeal) were granted the possibility of accumulating some tax benefits provided for by Italian law. The entry into force of an "interpretative law" which established that the tax benefits could not be accumulated made it pointless for the applicants to carry on the litigation. Thus, the law had the effect of definitively modifying the outcome of pending litigations in favour of the State. Relying on its settled jurisprudence on the issue, the ECtHR found a violation of article 6 ECHR. Even accepting that the legislative intervention was necessary to eliminate any doubt about the extent and method of application of the benefits at issue, the Court was unable to identify in the circumstances of the present case any compelling general-interest reason capable of outweighing the dangers inherent in the use of retrospective legislation which had the effect of influencing the judicial determination of a pending dispute to which the State was a party. On the contrary, in respect of article 1 Protocol I ECHR, the Court found no violation. The same reasoning was followed by the Court in the second case which concerned the enactment of an "interpretative law" that retroactively impacted on the outcome of pending proceedings initiated by members of the administrative judiciary to obtain the recognition of a higher salary level.

Questions related to a group of employees of different Italian provinces transferred to the Ministry of Education that only had a partial recognition of their length of the service completed with their previous employer (see *Agrati and Others*, *2012 Yearbook*, pp. 346–347 and *De Rosa*, *2013 Yearbook*, pp. 369–370), are raised in the cases *Montalto and Others* (14 January), *Biasucci and Others* (25 March), *Peduzzi and Arrighi* (13 May), *Caponetto* (13 May). In all these cases, the Court found a violation of article 6 ECHR (due process) for having the State interfered with retroactive legislation in legal proceedings which had been, until that moment, generally favourable to the applicants. In *Marino and Colacione* (13 May) and *Caligiuri and Others* (9 September), the Court also found a violation of article 1 of Protocol I ECHR (right to peaceful enjoyment of property) on account of the fact that the legislative measure adopted by the State constituted a disproportionate interference with the right of "property", the latter being represented by the legitimate expectation of the transferred employees to have full recognition of their length of their service completed with their previous employer. In *Bordoni and Others* (13 May), the Court also established the amount of the compensation.

Circumstances analogous to those described in *Maggio and Others* (see *2012 Yearbook*, pp. 347–348), and thus concerning the case of Italian citizens who had worked in Switzerland whose pension had been reduced on the basis of an "interpretative law" which retroactively impacted on legal proceedings which had been, until that moment, generally favourable to them, are dealt with in *Stefanetti and Others* (15 April), *Cataldo and Others* (24 June), and *Biraghi and Others* (24 June). As in *Maggio*, the ECtHR found a violation of article 6 ECHR on account of the fact that any interference in the administration of justice designed to influence the outcome of proceedings that are still pending must be justified by overriding reasons of general interest that, in the present case, are inexistent. Differently from *Maggio*, however, in *Stefanetti and Others*, the Court also found a violation of article 1 Protocol I ECHR on the ground that by losing 67% of their pensions the applicants had suffered a disproportionate burden.

The case *Dhahbi v. Italy* (No. 17120/09), decided on 8 April 2014, concerned the inability of an immigrant worker of Tunisian origin to obtain payment from the Italian public authorities of a family allowance provided for under the Association agreement between the EU and Tunisia (Euro-Mediterranean agreement). Relying on article 6 ECHR (right to a fair trial), the applicant alleged that the Italian Court of Cassation ignored his request to have a preliminary question referred to the ECJ. Relying also on article 14 ECHR (prohibition of discrimination) taken in conjunction with article 8 ECHR (right to respect for private and family life), he submitted that he had been discriminated against on grounds of his nationality regarding an award of the allowance payable under l. 448/1998.

In respect of the alleged violation of article 6 ECHR, the Strasbourg Court found a violation of the invoked provision on account of the fact that the judgment of the Italian Court of Cassation had included a reference neither to the request for a preliminary ruling submitted by the applicant nor to the reasons why the Court of Cassation had deemed that the question raised should not be referred to the ECJ. According to the ECtHR, indeed, the Italian Court of Cassation should have set out its reasons for considering that the question was not relevant, that the provision had already been interpreted by the ECJ, or that the correct application of EU law was so obvious as to leave no scope for reasonable doubt. As for the second part of the complaint, the ECtHR observed that the national authorities' refusal to grant the applicant the family allowance had been based exclusively on the fact that he was not a national of a EU Member State. Since the budgetary reasons mentioned by the Government were insufficient to persuade it that the difference in treatment complained of was proportionate, the Court concluded that there has been a violation of article 14 ECHR in conjunction with article 8 ECHR.

Several decisions condemning Italy for the excessive length of domestic proceedings, including the unreasonable length of "Pinto" procedure, were issue by the European Court of Human Rights also in 2014. In the framework of the same decisions, the ECtHR had also often found that the delay in paying the compensation awarded under the "Pinto" procedure was contrary to article 6 ECHR (execution of judgments). On the other hand, the allegations based on article 13 ECHR concerning the non-effectiveness of the "Pinto" procedure by reason of the reduced compensation awarded were held unfounded. Among this group of decisions, it is possible to mention *Bifulco and Others* (22 July) and *Zucchinali and Others* (21 October, in this case the delay in the payment of the "Pinto" compensation was considered contrary to article 1 Protocol I ECHR as well).

In *Giannini and Others* (3 June), *Miele* (16 September), *Siciliano and Gagliardi* (16 September), *Pubblicità Grafiche Perri s.r.l. and Others* (14 October), having took note of the unilateral declaration lodged by the Italian Government aimed at resolving the matters raised by the complaints, the ECtHR concluded that it was no longer justified to continue the examination of the applications and decided to strike them out of the list of cases pursuant to article 37 ECHR. The case *Fedele and Others* (14 October) was struck out of the list on account of the friendly settlement reached by the parties.

In *Panetta v. Italy* (No. 38624/07) the applicant had dual French-Italian citizenship. Relying on article 6 ECHR (right to a fair trial), Ms Panetta complained about the inaction of Italian authorities in dealing with her requests for maintenance payment from her former husband. After their divorce, indeed, the latter had settled in Italy. Having considered that the proceedings for the execution of the French court's judgment setting the level of maintenance to be paid by the applicants' former husband took thirteen years and eleven months and that the case had been neither complex nor characterised by uncooperative behaviour of the parties, the ECtHR found a violation of article 6 ECHR on account of the unreasonable length of the proceedings. In addition to costs and expenses, the applicant was granted 18,750 euro in respect of non-pecuniary damages.

In *Stefanelli v. Italy* (No. 13139/08), the applicant is a high school teacher whose alleged involvement as a leader of a satanic group became public as a result of a press conference organised by the prosecutor in charge of the investigation. Relying on article 6 ECHR, the applicant, against whom all charges had meanwhile been dismissed, lamented that the press conference and its echoes violated his right to presumption of innocence. In the absence of the text or the record of the contested press conference, the ECtHR examined newspaper articles based on the information disclosed by investigators during such event. From the analysis made, the Court noted that no statement reflecting the sentiment that the applicant was guilty had been used. Rather, as the Court observed the use of several precautions, as the conditional tense, it found no violation of the principle of presumption of innocence and declared the case inadmissible. The part of the complaint alleging a violation of article 8 ECHR in relation to the same facts was rejected for non-exhaustion of domestic remedies.

In *Dalla Santa v. Italy* (No. 353/10), the ECtHR held that, in the absence of the explicit request of the detainee to appear during the appeal hearing against a judgment issued in the context of an abbreviated trial procedure (*rito abbreviato*), the Italian authorities acted in conformity with article 6 ECHR when they concluded that there had been an implicit withdrawal of such right on the part of the applicant. Considering that the obligation on the applicant to manifest his intention to appear at the hearing did not require complex formalities and that during the hearing the latter's lawyer had not raised the issue of the absence of his client, the Court declared the application inadmissible as manifestly unfounded.

In *Pahor and Others v. Italy*, the applicants, members of the Slovenian minority in Italy, filed several criminal complaints against a number of Italian politicians, public officials and judicial officers who had allegedly failed to adopt adequate legislation for the protection of the Slovene minority and who had allegedly been trying to prevent the exercise of the applicants' minority rights. After all proceedings had been discontinued at national level, the applicants lodged an application before the Strasbourg Court. Relying on articles 6 and 13 ECHR, they complained about the unfairness of criminal proceedings as well as the ineffectiveness of the criminal investigation. They further complained under article 14 ECHR that they could not use their mother tongue. In respect of article 6 ECHR, the ECtHR declared the application incompatible *ratione materiae* with the provisions of the Convention on the ground that the rights claimed by the applicants were political, and not civil in nature, as they concerned the action of the public authorities, and in particular of the legislature. Having established that article 6 ECHR was inapplicable, the Court held that neither article 14 ECHR could be taken into account.

The case *Vianello v. Italy* (No. 27516/09) was declared inadmissible as manifestly ill-founded. The applicant alleged a violation of the fairness of the proceedings he was subjected to (article 6 ECHR) and of the principle of non-retroactivity of criminal law (article 7 ECHR) on account of his conviction for fraudulent bankruptcy under articles 216(1) and 223 of the Bankruptcy act. According to the applicant, in particular, having the domestic courts failed to interpret the abovementioned provisions in conjunction with article 2634 civil code (according to which the profit of a company is not to be considered unfair if it is outweighed by the benefits, earned or predictable, arising from the company being part to a group), he was convicted for acts that were no longer considered crimes by law.

III. Freedom of Movement, Right to Life

In the case *Battista v. Italy* (No. 43978/09), decided on 2 December 2014, the ECtHR had to assess the compatibility with the Convention of restrictions imposed by the Italian legislation on the freedom of movement of individuals in debt of particularly significant credits towards third parties, such as maintenance payments. The applicant in the present case, after having asked the guardianship judge to issue him with a new passport, requesting that the names of his children also be entered in it, was ordered to hand in his passport to the police. His identity card was then amended, making it invalid for foreign travels on account of failure to make maintenance payments. Relying on article 2 Protocol IV ECHR, the applicant complained about the violation of the freedom of movement and the freedom to leave one's Country.

The ECtHR first of all observed that the applicant had been deprived of documents valid for foreign travel since 2008, a period during which domestic courts had failed to carry out any fresh review of the justification and proportionality of the measure he was subject to. According to the Strasbourg Court, indeed, national courts did not consider it necessary to examine the applicant's personal situation or his ability to pay the amounts due. The only factor taken into consideration was the property interests of the maintenance recipients. Moreover, on the issue of the recovery of maintenance payments outside national borders, the Court found that national authorities failed to take into account the multiplicity of existing methods for obtaining recovery of such debts. In light of these considerations, the Court considered that the automatic imposition of such a measure for an indeterminate period without any regard to the individual circumstances of the person concerned could not be described as necessary in a democratic society. Having found a violation of the invoked provision, the Court considered it appropriate to award the applicant 5,000 euro in respect of non-pecuniary damage.

In its judgment of 13 November 2014 in the case *G.G. and Others v. Italy*, the ECtHR held Italy responsible for the violation of the procedural limb of article 2 ECHR (right to life) on account of the length of civil proceedings brought by the applicants (or their deceased relatives) seeking compensation for the damage they had allegedly sustained after they (or the deceased) had been infected with various viruses in the course of blood transfusions carried out in public hospitals. Having ascertained that the civil proceedings initiated by the applicants lasted from seven to fifteen years at first instance, and from ten to fourteen years, for two, three or four stages of judgment, the Court held that the length of proceedings had been excessive and concluded that the Italian authorities failed in offering an adequate and rapid response as required by the procedural obligations under article 2 ECHR. Several hundreds of thousands of euro were granted in respect of non-pecuniary damages.

A case presented by the mother and the siblings of an inmate of the prison of Voghera who had died as a result of overdose was declared inadmissible as manifestly ill-founded (*Marro and Others v. Italy*, No. 29100/07). The applicants, relying on article 2 ECHR (right to life), complained that the failure of authorities to prevent the entrance of drugs in prison and the decision to place their relative in a cell with another prisoner who had been charged with drug-trafficking and had tested positive for drugs had caused the death of their beloved. The Court, while acknowledging States' obligation to adequately ensure the health and well-being of prisoners, and in particular of vulnerable groups such as drug-addicted prisoners, excluded that that the mere objective fact that a prisoner might have had access to narcotic substances constitutes a breach by Italy of its positive obligations under article 2 ECHR. Indeed, while authorities have the duty to adopt anti-drug-trafficking measures, they are bound by an obligation as to measures to be taken and not as to results to be achieved.

IV. Property Rights, "Indirect Expropriations"

The case *Valle Pierimpiè Società Agricola S.p.a. v. Italy* (No. 46154/11) concerned the legal status, public or private, of the fishing valley situated on a lagoon in the province of Venice. The applicant in the case was the agricultural company Valle Pierimpiè Spa which had acquired the fishing valley on the basis of a notarised deed of sale and which carried out a particular form of fish rearing on the site. Following a judgment of the Italian Supreme Court ruling that the fishing valley belonged to the public maritime domain, the applicant lodged a complaint before the ECtHR alleging a violation of article 1 Protocol I ECHR on account of the fact that it had been deprived of the fishing valley without compensation and, contextually, it had been ordered to pay compensation for unlawful occupation of the site.

The ECtHR first of all observed that the State interference with the applicant company's right to the peaceful enjoyment of its possessions had a sufficient legal basis in Italian law and had pursued the legitimate aim of preserving the lagoon ecosystem and of ensuring that the latter was actually designated for public use. On the other hand, the Court considered that the State had not struck a fair balance between the public and private interests at stake. Indeed, not only the interference in question had not been accompanied by any compensation, but the applicant had been ordered to pay a fine for unlawful occupation. In conclusion, as there was no evidence that the applicant had not acted in good faith and in consideration of the failure on the part of the authorities to take any steps to lessen the financial impact of the interference, the Court found a violation of article 1 Protocol I ECHR.

In the case *Ceni v. Italy* (No. 25376/06), decided on 4 February 2014, the ECtHR had to deal with a complex situation concerning the ownership of a flat in the context of an insolvency proceedings. In short, the construction firm with which the applicant had signed a preliminary contract of sale for the off-plan purchase of a flat refused, despite the payment of the full price, to sign the final contract of sale. Having the construction firm declared insolvent, the liquidator decided to cancel the preliminary contract and to sell the flat at auction pursuant to article 72(4) of the Bankruptcy act. During the long judicial battle that followed, the applicant was ordered to pay a compensation for unlawful occupation, had part of her salary seized and eventually become the owner the flat only after she had bought it back from the new owners. Relying on article 1 Protocol I ECHR, the applicant complained that she had been deprived of her right to become the owner of the flat in question, without any compensation, because of the discretionary decision of the liquidator to unilaterally cancel the preliminary contract.

First of all, the ECtHR dismissed the claim of admissibility raised by the Italian Government according to which the provision invoked by the applicant would be inapplicable on account of the fact that under Italian law a preliminary contract does not operate a transfer of ownership of the good. The Court, indeed, considered that the legitimate expectation of the applicant linked to economic interests such as the full payment of the sale price and the purchase of the flat were of sufficient relevance to be considered a "possession" within the meaning of article 1 Protocol I ECHR.

On the merit, although the Court did not consider the Italian State directly responsible for the actions of the court-appointed liquidator, it concluded that Italy had not fulfilled its positive obligations under article 1 Protocol I ECHR by reason of the applicant's inability to secure a review of whether the liquidator's decision to cancel the preliminary contract for the sale of the flat had been necessary and proportionate. The latter, indeed, had exercised a discretionary power which could not be subject to any form judicial review at the request of one the parties to the cancelled contract. Therefore, the applicant had been deprived of any effective protection against the loss of the flat and of the sums she had paid to purchase it, thus obliging her to bear an excessive and impracticable burden. Lastly, as the applicant had been unable to secure a review of the measure taken by the court-appointed liquidator at the national level, the Court found also a violation of article 13 ECHR in conjunction with article 1 Protocol I ECHR. In a judgment of 16 December 2014, the Court ruled on the question of just satisfaction sought by the applicant. Taking into account the feelings of powerlessness and frustration suffered, the Court considered it appropriate to award 50,000 euro in respect of non-pecuniary and pecuniary damage combined, plus 15,000 euro of expenses.

In 2014, in more than one occasion, the ECtHR condemned Italy for the violation of the right to peaceful enjoyment of property in connection with cases of "indirect expropriation". In *Pascucci* (14 January), *Giannitto* (28 January) *Pagnozzi* (4 February), *Benenati and Scillamà* (4 February), *Maiorano and Serafini* (25 November) and *D'Asta* (16 December), the Strasbourg Court reviewed the practice of Italian courts to consider, in application of the indirect expropriation procedure, the applicants to be deprived of their possession as of the completion of the public works. The Court, however, noted that in the absence of a formal act of expropriation, the applicants could have had legal certainty concerning the deprivation of the land only from the date on which a finding of unlawfulness had become final. Not considering the situation as "foreseeable", and therefore inconsistent with the principle of legality, the Court held that there had been a violation of the applicants' right to peaceful enjoyment of property. In all cases, but in *Giannitto*, *Pagnozzi* and *D'Asta*, the ECtHR awarded the applicants just compensation according to criteria established by the Grand Chamber in the case *Guiso-Gallisay v. Italy* (22 December 2009). Again in relation to cases of "indirect expropriation", the ECtHR stroke out from the list of cases *Rossi and Variale* (No. 23180/04, after the Italian government had lodged a unilateral declaration aimed at resolving the dispute) and *Canestrari and Uguccioni* (No. 63243/00, after the parties had reached a friendly settlement).

A sales contract with the postal administration not approved by the Minister or his delegate does not constitute a "possession" within the meaning of article 1 Protocol I ECHR if the approval is a condition of the validity of such contract. This was the determination of the ECtHR in the case *Romanazzi and Others v. Italy* (No. 18931/09) which had been declared inadmissible as incompatible *ratione materiae*.

V. Right to Private and Family Life

Cusan and Fazzo v. Italy, No. 77/07, was a case lodged by an Italian married couple who claimed the right to give their new-born the mother's surname. After their request was dismissed by the register of births, marriages and deaths and having exhausted all possible domestic remedies, the applicants claimed that the impossibility under Italian law to register their child under the mother's surname violated their right to respect for private and family life (article 8 ECHR) in conjunction with article 14 ECHR (prohibition of discrimination) as well as the principle of equality between the spouses (article 5 Protocol VII ECHR).

With a judgment issued on 7 January 2014, the ECtHR concluded (6 votes to 1) that there had been a violation of article 14 ECHR in conjunction with article 8 ECHR on account of the fact that the Italian provision according to which "legitimate children" are with no exception registered under the father's surname was based solely on a discrimination grounded on sex. While such rule could be necessary in practice and was not necessarily incompatible with the Convention, the absence of any possible derogation when registering a new child's birth was excessively rigid and discriminatory towards women.

The applicant in the case *Zhou v. Italy* (No. 33773/11) was Jiaoqin Zhou, a Chinese national who, unable to look after her son, complained that the Juvenile Court of Venice had declared her child eligible for adoption interrupting all contact with her. In examining the case, the ECtHR observed that not only the Italian authorities had not made sufficient efforts to preserve the maternal affiliation between the applicant and her son, but that they had not made appropriate or sufficient efforts to permit the child to live with the biological mother before opting for the adoption procedures. For these reasons, the Court concluded that the applicant's right to live with her child had been violated, thus breaching her right to respect for her private life, guaranteed by article 8 ECHR. Italy was therefore ordered to pay 40,000 euro in respect of non-pecuniary damage and the additional sum of 17,000 euro for costs and expenses.

Among the different provisions relied on by the applicant in the case *Bellomonte v. Italy* (No. 28298/10), it is worth mentioning the alleged breach of article 8 ECHR. The applicant, of Sardinian origin, was accused of being part of an extreme-left terrorist group and placed in custody in a high security prison. According to a distribution plan implemented by the prison administration, the applicant was then placed in a prison in Catanzaro. Relying on article 8 ECHR, the applicant claimed that his placement outside Sardinia had compromised his right to respect for private and family life to the extent that had considerably limited contact with his wife and family. Considering that the distance between Sardinia and Catanzaro was not disproportionate and that the absence of direct flights linking these two cities could not, by itself, amount to a violation of article 8 ECHR, the Court dismissed the case as manifestly ill-founded.

In *Durisotto v. Italy* (62804/13), relying on articles 2 ECHR (right to life) and 8 ECHR (right to respect for private and family life), the applicant claimed a violation of his daughter's right to life and health on account of the fact that it was impossible for her to obtain the compassionate therapy known as "Stamina". Moreover, relying on article 14 ECHR (prohibition on discrimination), the applicant maintained that the entry into force of l.d. 24/2013 had introduced a discrimination in access to care between persons who had already begun treatment prior to the entry into force of the decree and those who – like his daughter – were not in that situation. Examining only the allegations brought under articles 8 and 14 ECHR, the ECtHR rejected the case as manifestly ill-founded. With respect to article 8 ECHR, the Court reiterated that in cases concerning prohibitions on access to compassionate care in respect of persons suffering from serious illnesses, States Parties enjoy a wide margin of appreciation. Considering that a scientific committee set up by the Ministry of Health had issued a negative opinion on the therapeutic method "Stamina", the Court concluded that the interference in the applicant's daughter right to private life could be considered as necessary in a democratic society. As for article 14 ECHR, the fact that certain courts had authorised access to this treatment for persons in a similar state of health to the applicant's daughter was not sufficient to amount to a violation of the prohibition of discrimination.

The allegations raised in the case *Briani v. Italy* (No. 33756/09) could not be considered as falling within the notion of "respect for the private and family life" under the meaning of article 8 ECHR. The applicants in the case complained about the failure of the State to take positive measures aiming at guaranteeing the proximity between the applicant and his disabled daughter, while preserving the father's career in the army. Absent a direct and immediate link between, on the one hand, the measures requested by the applicants and, on the other hand, their private and family life, the ECtHR dismissed the case as incompatible *ratione materiae*.

The case *X and Y v. Italy* (No. 41146/14) was declared inadmissible for non-exhaustion of domestic remedies. Relying on article 8 ECHR, the applicants complained that their right to respect for their private and family life has been violated since their embryos have been wrongly implanted in another woman's uterus as a consequence of a mistake made by a public hospital. Noting that the applicants have failed to introduce at domestic level any action – civil or criminal – in order to seek damages for the alleged medical negligence or to establish the possible criminal responsibility of the persons concerned, the ECtHR concluded that they had failed to give to the respondent State the opportunity of preventing or putting right the violations alleged.

The same conclusion was reached by the ECtHR in *De Ciantis v. Italy*, decided on 16 December 2014. The applicant in this case, relying on various provisions of the Convention, maintained that, by failing to adopt the necessary measures to ensure that waste deposited in the Castelliri landfill were eliminated and to clean up the site, public authorities had put in danger his family and his own life and health. Having decided to consider the complaint under article 8 ECHR, the Strasbourg Court dismissed it for non-exhaustion of domestic remedies. The applicant, indeed, could have introduced a legal action either before civil courts in accordance with article 844 civil code or before administrative courts.

Italy in the Case-law of the Court of Justice of the European Union

A. *Fixed-term Employment, Non-discrimination*

The requests for a preliminary ruling from the Italian Constitutional Court and the Court of Naples to the Court of Justice of the European Union (ECJ) in Joined Cases C-22/13, C-61/13, C-62/13, C-63/13 and C-418/13 concerned the compatibility with EU law of the Italian legislation on fixed-term employment contracts in the school sector. The main proceedings concerned a group of employees of publicly-maintained schools (teachers and administrative staff) recruited under successive fixed-term employment contracts. Taking the view that those contracts were unlawful, they had brought actions at national level seeking the conversion of the contracts into employment relationships of indefinite duration, the payment of the salaries corresponding to the periods during which their employment was interrupted, and compensation for the damage suffered. In the context of such proceedings, the referring courts questioned the compatibility of the Italian legislation with the Framework agreement on fixed-term work annexed to directive 1999/70/CE. Making particular reference to article 5(1) of the abovementioned Framework agreement on measures States should adopt to prevent abuse arising from the use of successive fixed-term employment contracts or relationships, the referring courts asked the ECJ if the latter must be interpreted as precluding national legislation from authorising the renewal of fixed-term employment contracts to fill posts that are vacant and unfilled, pending the completion of competitive selection procedures for the recruitment of tenured staff of schools administered by the State, without stating a definite period for the completion of those procedures and while excluding any possibility, for those teachers and staff, of obtaining compensation for any damage suffered on account of such a renewal.

In its judgment of 26 November 2014, the ECJ first of all noted that in the Italian system the renewal of fixed-term employment contracts in order to cover posts that are vacant and unfilled on the basis that completion of competitive selection procedures is awaited is used to cover needs which are, in fact, not temporary in nature but, on the contrary, fixed and permanent because of the structural shortage of posts for tenured staff in the Member State concerned. In this connection, the budgetary considerations invoked by Italy cannot, under EU law, justify the lack of any measure preventing the misuse of successive fixed-term employment contracts. The ECJ thus concluded that EU law should be interpreted as precluding a national legislation which does not permit objective and transparent criteria to be identified in order to verify whether the renewal of those contracts actually responds to a genuine need, is capable of achieving the objective pursued and is necessary for that purpose, and does not contain any other measure intended to prevent and punish the misuse of successive fixed-term employment contracts.

By its order of 4 September 2014 in the case C-152/14, the ECJ answered the request for a preliminary ruling submitted by the Supreme Administrative Council in the context of a dispute between the Authority for Electricity and Gas (AEEG) and some of its employees. As in the *Rosanna Valenza et al. v. AGCM* case decided by the ECJ on 18 October 2012 (see *2013 Yearbook*, p. 380), the referring court asked the ECJ to consider whether the national legislation which completely disregards periods of service completed under fixed-term contracts in cases where the workers concerned are recruited under a stabilisation procedure is contrary to EU law and, specifically, to the Framework agreement on fixed-term work annexed to directive 1999/70/CE. The Court, reaffirming the principles established in the *Rosanna Valenza* case, excluded that the mere temporary nature of an employment relationship is sufficient to justify any difference in treatment between temporary and permanent workers. Moreover, the objective of preventing reverse discrimination against career civil servants recruited after passing a general competition cannot constitute an "objective ground" for the purposes of clause 4 of the Framework agreement if, such as in the present case, the national legislation completely and in all circumstances prohibits all periods of service completed by workers under fixed-term employment contracts being taken into account in order to determine the length of service of those workers upon their recruitment on a permanent basis. It is however up the national court to determine whether or not there are other "objective reasons" to justify any difference in treatment.

Another request for a preliminary ruling concerning the interpretation of the Framework agreement on fixed-term work annexed to directive 1999/70/CE (clauses 3 and 5) was submitted by the Court of Cassation in Joined Cases C-362/13, C-363/13 and 407/13, *Fiamingo and Others*. The case in the main proceedings concerned a dispute between the Rete Ferroviaria Italiana (Italian Railway) and a group of its employees recruited as seafarers under successive fixed-term contracts. By its judgment of 3 July 2014, the ECJ concluded that the provisions of the Framework agreement must be interpreted as not precluding national legislation which provides that contracts of fixed-term employment have to indicate their duration (in this case, a maximum of 78 days) but not their termination date. Moreover, the Court held that clause 5 of the Framework agreement must be interpreted as meaning that it does not preclude, in principle, national legislation, such as that at issue in the main proceedings, which provides for the conversion of fixed-term employment contracts into employment contracts of indefinite duration only in circumstances where the worker concerned has been employed continuously under such contracts by the same employer for a period longer than one year (the employment relationship being considered to be continuous where the fixed-term employment contracts are separated by time lapses of less than or equal to 60 days). It is, however, for the referring court to satisfy itself that the conditions of application and the effective implementation of that legislation result in a measure that is adequate to prevent and punish the misuse of successive fixed-term employment contracts or relationships.

The case C-221/13 concerned the request for a preliminary ruling submitted by the Court of Trent in the context of a dispute between the Ministry of Justice and one of its employee concerning a decision ordering the conversion of the latter part-time employment relationship into a full-time employment relationship. According to the ECJ, clause 5(2) of the Framework agreement which provides that "[a] worker's refusal to transfer from full-time to part-time work or vice-versa should not in itself constitute a valid reason for termination of employment, without prejudice to termination (...) for other reasons such as may arise from the operational requirements of the establishment concerned" does not require Member States to adopt rules making the conversion of a worker's part-time employment relationship to a full-time employment relationship subject to his consent. That provision seeks merely to exclude the refusal of a worker, as regards issues such a conversion of his employment relationship, from being the only reason for the termination of his employment in the absence of other objective reasons. It follows that clause 5(2) of the Framework agreement does not preclude legislation which allows an employer to order, for such reasons, the conversion of a part-time employment relationship into a full-time employment relationship without the consent of the worker concerned.

The case C-89/13 concerned another request for a preliminary ruling decided by the ECJ on the compatibility of the Italian legislation with article 4 of the Framework Agreement on fixed-term work. Submitted in the context of a dispute between Poste Italiane (National postal service) and one of its employee concerning the insertion of a fixed-term clause into the employment agreement they had concluded, the case involved the disparity of the economic consequences in the event of unlawful suspension of the employment contract between temporary and permanent workers. The referring court, in particular, asked the ECJ to assess the compatibility of l. 183/2010 (Provisions on fixed-term work) with article 4 (principle of non-discrimination) of the Framework agreement to the extent that the compensation paid in the event of unlawful insertion of a fixed-term clause in an employment contract and that paid in the event of unlawful termination of a contract of indefinite duration is significantly different and disadvantageous for temporary workers. As in the *Carratù* case (C-361/12, see *2014 Yearbook*, pp. 337–338), the ECJ concluded that article 4 of the Framework agreement does not apply in the present case. This is because the principle of non-discrimination between temporary and permanent workers does apply only whether the persons concerned can be regarded as being in a comparable situation, while the present case concerns workers whose employment contract was concluded unlawfully and workers who have been dismissed. Consequently, while the Framework agreement does not preclude Member States from granting fixed-term workers more favourable treatment than that provided for by the Framework agreement, EU law must be interpreted as not requiring the compensation paid in respect of the unlawful insertion of a fixed-term clause into an employment relationship to be treated in the same way as that paid in respect of the unlawful termination of a permanent employment relationship.

By its judgment delivered on 13 February 2014 in the case C-596/12, *European Commission v. Italy*, the ECJ granted the Commission's action and condemned Italy for having failed to fulfil its obligations under directive 98/59/EC on the approximation of the laws of the Member States on collective redundancies. Italy, in particular, had excluded the category of "magagers" from the scope of the mobility procedure provided by articles 4 and 24 of l. 229/199123, relating to provisions on technical lay-offs, mobility, unemployment benefit, implementation of Community directives, employment services and other provisions relating to the employment market.

B. Equal Opportunities in Employment and Occupation

The case C-595/12, decided by the ECJ on 6 March 2014, concerned the reference for a preliminary ruling submitted by the Lazio Regional Administrative Court in the context of a dispute between the Ministry of Justice and Ms Napoli regarding the latter's exclusion from a training course to become a deputy commissioner in the prison service as a result of her absence from that course for a period of more than 30 days, even though the reason for that absence was compulsory maternity leave. According to the national legislation (lgs.d. 146/2000), not only such an exclusion was justified on the ground that public interest demands that only candidates who have been adequately prepared through the training course are employed in the prison service, but it was not considered at variance with the rights of women at work to the extent it guaranteed their right to participate to a subsequent course, the date of which was nevertheless uncertain. The referring court asked the ECJ to consider whether the provisions of directive 2006/54 on the implementation of the principle of equal opportunities and equal treatment of men and women in matters of employment and occupation should be interpreted as precluding national legislation which, for reasons of public interest, exclude a woman on maternity leave from a training course which forms an integral part of her employment and which is compulsory in order to be able to be appointed definitively to a post as a civil servant and in order to benefit from an improvement in her employment conditions, while guaranteeing her the right to participate in the next training course organised, the date of which is nevertheless uncertain.

The ECJ first of all considered that the exclusion from the vocational training course as a result of having taken maternity leave had had a negative effect on Ms Napoli's working conditions and must therefore be regarded as constituting unfavourable treatment for the purposes of article 15 of directive 2006/54. Moreover, the fact that there was uncertainty as to the start of the next training course, the measures adopted by the State in order to guarantee public security are not proportional with respect to possible derogations from a right fundamental, such as the equal treatment of men and women. According to the ECJ, although national authorities have a certain degree of discretion in order to achieve the substantive equality between men and women pursued by directive 2006/54, it seemed possible to conceive measures which would interfere less with the principle of equal treatment between men and women than the measure at issue in the main proceedings, for example by providing, for a female worker who returns from maternity leave, parallel remedial courses equivalent to the initial training course so that that female worker may be admitted within the prescribed period to the examination enabling her to be promoted, without delay, to a higher grade and also meaning that the development of her career is not less favourable than that of the career of a male colleague who has been successful in the same competition and admitted to the same initial training course.

C. *Terms for Conferring Long-term Resident Status*

The case C-469/13, decided on 17 July 2014, concerned a request for a preliminary ruling submitted by the Court of Verona in the context of a dispute relating to the terms for conferring long-term resident status to a person with family connections to a long-term resident. The referring court, in particular, asked the ECJ whether EU legislation concerning the status of third-country nationals who are long-term residents (directive 2003/109) is to be interpreted as meaning that the requirement of legal and continuous residence for five years in the Member State, documentary evidence of which must be submitted when an application for a long-term residence permit is made, may also be applied to a person, other than the person making the application (in the present case, the applicant's husband who already was a long-term resident). Secondly, the referring court asked the ECJ whether one of the more favourable term according to which Member States may issue EU long-term resident permits (article 13 (1), directive 2003/109) is that, where a person has already acquired long-term resident status, having satisfied the pre-condition for receiving that status laid down in article 4(1) of that directive, under which legal and continuous residence in the Member State concerned for five years is required, members of that person's family are to be deemed also to have satisfied that pre-condition, irrespective of the length of time for which they have resided in the national territory of the Member State.

The ECJ stated that article 4(1) and 7(1) of directive 2003/109/EC must be interpreted as meaning that family members of a person who has already acquired long-term resident status may not be exempted from the condition under which, in order to obtain that status, a third-country national must have resided legally and continuously in the Member State concerned for five years immediately prior to the submission of the relevant application. Moreover, article 13 of the same directive must be interpreted as not allowing a Member State to issue family members with EU long-term residence permits on terms more favourable than those laid down by EU law.

D. Ne Bis in Idem

The request for a preliminary ruling in the case C-398/12 was submitted by the Court of Fermo in the context of a criminal proceedings brought against an Italian citizen on the basis of the same facts as those which had been the subject of a parallel investigation in Belgium, ended with a decision not to prosecute (now *res judicata*), on the ground that he had committed, between May 2001 and February 2004, on the territory of that latter Member State, acts of sexual violence against a child. The proceeding in Belgium had concluded with a finding that there was no ground to refer the case to a trial court because of insufficient evidence. The referring court, in particular, asked the ECJ whether article 54 of the Convention implementing the Schengen Agreement, which provides that no one may be prosecuted in a Contracting Party for the same acts for which he or she has already been finally acquitted or convicted in another Contracting State, must be interpreted as meaning that the final judgment of *non-lieu* taken by the Belgian judicial authorities must be considered as a final judgment notwithstanding the fact that the Belgian code of criminal procedure permit the reopening of the case if new evidence emerge.

Recalling article 50 CFREU on *ne bis in idem* and the corresponding provision enshrined in the ECHR, the Luxembourg Court noted, first of all, that the assessment of the "final" nature of the criminal ruling at issue must be carried out on the basis of the law of the Member State in which that ruling was made. In the present case, following the judgment delivered by the Belgian Court of Cassation, the order making a finding of "*non-lieu*" acquired the force of *res judicata* as it precluded, in Belgium, any new criminal proceedings against the Italian citizen concerned for the same acts and on the basis of the same body of evidence. The possibility provided by the Belgian code of criminal procedure to reopen the criminal investigation if new facts and/or evidence become available cannot affect the final nature of the order making a finding of "*non-lieu*" at issue in the main proceedings. According to the ECJ, indeed, that possibility involves the exceptional bringing of separate proceedings based on different evidence, rather than the mere continuation of proceedings which have already been closed. Article 54 of the Convention implementing the Schengen Agreement must therefore be interpreted as precluding new proceedings against the same person in respect of the same acts in Italy.

E. Failure to Fulfil Obligation in Waste Management

By its judgment delivered on 15 October 2014 in the case C-323/13, the ECJ condemned Italy in the context of the infringement proceedings brought by the European Commission for not having taken all the necessary measures to ensure that part of the municipal waste going to the landfills of Rome and Latina SubATO undergoes treatment, including a proper sorting of the various fractions of the waste and the stabilisation of the organic fraction, and by failing to establish in the Region of Lazio an integrated and adequate network of waste management installations which takes into account best available techniques as required by directive 1999/31/CE on the landfill of waste and directive 2008/98 on waste.

By its judgment of 6 November 2014 in the case C-385/13 P, the ECJ dismissed the appeal brought by Italy seeking the setting aside of the judgment of the General Court of the European Union (T-99/09 and T-308/09, Italy/European Commission). By that judgment, the General Court had dismissed the appeals brought by Italy seeking the annulment of a number of acts adopted by the European Commission which had declared unacceptable the requests for interim payments by the Italian authorities aimed at obtaining the reimbursement of expenditure incurred for improving and promoting the collection system and waste disposal in Campania, co-financed by the European Regional Development Fund (ERDF). On the basis of the outcome of the infringement procedure 2007/2195, indeed, the European Commission decided to suspend all payments due to concerns about the correctness of the management of the measures aimed at improving and promoting the collection system and waste disposal. As a consequence of the ECJ decision to uphold the General Court judgment, the Italian treasury lost more than 31 million euro of EU funding.

F. EU Citizenship, Non-discrimination

In the case C-322/13, decided by its judgment of 27 March 2014, the ECJ considered the request for a preliminary ruling made by the Court of

Bolzano in the context of a dispute between a German and a Polish citizen concerning an action for damages following a skiing accident occurred in the Province of Bolzano. The question referred to the ECJ concerned articles 18 and 21 TFEU on non-discrimination and citizenship of the Union. In particular, the referring court asked the ECJ whether these provisions should be interpreted as precluding the application of the Italian legislation (d.p.r. 574/1988), which grants the right to use the German language in civil proceedings pending before courts in the Province of Bolzano only to Italian citizens domiciled in the Province of Bolzano, but not to nationals of other EU Member States, whether or not they are domiciled in that Province.

The observation of the Italian Government, according to which there is no reason to extend the right to use the ethnic and cultural minority language to a citizen of another Member State who is present on an infrequent and temporary basis in the Province of Bolzano, was rejected by the Luxembourg Court. In the Court's opinion, indeed, unless it is based on objective considerations independent of the nationality of the person concerned and proportionate to the legitimate aim of the national provisions, the legislation at issue in the main proceedings run counter to the principle of non-discrimination. As regards the observation made by the Italian Government relating to the extra costs which would be incurred by the Member State concerned, the Court reiterated his settled case-law according to which aims of a purely economic nature cannot constitute pressing reasons of public interest justifying a restriction of a fundamental freedom guaranteed by the Treaty.

The case C-270/13 concerned the request for a preliminary ruling made by the Italian Supreme Administrative Council in the context of a dispute between Mr Casilli and Mr Haralambidis, a Greek citizen, on the appointment of the latter as President of the port authority of Brindisi. The referring court asked the ECJ whether EU law, and in particular article 45 TFEU must be interpreted as not authorising a Member State to reserve to its nationals the post of President of a port authority. More specifically, the question that the ECJ had to answer was whether, for the purposes of EU law, the presidency of a port authority should be considered as an employment in the public service provided that the fundamental principle of the freedom of movement for workers and the abolition of all discrimination based on nationality between workers of the Member States (article 45(4) TFEU) does not apply to such category of employment.

Established that the concept of "public service" within the meaning of article 45(4) TFEU covers posts which involve direct or indirect participation in the exercise of powers conferred by public law and duties designed to safeguard the general interests of the State or of other public authorities, and thus presume on the part of those occupying them the existence of a special relationship of allegiance to the State and reciprocity of rights and duties which form the foundation of the bond of nationality, the Court held that the exercise of powers of a public authority only occasionally, or indeed exceptionally, by the president of the port authority did not compromise the protection of the general interests of the State. In this context, therefore, a general exclusion of nationals of other Member States from access to the post of President of an Italian Port Authority constitutes a discrimination on grounds of nationality prohibited by article 45(1) to (3) TFEU.

Index

Table of Cases

Constitutional Court

Court of Cassation, Civil Division

Court of Cassation, Criminal Division

Supreme Administrative Council

Regional Administrative Tribunals (TAR)

Ordinary Tribunals

European Court of Human Rights

Court of Justice of the European Union

European Committee of Social Rights

Research and Editorial Committee

Andrea Cofelice, MA in Institutions and Policies of Human Rights and Peace, University of Padua. PhD Candidate in Political Science – Comparative and European Politics, University of Siena.

Pietro de Perini, MA in Institutions and Policies of Human Rights and Peace, University of Padua. PhD Candidate, Department of International Politics, City University London.

Paolo De Stefani, Aggregate Professor of International Protection of Human Rights in the Degree Course in Political Science, International Relations and Human Rights at the University of Padua. In the same University he also teaches International Criminal and Humanitarian Law. He is National Director for Italy of the European Master in Human Rights and Democratisation (E.MA).

Marco Mascia, Associate Professor of International Relations and Jean Monnet Chair in Political System of the European Union at the University of Padua. In the same University he is Director of the University Human Rights Centre and Director of the Master's Degree Programme in Human Rights and Multi-level Governance.

Antonio Papisca, Professor Emeritus of the University of Padua and UNESCO Chair in "Human Rights, Democracy and Peace", he promoted in 1982 the establishment of the Human Rights Centre within the University of Padua. In the period between 1994 and 2002 he has been member of the Italian Inter-Ministerial Committee for Human Rights at the Ministry of Foreign Affairs and of the Italian Human Rights Commission at the Presidency of the Council of Ministers.

Claudia Pividori, MA in Institutions and Policies of Human Rights and Peace, University of Padua. PhD in International Order and Human Rights, University of Rome – La Sapienza.

Peter Lang – Italian Yearbook of Human Rights Series

The legal and political significance of human rights has increased enormously at the international and European levels. Awareness has risen that the respect and the promotion of human rights must be at the centre of States and local communities' public policies and that human rights are at the basis of civil society initiatives and movements. There is a large machinery monitoring, at all the levels of governance, the way in which States implement the obligations assumed toward each person under their sovereignty.

The **Italian Yearbook of Human Rights Series** provides year by year, a dynamic and up-to date overview of the measures Italy has taken to adapt its legislation and policies to international human rights law and to comply with commitments voluntarily assumed by the Italian Government at the international level. The Series thus intends to contribute to the continuous monitoring activity on the situation of human rights in Italy undertaken at the local, national and international levels by relevant intergovernmental and civil society actors.

Each volume of this series surveys the activities carried out, during the year of reference, by the relevant national and local Italian actors, including governmental bodies, civil society organisations and universities. It also presents reports and recommendations that have been addressed to Italy by international monitoring bodies within the framework of the United Nations, the Council of Europe and the European Union. Finally, each Yearbook provides a selection of examples from international and national case-law which cast light on Italy's position vis-à-vis internationally recognised human rights.

The Yearbook is edited by the Human Rights Centre of the University of Padua, in cooperation with the UNESCO Chair in Human Rights, Democracy and Peace of the same University, and with the support of the Region of Veneto. The Centre, established in 1982, carries out research and education following a global and interdisciplinary approach. It hosts the Jean Monnet Centre of Excellence on intercultural dialogue, human rights and multi-level governance.

Editorial Board
Léonce Bekemans, *University of Padua*
Bojko Bucar, *University of Ljubljana*
Gabor Halmai, *Eötvös Lóránd University, Budapest*
Jean-Paul Lehners, *Université du Luxembourg*
Gianni Magazzeni, *Office of the UN High Commissioner for Human Rights*
Marco Mascia, *University of Padua*
Antonio Papisca, *University of Padua*
Stelios Perrakis, *Panteion University, Athens*
Ugo Villani, *LUISS University, Rome*
Peter G. Xuereb, *University of Malta*

www.peterlang.com

For the avoidance of doubt, input of the whole or any part of this publication into any generative artificial intelligence model, chatbot, program, software or technology is expressly prohibited without the prior written consent of the publisher.